AQA
Law in Focus
AS Level

Simon Jackson

Causeway Press

Contents

Module 1 - Law-making

Module 2 - Dispute solving

Module 3 - The concept of liability

1.1 What do we mean by 'law'?

Laws are rules that society, or the population as a whole, is required to follow. Laws are not the same as social rules, though. Never washing your hair or wearing the same socks for a week would break social rules but would not involve breaking any law. Nobody appears in court on a charge of having smelly socks. So, some rules of society cannot be described as laws. A better definition of law is to say that laws are rules of society that can be enforced in the courts. Where legal rules are broken, there is the potential that the state, through the court system, will either punish someone (in the case of criminal law) or require another person to provide compensation (in the case of civil law).

1.2 Morality and justice

If law involves rules, then we would expect society to regard breaking these rules as wrong in some sense. In other words, we would expect most people to regard the breaking of the law as immoral. The law and morality are related. It is wrong to commit murder, for example, and it is against the law. However, the relationship between the law and morality is not always so straightforward as is suggested by that example.

The term 'morality' refers to principles which seek to distinguish between ideas of right and wrong. In Western society, morality and laws draw heavily on the Christian tradition. The Christian faith provides a clear-cut set of ideas about right and wrong. It is interesting to note that the ancient origins of English law are found in laws created by church authorities. At one time in Britain, almost everyone was deeply religious. This is no longer the case. Consequently, today, the law draws on other traditions and other sets of values.

Sometimes the law is regarded by some sections of society as immoral and by others as perfectly acceptable. For example, many Christians are deeply opposed to abortion. Within certain boundaries, however, the law permits abortion. Supporters of abortion argue that to make abortion unlawful in any circumstances would be wrong since it would deny women a basic right to determine the course of their own lives.

The law is not fixed. It changes as society changes and as ideas of right and wrong change. Moreover, at any one time there are competing sets of morality and, therefore, competing ideas about what the law should be. In practice,

therefore, law and morality are not the same, though they do overlap a great deal.

Justice is about fairness and treating everyone equally. Are law and justice the same thing? Claimants and defendants, the prosecution and the accused, all say that they wish to obtain justice from the courts. Often what they really mean is that they want their version of the facts to be preferred over that of the other side. A more complex issue is whether the law itself always provides justice. This issue is discussed in Box 1.1.

Box 1.1 *Does the law itself always provide justice?*

Certainly, some laws aim to bring justice in the sense that they aim to ensure that everyone is treated in a fair way. For instance, before the Sex Discrimination Act was passed in 1975, an applicant for a job who was rejected solely on the grounds of gender was powerless to do anything about it. The Act - a new law - provided the right for women (and men) to receive compensation from employers in such cases. This law, like many others, sought to ensure that everyone is treated fairly.

To take another example, in the UK the police have considerable powers to arrest and detain suspected offenders under the Police and Criminal Evidence Act 1984 (or 'PACE' as it is often known). At the same time, the courts are able to disregard confessions and other pieces of evidence that seem to have been obtained in breach of the PACE code of practice on the treatment of suspects. This rule is aimed at preventing the police obtaining a confession in an unfair way. On the one hand, therefore, the law provides powers to help bring suspected criminals to justice. On the other hand, it seeks to ensure that people receive a fair trial. A fundamental purpose of the law, in other words, is to provide justice.

But is the law always used to provide justice? There are examples where this is very obviously not the case. In Nazi Germany, the persecution of Jews was carried out through the use of the legal system, including the courts. In apartheid South Africa, the law enforced a system which denied black people the same rights as white people. When these extreme examples are considered it might be tempting to think that the law and the legal system in England and Wales is fair to everyone. This, however, is a dangerous assumption. Some laws, it could be argued, are inadequate as a means of securing justice. Others can, with justification, be regarded as downright unfair. Law and justice, like law and morality, may overlap but they are not really the same thing.

This book includes discussion of areas where the law and the workings of the legal system are in need of reform. Sometimes reform is needed because particular laws are too difficult to enforce, too complicated or too ambiguous to achieve their aim effectively. In other cases, questions can be asked about the law because of perceived injustices. Three examples can be given to illustrate this:

1. Home Office figures for 2002 indicate that black people were eight times more likely to be stopped and searched by the police in Britain than white people. Should the powers given to the police by law be reviewed?

2. While successful lawyers can charge anything up to £400 per hour, the volume of complaints about the legal profession is spiralling. The results of a survey carried out in 2001 showed that 60% of those surveyed said their solicitor had made a basic and potentially serious mistake. Is the legal profession itself in need of reform? This is discussed in Unit 13.

3. Recent legislation has enabled the government to place a limit on how much money may be allocated to helping people on lower incomes with the legal costs of bringing a court action. Whole categories of cases have been taken out of the legal aid system altogether. This means that some potential claimants, no matter how strong their case may be, are being denied justice. Is this legislation acceptable? This is discussed in Unit 17.

Activity 1.1

Imagine that you are walking home and you come across a little green man from Mars. You strike up a conversation. When the Martian learns that you are studying law, he looks puzzled. It turns out that the concept of law does not exist on Mars. Provide a brief explanation of the term for him. (6)

1.3 What types of law are there?

The law in the United Kingdom can be classified in various ways. Three ways of classifying it are:

- by dividing it into civil law and criminal law
- by dividing it into private law and public law
- by listing the various sources of law - the places where the law comes from.

While it is not the purpose of this book to examine all of the actual rules of law that are upheld by the courts, it is helpful to understand the first two ways of classifying law, and to be able to distinguish in general terms between different types of law. Box 1.2 provides a summary of the different categories of law.

Box 1.2 *Different categories of law*

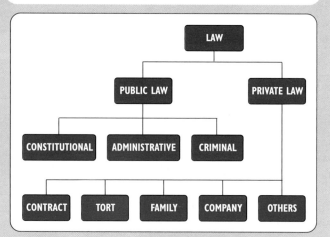

The law is usually divided into the categories shown in this diagram.

Civil law and criminal law

Civil law covers various areas of law, each of which works in quite different ways. These are:

- contract (the law of legally binding agreements)
- torts (which is a term used to cover civil wrongs other than contract - the most important of which is negligence)
- succession (which is the law relating to wills and related matters)
- family law (which includes divorce and laws relating to children, such as adoption)
- company law
- others.

Criminal law covers a wide range of offences (murder, manslaughter, assault, theft and others), but the legal rules relating to all of them have a great deal in common, so they may be seen as being within one category in a way that is not possible with civil law.

1.4 Civil law

When the courts deal with civil law cases, they are concerned with resolving disputes between two parties rather than punishing people for committing crimes. This is not to say that civil law does not involve wrongdoing, merely that this sort of wrong is treated differently by the legal system.

The role of the court is to consider, by application of the law, which of two sides in a dispute is in the right. If the court finds in favour of the person who has brought the claim to court (the claimant), it orders the defendant to do something for the benefit of the claimant. Most often, this takes the form of damages - a sum of money paid as compensation. It is important to note that a legal action only reaches the civil courts if someone starts an action after suffering loss. A criminal action, on the other hand, involves prosecution by the state through the police and the courts. Victims of crimes hardly ever bring about a court action (private prosecutions brought by the victim of a crime are possible but are extremely unusual).

Contract

A contract is a legally binding agreement. In other words, it is an agreement that the law will enforce. Contracts are part of everyday life. Anyone who has a job has a contract of employment between themselves and their employer. Anyone who drives a car must be covered by a contract of insurance, which is an agreement between an insurance company and the owner of the vehicle. Even buying something in a shop involves the creation of a contract, however small a purchase may be involved. Contracts may be written down or based on verbal agreements. It is wrong to think that only written contracts are legally binding.

What do we mean by 'the law will enforce'? Where a contract exists, one of the two parties involved in the agreement may start a court action if the other seems to have broken the agreement in some way. Not all disputes about contracts are brought before the courts, however, largely because of the expense and time involved.

Not all agreements are legally enforceable. For example, it is obvious that if you agree to go out with a friend to the cinema and later cancel the arrangement, your friend is not able to start legal proceedings against you. But how does the law distinguish legally enforceable agreements from other sorts? Box 1.3 shows that there are four essential ingredients.

As a rule, contracts only give rights to those who are a

Box 1.3 *Essential elements to form a valid contract*

Offer and acceptance
If one person makes an offer and another accepts, there is clearly an agreement.

Consideration
Both parties must give something of value - for example, money in exchange for goods. The technical term for this is 'giving consideration'.

An intention to be legally bound
One of the things that prevent an agreement to go the cinema from being a contract is the fact that neither person for one moment thinks 'stand me up and I will consult my solicitor'.

Capacity
Where the other three elements are present, the law regards agreements involving children, the mentally disordered and (sometimes) companies in a different light from other contracts.

Activity 1.2

(a) **Give four examples of contracts. (2 marks each)**

(b) **State whether or not a legal contract exists in the following situations:**

- **Jane Smith goes to watch a Premier League football match with her friends.**

- **Jane's mother promises that she will lend Jane her car for the day if Jane cuts the lawn in return. (4 marks each)**

---

party to it (for example, to the buyer and the seller). This may cause problems. For example, if someone is given something as a gift, only the actual buyer has legal rights against the seller if the goods are defective.

Tort

Tort covers many civil wrongs other than breach of contract. The most important type of tort is negligence which is examined in Unit 22.

The modern law of negligence began with the case of *Donoghue v Stevenson (1932)*. Ms Donoghue went to a café in Paisley with her friend. The friend bought her a bottle of ginger beer (in a coloured glass bottle, so that the contents were not visible). After drinking most of the bottle, she tipped the remainder into her glass. To her horror Ms Donoghue found a decomposed snail in her drink. Afterwards, she became ill.

Although Ms Donoghue had no contractual rights, either with the café or the manufacturer of the ginger beer, as she had been given the drink as a gift, it was argued on her behalf that the manufacturer was at fault and should, therefore, provide damages. The case went all the way to the House of Lords, the highest appeal court in the United Kingdom. The Lords ruled in favour of Donoghue. Lord Atkin created the concept of a *duty of care*. The famous quote from his judgement is:

> *'You must take reasonable care to avoid acts and omissions which you can reasonably foresee would be likely to injure your neighbours.'*

He went on to say, in effect, that 'your neighbour' is anyone who would be directly affected by your act and it is your duty, when acting, to consider the possibility of personal injury or damage to property. In simple terms, Lord Atkin was saying that carelessness leading to injury or damage could give rise to a claim for damages. Today, this simple and generalised rule enables a multitude of claims in negligence. Car drivers, doctors, and employers are among those who must take reasonable steps to avoid injury to others. This applies whether or not there is a contractual relationship.

Other torts are listed in Box 1.4.

Box 1.4 *Torts other than negligence*

1. Nuisance

Nuisance covers situations where a continuing state of affairs causes problems. A common example is where the dust and noise from a factory affects the health and peace and quiet of local residents.

2. Defamation

If someone is wrongly accused of having done or said something that will affect their reputation, they may bring an action in the tort of defamation, usually against the media.

3. Assault

Although assault is a crime it can also give rise to a claim for damages in the civil courts.

4. Trespass

Though many farmers might want trespass to be a crime, it is only a tort. If trespass is accompanied by theft or deliberate damage to property that is a different matter.

1.5 Criminal law

Criminal trials involve an investigation into whether a person has committed an offence. Although there are limited opportunities for the court to order the offender to compensate the victim for loss, this is not the basic purpose of a criminal trial. Defendants who are found guilty are normally punished, or 'sentenced', in some way. By no means all offenders are sentenced to prison. In fact, only a minority end up going to prison. Most offenders serve some type of community-based sentence or are fined.

A criminal trial is not about resolving disputes. It is about the state, through the police and the courts, investigating whether the criminal law has been broken and, if necessary, dealing out punishment.

Contrary to the impression that is given in some newspapers, the UK is not swarming with murderers, rapists and paedophiles. As many as 95% of criminal trials are for relatively minor offences such as motoring offences, disorderly conduct, minor theft, minor assault and so on. Such cases are heard by magistrates, who are part-time, unpaid volunteers. Serious crimes such as murder, rape, and 'GBH' (grievous bodily harm), are still quite unusual. These are heard by a judge and jury in different courts from those used for civil trials.

1.6 Private and public law

Private law is the same as civil law. Constitutional and administrative law, which are concerned with the nature and powers of the state, together with criminal law, make up public law.

Summary ● ● ●

1. *What do we mean by law?*

2. *Does the law always provide justice?*

3. *What types of law are there?*

4. *What is the difference between civil and criminal law?*

5. *What is the difference between public and private law?*

Case study • *The law in action*

Item A *Law in Afghanistan*

Shazia, aged 13, crouched on the floor inside the miserable Kabul Provincial Jail for women. When adults were present, she bit her nails and tugged at her black scarf, covering her face and hazel eyes. Her crime was running away from the middle-aged husband she was forced to marry. The jail is full of teenage girls accused of crimes ranging from falling in love to having affairs, from leaving harsh parents to running away from abusive husbands. Taliban-style executions may be gone, but Islamic law and rigid cultural traditions persist in Afghanistan. The country still relies on Islamic law dating back to the 7th century.

Adapted from the *Chicago Tribune*, 28 April 2002.

Item B *A day in the life of Sam Jones*

Sam Jones purchased a chocolate bar in the newsagent. As he drove along, munching chocolate, he answered his mobile phone. It was Susan, his girlfriend. He promised to buy her a meal in a restaurant the next day. A moment later he crashed into the back of the car in front of him, injuring the other driver and writing off both cars. Sam was released from hospital the same day but later became ill from very severe food poisoning. This prevented him from taking Susan out. The cause of this illness was identified as the chocolate bar he bought. Susan is now shocked to find that because it is her car that Sam was driving, the local newspaper mistakenly names her as the driver.

Questions

(a) Using Item A, explain the difference between law, morality and justice. (10)

(b) Look at Item B.
   i) Identify possible civil and criminal court actions. Explain what type of law is involved in each case. In relation to civil cases, be as specific as possible. (10)
   ii) Explain who would be the defendant and the claimant (in any civil cases) and who would be the prosecution and the defendant (in any criminal cases). (8)

2 (Parliament

2.1 What is Parliament?

Box 2.1 *The Houses of Parliament*

This photo shows the Houses of Parliament in Westminster, London.

Parliament is the UK's main law-making body - its 'legislature'. The origins of Parliament can be traced right back to the 11th century when Saxon kings sought advice from the 'Witangemot' (Saxon for 'the assembly of the wise'). Parliament today consists of the House of Commons and the House of Lords. Both Houses are situated in Westminster, London (see Box 2.1). Whether it is, or has ever been, a place of wisdom is open to debate but the purposes of this unit are to explain what Parliament is and how laws are made in Parliament.

Government and Parliament are two different things, and care should be taken not to confuse these terms. Government - the executive - is made up of ministers supported by civil servants. Ministers are normally Members of Parliament or peers (members of the House of Lords). In simple terms, the government is responsible for running the country rather than creating laws, though, as explained below, it is the government which puts forward most of the proposals for the laws voted on by Parliament.

Some law is made by judges (the 'common law' - see Unit 7), but far more law is created by Parliament, and this law takes precedence over judge-made law. A draft law introduced in Parliament is known as a 'Bill'. A law that has been passed by Parliament and which has received Royal Assent is known as an 'Act' or a 'statute'.

The UK Parliament website describes the four main functions of Parliament:

- examine proposals for new law
- provide, by voting for taxation, the means of carrying on the work of government

- scrutinise government policy and administration, including proposals for expenditure
- debate the major issues of the day.

2.2 Types of Act

Acts of Parliament can be distinguished on the basis of the function they serve. Some introduce entirely new legal rules, but others deal with existing law. Legislation fits into one of four categories.

1. Original legislation
Original legislation is entirely new law.

2. Consolidating legislation
Consolidating legislation is designed to bring together laws previously contained in a number of Acts purely so that they can be found all in one place. There is no real change in the law at all. The Companies Act 1985, for example, brought together numerous Companies Acts from the previous 37 years.

3. Codifying legislation
Codifying legislation brings Acts together in the same way as consolidating legislation but also incorporates common law into statute. The Sale of Goods Act 1979, which deals with contracts for the buying and selling of goods, is a major example of a codifying Act.

4. Amending legislation
Amending legislation is designed to alter an existing Act. These alterations may be minor in their effect or they may represent quite substantial changes in the existing Act.

2.3 The House of Commons

The Commons (see Box 2.2) is the more powerful and important of the two Houses of Parliament. Because the general population elects MPs, the Commons is seen as central to the existence of a democratic state. When the Commons scrutinises the actions of government and debates government proposals for new laws it is, in theory at least, acting on behalf of the electorate.

Acts of Parliament are effectively created through the will of a majority in the House of Commons. The Boundary Commission determines the number of MPs. At the time of the 2001 general election, there were 659 MPs. Each MP represents a specific constituency (area). General elections are held at least once every five years. If an MP resigns or dies during the lifetime of a Parliament, a by-election is held to replace them.

Parliament Acts of 1911 and 1949 effectively made the Lords subordinate to the Commons, by allowing the Commons to bypass the Lords if it opposes Bills. At one time, the Lords had the power to vote Bills out of Parliament (see Section 2.9 below).

Following the passage of the House of Lords Act in November 1999, the composition of the Lords has changed. Before the passage of the Act, many peers were hereditary peers - peers who had inherited their title through their family. Indeed, hereditary peers had enjoyed the right to sit in the House of Lords for over 700 years. Following the passage of the Act, however, the number of hereditary peers was reduced to 92. As a result, from November 1999, life peers - peers appointed to be members of the House of Lords for life (but whose title would not be passed on to their children) - made up the majority in the Lords. In April 2001, 561 peers were life peers out of a total of 679. Many were former MPs. Life

---

Box 2.2 *The House of Commons*

This photograph shows the former Leader of the House of Commons, Robin Cook, at the dispatch box in the House of Commons in 2002.

For centuries, most MPs in the Commons have belonged to one of two major political parties. In the 19th century, the two main parties were the Conservative Party and the Liberal Party. Since the 1930s, the Labour Party has replaced the Liberal Party as the other main party. Normally, the party which holds the most Commons seats forms the government. The Leader of that party is invited by the monarch to become Prime Minister. The Prime Minister then appoints a Cabinet (a group of senior ministers) and other, more junior, ministers. The party with the second highest number of seats in the Commons is known as the 'Official Opposition'. The Leader of the Opposition appoints a 'shadow Cabinet' (a group of would-be senior ministers) and other, more junior, shadow ministers. MPs who do not hold ministerial or shadow ministerial jobs are known as 'backbenchers' because they sit behind ministers and shadow ministers in the Commons.

2.4 The House of Lords

Like the House of Commons, the House of Lords (see Box 2.3) debates and votes on Bills. In 2002, peers were unpaid and unelected (the government was considering plans to reform the Lords). The Lords generally acts in a way that complements the work of the Commons rather than acting in opposition to it. It revises proposals for legislation and scrutinises the work of government. Many Lords amendments to a Bill aim to tidy it up to make a workable law. The Commons is the driving force behind most Acts in the sense that it is more important that a Bill is approved by the Commons than the Lords. The

---

Box 2.3 *The House of Lords*

This photo shows the House of Lords in session.

peers were first appointed under the Life Peerages Act 1958. In addition to the 92 hereditary peers and the life peers, 26 bishops from the Church of England sit in the Lords and a small number of senior judges (Law Lords) are appointed to the Lords to sit in the Judicial Committee - the UK's highest appeal court. Law Lords are also entitled to participate in debates on Bills and other parliamentary business.

The second stage of reform

The House of Lords Act 1999 was intended as a first stage in a process of reform of the House of Lords. Also in 1999, the government appointed a Royal Commission on Reform of the House of Lords, under the Conservative peer, Lord Wakeham, to make recommendations for the second stage of Lords reform. The commission published its report in January 2000. The Wakeham Report made 132 wide-ranging proposals on the recruitment of peers and changes to the procedures of the House.

In November 2001, the government published a White Paper announcing its plans for the second, and final, stage of the reform process. In broad terms, the plans followed

the recommendations of the Wakeham Report. The main proposals were concerned with the composition of the new House. The recommendations included:

- the removal of the remaining hereditary peers
- 20% of the House to be directly elected - by proportional representation in large, multi-member regional constituencies
- 80% of the House to be appointed.

However, this White Paper was not well received by Labour MPs, many of whom felt that far more than 20% of the second chamber should be elected. The government set up a Joint Committee of both Houses in May 2002 to give further consideration to what should happen. For the time being, further changes seem to have been postponed.

2.5 Influences on Parliament

Because the government of the day has a Commons majority it obviously has the greatest influence on what laws are made by Parliament. Most legislation stems from government plans. However, the government is heavily influenced by other groups - for example:

1. The European Union - membership of the EU involves a commitment to incorporate EU directives into legislation (see Unit 6).
2. Those bodies whose role it is to suggest practical reforms to the existing law (see Unit 9).
3. Groups known as pressure groups, which represent particular interests and concerns - for example, employer bodies and environmental campaigners (see also Unit 9).

2.6 Types of Bill

There are three types of Bill.

1. Private Bills

These are Bills that apply only to a particular area, a specific organisation or a certain section of the population, rather than to the country as a whole. In recent decades only a very small number of private Bills have been passed. In the 19th century they were more widely used, for example to enable the construction of the Manchester Ship Canal and other very big projects that it would have been difficult for local councils to achieve on their own.

2. Public Bills

The vast majority of Bills passing through Parliament are aimed at the public as a whole. Most public Bills are introduced by the government and, therefore, described as 'government Bills'.

Activity 2.1

Composition of the Lords

If the power of hereditary peers is illegitimate because it has never been subject to democratic consent, then the same formula surely applies to the power of appointed peers. The trouble is that a second chamber controlled by appointees is simply too convenient to discard. Yet, with a few striking exceptions, appointments to the House of Lords amount to a monumental role of dishonour. Life peerages are handed to people who have performed 'political services' (stuffing their party's pockets), 'services to wealth creation' (stuffing their own pockets), or 'public services' (stuffing the rest of us). What remains after the House of Lords Act 1999 is a gigantic, politically appointed organisation that is linked closely to government. So how should we replace it? Should we encourage the government to establish an elected second house as soon as possible? This carries the danger of constructing a rival decision-making body, rather than an effective revising chamber.

Adapted from the *Guardian*, 29 July 1997 and 8 November 2001.

(a) How was the Lords reformed in 1999? Suggest why the Lords was reformed. (4)

(b) Summarise the arguments for and against creating a new second chamber made up of appointed peers. (4)

3. Private Members' Bills

Private Members' Bills are Bills introduced by backbench MPs. Around 10% of Commons time is spent on this type of Bill. There are a number of ways in which Private Members' Bills can be introduced into Parliament but the most common is through a ballot that is held every 12 months. MPs who wish to introduce a Private Members' Bill can enter their names in the ballot and 20 names are drawn.

Largely because very limited time is set aside for debating these Bills, the chances of a Bill becoming an Act are small. However, there are a number of important statutes resulting from Private Members' Bills. One example is the Abortion Act 1967, which legalised abortion in the United Kingdom.

2.7 Green and White Papers

Before a Bill is drafted and introduced into Parliament by the government, there is often a period of consultation. Professional organisations, employer bodies, trade unions, and charities are examples of the kind of organisations which may put forward a view on the merits or otherwise of proposed laws. Groups of people campaigning on specific issues often actively 'lobby' (seek to influence) MPs to try and win their support for changes in the law. Greenpeace and Age Concern are examples of pressure groups.

Part of the consultation process may be the publication by the government of a Green Paper. In this, the government sets out its reasons for wishing to create new laws and it puts forward broad proposals as to what form new laws will take. Responses are invited to the Green Paper. Sometimes the views expressed in a consultation period change the government's thinking on the form that new laws should take.

Later, a White Paper is produced, containing more detailed proposals for law. The approach contained in a White Paper is likely to be the one used in a Bill. An example is the White Paper *Justice for All* (published in 2002) which set out some significant changes to the way in which the criminal courts operate (see Unit 12).

Bills are worded in dry and precise language because of the need for certainty and precision in the law. Green and White Papers, on the other hand, are formal reports discussing issues and containing a summary of proposals. People without legal training can read them more easily. Not all Bills are preceded by Green and White Papers. Green Papers have been used less often in recent years, in favour of more informal consultation papers.

Once consultation is over, a Bill is drafted and put before Parliament.

2.8 From Bill to Act of Parliament

A Bill has to pass through a number of stages in both the Commons and the Lords before it can be given Royal Assent and become law (see Box 2.4). Most Bills can start off in either House, but it is usual for Bills where there are likely to be major differences of opinion between MPs to start in the Commons. Public Bills involving changes in taxation or public spending must begin in the Commons.

The stages are almost the same in both Houses. Remember that if a Bill fails to win a majority vote in a vote in either House it will not become law unless there is another attempt to take it through the different stages in Parliament at a later date.

Box 2.4 *The passage of a Bill through Parliament*

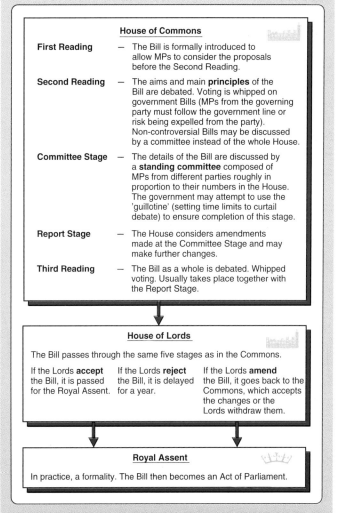

This diagram shows the stages a Bill has to pass through before it becomes law.

First Reading

The First Reading is a brief formality. The name and main aims of the Bill are read out. Usually there is no debate but a vote is taken on whether the House wishes to proceed to the next stage.

Second Reading

A lengthy debate takes place. The government minister from the department responsible begins the debate (the Education Minister would speak first in the Second Reading on a Bill affecting schools or colleges, for example). The main principles of the proposed new law are outlined and the most important clauses summarised. The shadow minister then responds. During the debate that follows, other MPs have the chance to comment. A vote is then taken as to whether the Bill should proceed further.

When Public Bills refer exclusively to Scotland or Wales, the procedure may sometimes be different. The Welsh or Scottish Grand Committees consider the principles of the Bill, and the Second Reading is a formal vote, held without debate.

Committee Stage (Commons)

If it has received approval in the vote taken in the Second Reading, a Bill is then scrutinised in some detail by a 'standing committee' of MPs drawn from all parties. Committees range in size from 16 to 50 MPs. After analysing the way each section of the Bill is worded and the intention of the proposed change in the law, amendments may be made by the committee. For Bills of constitutional significance and Bills concerned with taxation (Finance Bills), the whole House may sit as a committee at this stage.

Committee Stage (Lords)

In the Lords, there are no standing committees. After the Second Reading of a Bill, all peers are entitled to take part in a detailed examination of the Bill. As with the Commons, the Committee Stage in the Lords also involves detailed scrutiny.

Report Stage

The Bill then returns to the whole House of Commons, where the changes suggested at the Committee Stage are considered. All MPs are entitled to speak in the debate that takes place and a vote is taken on whether to accept or reject each amendment. One function of the Report Stage is to enable the House of Commons to ensure that the small number of MPs in committee have not amended a Bill in a way that would not be agreed in a vote of the whole House. Another is to benefit from the time that has

elapsed and discussion that has taken place since the Second Reading. It may be that individual MPs have changed their minds and take a different view of what the law should be.

Third Reading

It is common for the Third Reading to take place immediately after the Report Stage. A Bill is reviewed in its final version. Major changes cannot be made at this point. The Third Reading is generally short. There is only a Commons vote if a minimum of six MPs requests it. If the Bill is approved in this final vote it will pass to the other House of Parliament and then receive Royal Assent.

Royal Assent

When a Bill has passed through all of its five stages in both Houses, it receives Royal Assent (approval) from the monarch. This is a formality. The last time a monarch refused to add her signature was Queen Anne in 1707. In a modern democracy, it is unlikely that the monarchy would continue in its present role if it began to refuse Royal Assent.

Bills nearly always take many months to become Acts. However, there have been a few occasions over the years where all parties have recognised the need for speed and an Act has been passed within a day. For example, during unforeseen national emergencies the government may need to be given extra powers on top of those it has already.

2.9 Bills and rejection by the Lords

If a Bill is amended at some stage in the Lords it must return to the Commons for those amendments to be considered. MPs and the government may have little difficulty in agreeing with these (often minor) amendments. However, it is possible that a majority in the Lords might vote against an entire Bill. Under the Parliament Acts 1911 and 1949, the effect of such a vote in the case of a Public Bill would be to cause delay only. A Public Bill rejected by the Lords may return to the Commons and pass through all stages again. The need for a vote in the House of Lords can be sidestepped.

It should be noted however that the House of Lords still has the potential to be a significant thorn in the side of any government. Given the constant pressures of a busy law-making timetable, no minister wishes to see a Bill taking up extra time in Parliament. It is very rare for the Lords to vote against a government Bill. A little more often, however, peers force the government to change its ideas by indicating they are intending to vote against a Bill.

Activity 2.2

Standing committees

The most shocking thing about the Commons is the way in which laws are made. If you want to see what it is like, sit on a standing committee. A Bill is produced and that Bill has to be defended and go through the Committee Stage. The government has a majority on that committee and it selects the members of the committee. It doesn't pick people who are going to be difficult - it is a handpicked tame majority which can be relied on to defend the measure and uncritically see it through the process. And then, ministers will say 'Parliament has decided'. I'm not easily shocked, but I was in respect of what became the 1993 Education Act. Members of the government party on that Bill spent their committee time writing their Christmas cards. This is the reality of how legislation is scrutinised in standing committee. People stay out of the room, except for crucial votes. Government MPs are told to say nothing so that a Bill can go through as quickly as possible. The opposition simply engages in a tactic called 'delay' - talking about anything remotely connected to the Bill in the vain hope of extracting some political benefit. David Butler has described the Committee Stage as a 'futile marathon'. He cites a standing committee which met for two months in 35 separate sessions for a total of 120 hours. Yet, no fewer than 35 hours were spent on the first two clauses and, when only 17 of the 129 clauses had been examined, a guillotine was applied, depriving most of the details of the Bill from any scrutiny at all. There were 173 votes on the Committee Stage and, surprise surprise, the government won them all. You could replay the same story for any major piece of legislation. This is why we have such bad legislation. It is a shocking state of affairs.

Adapted from Wright, Tony, 'Does Parliament work?', *Talking Politics*, Vol. 9.3, Spring 1997 (at the time of writing, Tony Wright was Labour MP for Cannock and Burntwood) and the House of Commons Information Office, 5 November 1998.

The Standing Committee on the Social Security Bill in the 1997-98 parliamentary session

Sittings of committee	14
Amendments made to Bill	131
Ministerial amendments carried	131
Amendments moved by government backbenchers	0
Amendments moved by opposition MPs	173
Opposition amendments carried	0
Votes on opposition amendments	10
Hours of deliberation in committee	28 hrs 27 mins

This table shows the work of the Standing Committee on the Social Security Bill in the 1997-98 parliamentary session.

(a) What is the supposed function of standing committees? (3)
(b) Summarise the drawbacks of the standing committee system. (8)

2.10 The monarch in Parliament

As discussed above, although the monarch is required to approve Bills before they become Acts, this is, in reality, a mere formality. In matters of government, the Crown (monarch) has considerable powers, but these powers are exercised by ministers, or those acting on behalf of ministers, not by the monarch themself. This system is known as a 'constitutional monarchy'. So, does the ruling monarch, as opposed to ministers, have any power in Parliament? The answer is, very little. But there are two areas where there is at least the potential for the personal exercise of power by the monarch.

1. **The power to appoint the Prime Minister**
   By convention, the monarch invites the Leader of the largest party in the House of Commons to form a government after a general election has been held. If, however, there is a 'hung' Parliament (ie no one party has an overall majority of seats in the Commons), it might not be obvious who should be asked to become Prime Minister. In this situation, the monarch would play a decisive role in determining the nature of the government.

2. **The power to dissolve Parliament**
   If a newly formed minority government wished to call a general election in the hope of increasing the number of seats it held, the monarch could decide not to dissolve Parliament and, instead, invite the Leader from another party to form a coalition government.

2.11 Scotland, Northern Ireland and Wales

There has been much debate for many years over the extent to which the Westminster Parliament should legislate for those parts of the UK other than England. Those in favour of devolution support a shift in power away from Westminster. In 1997-98, some significant constitutional changes were made. Following referendums in Scotland (1997), Wales (1997) and Northern Ireland (1998), Parliament handed over some of its powers to newly created assemblies.

Under the Scotland Act 1998, a new Scottish Parliament was given the power to create legislation on a wide range of matters (laws made by the Scottish Parliament have effect only in Scotland). However, some important areas are still under the control of the Westminster Parliament, including trade and industry, foreign affairs and defence. The Northern Ireland Act 1998 created a similar relationship between the Westminster Parliament and a new Northern Ireland Assembly.

In Wales, the position is different. The Government of Wales Act 1998 created a Welsh Assembly that does not have the power to make primary legislation (ie laws which have effect only in Wales). However, the Welsh Assembly is able to make delegated or 'secondary' legislation (regulations made under a pre-existing Acts of Parliament - see Unit 4). The delegated legislation made by the Welsh Assembly has effect only in Wales.

Summary ● ● ●

1. What is the difference between Parliament and government?

2. What are the differences between the House of Commons and the House of Lords?

3. What is a White Paper?

4. During which stages of a Bill's passage through Parliament are there lengthy debates and which stages may be seen as largely formal, with little debate?

5. Which of the Houses of Parliament is subordinate?

6. What was the effect of the Parliament Acts 1911 and 1949?

Case study ● Law-making

Item A   *Cartoonist Brick's view of Parliament*

This cartoon is entitled 'The Theatre of Parliament'. It was produced in 1999. Select committees are committees made up of backbenchers. Their job is to examine government policy and administration. Departmental select committees examine the work of specific departments (for example the Trade and Industry Select Committee examines the work of the Department of Trade and Industry). Non-departmental select committees examine particular areas of government activity (for example, the Public Accounts Committee checks the government's accounts).

Item B   *Andrew Adonis' view*

Andrew Adonis argues that Parliament performs an important scrutiny role that has been strengthened in recent years by the development of the committee system and by the rise of a new generation of full-time and more independent-minded MPs. He claims that what makes Parliament effective is that, although it does not govern itself, government takes place through Parliament. As a result, parliamentary committees are able to scrutinise the work of government, while the televising of Parliament means that ordinary voters can themselves scrutinise the behaviour of government and parliamentary activity. Adonis does concede, however, that there is widespread public discontent with the quality of parliamentary representation and government, and that less and less government is taking place through Parliament because of the growing influence of European institutions.

Item C Tony Wright's view

Tony Wright claims that Parliament doesn't really exist at all. He notes that a Labour MP recently remarked that it wasn't the job of the opposition to scrutinise and improve government legislation. Neither is it the business of government backbenchers. So, he asks, whose job is it? His stark answer is that it is nobody's job. Parliament does not exist collectively at all. What exists is government and opposition - engaged in a never-ending election campaign on the floor and in the committee rooms of the House of Commons. The only rules of the game are those agreed by the politicians themselves. There is nobody to speak for the public interest or to suggest that people are not well served by this cosy self-regulation. Government and opposition conspire to prevent reform to the system, Wright concludes, as they both benefit from it. The only losers are the public.

Item D *Extracts from the Licensing (Young Persons) Act 2000*

Licensing (Young Persons) Act 2000

Be it enacted by the Queen's most Excellent Majesty, by and with the advice and consent of the Lords Spiritual and Temporal, and Commons, in this present Parliament assembled, and by the authority of the same, as follows:

Amendment of Part XII of the Licensing Act 1964.

1. For Section 169 of the Licensing Act 1964 (serving or delivering intoxicating liquor to or for consumption by persons under 18) there shall be substituted the following sections-

Sale of intoxicating liquor to a person under 18.

169A. (1) A person shall be guilty of an offence if, in licensed premises, he sells intoxicating liquor to a person under eighteen.

(2) It is a defence for a person charged with an offence under sub-section (1) of this section, where he is charged by reason of his own act, to prove that he had no reason to suspect that the person was under eighteen.

(3) It is a defence for a person charged with an offence under sub-section (1) of this section, where he is charged by reason of the act or default of some other person, to prove that he exercised all due diligence to avoid the commission of an offence under that sub-section.

(4) Subsection (1) of this section has effect subject to Section 169D of this Act.

This Act makes provisions in connection with the sale and consumption of intoxicating liquor to people under the age of 18, and for connected purposes. It received Royal Assent on 23 November 2000.

Adapted from David Roberts (ed.), *British Politics in Focus* (Second Edition), Causeway Press, 1999 and www.open.gov.uk

Questions

(a) Using Items A and B explain what is meant by 'scrutiny'? How does Parliament scrutinise government? (4)

(b) Using Items A-C and your own knowledge, explain why it might be argued that it is not the job of the Opposition to scrutinise and improve legislation. (3)

(c) What are the arguments for and against the idea that the televising of Parliament distracts it from the serious scrutiny of proposals for new law? (6)

(d) i) What type of Act is shown in Item D?

   ii) As with all Acts, the monarch is mentioned at the beginning of the text. What is the monarch's role in the parliamentary process? (4)

(e) Why are Green and White Papers important to those with an interest in future Bills? (3)

(f) 'Parliament has little real influence on the process of creating legislation. The House of Commons is simply a rubber stamp.' Using Items A-D, give arguments for and against this view. (12)

Parliamentary sovereignty and human rights

3.1 What is meant by 'constitution'?

Clubs very often have a written constitution. This is a rulebook that sets out how the club will operate - how often meetings will be held, how those meetings will be conducted and so on. In relation to legal systems and governments the idea of a constitution works in much the same way. The constitution is the set of principles that determines the nature and powers of government. Constitutions describe:

- the powers a government has in a state
- the relationship between different parts of the state
- the relationship between government and the citizen.

This unit provides a brief explanation of the principles behind the UK constitution. It focuses, in particular, on the concept of parliamentary sovereignty.

3.2 Constitutional principles

Royal prerogative

Royal prerogative is the name given to certain privileges and powers that are still held by the monarch, dating from the time before Parliament became all-powerful or 'sovereign'. Today, almost all of these powers are exercised by the Prime Minister and the government on behalf of the monarch. The royal prerogative is very significant as it enables the government to take action in a number of circumstances without holding a vote in Parliament. The royal prerogative includes the powers to:

- declare war
- make treaties
- take possession of or give up territory
- issue orders to the Armed Forces
- control the civil service
- do anything necessary to defend the realm.

There are three broader principles underlying the constitution. These are:

- the separation of powers
- the rule of law
- the supremacy of Parliament.

1. The separation of powers

The ideas of Montesquieu (a French 18th-century philosopher) have been very influential in shaping the constitution of the UK. He said that all powers of the state could be divided into three types:

1. **The executive** - the government and those involved in the administration of government (civil servants), as well as organisations such as the police.
2. **The legislature** - the group which creates laws. In Britain, this is Parliament which create Acts of Parliament, also known as 'statutes'.
3. **The judiciary** - judges, who resolve legal disputes and enforce laws.

Montesquieu felt it was crucial that legislative, executive and judicial powers should each be exercised by a different person or group. This is known as the 'principle of the separation of the powers'. The object of such a principle is to avoid the concentration of power into the hands of a single person or group.

In a constitution with a clear separation of powers, the executive, legislature and judiciary are independent of one another and, as a result, more able to act as a restraint on each other in a way that benefits citizens. They are less able to oppress the people through excessive power. In Britain, for example, government ministers only have such powers as are defined by Parliament. The courts can be asked by anyone to prevent government from acting outside of these powers. This is done through a process called 'judicial review' (see pages 24, 80 and 128-29). Applications for judicial review by citizens may be in relation to grave matters of life or death or in relation to relatively everyday concerns. In 1999 alone, there were over six thousand applications for judicial review against government departments.

2. The rule of law

Crucial to a separation of powers is obedience to established law by citizens and all organs of the state (see Box 3.1). This principle of 'the rule of law' has three elements:

1. Nobody should be punished by the state unless they have broken a law.
2. The same laws should apply to officials of the state as to the ordinary people.
3. The rights of the individual are not determined by the executive, they arise out of decisions made in individual cases by an independent judiciary.

3. The supremacy of Parliament

Parliament is the supreme law-making body and, in this sense, has **'legal sovereignty'**. However, the 19th century constitutional expert A.V. Dicey argued that because the

Box 3.1 *Northern Ireland and the rule of law*

Critics of the UK constitution often refer to the breakdown of the rule of law in Northern Ireland. Detention of suspected terrorists without being charged with a criminal offence (the policy of 'internment') and the so-called 'shoot-to-kill' policy have been seen as breaches of the rule of law. This photo shows the homecoming of a Republican, Frank McGlade, who was arrested in August 1971 and 'interned' (detained without being charged) before being released in April 1972.

Box 3.2 *The two pillars of the British Constitution*

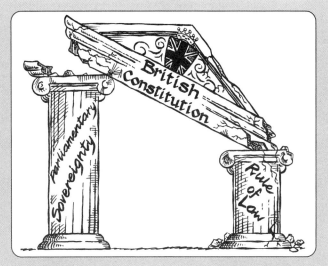

According to A.V. Dicey whose book *An Introduction to the Study of the Law of the Constitution* was first published in 1867, the British Constitution rests on 'twin pillars' - parliamentary sovereignty and the rule of law. This cartoon suggests that parliamentary sovereignty is the more important pillar.

people elect Members of Parliament, they have the power to determine policy and, therefore, have '**political sovereignty**'. Because ministers are accountable to Parliament for the actions of government, the executive is also brought under the influence of the electorate.

This idea of the supremacy of Parliament is sometimes called 'parliamentary sovereignty'. This means that Parliament is the highest source of English law. There are a number of strands to Parliamentary supremacy.

First, although the courts can and do make law (see Unit 7), they are obliged first and foremost to apply the laws created by Parliament. The courts have long since ceased being the primary creators of laws, the role that historically they once played. However well-established the common law (judge-made law) may be, if Parliament passes an Act of Parliament that changes the common law, judges are obliged to apply the Act when deciding cases,

whether or not they think it is 'good law' and preferable to the old common law.

Second, sometimes Parliament gives other people, such as government ministers or local authorities, the right to create binding laws. These laws are known as 'delegated legislation' (see Unit 4). This does not affect parliamentary supremacy because the legal entitlement to make law can be altered or taken away altogether by Parliament and because the individual laws created by those given such power by Parliament can be altered or eliminated by an Act of Parliament.

Third, in theory at least Parliament is free to create 'bad' laws. If an Act of Parliament were passed requiring all grandmothers to be hung drawn and quartered for purchasing custard cream biscuits, it would have to be enforced by the courts and the police. A key theoretical part of parliamentary supremacy is that Parliament is not bound to create laws that comply with any particular notion of right or wrong. Many other countries do bind their Parliament to comply with fundamental principles of human rights set out in a separate document (known as a Bill of Rights). The USA, for example, has a Bill of Rights that enables a court to strike down laws as 'unconstitutional'. Similarly, some countries have adopted the European Convention on Human Rights as part of their constitution. Again, this means that any laws created must comply with the broad principles set out there. In

Britain, despite the Human Rights Act 1998, this is not the case.

Fourth, Parliament cannot bind itself. Because the House of Commons is elected at least once every five years, the body of people involved in deciding on what the law should be is very fluid. It is part of the constitution that any Act passed can be later repealed (voted out) either by the same Parliament or by any subsequent Parliament.

Limits to parliamentary supremacy

There are at least three ways in which the idea of an all-powerful Parliament is not altogether valid:

1. The international treaties by which the UK is bound by virtue of its membership of the European Union (EU) mean that in relation to many areas of civil law, particularly those affecting business, trade and employment, EU law takes precedence over Acts of Parliament. Moreover, the European Communities Act 1972 specifically spells out this surrender of sovereignty to Europe, although, as explained above, Parliament cannot bind itself.

2. The House of Commons effectively dictates what Acts of Parliament are passed. The Commons is controlled by the party that holds a majority of Commons seats. As this party also forms the government, there is a tendency for Parliament effectively to be dominated by government when the government has a large majority in the Commons.

3. The creation of national assemblies for Scotland and Northern Ireland represents a transfer of power and a reduction in the sovereignty of Parliament within the United Kingdom.

3.3 What are 'human rights'?

Today, it is generally agreed that freedoms - what are usually called 'civil liberties' or 'human rights' - are essential ingredients in a democratic society. The extent to which civil liberties are recognised varies in different legal systems but all democratic states recognise the following to some degree:

● **freedom of speech**, which includes press and broadcast media which are not controlled or restrained by government

● religious freedom or **freedom of belief**

● freedom to meet with others, for example in trade unions or political parties, also known as **freedom of assembly**

● **freedom to protest peacefully**

Activity 3.1

'The UK government has seated Parliament on two horses, one straining towards the preservation of parliamentary sovereignty, the other galloping in the general direction of Community [EU] law supremacy.' (De Smith in Street & Brazier 1981, p.91)

What point is being made about parliamentary sovereignty in this cartoon? How vaild is the point? (4)

● **freedom from imprisonment** or other punishment when no law or no just law has been broken

● **the right to a fair trial**.

Worldwide, many countries have a special constitutional document or **Bill of Rights** defining civil liberties. The rights given to individuals in such documents cannot be removed by the national government or Parliament and must be enforced by the courts since the rights laid down in a Bill of Rights are regarded as superior to any conflicting law that might be created. For example, since the USA became independent over 200 years ago, laws and government activities have been able to be challenged as being 'unconstitutional' in that they infringe one of the special amendments to the United States constitution. These amendments form the USA's Bill of Rights.

Britain is almost unique among democracies in that it has neither a written constitution nor a Bill of Rights to protect individual freedoms. In Britain, until the Human Rights Act 1998 came into force (see below), civil liberties were traditionally regarded as **residual freedoms**. In other words, the courts regarded people as free to do anything so long as the law did not restrict it. It was the role of Parliament to curb individual freedom only where it was seen as essential for the wider public good. So, for example, freedom might be restricted where it was seen as necessary to ensure public order or national security.

Beyond that, people could live and behave as they chose. Any unlawful attempt to limit freedom could be prevented by seeking remedies from the courts developed as part of the ordinary law of the land.

It has often been argued that one way of strengthening human rights is to incorporate the European Convention on Human Rights into UK law. This, broadly speaking, was achieved by the Human Rights Act 1998.

Activity 3.2

Suggest why it may be necessary to restrict freedoms in the following situations:

- **The BBC plans to broadcast a programme about a new fighter plane.**

- **A newspaper publishes an article alleging that a politician has had an extra-marital affair.**

- **A peaceful demonstration is held on the hard shoulder of the motorway.**

- **The police wish to question a suspected armed robber. (4 marks each)**

3.4 The European Convention on Human Rights (ECHR)

The European Convention on Human Rights (ECHR) is an international treaty that contains 66 articles and five protocols defining, in the words of the introduction to the treaty:

'Fundamental Freedoms which are the foundation of justice and peace in the world and are best maintained on the one hand by an effective political democracy and on the other by a common understanding and observance of the human rights upon which they depend.'

In other European countries, the ECHR has been adopted as part of domestic law, effectively making it a Bill of Rights. Britain was the first country to sign the ECHR and, since 1966, British citizens have been able to pursue complaints in the Strasbourg Court of Human Rights. Until recently, however, the ECHR was not part of UK domestic law.

Britain and the other members of the Council of Europe signed the ECHR in 1950. The ECHR stemmed from a determination to prevent a repeat of the horrors inflicted upon the ordinary people of Europe during the Second World War. The ECHR not only set out the rights which all citizens in Europe could expect, it also established a Commission of Human Rights and a European Court of Human Rights to enforce it (in 1998, the Commission was merged into the Court).

It should be noted that the Council of Europe and the Court of Human Rights are separate organisations from those existing within the European Union discussed in Unit 5. It should be noted that the rights set out in the ECHR are not absolute. For example there is scope under the treaty for states to restrict freedoms where there are issues of national security or public order. Box 3.3 contains a summary of the ECHR.

Box 3.3 *The ECHR*

The European Convention on Human Rights

Article 2 Right to life.
Article 3 Freedom from torture or inhuman or degrading treatment or punishment.
Article 4 Freedom from slavery or forced labour.
Article 5 Right to liberty and security of person.
Article 6 Right to a fair trial by an impartial tribunal.
Article 7 Freedom from retroactive criminal laws.
Article 8 Right to respect for private and family life, home and correspondence.
Article 9 Freedom of thought, conscience and religion.
Article 10 Freedom of expression.
Article 11 Freedom of peaceful assembly and association, including the right to join a trade union.
Article 12 Right to marry and found a family.
Article 13 Right to an effective remedy before a national authority.
Article 14 Freedom from discrimination.

Protocol 1
Article 1 Right to peaceful enjoyment of possessions.
Article 2 Right to education; and to education in conformity with religious and philosophical convictions.
Article 3 Right to take part in free elections by secret ballot.

Protocol 4
Article 1 Freedom from imprisonment for debt.
Article 2 Freedom of movement of persons.
Article 3 Right to enter and stay in one's country.
Article 4 Freedom from collective expulsion.

3.5 The European Court of Human Rights

The European Court of Human Rights sits in Strasbourg and exists solely to deal with breaches of the ECHR. In May 2001, the Court had 41 judges - one for every member state of the European Council. The European Council elects them for a six-year term of office. In recent years, the workload of the Court has increased enormously. The Court dealt with seven cases in 1981 and 119 in 1997.

The Court only has the power to hear cases when all domestic procedures have been exhausted. In other words, a UK citizen would have to seek an appeal in the normal way before resorting to the Court of Human Rights. The Court can only hear cases brought against a public authority, such as a court of law or a government department. It has no power to hear cases brought against an individual or a private organisation. The Court can never alter decisions of a national court. It is not, in this sense, a court of appeal.

The European Court of Human Rights is able to award compensation to applicants. But unlike a national court, it has no way of enforcing its decisions through court orders. However, states that are found to have breached the ECHR generally change their laws if the Court rules against them. Examples of UK laws changed as a consequence of Court of Human Rights' decisions include:

- the Contempt of Court Act 1981
- the Interception of Communications Act 1985.

3.6 The Human Rights Act 1998

Partly because of concern over the worrying number of cases in which the UK was seen to be in breach of the ECHR, momentum grew for some kind of incorporation of the ECHR into the English legal system. In 1993, for example, Lord Bingham, then Lord Chief Justice (head of the Criminal Division of the Court of Appeal), argued that:

> 'The ability of English judges to protect human rights...is inhibited by the failure of successive governments over many years to incorporate into United Kingdom law the European Convention on Human Rights.' (*Law Quarterly Review*, 1993, p.109)

The Labour Party promised to incorporate the ECHR and, in 1998, the Human Rights Act (HRA) was passed. The Act did not come into force until October 2000 so that the government, the courts and the legal profession might be fully prepared for such a significant change in the legal system. The Act stops short of making the European Convention into a UK Bill of Rights, but it does enable judges in the UK to look at legislation and the acts of public authorities in light of the ECHR. It is no longer necessary to apply to the European Court of Human Rights in Strasbourg to enforce these rights. Some key provisions of the Act are as follows.

1. Legislation must be read and given effect by the courts in a way that is compatible with the ECHR

This means that the wording of Acts must be read in light of the ECHR. This applies to both Acts of Parliament and delegated legislation (see Unit 4 for information on delegated legislation). Crucially however, if laws are found by the courts to be conflict with the ECHR, **they will**

continue to be valid. The constitutional principle of parliamentary sovereignty - of Parliament being free to make whatever laws it chooses - remains.

2. Higher courts may make a declaration of incompatibility with the ECHR

The High Court, the Court of Appeal and the House of Lords may clearly state that legislation and delegated legislation is seen as in breach of the ECHR. It is then for Parliament to decide whether or not the particular law should be altered. The courts cannot strike down an Act, but they may tell the government and Parliament where there are problems.

3. The courts must take into account the decisions of the European Court of Human Rights

This applies to all courts and tribunals, not just the higher courts. A whole new area of case law must now be reviewed before any judgement is made.

4. Actions of public authorities must be compatible with the ECHR

Schools, hospitals, local councils and government departments may find themselves facing court action brought by members of the public. The courts will be able to award damages (compensation) where an Article has been breached. Parliament is not counted as a public authority under the HRA, though the courts themselves are.

5. There is a procedure where a minister may declare in advance that a particular Bill will not be affected by the ECHR

Under the Human Rights Act, if Parliament wishes, it could pass legislation that deliberately contravenes the ECHR, but the government must publicly announce that it intends to do this.

6. Existing laws protecting human rights remain in force

The Human Rights Act does not remove previous existing statutory or common law rights under UK law. These continue in force, alongside the ECHR.

3.7 Has the Human Rights Act 1998 weakened parliamentary sovereignty in the UK?

The Human Rights Act clearly represents a new departure in the English legal system. But has the Act affected the principle of parliamentary sovereignty? Although the Act does give the ECHR a special status, the supremacy of Parliament has not been weakened. This can be explained as follows.

Box 3.4 *The impact made by the Human Rights Act 1998*

Before the Human Rights Act 1998 came into force

1. Residual freedoms: patchwork of UK laws restricting freedoms where necessary.
2. European Convention on Human Rights only **influences** UK courts.
3. Government has no obligation to alter UK legislation to comply with ECHR.
4. Legal action under ECHR only possible through European Court of Human Rights.

After the Human Rights Act 1998 came into force

1. Residual freedoms remain but ECHR incorporated into UK law too.
2. UK courts **must** consider whether laws and actions of public authorities are compatible with ECHR.
3. Courts may make a declaration of incompatibility but Parliament is still not obliged to make changes to legislation.
4. Legal action for breach of ECHR possible in UK courts and the courts might award damages.

1. It is still possible for Parliament to create laws that are a clear breach of the ECHR

Parliamentary sovereignty remains intact. The ECHR has not been given the full status of a Bill of Rights that binds law-making authorities absolutely.

2. The courts are only able to declare legislation incompatible

The courts might have been given stronger powers to disregard or remove incompatible legislation but they were not.

3. A government may choose to declare that a particular Bill is a deliberate derogation from the ECHR whenever it feels it is convenient to do so

A 'derogation' from the ECHR means a deviation from the ECHR. The government may do this irrespective of whether or not it can really be justified.

Box 3.4 shows the impact of the Human Rights Act 1998.

Summary ● ● ●

1. What is meant by 'the separation of powers' and 'the rule of law'?

2. What is meant by 'parliamentary sovereignty' and what consequences result from it?

3. What was the approach to human rights used within the UK prior to 1998?

4. What is the European Convention on Human Rights?

5. What new powers have the courts been given by the Human Rights Act 1998?

6. Does the Human Rights Act 1998 fully incorporate the ECHR into English law?

Case study ● Parliamentary sovereignty and the Human Rights Act

Item A *Our constitutional arrangement*

Our constitutional arrangement might be considered to be an odd one in a system so apparently committed to the separation of powers. Not just the same party, but essentially the same people, run both legislature and executive. In other Western democracies this is not the case. In the USA, for example, the executive, led by the separately elected President, consists of quite different people from the elected legislature (though admittedly the President usually belongs to one of the two big political parties that hold seats in the legislature). In the British system, the supremacy of Parliament can more aptly be described as 'the supremacy of the political party holding the most Commons seats'.

Adapted from *Web Journal of Current Legal Issues*, Vol.1, 1998. and the *Chicago Tribune*, 28 April 2002.

Item B *The Human Rights Act (HRA)*

In the House of Lords in 1997, Lord McCluskey unsuccessfully opposed the passage of the Human Rights Bill on the grounds that it would provide 'a field day for crackpots, a pain in the neck for judges and legislators and a goldmine for lawyers'. While it is true that one man threatened to take court action against the failure of his local council to

The European Court of Human Rights in Strasbourg.

collect a wheelie bin, there has been no flood of hopeless cases since the HRA came into force. All the rights guaranteed under the ECHR are already part of the common law. And, since 1966, it has been possible to bring a claim before the European Court of Human Rights in Strasbourg. Since the HRA was passed, however, it is no longer necessary to wait for ten years for a visit to the European Court. The UK courts, which for many years have tended to refer to the ECHR when considering human rights cases, can fully apply the Articles of the Convention.

Item C *The impact made by the HRA*

In the three months after the implementation of the HRA, there were just 168 cases in the Crown Court (where more serious criminal offences are tried) in which human rights issues were raised. This is less than half of 1% of Crown Court cases. Between 2 October 2000 and 31 January 2001, 277 of 2,491 Court of Appeal Criminal Division cases contained human rights points. The criminal courts have certainly adopted what might be described as a 'softly, softly' approach to human rights arguments. The general approach is that the common law is compatible with the ECHR and that the appeal courts should deal with any shortcomings. The courts try hard to interpret legislation in a way that makes it compatible with the ECHR, even if this is sometimes straining the normal meaning of the words used in an Act. The Attorney General stated in March 2001 that:

> 'The overwhelming majority of the challenges prosecutors have faced in practice so far - and it is early days - have been dealt with at first instance in the Crown Court or the Magistrates' Courts and resolved in favour of the prosecution.'

Some lawyers predicted that the HRA would have a very dramatic effect on the courts. So far this does not appear to have occurred. While the number of cases involving consideration of the ECHR by the UK courts rose dramatically in the first 12 months after the HRA, only two of these led to a declaration of incompatibility.

Adapted from the *Times*, 3 October 2000 and Bobb-Semple, C., 'Recent human rights developments in criminal litigation', *Student Law Review*, Vol.33, Summer 2001.

Questions

(a) Item A questions whether Parliament really is supreme. What are the limits to parliamentary sovereignty? (10)

(b) i) Using Item B, put forward arguments for the idea that the Human Rights Act represented a natural progression rather than a legal revolution. (4)

   ii) Are the courts a 'public authority' within the Human Rights Act? What are the implications of this? (5)

   iii) What legal action could be taken by an individual for breach of the European Convention on Human Rights before the Human Rights Act was passed in 1998 and after the Human Rights Act came into effect in 2000? (10)

(c) Using Item C, explain what sort of impact the Human Rights Act has made on decisions taken by the courts. (8)

4.1 What is 'delegated legislation'?

Delegated or secondary legislation consists of laws created under the authority of Parliament but not actually by Parliament. Some Acts of Parliament lay down broad principles rather than provide detailed laws. The Act specifies who has the power to make further, more specific laws and the extent of that power. An Act of this kind is called an Enabling Act, or a Parent Act. Delegated legislation takes a number of forms - see Box 4.1.

Box 4.1 *Types of delegated legislation*

Statutory instruments

Made by:	Government ministers
Examples of use:	Wide-ranging - to assist government departments

Orders in Council

Made by:	Queen and Privy Council
Examples of use:	For emergencies, when Parliament is not sitting
	Transfer of power between ministers

Bylaws

Made by:	Local authorities and public corporations
Examples of use:	Improving the appearance of local areas
	Ensuring the safety of a particular location

Statutory instruments

Statutory instruments (SIs) are often called 'regulations'. Government ministers are given the power to create statutory instruments by Parliament in relation to the work of departments. A common example of the use of SIs is where time limits, fines or fees are set. If the Parent Act set these out, they would require regular updating to allow for inflation, for example. Without SIs there would need to be an entirely new Act when a fee had to be increased.

R v Secretary of State for the Home Department, ex parte Simms (1999) provides an example of the use of regulations by the Home Secretary to control visits to prisoners. The claimants were in prison, having been convicted of murder. They claimed that they were innocent and fought for their acquittal. Some journalists visited them in prison, interested in giving publicity to this campaign. On becoming aware of this, the prison

authorities refused to allow the journalists access to the prisoners, acting within very wide-ranging regulations created by the Home Secretary. The prisoners applied to the High Court. Part of their argument was that the Home Secretary was acting outside of his statutory powers in creating the rules about visits by the press. The High Court granted a court order to the prisoners, which the Court of Appeal reversed. The House of Lords, after a further appeal, found in favour of the prisoners.

Another example of statutory instruments being used is to be found in *R v Secretary of State for Social Security, ex parte Joint Council for the Welfare of Immigrants (1996)* which is discussed in Activity 4.2.

Orders in Council

Orders in Council are made by the Privy Council and signed by the monarch. The Privy Council exists to advise the monarch and is made up of current and former Cabinet ministers and other senior politicians. In practice, government departments draft Orders in Council. As with statutory instruments, the power to create Orders in Council stems from an Act of Parliament.

Orders in Council are used for a variety of purposes, but most frequently when statutory instruments would be inappropriate. For example, Orders in Council are used to transfer responsibilities between government departments. They were used to transfer power from ministers of the UK government to those of the devolved assemblies in Scotland and Northern Ireland, for example. Parliament only sits for a part of the year so Orders in Council are a helpful device in times of emergency, as it is easier to call a meeting of the Privy Council (a relatively small group) than to recall Parliament. Orders in Council are also used to bring Acts of Parliament into force.

Bylaws

Bylaws are made by local authorities (for example, County Councils) to deal with matters within their area. They apply only to that area. A bylaw might set rules regarding the use of footpaths in a particular area, for example. Some public corporations (government-controlled organisations) also have statutory power to make bylaws. For example, safety rules on the London Underground have legal force as bylaws.

4.2 Why is delegated legislation used?

Although delegated legislation rarely receives as much media attention as Acts of Parliament, it is an extremely important form of law-making. About 3,000 statutory instruments are created every year. Delegated legislation offers a number of advantages over Acts.

1. Time

Although Parliament has been known to create an Act in 24 hours, this is rare. Parliamentary procedures are cumbersome and complicated. Moreover, Parliament does not sit for the whole year. At the same time, there is often a great deal of pressure on Parliament to fulfil a government's law-making programme. Delegated legislation provides a way of allowing the details of law reforms to be filled in later so that MPs can focus on considering new Bills.

2. Flexibility

Delegated legislation can not only be put into action more quickly than an Act, it can also be changed more quickly as unforeseen circumstances arise. An Act can only be repealed (removed) by another Act. Again, this is likely to take considerable time.

Activity 4.1

Suggest which type of law is most likely to be used in the following situations, giving reasons why they would be used:

(a) The transfer of responsibility for international development from the Foreign Office to a newly created ministry. (4)

(b) A law re-routing a public footpath. (4)

(c) Laws dealing with the storage of dangerous chemicals. (4)

(d) An increase in the maximum penalty for speeding. (4)

(e) An entirely new kind of criminal offence, aimed at preventing 'stalkers'. (4)

3. The need for local or specialist knowledge

Bylaws allow local or specialist knowledge to be taken into account. Local councillors have a better personal knowledge of a local area. Equally, the engineers and other professionals who work for the London Underground are much better equipped than MPs to understand what safety issues are important for the protection of the public.

4.3 Control of delegated legislation

Delegated legislation is subject to different kinds of control and monitoring to ensure that law-making powers that have been delegated by Parliament are not used inappropriately - see Box 4.2.

Box 4.2 *Control by Parliament*

1. **Legislation**
   Parliament can revoke delegated legislation or pass an Act on the same subject.

2. **Negative procedure**
   An SI becomes law **UNLESS** Parliament votes against it.

3. **Affirmative procedure**
   An SI becomes law **IF** Parliament agrees it should do so.

4. **The Scrutiny Committee**
   The Scrutiny Committee looks out for problematic SIs.

5. **Standing committees on delegated legislation**
   Standing committees on delegated legislation consider SIs, instead of the whole House of Commons doing so.

The main forms of control and monitoring are as follows.

1. Legislation

Parliament can revoke delegated legislation or pass an Act on the same subject.

2. Negative procedure

Some delegated legislation can be cancelled if either of the Houses of Parliament passes a motion calling for annulment within a specified number of days (usually 40 days). Such a motion is known as a 'prayer'. A motion put down by the Official Opposition is usually debated, but where an ordinary backbench MP puts down a motion it is less likely to be accommodated. If there is no motion, or the motion is not passed, the delegated legislation becomes law. Most Parent Acts specify that delegated legislation is subject to the negative procedure.

3. Affirmative procedure

The affirmative procedure is less common than the negative procedure. Under some Enabling Acts, delegated legislation must be approved by both Houses (or just the Commons where financial matters are concerned) within a certain number of days. Either House can reject it. Because delegated legislation can only become law when approved by Parliament, this procedure represents a stricter control than negative procedure, as the delegated legislation is always considered by Parliament, rather than being considered only in certain circumstances.

4. The Scrutiny Committee

This is a joint committee, including members of both Houses of Parliament, that hears evidence from government departments on SIs. The committee cannot consider whether the delegated legislation is good or bad law but it may recommend that Parliament reviews SIs when it considers:

● the authority of the Parent Act has been exceeded

● unexpected use has been made of powers given to ministers

● there is defective drafting (the SI has not been properly worded)

● the instrument requires further explanation.

5. Standing committees on delegated legislation

Standing committees on delegated legislation were first set up in order to relieve pressure of time in the House of Commons. Standing committees usually have 17 members. Although only committee members may vote, any member is allowed to attend and speak. SIs are referred to a committee by a minister, subject to the approval of the whole House, so that Parliament can scrutinise delegated legislation without taking up time on the floor of the House.

4.4 Control by the courts

The validity of delegated legislation can be challenged in the courts. This may be through the process of **judicial review** in the Queen's Bench Divisional Court (see page 80). Alternatively, it may arise in a civil claim between two parties. The courts may be asked to examine whether or not delegated legislation is *ultra vires* (ie beyond one's legal power or authority).

1. Procedural ultra vires

Procedural *ultra vires* involves a complaint that the procedures laid down in the Enabling Act have not been adhered to. For example the courts have occasionally ruled Orders in Council and SIs to be invalid where there is a statutory requirement to consult with various parties beforehand and this has not been done properly.

2. Substantive ultra vires

Substantive *ultra vires* is judged to have occurred where the rules created under an Enabling Act go beyond the powers delegated by Parliament. It is not the way that delegated legislation is made that is at issue here, but whether the delegated legislation is permitted by the Enabling Act at all.

A second kind of substantive *ultra vires* is unreasonableness under the principle established in *Associated Provincial Picture Houses v Wednesbury Corporation (1948)*. If rules are obviously unjust, to the extent that no reasonable body would have made them, the courts can rule them to be invalid. An example would be new regulations that have a direct and beneficial effect on the personal interests of the minister that created them.

Prerogative orders in judicial review cases

Remedies are the court orders that may be issued when a case has been decided by the court. The normal remedies of damages, injunction and declaration are available in judicial review cases. In addition, there is the discretion to make other kinds of order, known as prerogative orders. There are three types of prerogative orders.

1. Quashing

This order cancels an *ultra vires* decision. For example it might be used to reverse the decision of a local authority to allow the construction of a new drive-in McDonalds. Of course this would only be possible where the local authority had acted *ultra vires*.

2. Mandatory

This is an order to do something. If, for example, a court lower than the High Court had improperly refused to hear a case, a mandatory order might be issued. It is not unusual to request both the quashing and mandatory orders.

3. Prohibition

A prohibition order is used to prevent something happening in the future. A prohibition order might provide the means for an applicant to prevent a tribunal going ahead with a hearing that is outside its powers, for example. Where the plans of a public body are known in advance, the order of prohibition allows the courts to prevent illegal behaviour in advance of it actually occurring.

It should be emphasised that all three of these orders are discretionary. In other words, even if a judicial review case is won, the court may feel that it is only appropriate to award damages. For instance, if there is an appeal system which has not been utilised, the court will tend to avoid using a prerogative order.

4.5 Consultation

Quite often powers created by an Act to make delegated legislation must only be used after consultation with various named organisations or persons. For example s.114 of the Learning and Skills Act 2000 gives the Secretary of State for Education power to 'provide or secure the provision of services which he [*sic*] thinks will encourage, enable or assist...effective participation by young persons in education or training.' However, s.115 requires the Secretary of State for Education to consult with a range of bodies including a local authority, a health authority, the police, GP Trusts and others before making such arrangements.

Those involved in consultations of this kind have no power to insist on changes to government proposals. However, effective arguments made against particular points sometimes cause changes to be made to the wording of rules.

4.6 Are there any problems with delegated legislation?

1. Absence of democratic involvement and public awareness

A very large number of laws are made every year by civil servants rather than elected Members of Parliament. Delegated legislation is a useful way of avoiding tying up parliamentary time in relatively trivial matters, as discussed earlier. However, there have been occasions when governments have been criticised for introducing important new laws through delegated legislation without proper parliamentary debate. This is particularly true where very wide discretionary powers are given to a minister by an Act. Use of these powers has sometimes been described as a method by which government sidesteps Parliament and democratic accountability.

A second point is that, sometimes, the public does not even know about the existence of delegated legislation. Full parliamentary debate ensures at least some degree of press coverage. SIs and Orders in Council, briefly considered by a delegated legislation standing committee, may affect people who are quite unaware of an impending change in the law.

Where ministers are given discretionary powers, the practical reality may be that these powers are exercised by civil servants and 'rubber stamped' by the minister. Ministers, as Members of Parliament, have to be elected every five years. This is not true of the relatively anonymous, permanently employed civil servants who work for governments.

Activity 4.2

R v Secretary of State for Social Security, ex parte Joint Council for the Welfare of Immigrants (1996)

Immigration control at Heathrow airport.

Asylum seekers are citizens of one country who seek to live in another country because they are persecuted for their political beliefs or otherwise in danger. The UK receives a significant number of applications from asylum seekers every year. The Asylum and Immigration Act 1993 created rules for determining asylum applications and appeal routes. It also said that asylum seekers could claim social security benefits while waiting within the UK for their asylum hearings.

In 1993, the Conservative Government was concerned that many asylum seekers were actually seeking to enjoy a higher standard of living than they would have in their own country, rather than an escape from persecution. The Secretary of State for Social Security, therefore, exercised powers under the Social Security Administration Act 1992 to make regulations, which were approved by Parliament. These regulations withdrew the right to benefits from those who sought asylum after entering the UK.

The Joint Council for the Welfare of Immigrants brought an action for judicial review, claiming that the regulations fell outside the terms of the Social Security Act 1992. The Court of Appeal agreed with this view. The 1992 Act, it ruled, gave asylum seekers new legal rights to have their case for asylum considered. Mere regulations (rather than a new Act) could not take these rights away. But that was the practical effect of depriving asylum seekers of the right to money for living expenses, while waiting for their case to be heard. The Court of Appeal ruled that Parliament could not have intended, when the 1992 Act was passed, to give the Secretary of State power to remove later statutory rights. The regulations were *ultra vires*.

(a) Does this case represent an example of *substantive* or *procedural ultra vires*? **(2)**

(b) What kind of order might be sought in a case of this kind? **(3)**

(c) Why might this case be seen as an attack by the courts on the power of the legislature? **(4)**

2. Lack of effective supervision

Judicial review only occurs when an individual has the resources and determination to challenge a particular law. It may be that many others have simply suffered in silence from the abuse of delegated powers. Moreover, if a very wide discretion is provided to a minister or other party under an Enabling Act, the courts are normally unable to challenge laws created. Judges may only question delegated legislation where it appears to be outside of the framework put in place by an Act, not just because it appears to be an abuse of power by a government or is otherwise inappropriate.

Parliamentary controls have also been seen as problematic. The Commons Select Committee on Procedure made a number of criticisms in a report published in 2000. The committee said:

> 'In devising an effective system of scrutiny of delegated legislation, the key question is how best to target Parliament's over-stretched resources of time and expertise. There is widespread agreement that, at present, those resources are ineffectively targeted.'

It was argued that statutory instruments 'do not receive scrutiny in proportion to their merits'. The current system works on the basis that SIs with an affirmative procedure are automatically more worthy of debate than those with a negative procedure. In fact some negatives are concerned with important matters and some affirmatives are concerned with trivial and uncontroversial matters. 'As a result', the select committee noted, 'the time and expertise of members [MPs] is frequently wasted in attendance at delegated legislation committees to consider trivial affirmatives, often meeting for a few minutes only, whilst significant changes to the law may pass through Parliament unregarded and undebated because contained in negative instruments' (HC 48 of 1999-2000 para. 11).

Summary

1. What are the differences between the three types of delegated legislation?

2. How is delegated legislation controlled?

3. Why might judicial review not always prevent undesirable regulations taking effect?

4. What are the problems with parliamentary scrutiny of delegated legislation?

5. What are the advantages of delegated legislation?

Case study *Delegated legislation*

Item A *The Lords and scrutiny of delegated legislation*

The Salisbury Convention is an agreement made in 1945 between the Lords and the Commons that the Lords would not defeat manifesto commitments of the governing party. Since then, this convention has been applied to both Bills and delegated legislation. One recommendation of the Wakeham Royal Commission on the Reform of the House of Lords, however, was that the Salisbury Convention should be set aside so that the Lords could extend its role in scrutinising secondary legislation. At the same time, it was proposed that any vote in the new second chamber could be overruled by an affirmative vote in the Commons. The Wakeham Report suggested that this would provide a mechanism for enabling the Lords to delay and demonstrate concern about specific statutory instruments. It stated: 'The House of Commons should have the last word but would

Lord Wakeham who chaired the Commission which was set up by the government in 1999 to examine reform of the House of Lords.

have to take full account of the second chamber's concerns, ministers' responses and public opinion.' Lord Strathclyde, the Conservative Leader in the Lords, said in a public lecture: 'Secondary legislation is now of such importance and complexity that it is surely time for both Houses to consider the case for amending it.'

Item B *Statutory instruments*

Statutory instruments are laws made by civil servants. A minister, usually not the Secretary of State (the most senior minister in a government department), does see and approve them, but the crucial decisions about what should be in regulations, their timing and, indeed, whether they should be made at all are taken in Whitehall, by civil servants. As citizens, we would probably object to our MPs spending too much time on the Thames Estuary Cockle Fishery Order 1994 or the Baking and Sausage Making (Christmas and New Year) Regulations 1985. Laws like these deal with uncontroversial issues such as food safety and food hygiene. They are based on scientific advice and, in many cases, nobody would dispute the need for them. The issues behind other regulations make headline news - such as the the Sierra Leone [UN sanctions] Order 1997 which banned the selling of arms to Sierra Leone or the Beef Bones Regulation of 1997 which banned the selling of beef on the bone. And there are many more big issues - such as sentencing criminal offenders - that do not make the front pages.

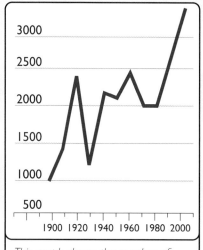

This graph shows the number of statutory instruments passed by Parliament per year between 1900 and 2000.

The problem is that there is simply no mechanism for airing the collective choices that are made every day on our behalf. Matters such as which particular bits of crime sentencing legislation should actually be brought into effect, whether discriminatory legislation preventing women entering the fire service should be removed or exactly how far we need to go to implement this or that EU directive are the bread and butter of everyday government in Whitehall. Yet, such regulations are created with little or no public knowledge and receive little real scrutiny in Parliament or in the media. There are several reasons why such topics are rarely raised by politicians, press, radio or TV. They may be technical issues. They may appear, at first sight, to affect only a few people. Alternatively, they may deal with matters that will only come into effect a long time in the future. But once they are on the statute book, they are difficult to remove. The Grey Squirrels (Prohibition of Importation and Keeping) Order 1937, for example, is technically still in force (requiring anybody who sees a grey squirrel on their land to report the sighting to the appropriate government department). A question arises. Is there sufficient consideration of all of the decisions made on our behalf by civil servants?

Adapted from *Report of the Royal Commission on the Reform of the House of Lords* 2000, the *Times*, 1 December 1999 and the *Guardian*, 19 January 2001.

Questions

(a) What arguments, connected with parliamentary supremacy, might be used against the proposal made by the Wakeham Commission outlined in Item A? (6)

(b) Using Item A, suggest why the Wakeham Commission argue for affirmative procedure, rather than negative. (6)

(c) Do you think it is likely that a government with a small majority in the Commons would be anxious to curb the use of delegated legislation? Explain your answer. (4)

(d) Using Item B, suggest when the use of delegated legislation is and is not justifiable. (6)

(e) Is there any reason why lobbying Parliament to amend or remove statutory instruments might be best done very early in the life of the instrument? (3)

5.1 What is the European Union?

Open any British newspaper and you are certain to find a reference to the European Union. But what exactly is the European Union and how is European law made? This unit addresses these questions.

The European Union (EU) is a group of nations bound together by the treaties they have signed. The treaty which set up the EU - or European Economic Community (EEC) as it was originally called - was the Treaty of Rome. This was signed by the six original members of the EEC in March 1957 (the EEC formally came into existence on 1 January 1958). By 2002, the number of members of the EU had grown from six to fifteen (see Box 5.1). Britain was not an original member of the EU. It joined the EEC in 1973.

Box 5.1 *Membership of the EU*

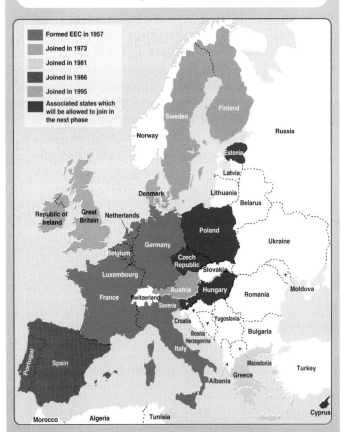

Formed EEC in 1957
Joined in 1973
Joined in 1981
Joined in 1986
Joined in 1995
Associated states which will be allowed to join in the next phase

This map shows the evolution of the EU. It shows the member states of the EU up to 2003 and the dates they joined. In 2003, there were plans for further enlargement. A further 12 countries had applied to join. Of these 12, it had been agreed, in principle, that six should be allowed to join in a first wave. These six 'associated' states are also shown on the map.

European law

The EU makes laws which must be respected by all member states. The body of European law is growing and will continue to grow. Since the aim behind the creation of new European laws is often to harmonise (standardise) laws between the different member states, it is inevitable that EU laws are passed which some member states do not like. Even if they do not like them, however, all member states have to obey EU laws. For members of the EU, it is no longer the case that only national governments can make laws within their territories.

5.2 The institutions - an overview

Decisions in the EU are made by four main institutions - the Council of Ministers, the European Commission, the European Parliament and the European Court of Justice. Each of these is examined below in detail, but the role of each is summarised in Box 5.2.

Box 5.2 *The EU's four main institutions*

1. The Commission
The Commission is the permanent bureaucracy of the EU. It is made up of commissioners appointed by member states and civil servants. Commissioners draw up proposals for new laws and ensure that member states follow existing EU laws. It is the job of commissioners to act in the interests of the EU as a whole.

2. The Council of Ministers
The Council of Ministers (the 'Council') is the EU's ultimate law-making body. Its job is to discuss and approve (or reject) proposals drawn up by the Commission.

3. The European Parliament
The citizens of each member state elect Members of the European Parliament (MEPs). In many areas of law, the Council needs the agreement of the European Parliament (EP) before new laws can be created. In other areas of law, the EP must be consulted during the law-making process.

4. The European Court of Justice
The role of the European Court of Justice (ECJ) is to interpret European law. The 15 judges in the ECJ have the power to resolve cases involving a breach of EU law or to settle disputes over the interpretation of European laws.

5.3 The European Commission

The Commission, more than any other EU institution, is the driving force of the EU. The Commission is the body that draws up proposals for new European laws. These proposals then follow a complicated consultation process before, finally, being adopted or rejected by the Council. In an average year, the Commission sends to the Council around 700 proposals for new laws.

It is important to note that only the Commission can draw up proposals for new European laws. The Council and EP can request the Commission to draw up proposals, but they cannot draw them up themselves.

Commissioners and civil servants

Members of the Commission are not elected. They are chosen by each member state. Each member state chooses one or two commissioners, depending on the population in the state. At the start of 2002, there were 20 commissioners, each appointed for a five year period. The Commission employs about 15,000 staff. This might seem a lot but it is fewer than the number employed in local government within a typical medium-sized city. The Commission is based both in Brussels and in Luxembourg.

Commissioners and civil servants working for the Commission must think and act independently of their national origins and in the interests of the EU as a whole.

Other powers

As well as drawing up proposals for new European laws, the Commission issues regulations (see Unit 6, Section 6.1). These regulations have the force of law. For example, each year regulations dealing with the prices of goods produced by farmers in the EU are issued by the Commission.

In addition, the Commission is responsible for making sure that all member states follow EU law. If it suspects that a member state is breaking EU laws, the Commission can take it to the European Court of Justice (see below). The Commission also has a number of other functions, including negotiating with states wishing to join the EU and managing the EU budget (spending plan).

5.4 The Council of Ministers

The Council of Ministers (the Council) decides whether proposals drawn up by the Commission should become law. The European Parliament has acquired a role in law-making in recent years (see below), but it is, ultimately, the Council that approves or rejects proposals.

The Council is, in reality, not a single council. It is a revolving council, made up of government ministers from each member state. When the Council is meeting about transport, ministers responsible for transport attend, for example. Every six months, a different state holds the Presidency of the Council.

Strictly speaking, the **European Council**, where all Heads of State (ie Presidents and Prime Ministers) meet, is a separate body. The European Council meets twice a year to discuss important issues and long-term policy.

Ministers who attend the Council are elected by the populations of their own countries and often put the interests of their own country first.

Voting procedure

When debating Commission proposals for new laws, the Council sometimes adopts them without alteration and sometimes makes amendments. On occasion, however, the Council rejects proposals outright. The voting procedure used by the Council depends on the matter under discussion. Three different voting procedures are used. Some matters require **unanimity** (all states must agree). Some matters are decided by a **simple majority** (each state has a single vote and the majority view is accepted). Most matters, however, are decided by **qualified majority** voting where the number of votes a country holds depends on its relative size.

Activity 5.1

Qualified majority voting

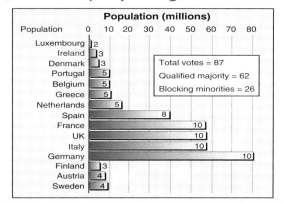

This bar chart shows the number of votes each member state had in the Council of Ministers in 2002. From 1998, a qualified majority required 62 votes. A measure could be blocked, therefore, by 26 (or more) votes - a minimum of two large states and either Spain or two small states.

Adapted from Hayes-Renshaw, F., 'Council of Ministers' in *Politics Review*, Vol.7.2, February 1998.

(a) **Why do you think that the qualified majority voting system is used for most matters? (3)**

(b) **Would you say that the qualified voting system is beneficial to small member states? Explain your answer. (4)**

(c) **Give arguments for and against the view that qualified voting should be the only voting system to be used by the Council. (6)**

COREPER

The Committee of Permanent Representatives (COREPER) assists the Council by doing a great deal of the day-to-day preparatory work. COREPER is made up of senior civil servants from the member states. Its members are based in Brussels. By working full-time on the proposals drawn up by the Commission, these civil servants provide a continuity which government ministers are unable to provide. Often the Council simply rubber stamps decisions taken by COREPER.

5.5 The European Parliament

The European Parliament (EP) is located in Strasbourg. Since 1979, its members, Members of the European Parliament (MEPs), have been directly elected every five years. The number of MEPs rose from 518 in 1979 to 626 in 1999. This reflects the growth of the EU.

Although the EP does not have the power to make laws (the Council has that power), it is involved in the law-making process in one of two ways.

1. The cooperation procedure

Under the cooperation procedure, the EP is allowed to suggest amendments to proposals drawn up by the Commission, but the Council does not have to accept these amendments (though it may do so).

2. The co-decision procedure

Under the co-decision procedure, both the EP and the Council must agree on the proposals drawn up by the Commission. Without the agreement of the EP, no laws can be created. Under this procedure, the EP is regularly able to force the Council to accept amendments to proposals since, if the Council fails to accept an amendment, the EP can prevent the proposal becoming law.

The 1997 Amsterdam Treaty extended the use of the co-decision procedure to all areas of EU law except those dealing with economic and monetary union. The aim was to provide the EP with a greater role in law-making.

Other powers

The EP also has the power to veto the annual EU budget put forward by the Commission and a 'power of censure' over the Commission (the EP can require the entire Commission to stand down if two-thirds vote in favour). In addition, the appointment of all commissioners and the signing of all international treaties must be approved by the EP.

Activity 5.2

The co-decision procedure

This cartoon illustrates a view that the EP is pointless and powerless. But how accurate a view is this?

In the vast semi-circular debating chamber of the European Parliament (EP) in Strasbourg, Neil Kinnock, one of Britain's two commissioners, is giving evidence. The dozen or so MEPs who are present are easily outnumbered by the translators in the booths surrounding the hall. To the casual observer, this scene might seem to illustrate the idea, widely held, that the EP is pointless and powerless. But this notion, if it was ever true, is out of date. The EP is far more powerful than most people in the EU realise. Last week, for example, the EP approved legislation that would lift the ban on the sale of new products containing genetically modified organisms. It also blocked measures to make company takeovers easier, much to the annoyance of the Commission. The EP can do this because it has the powers of 'co-decision'. Before the EP had the powers of co-decision, its views could be ignored. It had little power and little credibility. The Maastricht Treaty (which introduced the co-decision procedure in 1993) and the Amsterdam Treaty (which extended it in 1997) aimed to give the EP more credibility and more power.

Adapted from the *Economist*, 24 February 2001.

(a) **Describe the role that the EP plays in the EU's law-making process. (3)**

(b) **Explain why the introduction of the co-decision procedure was an important development. (5)**

5.6 The European Court of Justice (ECJ)

The European Court of Justice (ECJ) should not be confused with the European Court of Human Rights. The European Court of Human Rights is a quite separate court and is discussed in Unit 3, Section 3.5.

In January 2003, the ECJ had 15 judges, one from each member state. Occasionally all 15 judges sit (hear cases) together, but more often they sit in groups of five or three, known as 'chambers'. Nine Advocates General assist the court.

The ECJ's job is to ensure that EU law is applied in a uniform way throughout the member states. To achieve this it acts in two ways. First, it has a judicial role. It hears cases involving disputes both against member states and against other EU institutions. Second, it has a supervisory role. The ECJ ensures that courts in member states interpret EU law correctly. These two roles are described in more detail below.

It should be noted that decisions made by the ECJ cannot be challenged in any national court. European law, in other words, has supremacy over national law. In Britain, there was, for a while, some reluctance on the part of judges to accept that this was the case. So long as Britain remains a member of the EU, however, supremacy of EU law and institutions is undeniable whatever individual members of the legal establishment may feel.

1. The judicial role of the ECJ

If the government of a member state is seen as breaching European law, either the Commission or other member states can bring it before the ECJ. This is usually something of a last resort. As always, negotiation is to be preferred to court action.

Occasionally the Commission or Council finds itself before the ECJ when the legality of EU laws is brought into question. This happens if the Commission or Council is alleged to be:

● acting outside of its powers
● failing to follow procedures
● acting in a way not permitted by the various treaties.

Another EU institution or a member state can bring cases of this kind. Cases brought to the ECJ by private individuals are rare.

2. The supervisory role of the ECJ - Article 234

It is the job of the ECJ to ensure that courts in member states interpret EU law correctly. When a case comes

Activity 5.3

EC commission v UK re tachographs (1979)

Today in Britain, all lorries must be fitted with tachographs.

A tachograph is a device fitted to lorries that records the speed and distance travelled. An EU regulation requires that certain lorries should be fitted with tachographs. Checking tachographs allows the police or other authorities to stop drivers working over a certain number of hours on safety grounds. In Britain, the government was reluctant to implement this law, regarding it as an excessive burden on business. The Commission brought a complaint against the British government to the ECJ for failing to implement the regulation. The ECJ decided in favour of the Commission.

(a) Other than the Commission, who else might have brought this case? (1)

(b) Do the UK's highest appeal courts have the power to reverse this decision? Explain your answer. (3)

(c) Suggest why the Commission brought this case when Britain was clearly opposed to such interference with the transport industry. (3)

before a national court and EU law is an issue, under Article 234 (A.234) of the Treaty of Rome the case can be referred to the ECJ for a preliminary ruling. That does not mean that the ECJ takes over the case. Rather, it means that the ECJ is asked to make a ruling on the point of EU law affecting the case. The judge trying the case in the national court must then take this ruling into account when reaching a verdict. An A.234 preliminary ruling, therefore, is a little like deciding to ask a mechanic for expert advice on a difficult problem you are having with some repair work on your car. You seek advice and then go back to the work on your own. Unlike the advice of a mechanic, however, the ECJ's advice on EU law cannot be ignored.

It should be noted that Article 234 of the Treaty of Rome was Article 177 until the Treaty of Amsterdam, signed in 1997, renumbered the articles in the earlier Treaty of Rome.

Where the parties to a case disagree on the interpretation of a point of EU law and the case is being heard in the highest possible national appeal court (under English law, the House of Lords), there must be a referral to the ECJ. This is known as a **mandatory referral**. In effect therefore, A.234 limits the powers of the House of Lords. Other, lower courts have discretion. They may choose either to decide the matter themselves or to seek a ruling from the ECJ. This is known as a **discretionary referral**.

The ECJ, therefore, is not an appeal route from the English courts. If a case hinges on interpretation of EU law, A.234 provides the courts with a system for obtaining help in reaching the right decision. It is up to judges whether they employ that system or not (in all but the highest court, at any rate). Once a ruling has been sent from the ECJ back to the national court, the actual decision as to how the dispute should be resolved is left to the national court. The rulings given under A.234, however, are case law, or precedents (see Unit 7), that must be treated as binding in subsequent cases throughout the EU.

Discretionary Referrals

There has been debate among English judges for some time as to when a discretionary referral is appropriate. A.234 states that requests may be made to the ECJ where necessary for the court 'to enable it to give judgement'. This has been taken to mean that, if there is uncertainty as to the effect of a European law in relation to the case before the national court but a resolution of that uncertainty would make no difference to how that case was decided, no A.234 referral should be made.

Lord Denning ruling on the case of *Bulmer v Bollinger* (1974) in the Court of Appeal set out further guidelines as to when a discretionary referral should not be made:

- where it would not be conclusive of the case and other issues of law would still need to be decided
- where there has been a previous ruling on the same case
- where the court regards the point of EU law to be fairly clear
- where the facts of the case (rather than the law) have not yet been decided.

Denning highlighted the cost and delay involved in a referral to the ECJ and said that only where the point to be decided was 'really difficult and important' could the

use of the ECJ be justified. A contrary argument, however, is that an A.234 discretionary referral is to be preferred to the cost and delay of having to go through the appeals necessary to reach the House of Lords and a mandatory referral.

English courts still use these Bulmer guidelines, though, in recent years, there has been an increasing tendency to use A.234. In *R v International Stock Exchange, ex parte Else (1993)*, Lord Bingham, in the Court of Appeal, said that English courts should only decide on difficult points of EU law where they have real confidence in their decision and do not need the assistance of the ECJ.

The Court of First Instance

The Court of First Instance is a court which was set up to reduce the workload of the ECJ, and, therefore, to reduce delays. 'First Instance' means that the cases brought before it have not come through hearings in other courts. Its role is to hear cases involving:

- disputes between those employed by the European institutions and their employer
- competition law
- anti-dumping law
- cases involving the European Coal and Steel Community Treaty.

The Court has 12 judges, who hear cases in groups of six, four or three. Appeals on a point of law may be heard in the ECJ itself. Although it is a separate court, the Court of First Instance has a very narrow role compared to that of the ECJ.

Summary ●●●

1. What role is played in the law-making process by (i) the European Parliament, (ii) the Council of Ministers, (iii) the Commission and (iv) the European Court of Justice?

2. What is meant by the term 'qualified majority voting'?

3. What is the difference between the cooperation procedure and the co-decision procedure?

4. What is the purpose of an Article 234 ruling?

5. When are A.234 rulings mandatory and when are they discretionary?

Case study 〉 ● 〈 Sirdar v Army Board and Another (1997)

Sirdar v Army Board and Another (1997)

One principle of EU law requires that men and women should be treated equally. The French, Portuguese and United Kingdom governments all took the view that EU law permitted an exception to this in the case of the armed forces and, in particular, in the case of armed combat troops. Ms Sirdar, who had worked as a chef in the British Army since 1983, received, in 1994, an offer to transfer to the Royal Marines. But, she was later informed that the offer had been made by mistake and would have to be withdrawn, as she was ineligible by reason of her sex. Sirdar brought a claim before an Employment Tribunal on the grounds of sex discrimination. The Employment Tribunal sought a preliminary ruling from the ECJ on a number of issues,

Royal Marines set up a mortar in a combined Joint Forces Operation in May 1996.

including clarification of Article 297 of the Treaty of Rome (which is concerned with sex discrimination) and a relevant Council directive (Unit 6 explains what a directive is). The ECJ ruled first that:

> *An examination of the treaties and other EU laws did not allow work within the armed forces to be seen as an exception to the principle of sexual equality, even in relation to armed combat troops. Nevertheless, the Council directive did permit an exception to the equal treatment of men and women in matters of public security, so long as women were excluded where it could be justified as appropriate and necessary.*

The marines are a small force, intended to be the first line of attack. Chefs within the marines are also required to serve as front-line commandos. All marines are engaged and trained for that purpose. The second ruling of the ECJ, therefore, was that:

> *In these circumstances, the exclusion of women from certain parts of the armed forces, such as the British Marines, could in principle be justified.*

Adapted from the *Times*, 27 October 1999.

Questions

(a) Explain the difference between a mandatory and discretionary A.234 ruling. Was this matter dealt with by the ECJ as a mandatory referral or a discretionary referral? Explain how you know. (2)

(b) If the Tribunal had decided on these questions of EU law without an A.234 referral, what would Ms Sirdar have been obliged to do in the hope of getting the issues reviewed by the ECJ? (3)

(c) Would judges in countries other than the United Kingdom be obliged to refer to this ECJ ruling when deciding similar cases? Explain your answer. (2)

(d) Do you feel that the Employment Tribunal was likely to find that Ms Sirdar had been discriminated against, after receiving this A.234 ruling? Was it obliged to? Explain your answer. (4)

(e) The Court of Justice gave its ruling on October 26 1999. The Employment Tribunal reference was dated March 25 1997. Comment. (4)

(f) i) Suppose that the Commission decides to introduce a law giving women the right to be part of *all* combat units, without exception throughout the EU. Describe what would have to happen for this idea to become law. (3)

ii) Suppose that the EP proposes amendments to the Commission proposal. What would happen if the Council refused to accept these amendments? (4)

6.1 Primary and secondary sources of EU law

When talking about where exactly the law comes from, lawyers talk about 'sources of law'. There are two sources of European Union (EU) law.

1. Primary sources

Primary sources of EU law are treaties. Treaties are agreements signed by the Heads of State of all the member states of the EU. They set out the main principles and goals of the EU.

Treaties signed by members of the EU are different from other international treaties because failure to comply with EU treaties can sometimes lead to legal action being taken against a member state and to that member state being forced to comply with terms of the treaty. This is not necessarily the case with other international treaties. For example, almost every country in the world has signed the Universal Declaration of Human Rights. The third article of this treaty states that 'everyone has the right to life, liberty and security of person'. Despite this, there are many countries which regularly sentence criminals to death and execute them - something which is clearly in breach of this article. Although such countries are breaking the terms of the treaty, however, there is not really a legal process to force them to comply. With the various EU treaties on the other hand, there is such a process. The government of a member state may be brought before the European Court of Justice (ECJ - see Unit 5, Section 5.6).

2. Secondary sources

Secondary sources of EU law are:

- regulations
- directives
- decisions.

What these different types of law have in common is that they are all laws aimed at putting the general principles set out in the treaties into practice. Unlike treaties, however, they do not require the signature of Heads of State. They are proposed by the European Commission and approved by the Council of Ministers and the European Parliament (see Unit 5 for information on these institutions).

Treaties

Treaties are the highest source of EU law. Box 6.1 outlines the main provisions in the four treaties signed between 1957 and 2002.

Box 6.1 *Treaties of the European Union*

1. The Treaty of Rome, 1957

The European Economic Community (EEC) is created with the aim of 'ever closer union of the people of Europe'. Trade barriers and customs duties are abolished.

2. The Maastricht Treaty, 1993

The EEC becomes the European Union (EU). Everybody holding a passport from one of the member states of the EU becomes a citizen of the EU. There are new powers for the European Parliament (EP) and reform of other EU institutions. There is a commitment to monetary union (which some states, including the UK, opt out of). Employment rights are created.

3. The Amsterdam Treaty, 1997

There are more powers for the EP (the co-decision procedure is extended - see Unit 6, Section 6.5). Immigration laws are to be common between states. Human rights provisions are established.

4. The Treaty of Nice, 2001

Changes in the qualified majority voting system are agreed, a necessary preparation for a big increase in the number of member states. The idea that groups of countries will develop at different paces within the EU is agreed.

By signing a treaty, a member state makes a commitment to create new laws which fit with the principles and meet the goals laid down by the treaty. It is true that a member state can ultimately decide to leave the EU. But, the longer a member state remains in the EU, the more EU law becomes tangled up in its system. At some indefinable point, leaving the EU becomes almost a practical impossibility. For this reason, treaty obligations, the 'rules of the club', become binding and, in effect, have the force of law. Certainly, this is the way that the Commission and the ECJ view not only European treaties but also other types of EU law.

Directives

Directives are statements outlining the kind of national laws that member states are required to pass in order to meet the requirements of treaties. An extract from a directive is outlined in Box 6.2. Directives are issued under Article 249 of the Treaty of Rome. When a directive is issued, member states are given a date by which they must have passed laws meeting the criteria laid down by the directive. This date is known as the 'date for implementation'. Directives are more specific than treaties, which contain general principles. They direct member states to pass laws which meet certain criteria, though they leave it to the member states themselves to decide what form the laws will take. Sometimes a degree of flexibility and discretion is given to member states, with the result that different approaches are taken in different countries.

One example of a major Act of Parliament which was passed to comply with a directive is the Consumer Protection Act 1987. This legislation gave to consumers powerful new rights of action against the manufacturers of

defective products. Another example of a directive that has been incorporated into UK law is the Working Time Directive which was issued in 1993. This directive set out limits on hours of work and certain rest period and holiday entitlements for workers. It was implemented with the Working Time Regulations 1998.

Regulations

Regulations are detailed laws that apply to everyone in the member states. They are issued under Article 249 of the Treaty of Rome. Regulations are 'directly applicable'. This means that they become law automatically without member states having to pass their own laws to put them into effect. It was an EU regulation, for example which required certain lorries to be fitted with tachographs (see Unit 5, Activity 5.3). Another example of a regulation is provided in Box 6.3.

Box 6.2 *Directive 2000/79/EC*

The Council of the European Union, having regard to the treaty establishing the European Community and, in particular Article 139(2) thereof...has adopted this directive.

Article 1
The purpose of this directive is to implement the European Agreement on the Organisation of Working Time of Mobile Staff in Civil Aviation concluded on 22 March 2000...

Article 2
1. Member states may maintain or introduce more favourable provisions than those laid down in this directive.

2. The implementation of this directive shall under no circumstances constitute sufficient grounds for justifying a reduction in the general level of protection of workers in the fields covered by this directive...

Article 3
Member states shall bring into force the laws, regulations and administrative provisions necessary to comply with this directive not later than 1 December 2003 or shall ensure that, by that date at the latest, management and labour have introduced the necessary measures by agreement...

Article 4
This directive shall enter into force on the day of publication in the *Official Journal of the European Communities.*

Article 5
This directive is addressed to the member states.

An annex is attached providing the text of the European Agreement on the Organisation of Working Time of Mobile Staff in Civil Aviation.

Extract from Council Directive 2000/79/EC of 27 November 2000 concerning the European Agreement on the Organisation of Working Time of Mobile Workers in Civil Aviation.

Box 6.3 *Commission Regulation (EC) No 418/2001*

The Commission of the European Communities, having regard to the Treaty establishing the European Community, having regard to Council Directive 70/524/EEC of 23 November 1970 concerning additives in feedingstuffs, as last amended by Commission Regulation (EC) No 2697/2000 and in particular Article 4 thereof...has adopted this regulation.

Article 1
The preparations belonging to the group 'Micro-organisms' listed in Annex I to the present regulation are authorised for use as additives in animal nutrition under the conditions laid down in that Annex.

Article 2
The preparations belonging to the group 'Enzymes' listed in Annex II to the present regulation are authorised for use as additives in animal nutrition under the conditions laid down in that Annex...

Article 4
This regulation shall enter into force on the day following that of its publication in the Official Journal of the European Communities. It shall apply from 1 March 2001.

This regulation shall be binding in its entirety and directly applicable in all member states.

Extract from Commission Regulation (EC) No 418/2001 of 1 March 2001 concerning the authorisations of new additives and uses of additives in feedingstuffs.

Decisions and recommendations

Decisions are EU laws that have to be obeyed by a particular member state, individual person or organisation rather than by all member states or EU citizens. Decisions are issued under Article 249 of the Treaty of Rome and they are legally binding. Following Commission proposals, the Council, in consultation with the European Parliament (EP), passes decisions in much the same way as it passes directives and regulations (see Unit 5 for more detail on the law-making process). If, for example, a large corporation is acting in a way that is contrary to EU aims on competition or free trade, a decision might be passed in order to restrict its activities.

Also under Article 249, the Commission and the Council issue formal recommendations and opinions from time to time. These may be important statements of the views held by an EU institution on a particular matter, but they are not legally binding.

6.2 The impact of EU law on the UK

Before 1972, the UK had complete 'parliamentary sovereignty'. Parliament alone had control over the creation of laws (see Unit 3, Section 3.2). In 1972, however, this changed. The UK government's application to join the EU was accepted and Parliament passed the European Communities Act. This Act transferred some control over the creation of laws to EU institutions. It also gave the European Court of Justice (ECJ) the final say over the interpretation of EU laws. The ECJ, unlike UK courts, is quite beyond the control of Parliament and quite outside the English legal system. As a result of joining the EU, therefore, Parliament accepted that laws would be created outside the UK's national boundaries and that these laws would be binding on the UK whether or not the UK Parliament agreed with them. Only in areas of law not affected by the EU does Parliament remain sovereign, though, in theory, Parliament could, of course, pass a law which reverses the European Communities Act and leads to the UK leaving the EU.

The principle that, in the event of conflict between European law and national law, European law takes precedence was first established by the ECJ in *Van Gend en Loos (1963)*. In this case, the Dutch government unsuccessfully argued that the ECJ had no power to rule whether European law must take precedence over national laws about customs duties.

Activity 6.1

The Factortame case

In the 1980s, British fishing companies complained that Spanish businesses were taking a large amount of the quota of fish allocated to Britain by registering their fishing boats in Britain. The UK government responded to this concern by introducing a Bill into Parliament, which became the Merchant Shipping Act 1988. This Act stated that only boats on a new register would be allowed to fish in British waters. Essentially, only British boats were allowed to register.

Factortame, which was the owner of some Spanish boats, challenged this legislation in the High Court in 1990, on the grounds that it was in breach of EU trade laws. After a number of appeals, the case was eventually referred to the European Court of Justice. The ECJ ruled that the 1988 Act was in breach of EU law and could not be enforced against the Spanish boats.

Fishing off the British coast.

Before the case was decided, the Spanish fishing fleet had been deprived of the right to fish. In a later case, *Brasserie du Pécheur SA v Federation of Republic of Germany and R v Secretary of State for Transport, ex parte Factortame Ltd (No 4) (1996)*, the ECJ held that under EU law there was an individual right to compensation from a state in this kind of situation (the long case name is because the hearing before the ECJ involved two cases where the question of law to be decided was essentially the same - this is known as a 'joined case').

Adapted from Dowdle 1994 and the *Times*, 28 April 1998.

(a) **In light of the Factortame case, what legal advice would you give to an individual who appears to have been disadvantaged by UK legislation that contravenes the Treaty of Rome? (8)**

(b) **Explain how the Factortame case demonstrates the limits on Parliament's sovereignty. (6)**

(c) **Britain incorporated European Treaties into national law with the European Communities Act 1972. What arguments might be used in support of the view that parliamentary sovereignty has not been entirely lost in matters which are the subject of EU law? (4)**

Until the case of *R v Secretary of State for Transport, ex parte Factortame* proved otherwise (see Activity 6.1 above), there were lawyers who argued that, because of the doctrine of parliamentary sovereignty, the UK Parliament was unable to place limits on its own powers. No Westminster Parliament, they argued, could restrict the powers of a later Parliament or remove its right to reverse legislation. As a result, if, after Britain joined the EU, Parliament passed a law that went against an EU law, that law would be taken to be the will of Parliament and enforced in preference to the EU law. The Factortame case proved that this was not the case. It showed that, if Parliament passed a law which went against an EU law, then the EU law must be enforced, not the law passed by Parliament.

Direct effect and direct applicability

Laws give a group of people rights. These rights stem from the principles for regulating society which those making the law wish to create. Within national law, the mechanism by which individuals can enforce these rights is the courts. Acts of Parliament create rights for some groups, and usually impose obligations on others. For example, the Acts providing for unfair dismissal compensation create rights for employees and impose obligations on employers.

In the same way, principles of EU law can give one group rights and impose obligations on another. With European law, however, it is sometimes less clear-cut as to whether rights can be automatically enforced in national courts. If EU laws can be enforced in national courts in the same way as national laws, they are said to be **directly applicable**. Both EU Treaties and regulations are directly applicable. Directives on the other hand, because they are addressed solely to the governments of member states, are not directly applicable.

It was shown above that directives are, in one sense, not laws. They are instructions to governments to create laws in line with relatively generalised principles. Governments implement a directive by creating national legislation which complies with the directive within a certain timescale. Citizens can then enforce new legal rights in their national courts. Problems arise, however, when a particular member state does not really agree with a directive and either deliberately delays its implementation or creates laws which do not properly implement it. In these circumstances, two problems arise. First, it would appear that citizens are unable to obtain the benefit of particular legal rights to which they should be entitled. And second, the authority of European law is weakened. In response to these problems, the European Court of Justice has, over a number of years, developed the principle of direct effect.

What is direct effect?

The principle of direct effect allows a claimant to enforce the legal rights outlined within an EU directive in the courts, even though a national government has not yet implemented the directive. Claimants can do this in one of two ways (see Box 6.4). First, if they take action against the government for failing to implement the directive, they are attempting to show that the directive has **vertical direct effect**. And second, if they take action against the person or body who is required to do something by the directive, such as an employer, they are attempting to show that the directive has **horizontal direct effect**. It should be noted that both sorts of direct effect only become an issue where the government has not created appropriate laws under the directive. If such laws have been created, the laws are directly applicable in the normal way.

Box 6.4 *Direct effect*

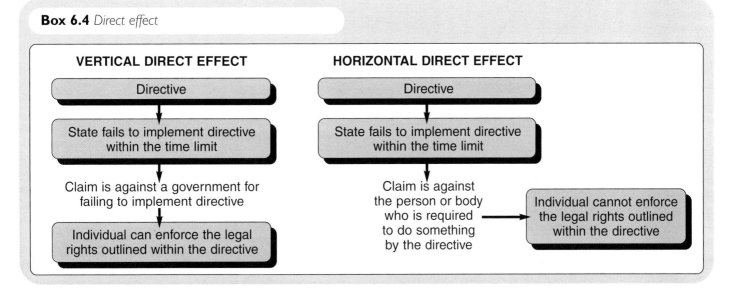

6.3 When do directives have direct effect?

Directives and vertical direct effect

There are a number of things to note about the way that the ECJ has judged directives to have vertical direct effect.

1. The directive must give specific rights to individuals

If a directive is clear, precise and unconditional it can have direct effect in the sense that it can be enforced by an individual against the state. A fairly vague directive, on the other hand, does not have vertical direct effect.

Van Duyn v Home Office (1974)

Van Duyn was a Dutch citizen who was a member of the Church of Scientology, a controversial religious group that the UK government wished to exclude from the UK following allegations that Scientologists were involved in a kind of 'brainwashing'. For this reason, the Home Office refused to allow Van Duyn to enter the UK. Van Duyn challenged this decision on the basis that it was contrary to articles of the Treaty of Rome allowing freedom of movement between member states. The Treaty of Rome allowed exceptions on the basis of 'public policy'. But, Van Duyn argued, an EU directive issued in 1964 limited the definition of 'public policy' to issues arising from personal conduct. Since, in her personal conduct, she had done nothing that would normally lead to exclusion, it was argued that she should be admitted. The ECJ ruled that, when a directive created clear rights and obligations, it should have vertical direct effect. It was not difficult to suppose what specific kinds of personal conduct would be unacceptable under the directive.

2. The term 'government' has been given a broad definition

While the notion of vertical direct effect restricts rights of action to those against the state, ECJ cases have shown that by 'government', the ECJ does not just mean the executive part of the state. The term 'government' includes government-funded bodies such as health authorities, and other 'arms of the state', even though they may be to some extent independent of government and are not involved in making laws.

Marshall v Southampton Health Authority (1986)

Ms Marshall, a dietitian who worked for Southampton Health Authority, was required to retire by her employer on the grounds that she was over 60. She, however, wanted to work until she was 65, as men were able to do. The employer's decision to force her to retire was legal under English law but illegal under a directive providing for equal treatment of men and women. Marshall claimed that she was being discriminated against. The national court made

an Article 234 reference to the ECJ (see Unit 5, Section 5.6), asking for directions on the interpretation of the directive. The ECJ found that English law was in conflict with the directive. They also found that Marshall, though not seeking enforcement of her rights from the government itself, was employed by a government-funded body and, therefore, able to rely on vertical direct effect as the government had obligations towards individuals working for bodies it funded.

3. Failure to implement a directive can result in the imposition of fines

The ECJ has also made it clear that, if a member state fails to create laws within the time limit specified by the directive, individuals may receive compensation from the national government.

Activity 6.2

Launch of a British Gas marketing campaign.

Foster v British Gas (1990)

Like the case of *Marshall v Southampton Health Authority (1986)*, the case *Foster v British Gas (1990)* also arose because of a dispute over the different retirement ages for men and women. In this case, however, the ECJ had to decide whether British Gas, a corporation created by government statute and with statutory duties concerning the supply of gas, could be regarded as part of the government (this case was brought before British Gas was privatised). The ECJ ruled that agencies which were 'subject to the authority or control of the state or had special powers beyond those which result from the normal rules applicable in relations between individuals' were part of the government. British Gas met these criteria and, as a result, Foster was able to rely on vertical direct effect.

(a) **Explain the difference between UK and EU law which was crucial to this case. (4)**

(b) **What is meant by vertical direct effect? Illustrate this concept using the case of *Foster v British Gas (1990)*. (8)**

(c) **Why do you think that the ECJ gave such a broad interpretation of the term 'government' in this case? (5)**

Italy v Francovich (1992)

A directive required member states to create a scheme to help employees of companies that became bankrupt. The aim was to ensure that employees received any overdue pay since, often, businesses on the verge of bankruptcy delay normal payment of wages. The Italian government did not implement the directive on time. Francovich lost his job in Italy when his employer became bankrupt and he was owed significant amounts of back pay. The ECJ ruled that compensation was due to him from the Italian government because of their failure to implement the scheme required by the directive.

However, in *Paola Faccini Dori v Recreb Srl (1995)*, the ECJ said that for there to be a right to compensation for failure to implement a directive, a number of criteria must be met:

- the directive must be one intended to give rights to individuals
- the nature of the rights must be clear from the directive
- there must be a clear connection between the state's failure to implement the directive and the individual's loss.

Directives and horizontal direct effect

Directives do not have horizontal direct effect. This means that directives which have not been implemented do not give an individual any rights against anyone other than the government. In *Duke v GEC Reliance Ltd (1988)*, Ms Duke was seeking to obtain the benefit of anti-discrimination rights set out in the Equal Treatment Directive. However she was not able to rely on the directive in an action against her employer as she was employed by a commercial business rather than by the government or an arm of the state.

In *Marleasing SA v LA Commercial Internacional de Alimentacion (1992)*, the ECJ ruled that where there was any ambiguity about a national law, national courts should interpret it, as far as possible, in light of any relevant EU directive. This applies even where the directive has not yet been implemented.

Treaties and direct effect

Not all articles in a treaty are capable of direct effect. That is because they are too vague to form the basis of rights or obligations for individuals. Take, for example, Article 4 of the Treaty on European Union (the so-called 'Maastricht Treaty' which was ratified in 1993). This includes the following provision:

'The European Council shall provide the Union with the necessary impetus for its development and shall define the general political guidelines thereof.'

The problems of treating this provision as having either vertical or horizontal direct effect are obvious. It would be ludicrous to suppose that an EU citizen could take court action to force a member state to 'provide the Union with the necessary impetus for its development'.

However, treaties can sometimes create rights and obligations which are enforceable by the courts even without new, more detailed laws being created. This was established in the case of *Van Gend en Loos (1963)*. The ECJ decided that treaty provisions could have both horizontal and vertical direct effect when:

- they were unconditional, clear and precise as to the rights and obligations that were being created
- no discretion was given to member states as to whether or not the provisions should be implemented.

So, when it is clear what rights and obligations are being given to EU citizens in a particular treaty provision and when that provision must be implemented by all member states, the provision has direct effect.

Direct effect and other EU laws

It was noted above that regulations are detailed laws that apply to everyone in the member states and that they are 'directly applicable'. Another way of saying this is that regulations have both vertical and horizontal direct effect.

Decisions are also directly applicable. Recommendations, on the other hand, are not legally binding and, therefore, do not have direct effect.

1. What does signature of an EU treaty involve for a member state?

2. Explain the difference between a directive and a regulation.

3. In relation to EU law, what is a decision?

4. What is a law which is 'directly applicable'?

5. What kind of EU laws are always directly applicable?

6. What is the difference between vertical and horizontal direct effect?

7. When will a directive have vertical direct effect?

Case study The Treaty on European Union

Article 29 of the Amsterdam Treaty, 1997

Without prejudice to the powers of the European Community, the Union's objective shall be to provide citizens with a high level of safety within an area of freedom, security and justice by developing common action among the member states in the fields of police and judicial cooperation and combating racism and xenophobia.

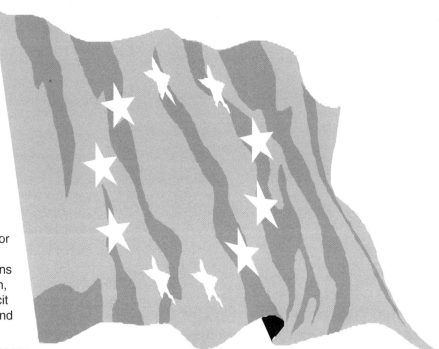

That objective shall be achieved by preventing and combating crime, organised or otherwise, in particular terrorism, trafficking in persons and offences against children, illicit drugs trafficking and illicit arms trafficking, corruption and fraud, through:

- closer cooperation between police forces, customs authorities and other competent authorities in the member states, both directly and through the European Police Office (Europol)

- closer cooperation between judicial and other competent authorities of the member states

- approximation, where necessary, of rules on criminal matters in the member states.

Extract from the consolidated version of the Treaty on European Union, incorporating the changes made by the Treaty of Amsterdam.

Questions

(a) Does Article 29 have direct effect? Explain your answer. (3)

(b) Give an example of a directive and a regulation which might be issued following the signing of this treaty. (6)

(c) Discuss what kind of specific details draft directives should contain to ensure that they have vertical direct effect. (6)

The common law and the doctrine of precedent

7.1 What is the 'common law'?

The 'common law' is judge-made law. In terms of civil law, the primary role of judges is to resolve disputes by applying existing law. In terms of criminal law, the primary role of judges is to oversee trials and to determine what sentence should be passed if the defendant is found guilty - again largely by applying existing laws. Much of the existing law is beyond the control of the courts. Parliament and the European Union have far more impact on the current law. Where an Act of Parliament is relevant to a case, a judge must apply the Act. This applies whether or not the judge sees the statute as leading to a fair or desirable resolution of the case.

However judges have the opportunity to create new law or change existing law in at least two circumstances:

- where it is necessary to decide what interpretation should be given to the language in which UK or EU legislation is written (see also Unit 8)
- where there is no legislation relevant to the case before the court.

Where there is no relevant legislation, the judge must decide whether and how to follow the decisions made by judges in earlier cases that had similar facts. In the words of Lord Simonds, speaking in the case of *Midland Silicones Ltd v Scruttons Ltd (1962)*, by making decisions in this way judges ensure that: 'the law is developed by the application of old principles to new circumstances'.

7.2 What is the 'doctrine of precedent'?

It is important to emphasise that, when making decisions in cases which mark a change in the law, judges do not begin with a blank sheet of paper. They are bound by strict rules known as 'the doctrine of precedent'. This can be defined as follows.

The common law is applied to a case by looking at earlier cases that appear to have similar facts. These cases are described as 'precedents'. They are also referred to as 'authorities'. If the rule created in a precedent appears to apply to the case that is presently before a judge then that rule must be followed. Judges write a statement, sometimes at considerable length, explaining the reasoning used, why they feel bound to follow one case rather than another and making other comments. This written statement is known as a 'judgement'. The judgement may itself become a precedent that is applied in later cases. The Latin term for this approach is *stare decisis* which means 'let the decision stand'.

At first sight, it may seem that the doctrine of precedent means that the common law will almost never alter. But, it would be an oversimplification to see the common law as a process of mechanically applying and restating rules of law that have already been created in the past. From time to time, cases arise that are so unusual that there is little or nothing in the way of case law. In addition, judges find ways to avoid applying an existing precedent. No two cases have identical facts. Judges generally have to choose which of a number of precedents apply to the current case. Earlier cases that are similar, but are in some crucial respect different, need to be **distinguished** from valid precedents. Higher courts may **overrule** or **reverse** the decision of lower courts (see pages 50-51 below for an explanation of these terms). Whether overruling or reversing of a precedent is possible depends upon the position of a court within a strict hierarchy.

7.3 Precedent and the hierarchy of the courts

As indicated above, there is a strict hierarchy of courts in England and Wales. Top of the civil court hierarchy is the European Court of Justice (ECJ), with the House of Lords the next tier down and the Magistrates' Courts at the bottom. Top of the criminal court hierarchy is the House of Lords, with the Court of Appeal Criminal Division the next tier down and the Magistrates' Courts also at the bottom. This hierarchy is important because lower courts are bound to follow the precedents set by higher courts. A precedent set by the ECJ, for example, must be followed by all courts since the ECJ is at the top of the hierarchy. Equally, a precedent set by the House of Lords must be followed by all courts except the ECJ since the House of Lords is the next court down the hierarchy. Since lower courts have no choice but to follow precedents set by higher courts, precedents set by higher courts are known as a 'binding precedents'.

The lower courts can create precedents. But, a precedent from a lower court can be overruled or reversed by one of the higher courts at a later date - see Activity 7.1. The relation between precedent and the hierarchy of the courts is explored in Activity 7.2.

Activity 7.1 — Lord Devlin's 'missing 10%'

Lord Devlin wrote in 1979 that 90% of judges, 90% of the time, are simply involved in the application of the law as it stands. He has a point. It would be wrong to imagine that many judges spend all their working days engaged in deep thought as to what the law really is, let alone what it ought to be. Most cases do not involve very difficult questions of law and the lawyers involved argue over questions of fact, not law. The law relating to most circumstances is clear-cut, well-established and frequently applied. What is at issue in most court hearings is primarily what happened, not what the law is. But, from time to time, the legal world becomes aware that the common law in a particular branch of law may change and it awaits the judgement of the court with interest. It is possible that cases involving arguments about the law will end up in the appeal courts - the Court of Appeal or the House of Lords. Judges at this level make up most of Devlin's 'missing 10%'. They are often engaged in creating 'new' rules of law. There are occasions where the judge is not only a referee in a dispute as to what happened but also a law-maker. Gradually, over the last two hundred years or so the role of the courts in law-making, as opposed to resolving disputes, has been greatly diminished. Parliament has become the most important source of law, both in terms of its supremacy over the courts and the amount of legislation created. But there are still significant areas of English law where there has been little legislative activity. Parliament has tended not to intervene a great deal in the development of the law relating to contracts, negligence and criminal law, for example. The common law has created many legal rules within these areas of law.

Lord Devlin

Adapted from *The Judge* by Lord Devlin, Oxford University Press, 1979.

(a) When do judges have a law-making role? (4)

(b) Which judges make the most of the common law? (2)

(c) Give examples of areas of law that are largely shaped by precedent. (3)

(d) Summarise the way in which judicial decisions become common law rules. (4)

Activity 7.2 — Binding precedents

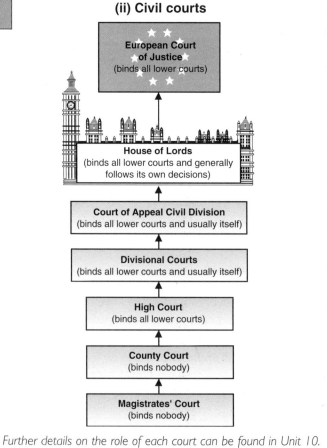

(i) Criminal courts

House of Lords
(binds all lower courts and generally follows its own decisions)

↑

Court of Appeal Criminal Division
(binds all lower courts and sometimes itself)

↑

Queen's Bench Divisional Court
(binds all lower courts and sometimes itself)

↑

Crown Court
(binds nobody)

↑

Magistrates' Court
(binds nobody)

Further details on the role of each court can be found in Unit 12.

(ii) Civil courts

European Court of Justice
(binds all lower courts)

↑

House of Lords
(binds all lower courts and generally follows its own decisions)

↑

Court of Appeal Civil Division
(binds all lower courts and usually itself)

↑

Divisional Courts
(binds all lower courts and usually itself)

↑

High Court
(binds all lower courts)

↑

County Court
(binds nobody)

↑

Magistrates' Court
(binds nobody)

Further details on the role of each court can be found in Unit 10.

(a) Supposing a precedent was set by a civil case in the Court of Appeal, which courts would be bound to follow this precedent? (2)

(b) Supposing a precedent was set by a criminal case in the Queen's Bench Divisional Court, which courts would be bound to follow this precedent? (2)

(c) Explain why the hierarchy of courts is an important part of the doctrine of precedent. (2)

7.4 The European Court of Justice (ECJ)

The European Court of Justice is a court that derives its authority from the member states of the European Union (EU), not just from English law (see Unit 5, Section 5.6). Since the UK is a member of the EU, decisions of the ECJ are binding on all UK courts. Some areas of law, including criminal law, remain unaffected by European law. In these areas, the House of Lords is, in practice, the supreme court. The ECJ is much more flexible about overruling its own past decisions than the House of Lords.

7.5 When is the House of Lords bound by its own decisions?

There has been considerable debate among the judiciary and legal academics for some years regarding the extent to which the House of Lords should see itself as bound by its own decisions. As the House of Lords is the highest court of appeal within the domestic UK system, this debate has a particular significance. The House of Lords has a choice between certainty and flexibility in the law.

The argument for certainty

Suppose that the Law Lords feel that there are good reasons for reforming certain areas of law, irrespective of well-established House of Lords precedents. Then suppose that, when opportunities arise to create reforms, Law Lords disregard these earlier cases in their judgements, and change the common law. One way of looking at this is to argue that the Lords have created regrettable uncertainty in the law. In such circumstances, it might be argued, lawyers will find it difficult to gauge what the common law is at any one time since major precedents are being created on the basis of the particular views of particular judges. This is a problem. For example, if a company has made a contract with another company, the company needs to know that it can enforce the agreement in the courts if the other side fails to comply with the terms of the contract. The strict rules of precedent help to prevent uncertainty. Because lawyers know what the precedents are, they can usually predict how a judge might regard the law. Practising lawyers, therefore, would prefer certainty to uncertainty.

The argument for flexibility

On the other hand, if the House of Lords is regarded as always bound by the decisions it made in the past, the law might not change fast enough. Few would argue, for example, that the moral principles underpinning the common law of the 19th century are always appropriate to modern society. Yet, because of the doctrine of precedent there have been occasions in the recent past when such principles remain within the common law. The case of *R v R (1991)* is as an extreme example of the potential danger of rigidly sticking to precedent. In this case the Lords said that, contrary to its own earlier decisions, rape could be a crime within marriage. Prior to *R v R (1991)*, a line of precedents stated that a married woman could not refuse sex with her husband. Obviously, most people would agree that the Lords were right to change the law, but it seems both worrying and surprising that it was not changed before 1991 (though it could be argued that Parliament, rather than the courts, had a responsibility to change the law).

7.6 The 1966 Practice Statement

Traditionally, the House of Lords has always preferred certainty to flexibility, but, in 1966, it issued a Practice Statement that indicated a willingness to be a little more flexible in the future.

Before 1966, the House of Lords followed the approach set out in *London Street Tramways v London County Council (1898)*. This case established that the Lords was always bound to follow its own decisions. The only limited exception to this was in cases where decisions were made 'in error' (known as '*per incuriam*'). The notion of 'error' was limited to instances where a decision had been made without any regard to relevant legislation or precedent. As a result of *London Street Tramways v London County Council (1898)*, the only way that most questionable House of Lords precedents could be undone was through legislation. It might be argued that this is not a good use of parliamentary time. Where the Lords had created or reinforced a poorly conceived rule, or in simple terms 'got it wrong', they ought at least to have the power to correct it. This is not inconsistent with the idea that major reform of the law is a matter for an elected Parliament.

In 1966, however, the Lord Chancellor issued the 'Practice Statement' - see Box 7.1. In future, the House of Lords would depart from its own earlier decisions when appropriate.

Developments since 1966

The common law system of precedent has not changed a great deal since 1966. On the whole, successive Law Lords have been cautious. There have been only a small number of occasions when the Practice Statement has been used. Alan Paterson in *The Law Lords* (1982) points out that Lord Reid, in various cases between 1966 and

Box 7.1 *The Practice Statement*

The 1966 Practice Statement was issued by the Lord Chancellor. It can be summarised as follows:

1. The Lords continue to regard the need for individuals to know more or less what the law is as crucial. The system of precedent helps to ensure this. Precedent is also seen as a good system for developing the law over time.

2. Sticking too rigidly to what was decided in earlier cases can lead to a situation where some individuals do not receive justice and the law changes too slowly. The House of Lords should continue to see itself as bound by its own decisions as a general rule but depart from a previous decision when it appears right to do so.

3. Contract law, property law, tax law and especially criminal law should not be changed lightly.

4. The Practice Statement only applies to the role of precedent in Lords decisions. It does not apply to the use of precedent in other courts.

3. Decisions concerning the interpretation of statutes should only be overruled in very exceptional cases.

4. (a) A precedent ought not to be overruled if the Law Lords could not predict the consequences of departing from the earlier rule and (b) a precedent ought not to be overruled if it would be better to reform a substantial area of law rather than one small part (since a sweeping overhaul of the law is best left to Parliament).

5. A precedent ought not be overruled merely because the Law Lords feel an earlier court's understanding of the law was wrong. There should be some other reason as well.

6. A precedent should be overruled if it has the effect of making the law very uncertain, so that lawyers cannot advise what the courts will decide on a particular matter.

7. A precedent should be overruled if it is clearly not in line with modern concepts of justice and social values.

The application of the Practice Statement is explored in Activity 7.3.

7.7 When is the Court of Appeal bound by its own decisions?

Within both the Criminal Division of the Court of Appeal and the Civil Division, earlier decisions are normally binding. This is the rule created by *Young v Bristol Aeroplane Company Ltd (1944)*. The three exceptions allowed by that case are as follows:

● where there are conflicting Court of Appeal decisions (in this situation the court may choose which of its earlier decisions it will follow)

● where there is a House of Lords decision which can be interpreted as overruling the Court of Appeal decision by implication

● where the earlier Court of Appeal decision was given *per incuriam*.

In addition there appear to have been some other minor exceptions to the rule in *Young v Bristol Aeroplane Company Ltd (1944)* created by later cases.

For a while during the 1960s and 1970s, the Court of Appeal and, in particular, Lord Denning sought in various judgements to overthrow the restrictions *Young v Bristol Aeroplane Company Ltd (1944)* creates. These efforts culminated in the case of *Davis v Johnson (1978)* - see Activity 7.4 on page 46.

After the retirement of Lord Denning there have been

1975, devised seven criteria to determine when the Practice Statement should be applied:

1. The Practice Statement should be used sparingly.

2. A precedent should not be overruled where it would create unfair problems for people who had settled their affairs properly assuming that the current law was that stated in the precedent.

Activity 7.3

Jones v Secretary of State for Social Services (1972)

The case of *Jones v Secretary of State for Social Services (1972)* concerned the interpretation of injury benefit legislation and whether the House of Lords should depart from its own decision in *Re Dowling (1967)*, under the 1966 Practice Statement. Out of seven Law Lords, four felt that Dowling was wrong but only three of these were prepared to use the Practice Statement. Lord Pearson was one of those who favoured certainty. He said that the earlier decision of the Lords had the distinct advantage of being final both in the sense that it put to an end to litigation (ie legal action) between the parties and in the sense that a principle embodied in the *ratio decidendi* was established (see page 46 for a definition of the term '*ratio decidendi*'). 'A firm foundation' on which commercial, financial and fiscal arrangements could be based was created. He said: 'This distinctive advantage of finality should not be thrown away by too ready use of the recently declared liberty to depart from recent decisions.' Lord Diplock on the other hand was in favour of overruling Dowling. He said that, although Dowling was a recent case, there was no sense in allowing long-standing errors to go uncorrected. The decision could be reversed by Parliament through legislation but this would take a long time and, in the meantime, the victims of accidents at work were losing out.

(a) **Does Lord Pearson seem to favour certainty or flexibility in the law-making role of the Lords? Explain your answer. (4)**

(b) **Which of the seven criteria laid down by Lord Reid do you think Lord Pearson would have used when coming to his decision? Explain your answer (6)**

(c) **Using the case of *Jones v Secretary of State for Social Services (1972)* assess the impact of the Practice Statement and the difficulties of applying it. (6)**

few occasions when the Court of Appeal has not followed its own decisions. An argument in favour of allowing the Lords to determine where precedent should be abandoned is the fact that the Lords hears far fewer cases than the Court of Appeal and has the most experienced judges. It should be able to take a wider and more long-term view on the need to change the common law. The Court of Appeal often deals with more everyday cases and has a greater workload. All but the most able of judges sitting there will find it difficult to consider cases in as much depth as the Lords.

The Court of Appeal Criminal Division

The Criminal Division is also bound by its previous decisions. The exceptions in *Young v Bristol Aeroplane*

Company Ltd (1944) apply. However, there is an important additional exception. In *R v Spencer (1985)* the Criminal Division said that there was no difference between it and the Civil Division in regard to precedent except that, when the liberty of a person was at stake, it might decline to follow one of its own decisions.

7.8 When are other courts bound by their own decisions?

The Divisional Courts of the High Court

The High Court contains three separate appeal courts, called Divisional Courts - The Queen's Bench, Chancery and Family (see Unit 10). All of them are bound by decisions of the Court of Appeal, the House of Lords and the ECJ. The Divisional Courts are generally bound by their own decisions. Exceptions to this rule are similar to those applying to the Court of Appeal. This was decided in *Police Authority for Huddersfield v Watson (1947)*. Like the Criminal Division of the Court of Appeal the Queen's Bench Divisional Court seems to have more flexibility to overrule its own decisions where personal liberty is involved - *R v Greater Manchester Coroner, ex parte Tal (1985)*.

The High Court

The High Court, which hears larger civil claims, is bound by the decisions of the Divisional Courts, the Court of Appeal, the House of Lords and the ECJ. Unlike all of these, however, it does not have to follow its own decisions - *Colchester Estates (Cardiff) v Carlton Industries plc (1984)*.

Crown Courts, County Courts and Magistrates' Courts

More serious criminal cases are heard in the Crown Court. The County Court deals with civil claims for small amounts. Less serious criminal cases are heard before the magistrates, who also have the power to hear a few kinds of civil cases. These three courts are 'inferior courts'. They are bound to follow all of the higher courts listed above. For all practical purposes they do not create precedents, though there have been a small number of exceptions to this in the case of the Crown Court.

The Human Rights Act 1998 and precedent

The Human Rights Act 1998 (see Unit 3, Section 3.6) marks a major development in the system of precedent. The Act gives all courts the freedom to ignore precedent when deciding points under the European Convention on Human Rights (ECHR).

Activity 7.4 *Davis v Johnson (1978)*

Domestic violence.

In the case of *Davis v Johnson (1978)*, the appellant was seeking to exclude her violent husband from the family home. Whether she was able to do this hinged upon interpretation of the Domestic Violence and Matrimonial Proceedings Act 1976. The Act was rather unclear as to whether a wife might obtain an injunction (a type of court order) excluding a husband, when he was a tenant or owner. Earlier Court of Appeal decisions ruled that the wording of the Act did not allow for this. Three judges out of five held that the Court of Appeal was free to depart from its previous decisions. In his judgement, Denning went the furthest. Denning discussed how he felt the earlier Court of Appeal decisions were wrongly decided. In other words, the court had been mistaken in their interpretation of the Act. He then asked whether he was at liberty to depart from these decisions. He took the view that the Court of Appeal should have discretion. Denning asked: 'What is the argument to the contrary? It is said that if an error has been made, this court has no option but to continue the error and leave it to be corrected by the House of Lords.' Three arguments against leaving it to the Lords to change the law were forcefully made:

- there might be a wait of many years before a case which created the chance for the law to be corrected was taken to the Lords
- even allowing for the existence of the state legal aid scheme, many people would not have the financial means to take a case to the Lords
- even if this particular case were appealed to the Lords, it would be many months before the further appeal was heard and, in the meantime, those women suffering domestic violence would be denied the protection Parliament intended them.

The case was appealed to the House of Lords. Although the Law Lords accepted the view of the Court of Appeal in this case regarding the correct interpretation of the Domestic Violence Act, they were very clear that the Court of Appeal majority was wrong to extend the exceptions to the rule in *Young v Bristol Aeroplane Company Ltd (1944)*. Lord Salmon said that one reason for this was the fact that there were 17 judges in the Court of Appeal. Any relaxation of *stare decisis* (let the decision stand - see page 41) would lead to a mass of conflicting decisions, uncertainty and confusion.

(a) What are the arguments for allowing the Court of Appeal more flexibility in whether to follow their own decisions? (6)

(b) What are the arguments against such a course of action? (6)

Section 6 of the Act makes it unlawful for a public authority, including courts, 'to act in a way which is incompatible with a convention right'. In other words, the courts must act in a way that does not contravene the broad principles of human rights set out in the ECHR. Section 2 provides that interpretation of the rights laid down by the ECHR must take into account the rulings of the European Court of Human Rights. UK courts must follow the decisions of the European Court even if that means disregarding the ruling of a UK court that would otherwise be seen as a binding precedent.

Section 2 will clearly have considerable impact on the doctrine of precedent as it means that lower courts may refuse to follow some decisions of higher courts. In *Re Medicaments (No 2), Director General of Fair Trading v Proprietary Association of Great Britain (2001)* the Court of Appeal refused to follow the House of Lords precedent of *R v Gough (1996)* because it conflicted with decisions of the European Court of Human Rights. The *Medicaments* case concerned an alleged breach of Article 2 (the right to a fair trial) due to the appearance of possible bias on the part of a tribunal member.

7.9 Finding the rule in a case: ratio decidendi and obiter dicta

The *ratio decidendi* of a case is the statement of what the law is in relation to the particular facts at hand. This principle, the core of a judgement, is known as the 'ratio' for short. Other things said in a judgement are known as *obiter dicta*.

Rupert Cross described the *ratio decidendi* as 'any rule expressly or impliedly treated by the judge as a necessary step in reaching his decision'. In future cases where the facts are essentially the same, it is only the *ratio* that binds judges. It follows, therefore, that any discussion of the law within a judgement that is not strictly necessary to the resolution of the case - the *obiter dicta* - does not bind future judges, although their thinking will often be influenced by the *obiter dicta*. The division between a *ratio* and *obiter dicta* is illustrated in Box 7.2.

In law books, it is common to talk about the *ratio* in a particular case as though it were immediately obvious from a brief reading of that case what the effect of the

Box 7.2 *Home Office v Dorset Yacht Company (1970)*

A damaged yacht.

The law of negligence places a general duty to take reasonable steps to prevent injury to others or damage to property. For many years, the exact extent of this general duty has been shaped by the common law. The important negligence case of *Home Office v Dorset Yacht Company (1970)* concerned some boys who escaped from borstal and, while on the run, caused damage to a yacht. The House of Lords was required to decide whether the officers in charge of the boys owed any duty to the public to prevent damage to property. In his judgement, Lord Reid ruled that the officers and their employers were liable in this situation. This was the *ratio*. However, the judgement also contained a lengthy discussion relating to the circumstances in which a duty of care in negligence did and did not arise in general. In particular, Reid said that it was not possible to claim for what is known as 'economic loss' - such as loss of profit or other purely financial loss - as opposed to physical injury or damage to property. Obviously, these remarks were *obiter*, as the loss in question resulted from damage to property. Nevertheless, Lord Reid's remarks greatly affected the way in which negligence law was viewed at that time.

particular judgement was on the law. In reality, very often, it is difficult to do this. It is only over time, as the courts encounter opportunities to interpret a judgement and apply it to different cases, that it becomes possible to say with any certainty what the essential principle created by a precedent, the *ratio decidendi*, really is.

How do you find the ratio decidendi?

There are two factors to bear in mind when trying to establish the *ratio* in any particular case. Taken together, these factors indicate why there may be scope for debate as to what the *ratio* is and, often, why there is no simple black and white answer to the question.

First, written judgements do not have headings. There is never a clear heading, 'the *ratio decidendi*'. The judgements in appeal cases often run to a dozen or more pages, including a careful review of a whole body of law. As a result, it is not always clear what is *ratio* and what is *obiter*.

Second, there is always more than one judge in the appeal courts. In the House of Lords there may be up to seven. Each judge is likely to give a separate judgement, containing a different set of reasons for deciding the case, and a different view of the law. Which judgement provides the *ratio*? Sometimes appeal judges simply limit themselves to saying that they agree with a colleague.

How influential are obiter dicta statements?

Obiter dicta statements often turn out to be influential in the evolution of the law and should not be seen as insignificant just because only the *ratio* binds the courts.

The most important *obiter* statements are comments on what should or could be regarded as the current position of the law in relation to a general type of case, not just the specific case at hand. These statements are not strictly necessary to the process of deciding the case in the sense used by Rupert Cross above. Nevertheless, today's *obiter* may become tomorrow's *ratio* where a judge is impressed with the reasoning contained within it. This can happen in one of two ways - see Box 7.3.

Box 7.3 *Obiter statements transformed into ratio*

There are two ways in which an *obiter* statement today may become *ratio* in the future. First, since the Lords is the highest court in the domestic legal system, *obiter* statements made in the Lords are treated as an indication as to what current Law Lords would do if confronted with different facts. Lawyers read the *obiter dicta* in Law Lords' judgements and then argue that, if a particular case were to reach the Lords on appeal, it might well be decided in line with these *obiter* statements. In other words, the *obiter* statements become *ratio*. Where a judge is faced with the difficult dilemma of choosing between two or more competing versions of what the law is and one of those is supported by *obiter* statements made in a superior court, this will obviously have great influence. It is also possible that *obiter* statements in a lower court will, in due course, be considered and approved by a higher court. Legal arguments in the appeal courts are not confined solely to consideration of appeal court cases. Where something about the facts of the case under consideration makes it of a kind little seen in the courts before, only High Court judgements may be available for analysis. *Obiter* statements made in lower courts can influence the House of Lords or the Court of Appeal in their search for a 'correct' statement of the law to form a *ratio decidendi*. *Obiter* statements are one example of 'persuasive precedents' - see page 48 below.

7.10 How the common law evolves

Judges are conscious of factors beyond the need to be fair in resolving an individual case. To some extent they take into account other considerations, but these considerations make them cautious about changing the existing law dramatically. The considerations judges take into account include the following.

1. The need for certainty in the law

If the courts stick to treating like cases in the same way, this is helpful to people who need to plan their affairs in light of the current law.

2. The role of Parliament

When they have an opportunity to create new laws, the courts are often loath to do so on the basis that this is a matter for Parliament, as a democratically elected body.

3. Policy arguments

Sometimes the courts are wary of creating new 'causes of action' (grounds for claiming in the courts). An example of this is the fear of excessive litigation - what is known as 'the floodgates' argument. This is particularly true in the law of negligence. The courts need to balance the rights of those injured by careless actions with the danger of creating a situation where the courts are swamped by large numbers of trivial or fictional claims. An example of this can be seen in the cautious development of the law relating to nervous shock cases discussed in Item B of the Case Study at the end of the unit.

None of this means that the common law is not capable of dealing with the needs of society and changing as society changes. Some common law judges, such as Lord Atkin who founded the modern law of negligence, have been responsible for major innovations. However, compared to law-making through legislation, the common law changes slowly and step-by-step.

7.11 Original precedents

An original precedent is one created where the courts have never had to decide the point of law before and where there is no relevant legislation. Because there are no earlier precedents to refer to, the judge examines cases that seem to be closest in principle and adapts these. This is called 'reasoning by analogy'. Because the system of precedent has been used for centuries, true original precedents are rare.

Historically, stating the common law in entirely new situations was regarded as a matter of finding or 'discovering' the law. This tradition in English law is based on the idea that judges do not create law, but merely state what it has always been. Given the infinite variety of human activity, no contemporary lawyer would suppose that precedents are anything other than judicial law-making, and the quaint common law pretence is no longer kept up.

7.12 Binding and persuasive precedents

A binding precedent is one that the judge is obliged to follow. When the courts consider whether they must follow a precedent two questions have to be answered. First, are the facts of the precedent sufficiently similar? Second, was the court that created the precedent at a higher level in the hierarchy? If the answer to both questions is 'Yes', the precedent is definitely binding.

A persuasive precedent is one that the judge is not **obliged** to follow but where the judgement is clearly influential as it offers useful guidance and may be followed. There are a number of categories of persuasive precedent.

1. Judgements made by courts lower in the hierarchy

In particular, it has not been unusual for the House of Lords to follow decisions made in the Court of Appeal.

2. Statements made obiter dicta

In *Wilson (1996)*, a man branded his initials on his wife's body with a hot knife. His defence to a charge of assault was that his wife consented. Could this be acceptable in law? In the Court of Appeal, the judge used *obiter* statements about tattooing from the Lords judgement in *Brown (1993)*. These cases are discussed in the Case Study at the end of this unit.

3. Decisions of the Judicial Committee of the Privy Council

The Judicial Committee is made up of judges from the House of Lords. It rules on cases from certain Commonwealth countries which still use the Lords as a final court of appeal. Because the judgements do not relate to UK law, they are not binding on UK courts. Nevertheless, on occasion, these judgements are followed and embedded into English law.

4. Dissenting judgements

Court of Appeal cases are normally heard by three judges. It may be that two judges reach the same decision but one disagrees or dissents. Because there is a majority decision, a precedent has been created. However the Lords may prefer the views stated in the dissenting judgement and overrule the Court of Appeal.

5. The decisions of courts in other countries

Courts in Canada, Australia, New Zealand and other countries also use a common law system with similarities to the one in England and Wales. When there is a lack of precedent, the decisions of these courts can be persuasive.

Activity **7.5** Donoghue v Stevenson (1932)

Donoghue v Stevenson (1932) is a major precedent, what is known as a landmark case, in the tort of negligence. It created a wide-ranging mechanism by which the common law might compensate those who had suffered loss or injury through the fault of others. This was based on the idea of a general duty of care owed to others.

The facts of *Donoghue v Stevenson (1932)* are straightforward. Ms Donoghue went to a café with a friend who bought her some ginger beer and ice cream. The proprietor of the café opened the ginger beer and poured out some of the contents. The bottle was opaque, so it was not possible to see inside it. When the glass was topped up, a partially decomposed snail came out of the bottle. As a consequence Ms Donoghue became quite ill.

When somebody buys something, the law of contract applies. If a term of a contract for sale is not met, the courts will allow the person who has lost out to obtain compensation. However, the right to sue for damages relating to breach of contract is only provided to parties to the contract, namely the buyer and the seller. Ms Donoghue was not a party to the contract, as she did not buy the drink. Was there any other way that she could recover damages for her illness, given the apparent carelessness of the manufacturer?

Lord Atkin gave the leading judgement in the House of Lords. He recognised that the law of negligence was very piecemeal. The courts had only ruled on each specific case as it came before them. The common law required plaintiffs to fit their case into a limited and elaborate classification. Ms Donoghue's case did not come within the existing types of negligence.

Lord Atkin regretted that no broad, 'catch-all' duty of care existed. He set about defining such a duty. But, his position within the common law required him, at least, to dress his reform of negligence in the language of precedent. In his judgement, he said: 'And yet the duty which is common to all the cases where liability is established must logically be based upon some element common to the cases where it is found to exist.'

Lord Atkin ruled that a manufacturer of products that could not be inspected before use owes a duty of care to all those who might be expected to consume their product. This was all that was necessary to decide the case.

However Lord Atkin also set out his general test, now known as the 'neighbour test' to establish when a duty of care might arise in all manner of cases. He wrote that: 'You must take reasonable care to avoid acts or omissions which you can reasonably foresee would be likely to injure your neighbour. Who then is my neighbour? The answer seems to be persons who are so directly affected by my act that I ought reasonably to have them in contemplation as being so affected when I am directing my mind to the acts or omissions which are called in question'. In other words everyone has a duty to avoid injuring those who it might reasonably be thought would be injured by a lack of care.

This brief statement can be described as the main root of modern negligence, but it was made within a discussion of the law unnecessary to decide the particular case. Lord Atkin's test has been applied in countless cases since 1932, ranging from medical negligence, to everyday road accidents, accidents at work and even the Hillsborough Stadium disaster.

(a) **What is meant by the term 'negligence'? (2)**

(b) **Explain what makes *Donoghue v Stevenson (1932)* a landmark case in the law of negligence. (5)**

(c) **What problem did Lord Atkin identify in the law of negligence at that time? (4)**

(d) **Which of the following may be identified as the *ratio* of Donoghue?**

   1. **People who fall ill after drinking negligently contaminated ginger beer can be compensated by the manufacturer.**

   2. **People who fall ill after drinking negligently contaminated drinks can be compensated by the manufacturer.**

   3. **Manufacturers owe a duty of care to all those who might be expected to consume their product, particularly when the product is not capable of prior inspection.**

Explain how you reached your answer. (2)

(e) **Was Lord Atkin's neighbour test in *Donoghue* part of the *ratio* or *obiter dicta*? (2)**

(f) **The only part of a case that takes effect as a binding precedent is the *ratio*. Give reasons why the *obiter dicta* is nevertheless important. (8)**

(g) **Discuss whether Lord Atkin was sticking rigidly to the doctrine of precedent. (8)**

7.13 Distinguishing cases - dodging the precedent

The *ratio* of a particular case binds a court that is presented with a case that has essentially the same facts. The court must follow the precedent. It follows from this that, if the judge can show that, although the facts of their case are the same in some respects but in other important respects different, there is no obligation to follow a previous case. This is known as distinguishing a case. Distinguishing involves making a decision about what are significant factual differences between cases.

Sometimes the way a case is distinguished is uncontroversial and has relatively indisputable logic. On other occasions, distinguishing is rather artificial. What happens in this second type of case is that the judge looks for a way to avoid implementing a precedent that, for some reason, is seen as problematic. To do this, the judge stresses the significance of certain factual differences (see Box 7.4).

An example of distinguishing can be seen in the two cases in Box 7.5, both of which are concerned with mistaken identity in a contract for sale. The law of

Box 7.4 *Distinguishing cases*

Red squirrels are an endangered species. It is an offence to kill one. How would you explain what distinguishes the two different events below?

A.   X kills a red squirrel with a shotgun.

B.   Y kills a grey squirrel with a hunting rifle.

There are two differences between these sets of events. First, in (A) a red squirrel is killed and in (B) a grey squirrel is killed. And second, in (A) a shotgun is used and in (B) a hunting rifle is used. However, only one difference relates to the material facts. Obviously, X has committed an offence and Y has not. If you understand this very simple example you can begin to identify how, in court cases with much more involved facts, the judge can find important differences between cases with apparently similar facts. The differences that are found are much more subtle, and harder to identify, but the principle remains the same.

Box 7.5 *Examples of distinguishing cases*

(i) Cundy v Lindsay (1878)

A man called Blenkarn wrote to Cundy from 37 Wood Street, Cheapside to order goods and signed his name so that it looked like 'Blenkiron & Co', a firm whose offices were also in Wood Street. Cundy knew this firm and saw them as reliable customers. Blenkarn tricked Cundy into thinking he was someone else. The goods were bought on credit and resold by Blenkarn to Lindsay. Blenkarn did not pay the money he owed to Cundy, however. The court held that the contract was void because of the reasonable mistake made regarding the identity of the buyer. Effectively, there was no contract between Blenkarn and Cundy. This meant that Lindsay had to return the goods to Cundy.

(ii) Phillips v Brooks (1919)

A man entered a jewellery shop and selected various items. He proposed to pay by cheque. The jeweller said that delivery of the goods would only be made when the cheque had cleared. The man then said (falsely) that he was Sir George Bullough, a well-known, respectable and wealthy man. He gave an address. The jeweller checked that this was indeed the address of Sir George and allowed the buyer to take the goods with him straightaway. The cheque bounced, but meanwhile the man pawned the jewels. The jeweller sought to recover them from the pawnshop.

Again, the court had to decide whether the contract between 'Sir George' and the jeweller was void for mistake as to identity. The court decided that it was not. How did the court in *Phillips v Brooks (1919)* distinguish *Cundy v Lindsay (1878)*? At first sight there may seem little difference between the facts of the two cases. The earlier one was distinguished on the basis that, in this case, the mistake was not about identity but about creditworthiness. In the case of face-to-face transactions the court held that it should generally be presumed that the person intends to sell to the person they actually meet. *Cundy v Lindsay (1878)* was about a transaction purely through correspondence. Although the facts of both of these cases are very similar, the court found an important difference that affected the decision reached. In the second case, the court was able to distinguish the earlier precedent.

A jewellery shop.

contract makes a contract void (ie without legal effect) in certain situations where a mistake has been made. The implication of this is usually that a seller is entitled to the return of goods. In both of the two cases, the mistake was a consequence of fraud. In this situation, where the original buyer has sold goods on to a second buyer and then disappeared, the unfortunate second buyer may be required to return goods they thought were theirs, with little chance of recovering their value.

7.14 Overruling and reversing

Overruling occurs when a court is asked to review whether a precedent created by a court at a lower level in the hierarchy is correct law. The European Court of Justice and the House of Lords also have the ability to overrule their own previous decisions, even if these have become quite well-established precedents (though the Lords is often reluctant to overrule itself).

An example of overruling can be seen in *Pepper v Hart (1993)*. This case concerned whether the true meaning of words used in legislation could be established by looking at the printed record of parliamentary proceedings (ie the publication known as 'Hansard'). In *Davis v Johnson (1979)*, the Lords ruled that *Hansard* should not be used. In *Pepper v Hart (1993)* they overruled their own decision and said that it was permissible (see page 67).

Another example of the House of Lords overruling its own previous decisions can be seen in the contrasting cases of *Murphy v Brentwood District Council (1990)* and *Anns v London Borough of Merton (1978)*, which concern the correct test for establishing whether a claim for negligence should be allowed. Both cases were concerned with whether a local council should be liable for negligent failure to check that a builder was complying with building regulations (councils have legal obligations with regard to this). In both cases, defective foundations had affected the value of a property. This only came to light after the builders had sold properties to the applicants.

Of course, the builders were primarily to blame. But could the purchasers also claim against the council? It might be argued that this would be reasonable as a council in this situation could foresee the consequence of failing to spot bad work done by a builder. A contrary argument is that this would place too much of a burden on councils and open the door to excessive legal claims.

In *Anns v London Borough of Merton (1978)*, the Lords decided that the local council was liable to the purchaser of the house for damages. This was a major change in the law of negligence. In *Murphy v Brentwood District Council*

(1990), a seven-member court overruled the decision in *Anns v London Borough of Merton (1978)*, partly because they believed that the earlier case represented too wide an extension of the law of negligence. The law of negligence was returned to something closer to its traditional form by the decision in *Murphy v Brentwood District Council (1990)*.

Reversing is a term used in relation to appeals within the same case. Although the appeal courts often approve of the statements of law made in the courts beneath them it is obviously a major function of the appeal courts to reverse 'incorrect' decisions on appeal. Where there are two opposing views of the law, the High Court, for example, may prefer one, only to be overruled by the Court of Appeal, which prefers the opposing argument.

One example of reversing can be seen in the case of *Sweet v Parsley (1970)*. The defendant, a teacher, rented a house to students. Aside from collecting the rent, she had little contact with the students. She was unaware that they were using drugs. Nevertheless, she was convicted of being concerned in the management of premises which were used for the purpose of smoking cannabis contrary to Section 5 of the Dangerous Drugs Act 1965. She was convicted in the Crown Court. On appeal, the Queen's Bench Divisional Court upheld the conviction. The Divisional Court felt that the wording of Section 5 meant that no guilty mind or knowledge was required for an offence to have been committed. The defendant made a further appeal to the House of Lords.

The House of Lords allowed the appeal. Lord Reid said that there had been a presumption for centuries that Parliament did not intend to make criminals of those who were not blameworthy and that, in this Act, it was appropriate to read words into the statute requiring a guilty mind. The Lords reversed the ruling of the Divisional Court on the matter of the required state of mind.

7.15 The advantages and disadvantages of precedent

The advantages and disadvantages of precedent are summarised in Box 7.6.

7.16 Judges, law-making and reform

Although Parliament is by far the most important source of law in the UK today and laws created by the courts can be altered at any time by Parliament, there are several broad areas of law where the courts have been

Box 7.6 *Advantages and disadvantages of precedent*

Advantages

1. Certainty

It is often argued that if judges were seen to create laws on the basis of their own personal opinion about what was right and just, even if this ran contrary to clear precedent, there would be less consistency in the law. In addition, everyone would tend to find it difficult to predict in advance what was lawful and what was unlawful behaviour. For this reason, the Law Lords in particular have often preferred certainty to the reform of outdated laws.

2. Consistency

A related aspect of treating like cases alike is that individuals are treated consistently by the courts. The same rules are applied to everyone.

3. Flexibility

As noted above, the system of precedent does not always act as a straitjacket on judges. Judges in the appeal courts can, and regularly do, overrule or reverse decisions. The creative use of distinguishing can also prevent a court from being forced to follow a precedent it is reluctant to apply.

4. Detailed rules compared to legislation

Few would suggest that the common law should replace legislation. However, as a way of building up a detailed and comprehensive body of law it has the advantage that cases are dealt with as they arise. In areas such as contract law, Parliament has interfered relatively little with the long-established body of common law. English contract law is highly regarded by lawyers abroad.

Although Parliament creates Acts using language that seeks to provide for as wide a range of factual situations as possible, no Act can provide a complete set of rules for every eventuality. The courts, on the other hand, are in a position to interpret legislation when disputes arise and fill in any gaps where there is no statutory provision. It would not be practical for Parliament to spend time constantly amending legislation. The courts however are able to build up detailed case law over time which can help make legislation clearer and more workable. An example of this can be seen in the Theft Acts 1968 and 1978. A large body of case law has the effect of explaining and illustrating the meaning of certain terms used within the Acts.

Disadvantages

1. Complexity and obscurity

In a civilised society it is desirable for the law to be accessible and comprehensible. For ordinary citizens, the common law often appears difficult to understand and confusing. There are hundreds of thousands of decided cases. As mentioned earlier, the *ratio* of a judgement may be buried in many pages of discussion and comment. Eminent legal scholars are sometimes unable to agree what reasoning was used to decide a case, even after the judge has explained this at length in a written judgement. The same process of distinguishing that allows for flexibility in the common law can also lead to obscure 'hair splitting' decisions. Much of what judges say in their judgements is couched in legal jargon and difficult English. Occasionally, very old precedents written in antiquated language must be studied. Contract law is a good example of this. A number of early 19th century sailing ship cases such as *Stilk v Myrick (1809)* are still referred to in legal texts today.

2. The slow pace of change

The common law has sometimes been criticised as being too slow to alter in response to changes in society. Judicial precedent involves judges having to follow a binding precedent even where they think it is bad law. The House of Lords has the power to change the common law but it tends to err on the side of certainty. Case law changes only in response to someone bringing a case before the courts. As Denning pointed out in *Davis v Johnson (1979)*, it may be that few litigants have the financial resources or the determination to take a case to the Lords. The Lords, even if they are willing to alter the law, may wait a long time for the opportunity to do so.

3. The retrospective effect of changes in the common law

Whereas legislation normally only applies to events after it comes into force, changes made by case law apply to events which took place before the law was changed. This can sometimes be unfair. For example a business needs to be confident that the courts will enforce a contract.

4. The system is undemocratic

Where judges do take it upon themselves to reform the law they are not accountable to the electorate, but are making changes to legal rules that may greatly affect society. Almost all judges would agree with the comments of Lord Scarman in *Stock v Jones (1978)* that Parliament is a better way to create major changes in the law.

responsible for creating many of the legal rules.

1. The law of contract is essential to the working of modern society. However, except for the law relating to employment contracts and some parts of consumer law, it is almost entirely the product of the common law.

2. Criminal law is also largely based on common law principles. There are detailed Theft Acts, but even these are derived from common law (they gather together precedents). Also, there is a large body of case law that it is often necessary to consult in order to apply the Theft Acts.

3. The law of negligence, together with other areas of the laws of tort, have been developed through decisions of the courts since the landmark judgement of Lord Atkin in *Donoghue v Stevenson (1932)*.

However, the very nature of how the common law works, namely by starting from what the law was seen to be in the past, means that reforms to the common law are usually slow and gradual. In the final analysis, whether the courts introduce reforms depends upon the inclinations of the very small number of judges who sit in the House of Lords at any particular time. These judges do not answer to the government or anyone else. Perhaps the greatest pressures upon them is the awareness that:

● what they decide will shape the law of the land

● the words of a written judgement will be painstakingly scrutinised and picked apart by lawyers seeking to apply it in future cases.

It is hardly surprising that different Law Lords come to a different view of what their exact role as judges and law-makers should be. Some are reluctant to disturb legal rules, even if they have reservations about whether particular laws are fair or whether they are practical. They prefer not to risk disturbing the settled law or to jeopardise the precious certainty which so many other judges before have valued. They may also be nervous because, even though a change in the law may seem just for an individual case, it will have unpredicted and undesirable repercussions in later cases. Lord Halsbury, for example, admitted that if the Law Lords regarded themselves as bound by their own decisions 'cases of individual hardship may arise'. However, he preferred this to a 'disastrous' uncertainty. Other judges, such as Lord Denning, have adopted a less cautious approach and are much more inclined to see reform and the updating of the law as an inevitable part of their job in providing justice. Judges like this are more likely to value justice in individual cases and improvements in the law above certainty.

Activity 7.6

Different judges, different philosophies

Michael Zander illustrates the very different philosophies of senior judges by comparing the views expressed by Lord Simonds who sat in the House of Lords from 1944 to 1962 and Lord Denning who was Master of the Rolls (the most senior judge in the Court of Appeal) between 1962 and 1982.

He describes how Simonds saw his role as the preservation of the status quo. In *Midland Silicones Ltd v Scruttons Ltd (1962)*, for example, Simonds said:

'Nor will I easily be led by an undiscerning zeal for some abstract kind of justice to ignore our first duty, which is to administer justice according to the law which is established for us by an Act of Parliament or the binding authority of precedent. The law is developed by the application of old principles to new circumstances. Therein lies its genius.'

At the opposite end of the spectrum is Lord Denning, who once wrote:

'The truth is that the law is uncertain. It does not cover all the situations that may arise. Time and again practitioners are faced with new situations, where the decision may go either way. No one can tell what the law is until the courts decide it. The judges do every day make law, though it is almost heresy to say so. If the truth is recognised then we may hope to escape from the dead hand of the past and consciously mould new principles to meet the needs of the present.'

Zander points out that, despite his 'reforming zeal', Denning never formulated principles to guide judges as to when they should intervene in the common law and when they should not.

Adapted from 'The Reform of Equity' in Hamson, C.J. (ed.) *Law Reform and Law Making*, 1953 and Zander, M., *The Law Making Process*, Butterworths, 1999.

(a) Would Simonds be likely to argue in favour of judges being able to exercise their discretion more? (4)

(b) What are the arguments for and against common law judges being active in law reform? (10)

(c) What do you think Denning might have meant by 'the dead hand of the past'? Provide an example. (8)

7.17 Law reporting

Since the whole basis of the common law is about following earlier decisions, an accurate written record of judgements is obviously critical. It is rather surprising, therefore, that it was not until 1865 that highly accurate word-for-word accounts became available. In that year, the ***Incorporated Council of Law Reporting*** was set up. These reports are still published and are organised according to the court where judgements were given. They should be cited in court in preference to others as the report of each case is checked for accuracy by the judges involved before publication.

Other significant law reports include the ***All England*** series and the ***Weekly Law Reports***, which also set out a full judgement. Newspapers and legal journals also publish law reports. However, these are normally only a summary of the main points where the law reporter has tried to pick out points of importance to lawyers. Although full reports are to be preferred, the advantage of newspaper and journal reports is that they may make a case available for consideration earlier.

It is normal for lawyers and academics to use the citation of a case. The citation identifies the year of the case and where it is reported. It may also indicate which court the case was heard in. Abbreviations are used when a case is cited in writing. In this book the abbreviated citation is given in the table of cases. The meaning of some of the standard abbreviations is given in Box 7.7.

Box 7.7 *Citations of cases*

Look at the following citation:

[1990] 2 All ER 88

This refers to ***All England Law Reports*** for 1990. This particular case can be found in volume 2 at page 88. Other abbreviations used in citations include:

ICLR = ***Incorporated Council of Law Reporting***

WLR = ***Weekly Law Reports***

LR = ***Incorporated Council Law Reports***

Ch. = ***Chancery Division of the High Court***

QB = ***Queen's Bench Division of the High Court***

HL = ***House of Lords***

AC = ***Appeal Cases***

The new system of reporting

Since 2001, all cases from the High Court, Court of Appeal and House of Lords have also been given a different form of citation. Each case is given a unique identifying number which is not tied to any law report series. For example:

2001 EWCA Crim 10

This is the Court of Appeal for England and Wales, Criminal Division, case number ten. EW is used for courts whose jurisdiction only covers England and Wales, whereas UK is used instead for courts (such as the House of Lords) whose jurisdiction covers the whole of the United Kingdom.

Examples of abbreviations are given in Box 7.8.

Box 7.8 *The new form of abbreviation*

UKHL = **House of Lords**

UKPC = **Privy Council**

UKCA Crim = **Court of Appeal, Criminal Division**

UKCA Civ = **Court of Appeal, Civil Division**

UKHC (Ch) = **High Court, Chancery Division**

UKHC (QB) = **High Court, Queen's Bench Division**

Cases are also given paragraph numbers, so that the precise place in the case may be cited. A more detailed citation of the case mentioned in the text might, therefore, be:

2001 EWCA Crim 10 at 22.

Law reports and technology

A set of law reports for useful reference fills a great deal of space and is expensive. A complete set of the official ***Law Reports*** runs to 480,000 pages and occupies 180 feet of shelf space. Law reports in printed form cannot easily be accessed by those studying law unless they have easy access to the law library of a local university. In the past 20 years or so, information technology has made a considerable impact on law reporting. A set of the official ***Law Reports*** fits onto a small number of CD ROMs. Butterworths, the legal publisher, produces a database called 'Lexis' which contains all of the cases published in the main reports since 1945, together with a large number of unreported ones, including the transcripts of unreported Court of Appeal cases. This has led lawyers to refer to unreported cases in their arguments far more often than in the past.

On a number of occasions, both the House of Lords and the Court of Appeal have expressed their disapproval of this trend. In *Roberts Petroleum Ltd v Bernard Kenny Ltd (1983)*, Lord Diplock laid down general rules to limit reference to unreported cases and said that in this particular case: 'the only result of lawyers referring to the transcripts was to extend the length of the hearing unnecessarily'.

Storage of case reports on the World Wide Web is also a very useful tool for practising lawyers. Butterworths and others have produced subscription sites for this purpose. Free access to some judgements from the mid-1990s onwards is available on a number of websites including that of the Court Service (www.courtservice.gov.uk) and the House of Lords (www.parliament.the-stationery-office.co.uk). For those readers without access to a law library this is a good way of looking at examples of judgements.

Summary

1. What is the doctrine of precedent and why is it important?

2. What part do ratio decidendi and obiter dicta play in the creation of precedent?

3. What is the significance of the 1966 Practice Statement?

4. When are courts bound by their own decisions?

5. What is the difference between an original precedent, a binding precedent and a persuasive precedent?

6. What does 'distinguishing a case' mean?

7. When is a precedent overruled or reversed?

8. What are the advantages and disadvantages of following precedents?

Case study) • Precedent and the changing law

Item A *Brown (1993)* and *Wilson (1996)*

In assault cases, the consent of the 'victim' may in certain circumstances act as a valid defence so that, although harm was inflicted on another person, no offence was committed. In some instances, such as doctors and dentists performing operations, recognising the defence of consent is little more than common sense. In other instances, however, judges have had to deal with difficult moral considerations. *Brown (1993)* was a case in which a group of men took part in sado-masochistic practices, at a private party in the home of one of the defendants. These sado-masochistic practices included whipping and other very painful activities. All participants fully consented and nobody present made a complaint to the police. Despite this, the men were convicted of assaults under s.47 and s.20 of the Offences Against the Person Act 1861.

In the case of Brown (1993) the Lords considered that those involved in body piercing were not guilty of assault.

On appeal to the House of Lords, the conviction was confirmed. 'I am not prepared to invent a defence of consent for sado-masochistic encounters which breed and glorify cruelty and result in offences', commented Lord Templeman in his judgement.

However, the Law Lords who judged the case recognised that there were circumstances where consent was lawful. These included ritual circumcision, tattooing, ear and body piercing and violent sports such as boxing.

The decision was seen as controversial. There was nothing to suggest that the defendants were anything other than willing participants in the events that took place. Critics of the judgement argued that the Law Lords were deciding the case more on the basis of moral disapproval than the law and that it was difficult to see how, for example, contestants in a boxing match were not committing assault whilst the individuals involved in the case were.

In *Wilson (1996)*, the defendant admitted using a hot knife to brand his initials on his wife's body. This was done with the wife's approval and encouragement. However when a doctor reported the injury to the police after a medical examination, Wilson was convicted of a s.47 assault.

In the Court of Appeal, the judge, Lord Russell found that there was no factual comparison to be made with *Brown (1993)*. Wilson was engaged in a form of body decoration no different in principle from the piercing of nostrils or tongues. He said:

'It is to be observed that the question certified for their Lordships in *Brown (1993)* related only to a sado-masochistic encounter.'

He went on to say:

'We are firmly of the opinion that it is not in the public interest that activities such as the appellant's in this appeal should amount to criminal behaviour.'

Item B *McLoughlin v O'Brien and others (1982)*

A serious road accident.

The way in which the common law works can be illustrated by looking at the process judges use to explain their decision in a major precedent. *McLoughlin v O'Brien and others (1982)* is an important negligence case from the House of Lords. It concerns a claim relating to severe mental distress caused to the applicant when other people were badly injured or killed by the defendant's negligence. Lawyers refer to cases of this kind as 'nervous shock cases'. The right to claim in such cases has slowly evolved within the common law over a period of about 50 years. The appeal courts have been cautious of allowing members of the public who happen to witness a serious accident to claim from those who caused the accident. It is felt that this would impose an unreasonably large financial burden on defendants, as very many people would witness some accidents. There are also evidential difficulties with problems of a purely mental nature, rather than physical injury. It might be possible to invent symptoms of severe distress and, even where such claims are genuine, it is difficult to evaluate what damages should be awarded.

Ms McLoughlin was at home when a witness to a serious road accident two miles away came to tell her what had happened. The accident involved her husband and three children. When she arrived at the hospital she found her family in severe pain and covered in blood, oil and mud. She was told that her daughter had died. Ms McLoughlin suffered severe and long-term psychiatric illness as a result of this experience. She claimed against the defendants whose negligence had caused the road accident.

The case was appealed to the House of Lords. Several Law Lords gave judgement in the case. Sometimes, when judges and academics look back at past cases, they decide that the judgement made by a Law Lord is the 'leading judgement' - the judgement which makes the case an authority. In this case Lord Wilberforce gave the leading judgement. Lord Wilberforce reviewed existing nervous shock cases to see where the law currently stood and what precedents must be followed:

1. *Bourhill v Young (1943)* recognised the possibility of claiming for nervous shock in principle.

2. *Dulieu v White and Sons (1901)*, together with *Hambrook v Stokes Bros (1925)*, were at one time thought to limit a claim for damages to situations where the plaintiff was afraid of immediate personal injury. Wilberforce said that these cases had 'not gained acceptance'.

3. In *Hambrook v Stokes Bros (1925)* it was determined that a plaintiff may only recover (ie receive damages) for nervous shock brought on by injury to a near relative (husband and wife or parent and child). Moreover, there was no liability where the injuries were learnt of through communication with others, rather than actually witnessing something.

4. Where the plaintiff arrives at the scene immediately after the incident, however, as was the case in *Boardman v Sanderson (1964)* and *Benson v Lee (1972)*, they may be able to recover for nervous shock (so the rule in *Hambrook v Stokes Bros (1925)* was modified).

5. In *Chadwick v British Railways (1967)* a man who arrived in the immediate aftermath of a serious accident was allowed to recover for nervous shock even though those injured were not related to him, on the basis that he acted as a rescuer.

Having set out what he took to be the current position on the law relating to nervous shock cases, Lord Wilberforce then considered the effect of these precedents on Ms McLoughlin's position. He pointed out that the facts of *Benson v Lee (1972)* also involved a mother who was told of her family's injuries by a bystander. In that case, the mother was 100 yards away from the scene of the accident and went straight there. Wilberforce could find no reason why this case should be decided any differently: 'Can it make any difference that she comes on them in an ambulance or, as here, in a nearby hospital, when as the evidence shows, they were in the same condition, covered with oil and mud, and distraught with pain?'

What makes the judgement in *McLoughlin v O'Brien and others (1982)* typical of the way that the common law operates is the process of logical sifting through earlier precedents. The Law Lords who decided to grant Ms McLoughlin's appeal will have spent considerable time in a library, reading and re-reading the written judgements of other judges in earlier cases. They did not simply judge the case in isolation.

Questions

(a) Using Item A and your own knowledge, answer the following questions.

  i)   Explain why you are not normally able to sue your dentist for assault. (2)

  ii) What did Lord Justice Russell seem to feel was the *ratio* of *Brown (1993)*? Did it bind the Court of Appeal in *Wilson (1996)*? (6)

  iii) Does it seem fair that Wilson was acquitted but the defendants in *Brown (1993)* were not? Explain your answer. (6)

  iv) How did *obiter dicta* in *Brown (1993)* support the decision of the Court of Appeal in the later case? (4)

  v)   Do you think that the Court of Appeal is distinguishing on the basis of factual differences that are obvious and fairly straightforward, or are they distinguishing to avoid applying *Brown (1993)*? (6)

(b) Using Item B, complete the following tasks.

  i)   What is a leading judgement? (2)

  ii) *McLoughlin v O'Brien and others (1982)* was heard by the Lords in 1982. In what year was nervous shock first recognised as a reason for damages? (1)

  iii) Which precedent does Wilberforce appear to follow here? Does he regard the precedent as fundamentally different from the facts of Ms McLoughlin's case? (6)

  iv) Using the precedents on nervous shock, explain how as a Law Lord you would decide the two cases below. State what your decision would be and whether you would be following, distinguishing, or overruling relevant authorities:

  A. Ms Jones was in her home in Devon when a policeman came to tell her that her son had been severely injured in a rail crash in Glasgow a week before. She travelled to Scotland to see him in hospital. She then claimed for nervous shock against the negligent railway company.

  B. Mr Smith was travelling home after spending Christmas with his parents. Half way home, he came upon the immediate aftermath of a very serious accident. One of the two vehicles involved was a small car which had crumpled up, trapping the driver, who was not at fault. Mr Smith gave basic first aid to the driver, who lost a great deal of blood and slipped fast into unconsciousness. When he arrived home Mr Smith, a very sensitive person, suffered from depression and nightmares for some months. He claimed against the other driver, who was at fault. (10)

8.1 Introduction

The law only exists as words. It is only possible to give effect to the law by interpreting those words and applying them to a particular set of facts. This is what lawyers and, in particular, judges, are paid to do. This unit examines the various rules that the courts have developed to assist in

Activity 8.1

Car pollution.

Why are rules of statutory interpretation necessary?

The government of Noland (a fictional place) was deeply concerned about pollution, accidents and noise caused by traffic in its small and over-crowded country. As car ownership and use grew, the Prime Minister decided she would have to take drastic steps. Her advisers said that much of the problem stemmed from the engines in older, fuel inefficient and poorly maintained cars. It was decided to pass an Act of Parliament removing these old cars from the road. Because the government was so anxious to tackle the problems, it rushed legislation through Parliament in half the normal time. Section 1 of the No Old Cars Please Act 2002 reads:

> 'It shall be an offence to use any motor vehicle made before 1 January 1991 on public roads.'

This law was very unpopular, particularly with those who owned older vehicles. Harry Sharp identified a possible solution for these people however. Aware that the engine of a car is the most expensive part, he set up a business making very basic, low-cost, kit cars that are sold without engines. The purchaser assembles the car and is able to install a wide range of engines from old cars. Those customers who used Harry's kit cars with engines made before 1991, and Harry himself, were prosecuted under Section 1 of the No Old Cars Please Act 2002. The defendants pleaded not guilty, arguing purely on a point of law. They argued that, on the basis of the words used in the Act, they had not broken the law.

(a) Will the courts have a straightforward job when interpreting the wording of this statute? (2)

(b) What arguments would you put (i) for the prosecution and (ii) for the defence in this case? (4)

(c) Carefully draft an improved version of Section 1 of the No Old Cars Please Act 2002, using different wording, which achieves the government's aim. (4)

the process of interpreting and applying Acts of Parliament (Acts of Parliament are also known as 'statutes' or 'legislation').

You will have realised that the language in which the law was written in Activity 8.1 was capable of distortion. It was given a meaning not envisaged by the government. In the real Parliament, Parliamentary Counsel, who are specialised barristers, choose the words used in a Bill. They create a draft of the Act. In Parliament, these words are examined carefully and may be altered before the Bill becomes an Act, but it is often difficult to find exactly the right words.

Although the fictional scenario in Activity 8.1 is far-fetched, it suggests the kind of problems with words that occasionally confront the courts in the real world when they have to interpret statutes.

Some problems of statutory interpretation include:

1. Some words are ambiguous, they are capable of more than one meaning, and the courts are not sure which meaning to use.

2. Defendants find ways of evading the law which were not predicted and, therefore, not covered by the words used.

3. A word is insufficiently precise. For example, does the term 'motor vehicle' in Activity 8.1 include motorised wheel chairs and electric-powered cars?

4. Simple error in the drafting phase, which goes unnoticed.

5. The meaning of words may change over time. For example, in Section 28 of the Town Police Causes Act 1847 the word 'passenger' meant a traveller on foot, which is certainly not the meaning it is given in modern English.

8.2 The three basic rules of interpretation

The three rules defined

There are three basic rules of interpretation. These can be defined as follows.

1. The literal rule

This is a simple rule. Words should be given their ordinary meaning, regardless of whether that is necessarily the one that might be expected. The reason behind this rule is that it would be wrong for the courts to guess what Parliament actually meant when the Act was passed. Lord Esher stated in *R v Judge of the City of London Court (1892)*:

'If the words of an Act are clear, you must follow them, even though they lead to a manifest [obvious] absurdity. The court has nothing to do with the question of whether the legislature has committed an absurdity.' Two examples of the application of the literal rule are shown in Box 8.1.

Box 8.1 *The literal rule in practice*

(i) ***London and North Eastern Railway Co. v Berriman (1946)***

A steam train in the 1940s.

A railway worker was run over and killed by a train. His widow attempted to claim damages from the railway company. The relevant Act of Parliament allowed employees to receive compensation where they were engaged in 'relaying or repairing' railway tracks. The man killed had only been providing routine maintenance and oiling the tracks. The court held that this could not be interpreted as relaying or repairing, so his widow could not receive compensation.

(ii) ***Mesure v Mesure (1960)***

Under the Matrimonial Causes Act 1950, it was possible for a divorce to be obtained where one spouse had received five years 'continuous treatment' for mental illness. Ms Mesure had been in a mental hospital between 1952 and 1959 except for eleven weeks in a sanatorium where she was treated for tuberculosis. It was held that no divorce could be granted, as the treatment for mental illness was not continuous.

---

2. The golden rule

The golden rule provides that, if in exceptional circumstances the literal rule produces a wholly unjust result, the meaning of words may be altered to avoid that result. This rule has been used in two sorts of cases:

- where the words of statutes are ambiguous and it is very hard to see which meaning is appropriate
- where words have only one meaning but to give them that meaning would be wholly unacceptable.

In *Grey v Pearson (1857)*, Judge Parke gave one of the earliest statements of the rule. He explained that, in understanding the meaning of statutes, the grammatical and ordinary sense of words should be maintained, unless that would lead to some absurdity or inconsistency. Where this was the case, the ordinary sense of the words could be modified so as to avoid the absurdity or inconsistency. However, this modification should go no further than that. In other words, the golden rule should be used sparingly.

The golden rule is examined in Activity 8.2.

Activity 8.2

The golden rule

(i) *Maddox v Storer (1963)*

The Road Traffic Act 1960 made it an offence to drive over 30 mph in a vehicle 'adapted to carry more than seven passengers'. The vehicle in this case was a minibus made to carry 11 people, rather than adapted to do so. The Oxford Dictionary definition of the word 'adapted' uses terms such as 'adjust' and 'make suitable'. Had an offence been committed? Did it matter whether the minibus was manufactured to carry 11 people or whether seats had been added? The court held that 'adapted to' would be taken to include for this purpose 'suitable for', so by use of the golden rule an offence had in fact been committed.

(ii) *R v Allen (1872)*

Allen was accused of bigamy. Under Section 57 of the Offences Against the Person Act 1861 it was an offence to marry while one's original spouse was still alive. It was suggested that the word 'marry' had two possible meanings:

- become legally married to another person
- go through a formal ceremony of marriage.

A newly wedded Victorian couple.

If the word in the statute was given the first meaning nobody who was already married could ever be guilty of the offence of bigamy because, at the time they attempted to legally marry a second time, it would be impossible for them to do so. The court held that this was absurd and said that the word 'marry' must mean 'go through a formal ceremony of marriage'.

(a) *Maddox v Storer* **and** *R v Allen* **illustrate the two categories in which the golden rule is used. Explain which case illustrates which category. (8)**

(b) Discuss whether it would have been appropriate to have used the golden rule in *London and North Eastern Railway Co. v Berriman (1946)* **- outlined in Box 8.1 above. (4)**

3. The mischief rule

This rule was first set out in *Heydon's Case (1584)*. It gives judges considerably more discretion than the other two rules. In its modern form the rule has three stages:

1. Identify what the problem was for which the law did not provide (the problem was defined as 'the mischief' in the 16th century language of the original judgement and this is the word lawyers still use in this context).

2. Identify what 'remedy' or solution Parliament was trying to put in place to deal with this problem.

3. Ask what was the true reason for this remedy.

The role of the judge is then to give words a construction that would deal with the problem and implement the remedy.

   An example of the mischief rule is outlined in Box 8.2.

Which of the three rules are used and when?

Before considering the value of these three rules of interpretation there are two points that need to be made.

   First, it is clear that judges are not required to use one rule rather than another. They may choose which of the three rules to use, though, unfortunately, this choice is not made in any systematic way. There is no way of telling which rule a court in any particular case will employ. Judges appear to choose which rule to use depending on their individual view of the exact boundaries between the law-making role of the judiciary and that of Parliament. It might be that sometimes the desired outcome in a particular case is taken into consideration when making this choice. This can be described as an **integrated approach**. It is fair to say, however, that the literal rule has been used most often for most of the past century.

   Second, the steady growth in the influence of EU law in recent times and the effect of the Human Rights Act 1998 mean that the judicial approach to statutory interpretation is increasingly moving away from the three rules outlined above in favour of what is known as the **purposive approach**. This is more concerned with the spirit and the intended purpose of legislation than the precise meaning of the language used in legislation, and allows judges to go further than the mischief rule. This change stems from differences in the way that EU laws and human rights treaties are written and in the way that European courts tackle statutory interpretation. This is discussed in more detail later in this unit.

Box 8.2 *Smith v Hughes (1960)*

Section 1(1) of the Street Offences Act 1959 states:

   'It shall be an offence for a common prostitute to loiter or solicit in a street or public place for the purpose of prostitution.'

A prostitute soliciting.

The case involved appeals against conviction by six different women. In each case, the women had been inside a building adjoining the street, for example, on a balcony or at an open window, not actually on the street. However, they sought to attract the attention of men by calling out or tapping on windows and gesturing to them to come inside. It was obvious that the women were soliciting but had they committed an offence under Section 1 of the 1959 Act?

The convictions were confirmed. Lord Parker used the mischief rule. In his ruling, he said:

   'For my part, I approach the matter by considering what is the mischief aimed at by this Act. Everybody knows that this was an Act intended to clean up the streets, to enable people to walk along the streets without being molested or solicited by common prostitutes. Viewed in that way, it can matter little whether the prostitute is soliciting while in the street, or is standing on the doorway or on a balcony, or at a window or whether the window is half shut or half open; in each case her solicitation is projected to and addressed to somebody walking in the street.'

So the mischief appears to be prostitution on the streets. Parliament has responded by making it an offence for a prostitute to loiter or solicit on the street. This is the 'remedy'. The aim behind this remedy is to stop prostitutes seeking business on the streets. As men were in fact being solicited, Lord Parker saw no difficulty in convicting under Section 1(1).

Activity 8.3

Elliott v Grey (1960)

Under the Road Traffic Act 1930 it was an offence for a car to be 'used on the road' without an insurance policy. The defendant argued that he had not committed an offence because, although his uninsured vehicle was on the road, it was jacked up and had no battery. The court held it that it was nevertheless a hazard of the kind the Act was designed to prevent so an offence had been committed.

Jacking up a car.

(a) **Was the golden rule or the mischief rule used in this case? Explain your answer. (6)**

(b) **If the literal rule had been used how would the court have decided the case? (4)**

(c) **Do you agree with the court's approach and final decision? Explain your answer. (4)**

8.3 What is the value of the three basic rules of interpretation?

The literal rule

Often the use of the literal rule is uncontroversial. It would be surprising if judges were allowed to alter the meaning of words in Acts of Parliament to suit themselves, given the supremacy of Parliament over the courts. Although it is difficult for Parliamentary Counsel to cover all situations in the words that are chosen for an Act, most situations will have been covered most of the time. Where the meaning of words used in a statute is obscure or otherwise problematic it is, after all, open to Parliament to amend the Act.

However the literal rule has been subject to severe criticism. The outcome of its application in cases such as *London and North Eastern Railways v Berriman (1946)* - see above - is certainly hard to support. In his book *The Law Making Process* (Butterworths 1999), Zander is scathing about the literal rule:

'The judge gives up the attempt to understand the document at the first attempt. Instead of struggling to discover what it means, he simply adopts the most straightforward interpretation of the words in question - without regard to whether this interpretation makes sense in the particular context.' (Zander 1999, p.106)

Lord Denning's dissenting judgement in *Magor and St. Mellons v Newport Corpn. (1950)* also contained many comments displaying an impatience with excessive reliance on the literal rule. He said:

'We do not sit here to pull the language of Parliament and of ministers to pieces and make nonsense of it. That is an easy thing to do, and it is a thing to which lawyers are too often prone. We sit here to find the intention of Parliament and of ministers, and carry it out, and we do this better by filling in the gaps and making sense of the enactment than by opening it up to destructive analysis.'

The golden rule

The golden rule protects the court faced with a difficult question of interpretation from reaching an unjust decision because it allows the judge to avoid absurd results. However, it is little more than an extension of the literal rule and, therefore, subject to the same criticisms. Those employing the golden rule have generally made it plain that it should only be preferred to the literal rule in exceptional cases. It may seem, at first sight, that where the golden rule is used the court is going beyond the words in the Act to look for its purpose. In fact, there is no factual examination at all of the background to the Act. The judge simply makes 'common sense' assumptions about what Parliament intended.

The rule also lacks clarity. It has never been obvious what is to be treated as 'absurd' and what is not. When will the consequence of a particular interpretation be seen as so absurd that a court will feel justified in departing from a plain meaning? There is any number of reported cases where judges have preferred the literal rule even though it led to what most of us would see as an absurdity. Why did the court ignore the golden rule in *London and North Eastern Railways v Berriman (1946)*, for example?

The mischief rule

The value of the mischief rule is that it recognises that to look only at the words of a statute is inadequate. It is often hard to understand language without knowing the circumstances or the context of its use. As Zander points out the phrase 'teach the children a game' is not likely to include strip poker. The mischief rule enables judges to bring into consideration why the Act was passed when considering what meaning to give words.

One problem with the mischief rule is its age. When *Heydon's Case (1584)* was decided, it was common to explain the purpose of an Act at the beginning. This practice later disappeared. Moreover, at that time it was judges who drafted statutes. Parliament did little more than rubber stamp them. In 1584, therefore, judges were well placed to know what the purpose of an Act was. Today, Parliament is the main source of law. The law is, therefore, made and applied by two different groups. This raises the question of where judges can look to establish the purpose of an Act. What aids to interpretation can be used? To understand fully how the courts interpret statutes this question needs to be answered.

Activity 8.4

Rogers v Dodd (1968)

It was a condition of a coffee bar's registration under the Brighton Corporation Act 1966 that it 'should not remain open after 1.00 am'. At 1.40 am at one coffee bar in Brighton, however, hot dogs were

The Lanes in Brighton in 1967.

being served through an open window. The door had been firmly locked and customers asked to leave before 1.00 am.

(a) **What is the particular word that would be argued over in court? (2)**

(b) **Explain what would result from an application of (i) the literal rule, (ii) the golden rule and (iii) the mischief rule in this case. (12)**

(c) **State, with reasons, which rule you think is most appropriate here. (6)**

8.4 How can Parliament's intention be found?

Intrinsic aids

Whatever approach is used, clues to interpretation can often be found within the statute itself. These clues are known as internal or intrinsic aids. The following are permitted intrinsic aids.

1. The long and the short title

Acts are often created with a brief title and an alternative, more detailed one. It is well established that the long title may be used to provide clues to the meaning of words within the Act.

2. The preamble

Where there is one, a preamble is an introduction to the Act that may provide an indication of its the purpose. The Fur Trade Act 2000 commences with the following words:

'An Act to prohibit the keeping of animals solely or primarily for slaughter for the value of their fur; to provide for the making of payments in respect of the related closure of certain businesses; and for connected purposes.'

3. Marginal notes and headings

Marginal notes and headings summarise the effect of sections of an Act. Where the wording of either marginal notes or headings seem to have a contradictory meaning to the wording of the main body of an Act, the wording of the main body of an Act should be followed. Marginal notes and headings are inserted when the Act goes for printing, not during its progress through Parliament so are a little unreliable as an indication of Parliament's will.

4. Schedules

Schedules are extra details, a kind of appendix, which elaborate on the main sections of an Act. For example, Section 1 of the Postal Services Act 2000 set up a Postal Services Commission to ensure the provision of a universal postal service. Schedule 1 of the same Act sets out how many people the Commission consists of and how they are appointed.

5. Interpretation sections

Quite often Acts of Parliament specify exactly what meaning is to be given to a particular word or phrase. In many Acts, interpretation sections set out lists, sometimes quite long ones, of what meanings are intended for certain words used elsewhere in the Act.

Rules of language

Even those judges who favour a strict use of the literal rule will make use of a number of lesser rules that provide some order to the task of interpreting. These rules (which have Latin names) are as follows.

1. The ejusdem generis rule

This means that where particular words are used in a statute, (for example 'pen, pencil, crayon, felt tip pen'), and these words are followed by general words, (for example 'writing instrument'), the general words are defined by reference to the particular ones. So, in the example given, chalk would not be a writing instrument as it is not used for writing on paper.

An illustration of this rule can be found in the case of *Gregory v Fearn (1953)*. The Sunday Observance Act 1677 stated that 'no tradesman, artificer, workman, labourer or other person whatsoever' should work on a Sunday. In the case of *Gregory v Fearn (1953)*, the Court of Appeal held that the words 'or other person whatsoever' should be seen as a general term. As a result, the *ejusdem generis* rule meant that the Act did not apply to an estate agent (it might be thought that estate agents come into the category of 'tradesman' but they do not buy and sell houses, they act as an agent between the buyer and the seller).

2. Expressio unius exclusio alterius

This phrase means 'the mention of one thing excludes others'. Where there is a list of words but no general words follow after them, then the Act only applies to the particular items mentioned. This can be illustrated by the case of *Tempest v Kilner (1846)*. In this case, the court had to consider whether the Statute of Frauds 1677 applied to a contract for the sale of stocks and shares. The list 'goods, wares and merchandise' in the Act was not followed by any general words. The court held that the statute did not, therefore, concern stocks and shares.

3. Noscitur a sociis

This phrase means that a word is known by the company it keeps. The effect of this rule is that a word takes on meaning from other words around it. This can be illustrated by the case of *Inland Revenue Commissioners v Frere (1965)*. In this case, a section of an Act set out rules for 'interest, annuities or other annual interest' (an 'annuity' is an investment entitling the investor to a series of equal annual sums). Did the first word include interest paid monthly or daily? The court held that the presence of the words 'annual interest' meant that only interest paid annually was affected by the Act.

Presumptions

The court will make certain presumptions about the law unless the relevant Act makes it plain that the presumption is not meant to apply. The major presumptions are as follows:

1. It is presumed that the common law will apply unless the Act makes it plain that the common law has been changed.

2. It is presumed that criminal offences require intention to commit the offence, not just the physical process of committing it - see *Sweet v Parsley* on pages 51 and 173.

3. It is presumed that the Crown will not be bound by any statute unless the statute expressly says so.

Activity 8.5

Rules of language

Rugby balls.

In each question below, explain your answer.

(a) If a statute says it applies to 'rugby, football, cricket, netball, baseball, basketball and other such ball games' would you expect it to apply to snooker? (4)

(b) If a statute says that it applies to 'cricket, football, rugby, and other sporting activities' would you expect sailing to be affected? (4)

(c) If a statute says it applies to 'the sports of hockey and rugby' would you expect it to apply to netball? (4)

4. It is assumed that legislation does not apply retrospectively. So, a new Act does not change the legal position of people in relation to events that took place before the date the Act takes effect.

Extrinsic aids

Extrinsic aids to interpretation are those found outside the actual Act. The following extrinsic aids have been regarded as acceptable.

1. Dictionaries and legal textbooks

Dictionaries are an obvious tool to assist with the literal rule.

2. Other statutes

Earlier Acts have relevance in tracing the mischief that an Act was designed to tackle. The Interpretation Act 1978 defines particular terms that are found in a range of statutes.

3. Reports of the Law Commission and other law reform bodies

An Act is often preceded by an investigation by one of the bodies set up by the government to investigate options for reforming the law. These bodies produce reports on their findings and recommendations, which the government may adopt in a Bill (see Unit 9).

4. International treaties

It is presumed by the courts that Parliament does not legislate in a way that would be a clear breach of a treaty signed by the United Kingdom government.

5. Explanatory notes

Acts passed since 1999 have been accompanied by explanatory notes. These notes summarise the main provisions of the Act and explain the background to it. The government department responsible for the legislation writes them after the Act has been passed. For this reason, they should be regarded as extrinsic aids. The Fur Trade Act 2000, for example, though it is quite a short Act has an explanatory note some eight pages long. This explains the main purpose of the Act ('to prohibit fur farming'), as well as summarising and commenting on the various sections. It also states where discussion of the Bill can be found in *Hansard* (see below). Explanatory notes are written in much more readable language than Acts. Between 1999 and April 2003, there were no cases in which their use was considered. As a result, the way in which judges might use them is not yet clear.

To what extent can Hansard be used as an extrinsic aid?

Access to extrinsic aids is vital to the application of the mischief rule, but until quite recently the use of a key extrinsic aid was disapproved of. If the courts are to search for the intention of Parliament in passing the Act, an obvious way of doing this is to scrutinise what was said in Parliament when the Act was debated as a Bill. Full and careful written records are kept of debates in a publication known as *Hansard*. However, for many years it was well established that reference could not be made to *Hansard* in the judicial interpretation of statutes. This may seem surprising, given that the courts are allowed to look for the mischief that Parliament was seeking to address. Lord Denning sought to challenge the rule that judges should not turn to *Hansard* in *Davis v Johnson (1979)*. He said that to look for the meaning of an Act without reference to *Hansard* was like groping about in the dark without switching on the light. He also said:

'And it is obvious that there is nothing to prevent a judge looking at these debates himself privately and getting some guidance from them. Although it may shock the purists, I may as well confess that I have sometimes done it.'

On appeal to the House of Lords, all five of the Law Lords trying the case disagreed with Denning. Lord Scarman gave two reasons why *Hansard* was not appropriate reading material for a judge. First, what he called the 'cut and thrust' of debate did not always provide a very clear

explanation of the meaning of statutory language. This seems a valid point. MPs do not have it in mind that their words will be carefully picked apart by judges at a later date. Second, lawyers are not permitted to use *Hansard* in their arguments, so it seemed wrong to allow judges to do so. Lord Dilhorne added that allowing the use of *Hansard* would not be helpful in many cases. It would be time consuming and would add to legal costs.

Nearly a decade later, Law Lords took a different view. Very limited exceptions to the rule on *Hansard* were set out by the Lords in *Pickstone v Freemans plc (1988)*. Then, in *Pepper v Hart (1993)*, the House of Lords moved considerably further away from their earlier position. A special court of seven Law Lords ruled that where legislation was obscure, ambiguous or led to an absurdity, reference might be made to ministerial statements in Parliament where it was clear they would help. This ruling leaves some questions still unanswered. For example, how are we to know what is sufficiently 'obscure, ambiguous or absurd'? Lord Browne-Wilkinson, who gave the leading judgement in this case, was anxious to make it plain that *Hansard* should be used sparingly:

'In many, I suspect most, cases, reference to parliamentary materials will not throw any light on the matter. But in a few cases it may emerge that the very question was considered by Parliament in passing the legislation.'

However, since 1993, the courts have given a wide interpretation to *Pepper v Hart (1993)*. In *Warwickshire County Council v Johnson (1993)*, for example, the Lords themselves used *Hansard* even though there seemed little ambiguity in the statutory language.

What has created this new willingness to refer to parliamentary debates? It is partly because there has been a move away from the traditional three rules of interpretation and towards the purposive approach.

8.5 The purposive approach

The purposive approach involves interpreting statutes not only by looking at the dictionary meaning of words but also by conducting an investigation into why the law was created, and what the purpose of the legislation was. This includes looking at the context in which the law was created. In other words, it involves examining what the concerns of the government and Parliament were at the time the Act was created. In the purposive approach, external aids such as *Hansard* are obviously important. This is a departure from the traditional role played by English judges which has been to limit the search for meaning to the letter of the law.

Something like the purposive approach has always been used in countries where the law is codified. In codified systems of law, the law stems from one document or code, rather than from a multitude of cases and legislation as is the case in English law. The code is a fairly generalised statement of principle, designed to be capable of application to a very wide range of factual situations. In most continental court systems, therefore, judges are empowered to identify the spirit and the purpose of the law where detailed explanation of the effect of the law is not found in the code.

English courts have increasingly adopted the purposive approach. In *IRC v McGuckian (1997)*, Lord Steyn commented:

> 'During the last thirty years there has been a shift away from the literalist approach to purposive methods of construction. When there is no obvious meaning to a statutory provision, the modern emphasis is on a contextual approach designed to identify the purpose of a statute and to give effect to it.'

An example of a case where the purposive approach was used is *Bulmer v Bollinger (1974)* which concerned a dispute between Bollinger, a French champagne company, and Bulmer, owners of a sparkling pear wine, over the use of the word 'champagne' (details of the judgement in this case are given at the end of this unit).

Is there any difference between the purposive approach and the mischief rule?

In essence the purposive approach and the mischief rule are the same. However there is no longer the need to keep up the pretence of searching for 'mischief' within the terms of *Heydon's Case (1584)*. The purposive approach allows judges to abandon a rather outdated fiction and to be open about the fact that they are prepared to look at the background to legislation where necessary.

The growing importance of European Union law and the purposive approach

Under Article 234 of The Treaty of Rome, the European Court of Justice (ECJ) is the supreme court on issues of European law (see Unit 5, Section 5.6). Section 3(1) of the European Communities Act 1972 states that questions regarding the validity, meaning or effect of EU law are to be decided on the basis of ECJ rulings. The European Court is able to refer to formal documents produced by the European Council, separate from the law itself, which contain clear guidance on the intended purpose of the law. There is no direct equivalent of these in UK law. EU laws tend to be written in broad terms. The courts must consider the detail of exactly when EU laws do and do not

apply to a particular situation, as the laws themselves (unlike Acts of Parliament) do not provide this kind of detail. Not surprisingly, the ECJ, which is made up of predominantly continental judges, takes a European approach to interpretation. The ECJ's approach to interpreting law is very much a purposive one.

Inevitably, as the volume and importance of EU law affecting the UK has grown, the courts have had to adapt their approach to statutory interpretation, and the way that the ECJ approaches interpretation is bound to rub off. The 'literalist approach' is no longer appropriate, at least in cases involving EU law.

The Human Rights Act 1998 and interpretation

The Human Rights Act enables judges in the UK to look at legislation in light of the European Convention on Human Rights (ECHR - see Unit 3). Legislation must be read and given effect by the courts in a way that is compatible with the ECHR. The High Court, the Court of Appeal and the House of Lords may make a declaration of incompatibility with the convention. It is then for Parliament to decide whether or not the particular law should be altered or repealed (abolished). The courts cannot strike down an Act, but they may tell the government and Parliament where there are problems.

This marks a major change for a number of reasons. For the first time, UK courts are put in the position of formally assessing whether Parliament has acted in the right way. Judges may not be able to amend what an Act of Parliament says but, if their interpretation of part of an Act is that it contravenes the ECHR, then they have an obligation to spell out clearly why they think so. A shrug of the shoulders and saying 'this is a matter for Parliament', at least where the Human Rights Act is involved, is no longer enough.

Just as European Union treaties and other laws are written in very broad terms, setting out general principles, so is the ECHR. The European Court of Human Rights, whose rulings must be taken into account in matters relating to interpretation of the convention's articles, of necessity adopts a purposive approach. UK courts now have to adopt a more wide-ranging approach to interpretation as increasing numbers of Human Rights Act cases come before the courts.

8.6 Statutory interpretation - an overview

The table in Box 8.3 provides a summary of material covered in this unit.

Box 8.3 *Statutory interpretation - an overview*

1. Rules of interpretation

a. **The literal rule**
Give words their ordinary meaning - *London and North Eastern Railway Co v Berriman (1946)*

b. **The golden rule**
Words can be altered where the literal rule produces an unjust result (exceptional cases only) - *R v Allen (1872)*

c. **The mischief rule**
Identify what problem the Act was providing for and the solution Parliament sought - *Smith v Hughes (1960)*

d. **The purposive approach**
Interpret statute by considering the purpose of the Act and interpret in the spirit of that purpose - *Bulmer v Bollinger (1974)*

2. Aids to interpretation

a. **Intrinsic aids**
   i. Long and short title of Act
   ii. Preamble
   iii. Marginal notes and headings
   iv. Schedules
   v. Interpretation sections

b. **Rules of language**
   i. General words are defined by reference to particular words
   ii. Mention of one thing excludes others
   iii. A word is known by the company it keeps

c. **Presumptions**
   i. The common law will apply
   ii. Criminal offences require intention
   iii. The Crown will not be bound by Acts
   iv. Legislation does not apply retrospectively

d. **Extrinsic aids**
   i. Dictionaries and textbooks
   ii. Other statutes
   iii. Law Commission reports and other similar reports
   iv. International Treaties
   v. Explanatory notes
   vi. Hansard

Summary

1. What are the three basic rules of statutory interpretation and how do they differ?

2. What is the difference between an integrated approach and a purposive approach?

3. What difficulties arise from the use of each of the three basic rules of statutory interpretation?

4. How can Parliament's intention be found?

5. When can Hansard be used as an extrinsic aid?

6. Why is there a move towards the purposive approach?

Case study *Statutory interpretation*

Item A *The Renton Committee*

The Renton Committee on the Preparation of Legislation produced a report in 1975 making a large number of recommendations designed to improve the process by which Parliament drafted and published Acts. Some of these were:

● less detail should be included in legislation, and instead a more simple, continental style used

● Acts would benefit from the use of illustrative examples, showing the courts how the law was meant to be interpreted in particular situations

● Acts should be arranged for the benefit of those affected by them

● Acts could include text explaining their purpose in the same way as older statutes contained a preamble.

Most of the recommendations made in this report have not been implemented.

Item B *Bulmer v Bollinger (1974)*

Lord Denning's judgement in this case contains a discussion about the position of European law within the UK. In light of A.234 (ie Article 234) and the European Communities Act 1972 Section 3(1), Denning argues that English courts must adopt the same approach to interpretation as the European Court when they are looking at EU law (A.234 is discussed at length in Unit 5, Section 5.6). What does this involve?

Bulmer cider bottles.

English courts should stop looking at words in meticulous detail, debating precise grammatical meaning. He refers to the judgement of the European court itself in the *Da Costa (1963)* case, 'They must deduce from the wording and the spirit of the Treaty the meaning of the Community rules.' Denning recognises that this may involve finding gaps in meaning but says that it is legitimate for the judge to fill this gap. He says that the courts should do what those who created the law would have done if they had thought about it.

In the same case, Denning set out guidelines attempting to restrict Article 234 referrals to the European Court of Justice. He argued strongly in favour of adopting a European approach to interpretation while at the same time showing a reluctance to encourage the use of the European Court.

Item C *Lord Browne-Wilkinson and Hansard as an aid to interpretation*

In *Pepper v Hart (1993)*, Lord Browne-Wilkinson gave the leading judgement. He considered objections that the Attorney General raised against the use of *Hansard* and other parliamentary documents as an aid to interpretation. In the following summary of part of the judgement, these objections are shown in bold.

1. **Parliamentary materials are not easily available or understood by citizens and lawyers. Also, the cost of research would be high.**

Lord Browne-Wilkinson recognised that these materials were not easy to locate but they were available, although at some cost. This problem was not insurmountable. He also pointed out that statutes and delegated legislation were themselves not always accessible.

2. **Lawyers and judges are not familiar with parliamentary procedures and will find it difficult to know what weight to give to materials.**

Lord Browne-Wilkinson felt that significance should only be attached to clear statements made by a minister or someone else involved with the introduction of the Bill. He also stressed the importance of putting any statement made in Parliament about a Bill in context. For example, did the minister later change their mind on a particular point?

3. **Court time will be taken up by considering a large amount of parliamentary material and long arguments about its significance, increasing the expense of litigation.**

Lord Browne-Wilkinson was clear that this would not be a problem if the court insisted that only really relevant material of the kind already mentioned in Point 2 was introduced into arguments. He mentioned that in Australia and New Zealand, where a similar relaxation of the rules about parliamentary material had occurred, there was no evidence of complaints of this kind.

A pepper pot.

Questions

(a) Look at Item A and complete the following tasks.

   i)   Which of these recommendations has now been implemented? (3)

   ii) Suggest why continental legislation contains less detail. (3)

   iii) Who might benefit from the implementation of these recommendations and in what ways? Consider whether the law can be understood by the general public, certainty of the law and the costs of being legally represented in a court action. (9)

(b) Look at Item B and answer the following questions.

   i)   What are the two contrasting approaches to interpretation Denning discussed in *Bulmer v Bollinger (1974)* called? Briefly summarise them in your own words. (6)

   ii) What reasons would you suggest for a gradual shift from one approach to the other in relation to the interpretation of English law? (6)

   iii) On what grounds and when did Denning argue for a European approach to interpretation in relation to English law in English courts? (3)

(c) Look at Item C and complete the following tasks.

   i)   *Hansard* is an extrinsic aid to interpretation. Give three other examples of extrinsic aids. (6)

   ii) Give three examples of intrinsic aids. (6)

   iii) Does *Pepper v Hart (1993)* represent an abandonment of the previous rule on *Hansard* or a modification? (8)

   iv) An opposition MP makes a long speech about the purpose of a particular government Bill in a Commons debate. Explain why Browne-Wilkinson would not allow this speech to be brought into cases dealing with interpretation of the subsequent Act. (4)

9 Pressures for change and law reform agencies

9.1 Introduction

Unit 2 examines how Acts of Parliament are created. In other words, it explains *how* a Bill becomes an Act. This unit, on the other hand, looks at the background to why laws are proposed, and what influences reform and change in the law.

One or more of the following determine what laws are created by Parliament:

- public opinion
- political parties
- judges
- the media
- pressure groups
- law reform bodies, such as the Law Commission.

These groups also exert pressure on one another. For example, political parties are heavily influenced by the views expressed by journalists in the media, who have an important influence on public opinion.

9.2 Politics and changes in the law

During a general election campaign, each political party publishes a manifesto which sets out the election promises of the party (see Box 9.1). This manifesto outlines the Bills that the party proposes to put before Parliament.

These proposals for Bills - and the actual Bills that come before Parliament - fall into three categories.

Box 9.1 *Party manifestos*

The party manifestos produced by the three main parties during the 2001 general election campaign.

First, it would be wrong to assume that all Bills are politically inspired. Some meet with the broad approval of all political parties and pass through Parliament with little opposition. For example, the Law Commission's proposals for largely technical improvements to the law are often accepted by all the main parties.

The second category of Bills is made up of those which reflect public concerns in which party political loyalties are irrelevant. For example, a series of much publicised attacks by dogs on small children led to the Dangerous Dogs Act 1991. Similarly, the BSE crisis led to the legal regulation of the food industries.

The third category is those proposals for Bills which are inspired by purely political motives. Often, the aim of such proposals is to bring about a fundamental change in society. Take the trade union legislation passed by successive Conservative governments between 1979 and 1993. These laws were designed to weaken the trade union movement - a reflection of the Conservative Party's political belief (not necessarily shared by the other main parties) that trade unions had too much power. The Trade Union Reform and Employment Rights Act 1993, for example, made it easier for employers to challenge strike action in the courts. This was a highly political change in the law, reflecting the views of Conservative voters and their MPs about the balance of power between employers and employees.

9.3 Public opinion and the media

'The government should do something about it!', ordinary people often say when conversations turn to current affairs. 'Doing something about it', very often involves changing the law. The need for a change in the law might be because of a small number of isolated incidents or it might be the product of a long-term shift in the values and perceptions of society. Take the relaxation of the laws on homosexuality for example. In the 1950s, homosexual sex in private was a criminal offence. Today it is not and changing attitudes have resulted in the reduction of the age of homosexual consent from 21 to 18.

There is no doubt that the mass media influence the way in which people think about the world. It is, however, difficult to be sure whether public opinion is shaped by the media or whether the media simply reflect what people think. Either way, there are many instances where changes in the law stem from opinionated media coverage. Increasingly, pressure for law reform is a consequence of constant media debate over particular issues. One recent example of this can be seen in the understandable outrage generated by the murder of Stephen Lawrence - see Box 9.2.

Box 9.2 *Stephen Lawrence*

Stephen Lawrence was murdered by a gang of white youths in 1993. The failure of the police to make a serious investigation into his murder provoked outrage in the media.

The case of Stephen Lawrence became the focus of a great deal of criticism in the media of policing methods in general and of police attitudes to black and Asian people in particular. Eventually, three young men were tried in a private prosecution in a blaze of publicity. They were acquitted, despite evidence against them. The press continued to raise concerns about the handling of the investigation and raised serious questions about whether the acquittal was right. One newspaper even put the names and photographs of the chief suspects under the banner headline *Murderers*.

In response to all this criticism, the government set up an inquiry led by Sir William Macpherson, a retired judge. The Macpherson Report, published in February 1999, was highly critical of the Metropolitan Police Force, arguing that there was evidence of institutional racism. The report also questioned whether the double jeopardy rule was in need of review. The double jeopardy rule is the law that prevents anyone being prosecuted twice for the same particular offence. Jack Straw, then Home Secretary, asked the Law Commission to investigate whether the law should be changed. The Criminal Justice Bill of 2002 included clauses which enabled a second trial in some cases.

9.4 Pressure groups

Pressure groups are groups that attempt to influence policy-making and law-making without actually seeking to form a government. Like political parties, pressure groups put forward policies and seek support for them. However

Activity 9.1

Double jeopardy

The double jeopardy rule has been part of English common law for 800 years. It is, in effect, part of the rule that an accused is innocent until proven guilty. One argument against scrapping the rule is that the jury in a second trial would almost certainly be influenced by knowledge of the first trial. It has traditionally been accepted that it is better for some guilty defendants to go unpunished than run the risk of wrongful convictions. If the proposals in the Criminal Justice Bill 2002 are accepted by Parliament, it could be possible for the

The double jeopardy rule has inspired films and TV dramas.

three youths acquitted of murdering Stephen Lawrence to face another trial, but only if 'compelling' new evidence became available. The Appeal Court would also have to look at whether the men could ever have a fair trial, given the huge amount of publicity the case has received.

The Macpherson Report was critical of the double jeopardy rule. It said: 'We simply indicate that perhaps in modern conditions such absolute protection may sometimes lead to injustice.'

Some defendants have been acquitted but later admitted their guilt. Ronnie Knight, former husband of the actress Barbara Windsor, was acquitted in 1980 of the killing of Alfredo Zomparelli, but later wrote a book in which he admitted paying a man to kill him. In 2000, Freddie Foreman, once associated with the Kray twins (notorious gangsters), allegedly told a television documentary team that he helped in two murders for which he was cleared - that of Frank Mitchell, known as 'the Mad Axeman', and Tommy 'Ginger' Marks. After the documentary, Foreman - who served 16 years for disposing of the body of another Kray victim, Jack 'The Hat' McVitie - was told that he could not be retried.

Adapted from the Daily Telegraph, 6 March 2001 and the Guardian, 6 March 2001.

(a) What is the double jeopardy rule? **(2)**

(b) Explain why and how the press have sought to influence the law in relation to murder. **(4)**

(c) What concerns might there be about the way in which the media influences (i) law reform and (ii) the work of the courts? **(8)**

they differ from political parties in two ways. First, they do not normally put up candidates for election but seek to achieve their aims by putting pressure on those already in government. Second, they usually focus on a narrow range of issues while political parties cover a far broader range.

Protective and promotional groups

Pressure groups differ widely in their aims and methods of operation. A distinction is often made between protective and promotional groups. Protective groups - or 'sectional groups' as they are also known - aim to protect the common interests of a particular section of society.

Examples include trade unions and employer organisations. Other examples include Surfers Against Sewage and the British Diabetic Association. Promotional groups are often referred to as 'cause groups'. They are concerned with promoting a cause which is not necessarily of direct professional or economic benefit to the members of the group. Environmental groups such as Greenpeace and Friends of the Earth are examples of promotional groups. Others include LIFE, which seeks to change the law on abortion, and ASH which wants tighter legal controls on tobacco advertising.

Activity 9.2 — Pressure groups

Group	Aims	Supporters (members and/or donors)	Income	Staff*	Government contacts?**	Uses direct action?***
Charter 88	Campaigns for a written constitution and an entrenched Bill of Rights.	79,064 supporters	£750,000	14 ft 10 vols	✓	✗
British Union for the Abolition of Vivisection	Campaigns to halt the breeding and use of animals in experiments.	5,000 members 38,000 supporters	£1,210,682	18	✗	✓
Confederation of British Industry (CBI)	Promotes the interests of business and employers.	250,000 businesses	£4,329,000	200	✓	✗
Central Area Leamington Residents Association (CLARA)	Campaigns to preserve and improve the town of Leamington Spa and the surrounding area.	280 households	£840	vols	✓	✗
British Roads Federation	Aims to focus attention for a higher standard of service from the UK road network.	15 trade associations (representing 50,000 companies) and 80 individual business members	£500,000	9 ft	✓	✗
Earth First!	Campaigns against the destruction of the environment.	63 autonomous groups	not known	vols	✗	✓
Liberty	Campaigns to defend and extend human rights and civil liberties.	c.5,000 supporters	£500,000	10 ft 3 pt	✓	✗
Unison	Trade union for public sector workers.	1.3 million members and donors	£100 million	998	✗	✗
Friends of the Earth (FoE)	Campaigns to protect and conserve the environment.	200,000 members	£3,509,000	110	✓	✓

* ft = full time   pt = part time   vols = volunteers
** This column indicates whether a group has regular contacts with members of government (local or national) or with government officials (local or national)
*** This column indicates if a group uses direct action regularly

(a) Using the chart above, give an example of a protective group, a cause group, an insider group and an outsider group. (4)

(b) Give arguments for and against the idea that pressure groups might have a useful contribution to make to the formulation of proposals for new laws. (6)

Insider and outsider groups

Rather than classifying pressure groups in terms of what motivates their members, some authors classify them in terms of their status and the strategies they adopt. The distinction here is between 'insider' and 'outsider' groups.

Insider groups, such as the British Medical Association (BMA), are the groups which decision-makers consider to be legitimate and are, therefore, included in the consultation process. For example, insider groups might be involved in regular meetings with ministers or civil servants and they might be included on lists for circulation of new government proposals. Insider groups are similar in one respect. Generally, they abide by the 'rules of the game'. For example, they tend to respect confidences and not to make public attacks on decision-makers.

Outsider groups, such as Greenpeace, have none of the advantages of insider groups. They cannot expect to be consulted during the policy-making process, nor can they expect to gain access to ministers and civil servants. They have to work outside the decision-making process and, as a result, have fewer opportunities to shape new legislation.

Methods

Some of the methods used by pressure groups to try and influence the government and the law include the following.

1. Making contacts with MPs and political parties

Some groups employ people known as 'lobbyists' to bring matters to the attention of MPs. Other groups seek to recruit MPs as members. Many Labour MPs are sponsored by trade unions, for example.

2. Gaining public support

Pressure groups may use the mass media or advertising to gain public support. In addition, the work done by local branches can help gain public support.

3. Demonstrating levels of support

Pressure groups might, for example, demonstrate the level of support for a particular issue by collecting a petition and passing it to a government minister.

4. Involvement in consultations

Some pressure groups are consulted by decision-makers. This allows them to provide evidence to support their stance on particular issues. For example, the Law Commission consults relevant pressure groups when it investigates possible reforms to the law (see below). The present Labour government has been keen to encourage the general public to respond to government proposals for law reform through the internet, during a defined consultation period.

9.5 The Law Commission

The Law Commission is an independent body which was first set up in 1965 by Act of Parliament. It is the most important law reform body. It was set up to keep the law of England and Wales under review and to recommend reform when it is needed. Its proposals for law reform are based on research and consultation. Both relevant experts and those who will be affected by the reforms are consulted. The job of the Law Commission is to carry out this research and consultation and then to draw up proposals that will lead to a modernisation and improvement in the law. These proposals are put to Parliament and may eventually become Acts.

There are five Law Commissioners together with a small number of staff, including four or five Parliamentary Counsel (ie barristers who are skilled in drafting Bills). The Chair of the Commission, a High Court Judge, is appointed for a period of three years. The Law Commission works on law reform projects that have been approved by the government. The main areas include:

- trusts
- criminal law
- contract
- the law of landlord and tenant
- the law on transfer of land
- damages.

How does the Law Commission work?

The Law Commission has perhaps 30 or so projects at various stages of completion at any one time. The first stage is usually to study the existing laws and to identify where there are problems. This stage includes studying the law in other countries to see if this provides options for change.

The next stage is to issue a consultation paper which:

- sets out what the defects in the law are seen to be
- reviews the options for change
- asks for comments.

The consultation paper is circulated to practising lawyers, other relevant parties and the media. It is also made available to the public (for example, it is published on the Law Commission's web site).

After the consultation period, the Law Commission considers the various responses and, in light of these, produces a report that is sent to the Lord Chancellor with final recommendations. The report usually includes a draft Bill. Of course, to become law, the Bill must be debated and voted on by Parliament in the normal way.

The Law Commission and codification

In Britain, the law is a complex mass of separate pieces of legislation and case law. To understand the law in sufficient detail to conduct an action in the courts requires access to a whole range of case reports, statutes and other material. These are written in complicated language and piecing together the various strands is time-consuming and requires some skill. Most other countries have whole areas of law contained in a single document or code. This makes the law more accessible to citizens and, in theory at least, it makes it easier for the courts to understand the law and apply it. Instead of cross-referencing a number of sources of law, it is simpler to find a complete statement of the law in a single code. However, the codification of English law would inevitably involve changing and modifying the law so that laws that had evolved in a piecemeal way over centuries in the traditional English way could be brought together in one place.

When it was first set up in 1965, the Law Commission had ambitious plans for the codification of UK law. It was announced that it would begin to codify contract, landlord and tenant, evidence and family law. More than 30 years later the Law Commission has made very little progress towards achieving these goals. In 1989, the Law Commission published a draft Criminal Code but none of this has been turned into legislation. Only in family law has the Law Commission's work on codification led to legislation, though as several Acts rather than as one code. Work on contract, landlord and tenant and evidence codes has all been abandoned.

Consolidation and repeal

Consolidating legislation is designed to bring together laws previously contained in a number of Acts so that they can be found all in one place. There is little or no real change in the law. For example, in 1996, the majority of the law on education was consolidated into two new Acts as a consequence of Law Commission proposals.

A **repealing Act** is one that is used to remove existing legislation. As Parliament has been creating Acts for over 750 years, it is not surprising that some of them are now obsolete. Since 1965, about 5,000 enactments have been repealed by Statute Law (Repeals) Acts proposed by the Law Commission. Each of these Acts contains provisions repealing a large number of statutes in one go. These usually pass through Parliament with very little debate, but are preceded by consultation organised by the Law Commission. This process of 'tidying-up' is aimed at simplifying statute law. Some old laws still in force are described in Box 9.3.

Box 9.3 *Old laws still in force*

Some old laws still in force can only be described as bizarre. The following are examples.

1. It is legal for a male to urinate in public so long as he does it on the rear wheel of his motor vehicle, and his right hand touches the vehicle.

2. Until changes to the Sunday trading laws, only carrots could be sold on a Sunday.

3. The City Council of Chester was embarrassed by a local law which permitted the shooting of Welsh people with a bow and arrow inside the city walls after midnight.

How much has the Law Commission achieved?

If the Law Commission is measured against one of its original goals, namely to codify the law in England and Wales, it has not been a success. However, it may be that there is a fundamental problem with codifying English law rather than a problem with the Law Commission. Besides, codifying the law is by no means the Law Commission's only role. In relation to reform of the law in general, its record is impressive. In October 1997, out of 157 Law Commission reports published, 101 had been entirely or partially implemented. Achievements include:

● major changes in contract law, such as the Contract (Rights of Third Parties) Act 1999, which allows individuals who are not party to a contract to sue on it in certain circumstances

● reform of the law on conspiracy in the Criminal Law Act 1977

● important changes to public order offences which were enacted in the Public Order Act 1986

● the Family Law Reform Act 1987 which removed the legal disadvantages attached to illegitimacy

● the Children Act 1989 which reformed the whole of the law on children

● the Computer Misuse Act 1990 which introduced new criminal offences relating to the misuse of computers

● the Family Law Act 1996 which altered the law of domestic violence and of divorce.

However, during the 1990s, there was growing concern that too many reports were not being acted on by Parliament. One possible reason for this is lack of parliamentary time. The government often sees improvements in existing law as 'lawyers' law' and not as high a priority as the new laws it wants to create. In response to the growing backlog of Law Commission reports, the **Jellicoe Procedure** was introduced into the House of Lords in 1994. This enables the Special Public Bills Committee of the Lords to debate non-controversial Bills involving reform of the civil law. This allows reforms to be considered without them taking up the time of the whole of the Lords or the Commons. The use of the Jellicoe Procedure seems to have helped to reduce the backlog of Law Commission proposals.

9.6 Royal Commissions

Royal Commissions are set up by the government to study specific areas of law and to propose reforms. They are usually set up in response to public controversy. Whereas the Law Commission is a permanent body, Royal Commissions are disbanded when they have completed their work. Royal Commissions often take several years to investigate and report back. They are intended to be independent of government or political parties. The members of a Royal Commission are drawn from those who are considered to have particular expertise in the relevant field, not just from the legal world.

Recent examples include:

- the Royal Commission on Criminal Justice which reported in 1993
- the Royal Commission for the Reform of the House of Lords which published its report in January 2000 (see Unit 2).

Activity 9.3 *Reform of the Land Registration Act*

A new law is being devised to speed up England and Wales' antiquated conveyancing system. Clause 8 of the Electronic Communications Bill will enable documents needed to buy and sell a house to be transmitted in a legally binding form via the internet. But only after basic reforms are made to the Land Registration Act 1925 will the bureaucratic hold-ups of conveyancing be reduced. Under that Act, ownership of a house has to be registered with the government's Land Registry. Selling a house means the details held at the Land Registry have to be altered. Law Commissioner Charles Harpum summed up one view of the Land Registration Act, unchanged since 1925: 'It is a terrible piece of legislation. It is only because the staff at the Land Registry are remarkably sensible and efficient that it works at all.' It creates a system that means the register does not always show the true owner. There is a time lag between transfer of ownership and registration when the old owner's name is still shown on the register. This allows dishonest people to sell the same property twice. Although the Land Registry does pay compensation in that situation, the risk would be eliminated by making transfer and registration simultaneous. Better drafted legislation might have achieved that 75 years ago. The internet will make it simple. Once the law is changed, lawyers will make instantaneous pre-sales checks to find out who owns land. Once all the preparatory work is done, it will be possible to complete the formalities of buying a house within about an hour.

The Law Commission made recommendations in September 1998 that should make conveyancing faster and more secure. The reform process is slow. In May 2000, the legislation was being drawn up in Parliament, a process which was expected to take until the end of the year. Once the final draft had been completed, there would be further consultation. The new law might not reach the statute book for several years.

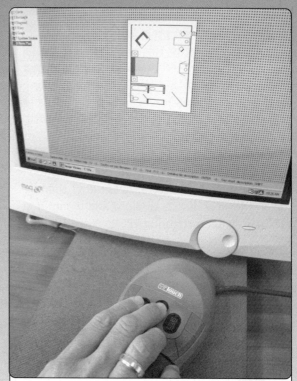

The Electronic Communications Bill will enable documents needed to buy and sell a house to be transmitted via the internet.

Adapted from the *Guardian*, 27 May 2000.

(a) **What problems are the Law Commission's proposed reforms of the Land Registration Act designed to tackle? (3)**

(b) **How would the reforms achieve this? (3)**

(c) **Implementation of the proposals is slow. Is this necessarily a bad thing? (3)**

(d) **Who might the Law Commission consult regarding these proposed changes in the law? (3)**

Royal Commissions are commonly named after the person who chairs them. The Royal Commission for the Reform of the House of Lords, for example, is often called the 'Wakeham Commission' after its Chair, Lord Wakeham.

Cynics might argue that governments often set up Royal Commissions when they have little intention of actually changing the law but want to give the impression that they are taking steps to deal with controversial issues. Certainly, there is often a considerable time lag between the start of an investigation and the publication of the final report and this time lag sometimes allows the government to avoid taking steps it is reluctant to take. In addition, governments can, and indeed often do, ignore recommendations made by Royal Commissions. For example, the government decided not to accept most of the 132 recommendations made by the Wakeham Commission. The Pearson Commission on Personal Injuries provides another example. When it was set up, this was seen as an indication that the government was keen to make much-needed changes to the way in which negligence claims are dealt with. In fact, very few of Pearson's proposals ever reached the statute book.

On the other hand, the 1981 Report of the Royal Commission on Police Powers played an important part in shaping the Police and Criminal Evidence Act 1984, a major and generally well received reform. Similarly, a Royal Commission on Police Powers was appointed in 1991 under Viscount Runciman to investigate the operation of the criminal justice system following public concern about an embarrassing series of proven miscarriages of justice (the Birmingham Six, the Guildford Four and others). Some, though by no means all, of the commission's proposals were implemented in the Criminal Justice and Public Order Act 1994. These included limitations on the right to silence and giving the police the right to take samples for DNA testing without the consent of the suspect.

9.7 The Criminal Law Revision Committee

The Criminal Law Revision Committee was a part-time body that sat between 1957 and 1984. Its membership consisted of both working lawyers and academics.

The main achievements of the committee were the Theft Acts 1968 and 1978. These Acts effectively codified the law on theft, representing a major overhaul. In fact, this reform was not a complete success as some sections of the 1968 Act were, to say the least, a source of confusion for lawyers and judges. This was reflected in a sharp rise in the number of appeals relating to points of the law on

theft in the years following 1968. Part of the purpose of the 1978 Act was to remedy a particular defect in the 1968 Act.

In defence of the the Criminal Law Revision Committee, Lord Scarman, writing in the *Times* in 1996, expressed the view that some poorly written legislation produced after 1984 might have been better drafted if the committee had still been available to assist the government.

The Criminal Law Revision Committee should not be confused with the Criminal Cases Review Commission (see Unit 12).

9.8 Other law reform bodies

The Law Reform Committee was set up in 1952. It is a part-time body that only considers a few branches of civil law. A major example of its influence is the Occupiers Liability Act 1957 which concerns the liability in negligence of those who have control over land.

Occasionally, judges are asked to investigate issues to do with the legal system. An important example of this is the Woolf Committee on Civil Justice, which was set up by the Lord Chancellor. This committee led to very significant changes in the operation of the High Court and the County Court (see Unit 10). In addition, the Arbitration Act 1996 (arbitration is a way of resolving legal disputes outside the courts of law) was a result of proposals generated by a committee set up by the Department of Trade and Industry and chaired by Lord Justice Saville.

Summary ● ● ●

1. How does public opinion influence law reform?

2. What part do the mass media and pressure groups play in law-making?

3. What is the Law Commission?

4. What have been the Law Commission's successes and failures?

5. Apart from the Law Commission, what other bodies play a part in law reform?

Case study ● Law reform agencies

Item A *The Law Commission*

The wording of a particular statute appeared to mean that a householder who split a house into two flats was not responsible when the roof leaked and flooded the flat that was sold. The Law Commission proposed changes in 1985. By 1994, nothing had happened.

Politicians like the broad brush. They like Bills that set out to transform the education system or privatise state-owned organisations. Modernising the shambolic English legal system, by contrast, involves uninspiring and complicated detail. But the government's failure to modernise hurts homeowners, businesses and victims. It also costs the government a great deal more to administer the courts.

The Honourable Mr Justice Brooke, former Chair of the Law Commission was quoted in the *Guardian* in 1994 as telling MPs: 'Substantial parts of our criminal law are a disgrace. They ought to be clear, consistent and coherent. Instead they are unclear, inconsistent and incoherent. The Law Commission does not undertake any law reform projects unless the relevant law is known to be bad. It is usually spoilt for choice.'

In Canada, it is possible to buy a copy of the criminal code for a few dollars. In Britain, the criminal law is a mishmash of case law and statutes dating back 300 years or more. The Law Commission is meant to have codified the criminal law and made it clearer. Its members include academics and barristers who consult widely and avoid party politics. They come up with sound proposals. But too many of them never become law.

Between 1989 and 1993, for example, ministers introduced only one of the measures the Law Commission presented to Parliament. Parliamentary time was occupied by bringing in the poll tax and then withdrawing it, privatising British Rail and considering various Bills on education. Perhaps politicians are concerned that law reform will not get them on television. But reform is needed - especially reform of the criminal law. The case of *Scarlett (1993)* provides an example. Mr Scarlett was the landlord of a pub who asked an extremely drunk man to leave the premises. In these circumstances, a landlord is permitted by law to use reasonable force. The man was pushed out of the pub into a lobby but fell down some stairs and died. The Crown Court convicted Scarlett for manslaughter. He spent five months in prison awaiting an appeal hearing, apparently for no reason other than confusion on the part of the trial judge as to the law in this type of manslaughter case, a confusion that the Court of Appeal seemed to suggest was understandable.

Adapted from the *Guardian*, 21 November 1994.

Item B *Should English law be codified? (i)*

This cartoon compares the rigidity of the American legal system with the flexibility of the British legal system.

Item C *Should English law be codified? (ii)*

Professor Hahlo, writing in the *Modern Law Review* in 1960, described how lawyers with experience of working in both codified and uncodified legal systems have felt that there are as many points of controversy in one as in the other and that the task of a French, Dutch or German lawyer in arguing a legal point is not substantially easier than that of their English counterpart. Hahlo points out that the immediate effect of introducing a code is twofold. On the one hand, it would settle previously uncertain issues. But on the other hand, it would create a long period of legal uncertainty while the exact meaning of the new laws is tested. For each controversy that has been removed, he argues, one or more new ones will arise. And it will only be decades later, after the code has become overlaid with case law, that the old measure of legal certainty will return. In addition to the growing body of case law, he argues, there will soon be an ever-growing body of amending legislation, followed in due course by judgements explaining the amending legislation, and amendments upon amendments.

Another objection to codification is that the law becomes fixed and rigid, and, therefore, unable to change over time in response to changes in society and unforeseen factual situations. The common law approach to building the law up over time as new cases come before the courts is seen by some as admirably flexible. The courts find the best way to interpret and apply relevant statutes and add to a detailed case law over time in a way that provides justice and fairness (see Unit 7). This flexibility would be lost, it is argued, if a system of codes were introduced since a code is designed to cover all situations and is more or less 'written in stone'. Critics of the codified approach argue that it is very hard to write a comprehensive code of law that would provide just law to all cases at all times, given the myriad range of different facts that come before the courts. Where a codified system is used, the codes of law cannot be amended without a special parliamentary procedure. To make it easy to disregard or amend the code and create exceptions to the rule would defeat the object of having one in the first place, as the law would tend to become piecemeal.

Questions

(a) Use Item A and your own knowledge to complete the following tasks.

   i)   What is the purpose of the Law Commission? (3)

   ii)   Why is clarity and certainty in criminal law particularly important? (4)

   iii)   Why does Parliament fail to act on many Law Commission proposals? (8)

   iv)   Item A is based on an article written in 1994. Explain the procedure that was introduced that year to get more Law Commission proposals into the statute book. (3)

(b) Use Items A - C and your own knowledge to complete the following tasks.

   i)   Explain what is meant by the term 'codification'. (4)

   ii)   Why might the codification of English law resolve the problem of confused criminal laws? (4)

   iii)   Summarise the arguments for and against the codification of English law. (10)

10.1 How do the civil courts work?

What areas of law are included in civil law?

Although few people are ever actually involved in a court action, the civil law runs through many aspects of everyday life. These are some of the areas that civil law deals with:

- divorce
- disputed wills
- negligence claims (common examples of these include accidents at work or on the roads)
- land and property
- the regulation of contracts.

Contract cases are the most common in the civil courts. Contract law is concerned with legally enforceable agreements. There are a multitude of agreements covered by contract law. Contract cases heard in the civil courts range from the simple collection of an unpaid debt owed to a small local firm, to highly complex disputes between giant corporations such as oil companies and banks.

How does a civil action differ from a criminal trial?

The aim and the end result of a civil action are both quite different from that of a criminal trial. A criminal trial is an exploration on behalf of the state into whether the defendant has broken the criminal law. If the defendant is found guilty, then some kind of punishment is inflicted on them by the state. The only part the victim or victims of the crime might play in court is to appear as a witness. The victim or victims do not benefit from the process, apart, perhaps, from gaining the satisfaction of seeing the accused punished by the state. A civil action is different - see Box 10.1.

Pre-trial procedure

A great deal of work goes on before the trial date. A whole series of formal documents are exchanged between the two sides. The first of these is sent by the claimant to notify the defendant that a case is being brought. The defendant has to respond to this with another document. Documents are exchanged outlining the facts, the legal basis for action and the documents that the parties propose to use in court. Parties can ask to see some or all of these documents in a process known as 'discovery'. Not everything can be used in evidence in court, and not all evidence can be raised at any time. There are a number of rules governing whether or not evidence can be admitted into court.

Box 10.1 *What is a civil action?*

A civil action is a contest between two parties (a party being an individual, a businesses or another organisation) where differences of opinion are settled by the courts. Since 1999, the party that brings the action has been known as the 'claimant'. Before that, they were known as the 'plaintiff'. The claimant is usually seeking financial compensation from the defendant. This compensation is known as '**damages**'.

In a sense, the claimant is the driving force behind a civil trial because the claimant is asking the court to make a judgement. There is no question of the state inflicting punishment on the losing side.

For the court to decide in favour of the claimant, facts that are central to the claimant's argument must be proven. But the burden of proof in a civil action is different from that in a criminal case. In a criminal case, the standard of proof required of the prosecution is 'beyond all reasonable doubt'. Basically, this means that a reasonable person could have no significant doubt that the defendant was guilty. In a civil case, on the other hand, the claimant has an easier task in proving facts. The standard of proof is 'on a balance of probabilities'. In other words, if it seems more likely than not that something occurred, that is sufficient.

The pre-trial process involves much more than simply preparing to appear in court. Both sides are anxious to know how strong the argument that will be used against them is, and what evidence will be presented to support this argument. But this only gradually unfolds. Many cases are won or lost without ever reaching court. The two sides probe each other's intentions, often acting like poker players trying to suggest that their hand is stronger than it really is. If the bluff is successful, the other side may drop out and settle the case out of court.

Cases are often settled out of court at some point in the months or years before they actually appear before a judge for trial. Settlement means either that the defendant makes an offer of payment that is accepted, or the claimant agrees to accept less than was earlier sought. Settlement out of court is mostly about a practical realisation that differences might be best resolved without running up further legal bills. If the defendant makes a formal **payment into court** before trial, the claimant runs a certain risk if they reject that offer of payment. Should the case then continue to full trial and should the court rule in favour of the claimant but award damages worth less than the earlier payment into court, the claimant then has to pay the defendant's costs from the date of the payment in.

The conduct of trials

The length of a trial and how it proceeds is mostly the outcome of choices made by the opposing advocates (lawyers). The English system works on the basis of what is known as **'the adversarial system'**. This means that opposing lawyers dominate the conduct of a trial, each presenting their side of the argument. The judge is there, mostly, to listen to the arguments presented and then to reach a decision on the outcome of the evidence presented in argument.

Paying lawyers to conduct a case in court is never cheap. In theory, whichever side loses has to pay the other side's legal costs as well as their own. But there are rules governing what costs will and will not be allowed by the judge. Court actions also involve paying fees to the court itself.

Are there any alternatives to court action?

Because of the time, expense and, sometimes, embarrassment involved in bringing a civil case to court, few people are keen on taking a dispute to court. Before resorting to legal action, negotiation takes place. Letters are written and discussions held. If this does not lead to settlement of the dispute, a solicitor's letter warning that legal action is a possibility may be sent. In matters such as simple debts, this often produces the desired result. If it does not, it may be possible to resolve disputes through both sides agreeing to put the matter before someone other than a judge. This is often known as **'alternative dispute resolution'**. A common example of this is arbitration. Here, the person, acting in private rather than in public as a 'judge' may be a lawyer, or it may be someone with appropriate non-legal expertise. For example, construction cases might be settled by reference to an arbitrator with recognised experience and expertise in the construction industry. Alternative dispute resolution offers a very cost-effective option (for further details see Unit 11).

What do we want from the civil courts?

In the 1990s, Lord Woolf led a major investigation into the civil justice system. His recommendations formed the basis of the Civil Procedure Rules which were introduced in 1999 and are often known as 'the Woolf reforms'. The standards that Lord Woolf said any civil justice system should match up to are outlined in Box 10.2

10.2 Civil courts of first instance

Which cases start in which court?

Civil cases may begin in one of three courts - Magistrates' Courts, County Courts and the High Court. Courts where

Box 10.2 *Lord Woolf and the standards of the civil justice system*

In his interim report which was published in 1996, Lord Woolf said that any civil justice system should match up to the following standards:

1. **It should be just in the results it delivers.** In other words, the court should provide a solution to the dispute that is fair.

2. **It should be fair in the way it treats litigants.** Not only the final decision but also the process experienced by those who are parties in a case should be unbiased.

3. **It should offer appropriate procedures at a reasonable cost.** If taking a court action proves to be excessively expensive, only the rich will be able to use the courts. It is obviously undesirable that only a section of society is able to access the courts.

4. **It should deal with cases with reasonable speed.** Delay can prevent justice. For example witnesses may find it difficult to recall exactly what happened, if the time lag between the events that gave rise to a court case and the trial is too great.

5. **It should be understandable to those who use it.** A common criticism of lawyers and judges is that they work with legal jargon that the ordinary person finds it difficult to comprehend, and that legal rules are sometimes unnecessarily complicated.

6. **It should be responsive to the needs of those who use it.** The courts should serve the needs of those who bring disputes before it. In simple terms, the courts should provide good service to its 'customers'.

7. **It should be effective.** The courts should be properly financed and organised.

cases begin are known as 'courts of first instance' (some civil cases are dealt with in tribunals - see Unit 11). If a legal action is started, the court a claimant should apply to is determined by the **jurisdiction** (legal authority) of the courts of first instance. Magistrates' Courts have a limited civil jurisdiction. For example, they can hear cases which deal with certain aspects of the law relating to adoption, maintenance of children and the licensing of premises involved in the sale of alcohol. Most civil cases begin in County Courts or the High Court. As a result, this unit will focus mainly on the County Courts and the High Court.

County Courts

County Courts were first established in 1846 to provide a

more local, simpler and, therefore, cheaper means of resolving relatively small actions than that provided by the High Court. County Courts handle contract and tort claims, but not usually those with a value above £50,000.

There are 240 County Courts scattered around the country. They are staffed by District Judges and the more senior Circuit Judges. Small-scale consumer disputes, up to £5,000 in value, can be heard before a District Judge within what is now known as the 'small claims track'. The County Court itself mainly deals with cases that have a value of more than £5,000 but less than £50,000.

The High Court

The High Court can hear cases that fit into one of the following categories:

- personal injury claims with a value of £50,000 or more
- other claims with a value above £15,000
- claims where an Act of Parliament requires an action to begin in the High Court
- certain specialist cases.

There are two elements to the High Court - it is a court of first instance and an appeal court. As a court of first instance, the High Court has three divisions. These are outlined in Box 10.3 below.

10.3 Civil courts of appeal

The High Court as a court of appeal

When the High Court sits as a court of appeal, it is also divided into three divisions. The jurisdiction of these **Divisional Courts** is outlined in Box 10.4.

The Queen's Bench Divisional Court and judicial review

The Queen's Bench Divisional Court may be asked to investigate and, if necessary, overturn a decision of a government department, some other public authority, a local authority, a lower court or a tribunal, by a party who has been disadvantaged by that decision. There are two grounds for judicial review. One is that the decision is *ultra vires*. An *ultra vires* decision is one made outside the legal power or authority of the person or body who has made it. The other is that it is against the rules of natural justice. There are two main rules of natural justice. First, no person is allowed to make rulings about a case in which they have an interest (*nemo judex in causa sua*). Second, both sides should be allowed to put their side of the story (*audi alterem partem*).

The Court of Appeal

No cases ever commence in the Court of Appeal. As its name suggests, the role of the court is purely to hear cases where one side or the other feels that some aspect of the decision made by a lower court is open to question. Although the 35 judges who sit in the Court of Appeal have a demanding workload of about 1,000 cases per year, this is only a tiny fraction of the millions of court actions that are started.

The judges in the Court of Appeal are called Lord or Lady Justices of Appeal (abbreviated to L.J. in law reports). The most senior Court of Appeal Judge is the Master of the Rolls, Lord Phillips in 2003.

Because only a few dozen cases are heard every year in the House of Lords, decisions of the Court of Appeal are quite often regarded as deciding the common law, though the Lords is the highest appeal court.

Box 10.3 *The three divisions of the High Court*

1. The Chancery Division

The jurisdiction of the Chancery Court includes the following:

- various matters of land law
- the law relating to mortgages
- the administration of deceased person's money and property, and disputes over wills
- bankruptcy
- the law relating to companies and partnerships
- tax law.

2. The Family Division

The Family Division deals with cases including the following:

- divorce and other matrimonial matters
- legitimacy of children
- adoption of children.

3. The Queen's Bench Division (QBD)

The Queen's Bench Division (QBD) is the part of the High Court that has the largest workload. Contract and tort cases are dealt with here. The QBD also includes an Admiralty Court, which deals with shipping cases. A High Court Judge presides over appeals from employment tribunals in the Employment Appeal Tribunal. Technically, this is not part of the High Court.

Box 10.4 *The jurisdiction of the three Divisional Courts of the High Court*

1. Chancery Divisional Court

In this appellate court (ie court of appeal), one or two Chancery Judges hear appeals from the Commissioners of Inland Revenue (regarding tax law) and certain County Court appeals, such as bankruptcy.

2. Family Divisional Court

In this appeal court, two High Court Judges hear appeals from decisions of Magistrates' Courts and County Courts in relation to certain matters of family law, largely to do with maintenance orders.

3. Queen's Bench Divisional Court

Two or three High Court Judges hear appeals in the following circumstances:

- appeals on a point of law by way of case stated from criminal cases in the Magistrates' Courts and certain tribunals
- applications for *habeas corpus* (an ancient court order that can be granted to persons who claim they are being unlawfully detained)
- judicial review.

The House of Lords

The House of Lords is the final court of appeal in the United Kingdom, for both civil and criminal cases. Only about 50 cases a year are heard by Law Lords (see Unit 14 for more information on Law Lords or 'Lords of Appeal in Ordinary' as they are called formally). Cases are normally heard by five Law Lords, but, in exceptionally important cases, seven may sit. The Lords also sits as the **Judicial Committee of the Privy Council**, which is the final court of appeal for certain Commonwealth countries.

For an appeal to move from the Court of Appeal or the Divisional Courts to the Lords, permission must be given by either the Lords themselves or by the lower court. Very occasionally, 'leapfrog' appeals from the Divisions of the High Court are also heard (see below for a definition of 'leapfrog' appeals).

The European Court of Justice

Although the European Court can only hear appeals relating to matters of EU law, EU law now represents a considerable part of the total body of UK law. In European law, the European Court is superior to the House of Lords (further details of the European Court of Justice are given in Unit 5, Section 5.6).

The overall structure of the system of civil courts is given in Box 10.5.

The appeal system in the lower courts

In almost all cases, permission to appeal is now required from the lower court. Permission is necessary when an appeal is sought to the County Court or the High Court. Permission is only given where there is a strong reason for

Box 10.5 *The overall structure of the system of civil courts*

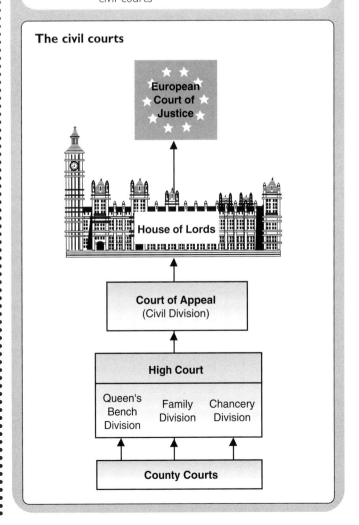

The civil courts

doing so. Appeals are limited to a review rather than a complete rehearing.

Appeals move between different levels of judge. The normal rule is that the appeal goes to the next level of judge in the hierarchy. In other words, appeals move from a District Judge to a Circuit Judge, from a Circuit Judge to a High Court Judge and from a High Court Judge to the Court of Appeal.

Leapfrog appeals

Perhaps one or two cases every year go straight from the High Court to the House of Lords, as what are known as 'leapfrog' appeals. For this to happen, three conditions must be met. First, both parties must agree. Second, the original trial judge has to indicate that the case involves a point of law of general public importance. This point must either be connected largely with statutory interpretation or it must be one where the judge was bound by a Court of Appeal or House of Lords decision. Finally, the House of Lords must give their permission. This permission is known as 'leave to appeal'.

10.4 Problems with the civil courts before 1999

Has there ever been a time where the courts worked well?

In 1985, the Civil Justice Review identified huge problems with the length of time it took for a case to reach the courts. It was recommended that one way of improving the civil justice system was to channel more cases away from the slower and more expensive High Courts to the quicker and cheaper County Courts. In the Courts and Legal Services Act 1990, the government drastically increased the size of claim that could be started in the County Court itself, and increased the upper limit for small claims cases. This meant that many more cases were started in the County Courts.

A few years later, the Woolf Report *Access to Justice*, published in 1996, was also extremely critical of the workings of the civil justice in England and Wales. The implementation of the recommendations made by Lord Woolf has made the biggest change to the way in which the courts operate for a hundred years. The problems which existed to make these drastic changes necessary are outlined in Box 10.6.

1. Excessive cost

It is not unreasonable for lawyers to expect to make a good living. They are skilled professionals who bear heavy

Activity 10.1

(1) Jane Osborne went into Notown Hospital a year ago for what should have been a routine operation to have her appendix removed. She believes that the surgeon, Dr Ying, made a mistake, the consequences of which have left her off work ill for many months. Dr Ying denies any liability. After an investigation within the hospital, the surgeon's employers also deny liability.

(2) Tony Williams died not long ago from cancer. He left a son, James, with whom he had little contact, and a married sister, Eileen Brown, who looked after him for several years during his illness. Under the law on wills, if Tony died without a will, all of his property would pass to his son. Eileen has produced a will which she claims was current at the time of Tony's death. Under the will, Eileen inherits Tony's property. James has found out something that leads him to question the validity of this will. He has instructed a solicitor and is prepared to go to court over the issue.

(3) John Jones has been purchasing diesel for his lorry on account from Malhi Garages over the past three years. At the end of every month, Jones receives a statement from the company, showing the amount due. This has to be paid within 30 days. Randip Malhi, the owner of Malhi Garages, is concerned that, despite several written reminders and a solicitor's letter, the account has not been paid for three months. The total owing is £350.

(4) David Morris has been refused planning permission for an extension to his office block from Thatplace Council, his local council. He feels that his application was not given fair or proper consideration by the council.

In each of the situations outlined above, identify:

(a) **who will be the claimant and who will be the defendant (2)**

(b) **in which court a legal action is likely to be started. (2)**

Box 10.6 *Lord Woolf's criticisms of the civil court system*

Lord Woolf identified the following problems:
- bringing a court action is much too expensive
- there are excessive delays in bringing cases to court
- the adversarial system too often results in tactical behaviour rather than cooperation between lawyers in the search for justice
- the complexity of court procedures limits access to the courts and imposes an unnecessary burden upon the parties
- hearings take too long.

responsibilities. But when the legal costs of both sides are paid by the loser, which is the normal rule, there is a risk involved in bringing a dispute before the courts. The higher the market price for a lawyer's services are, the more likely it is that those with limited finances will be afraid to go to court, no matter how strong their case actually is. Sir Thomas Bingham, former Master of the Rolls, described the expense of litigation as 'the cancer eating at the heart of the administration of justice'.

When Professor Hazel Genn conducted a survey for the Woolf inquiry, the most expensive type of cases studied were medical negligence, where average costs amounted to £38,252. How many people would be willing to risk such expense?

2. Delay

In 1994, High Court cases took on average 163 weeks in London and 189 weeks outside London to progress from starting the action to actually reaching a court hearing. The equivalent County Court figures were around 80 weeks. Lord Woolf described these figures as 'unacceptable in relation to the great generality of cases'.

Delay in reaching court is an additional problem for parties who have already suffered damage (see Box 10.7). It delays the compensation to which they may be entitled. In personal injury cases, this can lead to unnecessary suffering because the claimant is unable to afford proper care. It can lead to the collapse of relationships when the stress and worry of an unsettled court case is present for a long time. It makes it more difficult to establish facts because memories fade and witnesses cannot be traced. It may lead to people settling for inadequate compensation

because they are simply worn down by excessive delay or cannot afford to continue.

Delay is of more benefit to legal advisers than to the parties to the action. Judges told the Woolf inquiry that it was for the convenience of lawyers that many adjournments (postponements of the trial) were agreed. Too often, delay resulted in increased costs.

3. Problems with the adversarial system

Until 1999, the judge relied on lawyers to present their evidence in the way that they saw fit. It was not, to any great extent, the role of a judge to intervene in the interests of saving time and money for the parties concerned.

The Woolf inquiry reported aggressive tactics by some lawyers. Procedural rules, which might have prevented unfair tactics, were ignored on a vast scale. Timetables for the trial were too often ignored and other requirements were complied with only when it was convenient to the interests of one of the parties.

4. Complexity

This problem was most obvious when a party was not represented by a lawyer. But it also applied to confusion among the parties' professional advisers. For example, two weighty sets of civil procedure rules were in use. In the County Court, the 'Green Book' was used. In the High Court and the Court of Appeal, the 'White Book' was used.

5. Hearings take too long

In his interim report, Lord Woolf commented that, although time estimates were provided by parties and confirmed by the judge, these bore insufficient relation to reality. This approach was wasteful for all concerned. Judges did not intervene to curtail long-windedness or to focus presentation of the case, in case they gave grounds for appeal.

> **Box 10.7** *Problems faced by the civil courts before 1999*

Cartoonist Brick's view of the civil court system before 1999.

Activity 10.2

Lord Woolf set out various standards by which the civil courts should be judged. These are outlined in Box 10.2. Read Box 10.2 again and then briefly explain how, in the view of Lord Woolf and others, the civil courts failed to meet each of these standards before 1999. (12)

10.5 Current civil court procedure

The table in Box 10.8 sets out some of the key changes made in the new system introduced in April 1999.

Box 10.8 *Key changes to the system introduced in April 1999*

Pre-April 1999	Post-April 1999
The conduct of the trial is largely decided by the parties, the judge has a passive role.	The judge is involved in active case management.
Plaintiff decides whether the case is heard in the County Court or the High Court.	A judge decides where a case is tried, and which 'track' the case is allocated to.
Various complicated forms needed to start an action.	Single 'Part 7' claim form used to start an action.
Separate procedural rules for County Courts and High Court.	County Courts and High Court have same procedural rules.
Claims up to £3,000 automatically dealt with in small claims procedure - arbitration in private.	Small claims track allocated where it is felt appropriate in cases up to £5,000 - hearing in public.
Person starting an action described as a 'plaintiff'.	Person starting an action described as a 'claimant'.

The Civil Procedure Act 1997

How a case is handled by the courts, in terms of proceeding through the stages leading up to trial and the trial itself is set out in the Civil Procedure Rules (CPR). These rules were altered substantially following the recommendations in the Woolf Report. The following reforms have been made:

● judges were given a new duty to actively manage cases

● claim forms were simplified

● a new approach to allocating cases between the County Court and the High Court was introduced

● pre-action protocols (guidelines) were introduced to encourage settlement out of court

● judges were required to encourage the greater use of alternative dispute resolution.

Since 1999, parties to an action have had far less control over the speed with which the case progresses through the courts than in the past. The court now has a positive duty to manage cases. Litigants are not able to prolong a trial or delay it in the way that they once could because each case is subject to its own timetable. This timetable is monitored by court staff, using a computerised system.

The new approach to active case management by judges also includes the other elements outlined in Box 10.9.

Box 10.9 *The new approach to active case management*

The new approach to active case management by judges includes:

● encouraging the parties to cooperate with each other in the conduct of the action

● deciding which issues need full investigation and which can be dealt with fairly quickly

● helping the parties to settle the case (see below)

● encouraging the use of alternative dispute resolution (see below).

Although the adversarial system remains in place, judges are now required to intervene in the interests of dealing with a case justly.

Allocation of cases to 'tracks'

Once the court knows the defendant intends to defend an action, the District Judge (in the County Court) or the Master (in the High Court) sends out an **allocation questionnaire** to both parties. This is used to help determine the procedures that will apply to trial of the case. The system of selecting one of three distinct systems of court procedure is one the major innovations emerging from the Woolf Report. Each system is known as a 'track'. There are three possible tracks for the judge to choose from:

● **the small claims track**

● **the fast track**

● **the multi-track.**

The small claims track

Small claims cases are low value, straightforward cases. It is intended that the parties can effectively take part in a small claims hearing without the need for legal representation. Many small claims cases are dealt with in half an hour or so. There is little difference between the old (pre-1999) and the new method of handling small claims. Claims are still heard by a District Judge. They have the same relative informality and, basically, no costs can be awarded. However, several key changes were made in the new Civil Procedure Rules. These changes are outlined in Box 10.10.

Box 10.10 *Key changes to the small claims track*

The following are the key changes made to the small claims track in 1999:

1. The small claims jurisdiction was increased from £3,000 to £5,000.

2. The small claims track, unlike its predecessor, is not used more or less automatically for claims of a certain size. Rather, claims are allocated to this track after a decision-making process has been completed. Parties can consent to use this track even if the value of their case is above £5,000.

3. Hearings are usually in public (in the past, they were private).

4. The case can be tried on paper, without an actual hearing, if the parties consent.

5. Parties need not attend the hearing if they provide written notice that they will not be doing so.

6. The use of expert witnesses is only possible with the court's permission. This helps keeps the cost of a small claims action down.

The fast track

The idea of a relatively cheap fast track system is one of the key recommendations of the Woolf Report. The fast track aims to provide a streamlined, standardised procedure for the handling of 'middle value' cases where significant sums of money are at stake. In the past, the costs of this sort of trial too often escalated to levels out of all proportion to the amount claimed.

The multi-track

The multi-track does not have a standardised 'off the shelf' procedure, as is the case with the small claims and the fast track. Instead, it provides a flexible system for handling higher value, more complex cases (those over £15,000). A range of methods for managing the case is available to the judge. These methods can be used in combination to suit the needs of individual cases. Multi-track cases require lengthier debate than other cases.

There is some flexibility in the allocation rules. For example, if the parties agree, a case that might be expected to be tried using the multi-track may end up being tried in the fast track. Box 10.11 shows which court and which track a case is usually heard in.

Pre-action protocols (PAPs)

Pre-action protocols (PAPs) are guideline rules that the parties should follow. These rules are intended to focus

Box 10.11 *Allocating courts and tracks*

Value of claim	Likely court/track
Below £5,000	County Court/small claims
£5,000 to £15,000	County Court/fast track
£15,000 to £25,000	County Court/multi-track
£25,000 to £50,000	High Court or County Court/multi-track
Over £50,000	High Court/multi-track

the parties on the value of reaching a settlement without a trial. The rules require full and quick exchange of information at an early stage (as opposed to deliberate and tactical delays that too often have the effect of wearing the other side down).

Activity 10.3

Look at the cases described in Activity 10.1 and, for each case, suggest which track the case will probably be allocated to and what information, if any, you would require to help you allocate the case. (8)

Settlement out of court

Under the new Civil Procedure Rules (CPR), there is a greater incentive for parties to settle their dispute out of court than was the case in the past. If one side has refused a reasonable offer to settle and insisted on proceeding to trial, the court may take this into account when deciding how much costs should be paid by the other side. The implications of this rule are as follows.

Suppose that a defendant in an action makes a reasonable offer, that is close to what is being claimed and the claimant rejects this. The claimant will be aware that they may live to regret it. Even if the court eventually finds for the claimant and awards the damages originally sought, the judge, aware of the earlier offer, may reduce the costs that the claimant can recover from the defendant. In other words the claimant may have gained little or nothing by insisting on continuing with the court action.

However, for offers to be taken into account in determining costs, the offer must have been left open for at least 21 days. In the past it was possible to exert a great deal of pressure by, in effect, saying 'take it or leave it, this offer is only available for one day'. Under the new regime, there is time to consider whether the offer should be accepted or not in a more sensible way.

The increased use of alternative dispute resolution

Judges are now required to be more active in encouraging parties to use methods of resolving disputes other than full trial. Arbitration or other alternative dispute resolution methods are discussed in Unit 11. One way of doing this is by giving the parties a temporary halt in proceedings, known as a 'stay'.

10.6 How much has been achieved by the new Civil Procedure Rules?

It is probably much too early to say whether or not the changes sought by the Woolf recommendations have or have not been achieved. It would be surprising if such a major overhaul of the civil process were without its problems, despite the considerable amount of training that took place before the new rules came into force in 1999.

Despite this, there is already evidence that the reforms have made an impact. In 2001, litigation was down by 37%. This shows that the drive to settle more cases out of court and to increase the use of alternative dispute resolution (ADR) has worked.

Summary ● ● ●

1. How does a civil trial differ from a criminal trial?

2. What is the 'pre-trial procedure' and why is it important?

3. Which courts hear civil cases in the first instance and which on appeal?

4. What problems did civil courts face before 1999?

5. What steps were taken in 1999 to address the problems faced by civil courts?

Case study ● The civil courts

Item A *Happy Leisure plc v Aziz Ltd (an imaginary case)*

Happy Leisure plc, a national company, entered into a contract with Aziz Ltd., a large and reputable firm of builders, to build a conference and exhibition centre attached to a large hotel Happy Leisure plc owns in northern England. The centre was designed to provide an affordable venue for firms in the region to put on trade fairs and so on. Because Aziz did not complete the building until two months after the agreed date, Happy Leisure has lost a £30,000 contract for a conference (the organisers pulled out and went elsewhere). Aziz denied responsibility for the

delay, claiming that it was caused by last minute changes to the building specification made by Happy Leisure plc. Happy Leisure plc did not see it that way and brought a legal action against Aziz.

Item B *Boundary disputes and mediation*

In 1979, a court case between two neighbours over a tiny strip of land in the countryside started. It ended 20 years later when one of the parties was found hanged in a wood. A boundary dispute which started after the building of an extension on the defendant's family home escalated to the point where the defendant, faced with the possibility of having to lose his home so that £75,000 legal costs could be paid, committed suicide. His neighbour, formerly a close family friend, was faced with legal costs of £25,000.

Boundary disputes seem to bring out the worst in people. They may use up their life savings fighting a legal battle over a piece of land that could be worth only a few hundred pounds. Often the legalities are not clear-cut, sparking off appeals that push the costs higher than the value of the land in dispute.

The fence in this photo separates one person's property from another's. Disputes over boundaries can result in court cases like the one described in this item.

Mediation is an alternative to the painful and expensive war of litigation, which all too often leaves both sides losers. Cases go for mediation only if both parties agree. Whereas litigation can make the parties become permanent enemies, mediation can enable them to have a continuing relationship after the dispute is resolved. A neutral mediator acts as a go-between, not imposing a solution in the same way as a judge but helping the parties find something that both sides can accept. Instead of taking years, a case can be resolved in a day or less. Judge Neil Butter who, in 1996, established the first mediation scheme to be run by a court in Britain, says: 'Mediation is quick, cheap and informal. The striking feature of the whole process is the high level of consumer satisfaction'. The new civil court rules give judges much greater ability to actively manage cases. They now have the power, for example, to adjourn a case for the parties to try mediation or another form of alternative dispute resolution.

Hazel Genn, Professor of Socio-legal Studies at University College London, who has seen civil actions being settled by mediation says: 'having sat through hundreds of hours of mediation, I was quite impressed. It's just a way of short-circuiting things and letting people go away reasonably happy.

Adapted from the *Guardian*, 8 June 1999.

Questions

(a) Look at Item A. As a legal adviser for Happy Leisure plc, answer the following questions.

   i)   What size of claim for damages will Happy Leisure make? (1)

   ii)   Which court might the action begin in and which track it might be allocated to? How will the judge obtain information with which to make the allocation? (4)

   iii)   Roughly how long might this case take to reach trial? (2)

Further questions can be found on page 88.

Questions (continued)

(b) Look at Item A. As a legal adviser for Happy Leisure plc, answer the following questions.

   i) How might the judge dealing with this particular action comply with the duty to actively manage a case in relation to:
- avoiding the need for a trial? (8)
- reducing possible delay? (6)

   ii) What pre-trial procedures must be followed before the court hearing? (10)

   iii) Aziz Ltd have now examined the strength of the evidence against them, as set out in the particulars of claim. They are prepared to make an offer to settle of £27,000. Why might Happy Leisure plc do well to accept this offer, even though it is less than their original claim? (8)

(c) Using Item B, complete the following tasks.

   i) Explain why litigation 'all too often leaves both sides losers'. (6)

   ii) What is meant by 'alternative dispute resolution'? Why do you think judges now have a duty to encourage parties to attempt to resolve their differences through alternative dispute resolution? (8)

   iii) Explain why mediation may sometimes be preferable to a court action and when mediation will not be used. (6)

11 Tribunals and alternative dispute resolution

11.1 Introduction

Mahatma Gandhi (see Box 11.1) began his working life as a lawyer in South Africa during the 1890s. When he first arrived there from India, he acted for one of the parties in a complicated and long-running case being fought by two merchants. In his autobiography, Gandhi describes how during this time he learnt 'the true practice of the law'. He was worried that the legal fees were mounting so rapidly that the case would ruin the merchants, even though they had large businesses. The case occupied so much of their attention that that they had no time left for other work. Ill-feeling between the two men was steadily increasing. The winning party would not recover more than a proportion of their legal costs from the losing side because of the way that the court regulations worked.

'This was more than I could bear', wrote Gandhi. He suggested to his client that, if a person commanding the confidence of both parties could be appointed to resolve the dispute, the case would be quickly finished. 'I felt that my duty was to befriend both parties and bring them together. I strained every nerve to bring about a compromise...The lesson was so indelibly burnt into me that a large part of my time during the 20 years of my practice as a lawyer was occupied in bringing about private compromises of hundreds of cases.'

Over a hundred years after Gandhi's first experience of alternative dispute resolution, the incentives for avoiding court action remain very much the same. A court action is expensive, time consuming and something that, except for the very rich, should be seen as a last resort. There are other ways of resolving civil disputes.

11.2 Tribunals

What is the difference between a court and a tribunal?

A tribunal is a body that performs a function similar to that of a court of law but it is not a court of law. In the County Court and the High Court, a wide range of cases are dealt with, including a huge variety of contract cases, divorce cases, disputed wills, negligence claims (common examples of which include accidents at work or on the roads), and cases involving land and property. Tribunals, on the other hand, are more specialised. Each sort of tribunal hears only one type of case. For example, social security tribunals are only involved in benefit cases.

Judges in the High Court and County Court have to be experienced and senior professional lawyers before they become judges. Although some tribunals are chaired by lawyers, most people who make decisions on tribunals are not trained lawyers. A court of law is a very formal environment where there are many rules of procedure to understand and professional lawyers wear wigs and gowns. Tribunals, on the other hand, are designed to be less formal so that a person without a legal background should not be intimidated and not feel unable to speak for themselves. Wigs and gowns are not worn. Legal costs are not normally awarded to the parties in a tribunal hearing.

All tribunals recently came under scrutiny when the Lord Chancellor asked Sir John Leggatt, a former Lord Justice of Appeal to conduct a review. The **Leggatt Report**, published in 2001, contained a number of serious criticisms of tribunals in the UK and recommendations for reform. The report is discussed further below.

Types of tribunal

This unit focuses on **administrative tribunals**. Administrative tribunals are those that have been created by Act of Parliament to review decisions of government. Many were originally created in the 1940s and 1950s when the Welfare State was set up. The 'Welfare State' is the term used to describe the state provision of health care, education, state pensions, and various kinds of social security and employment entitlements. Tribunals were set up to deal with disputes about entitlement. There are 137

Box 11.1 *Mahatma Gandhi*

Mahatma Gandhi in 1900 when he was working as a lawyer in South Africa. Later, he led the struggle for Indian independence from the UK, promoting non-violent non-cooperation with the colonialists.

administrative tribunals today, dealing with over a million cases every year. This is considerably more than the number of contested cases dealt with by the County Court and the High Court combined.

Some important tribunals are listed in Box 11.2.

> **Box 11.2** *Important administrative tribunals*
>
> - **Social security tribunals** which deal with appeals against a decision to refuse payment in relation to various benefits
> - **Employment tribunals** which deal with many aspects of employment law, such as unfair dismissal and sex discrimination claims
> - **Rent tribunals** which are involved in fixing fair rents under the Rent Acts
> - **Immigration appeal tribunals** which hear appeals from decisions of the Home Office to refuse entry into the United Kingdom.

Employment tribunals

Employment tribunals (ETs) are perhaps the most significant, and certainly the most high profile, kind of tribunal. Under the Employment Tribunals Act 1996, they have authority to deal with a range of disputes between employers and employees, including unfair dismissal, sex or race discrimination, disability discrimination, disputes over maternity pay, and disputes over redundancy payments. Examples of unfair dismissal and discrimination cases are often reported in the newspapers. Unlike most other tribunal hearings, ET hearings are held in public.

Employment tribunals are found in major towns and cities. They normally have three members. The Chair, who leads consideration of the case, is legally qualified. One of the other two is drawn from a panel representing employers, and the other from a panel drawn up from trade union representatives. A lack of legal training is not necessarily a drawback as the non-legal members can often provide practical experience of employment matters rather than the knowledge of legal theory that is the strong point of the Chair.

The normal rules of court procedure do not apply. Parties can represent themselves, though they may, and often do, have solicitors, barristers or other people representing them. Trade unions often provide expert representation for their members. Tribunal hearings are heard in much simpler rooms than courtrooms. Tribunal members do not sit on a raised platform in the way that judges do and the atmosphere is less intimidating than a court.

Appeals on decisions of an ET are allowed on a point of law only. A High Court judge presides over appeals from employment tribunals in the **Employment Appeal Tribunal**.

Domestic tribunals

Domestic tribunals, as opposed to administrative tribunals, deal with matters relating to the internal workings of particular organisations, other than those that are part of the state. Examples of domestic tribunals include the disciplinary committees of the British Medical Association (the BMA, the professional body for doctors), the Law Society (the professional body for solicitors) and trade unions. Although such bodies are not usually created by statute but by agreement between members of the profession or union, they often have considerable power. For example, the disciplinary committees of the BMA and the Law Society have the power to prevent a person continuing to work within their profession.

Control of tribunals

The decisions and workings of both domestic and administrative tribunals are subject to control by the High

Activity 11.1

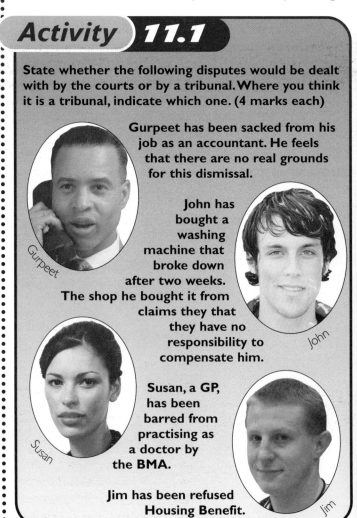

State whether the following disputes would be dealt with by the courts or by a tribunal. Where you think it is a tribunal, indicate which one. (4 marks each)

Gurpeet has been sacked from his job as an accountant. He feels that there are no real grounds for this dismissal.

John has bought a washing machine that broke down after two weeks. The shop he bought it from claims they that they have no responsibility to compensate him.

Susan, a GP, has been barred from practising as a doctor by the BMA.

Jim has been refused Housing Benefit.

Court. This may take the form of an application for judicial review on the basis of a breach of natural justice or that the tribunal has acted *ultra vires* (outside of its powers) - see Unit 10, Section 10.3.

The workings of certain specified tribunals are influenced by the Council on Tribunals. Members of the Council are appointed by the Lord Chancellor. The Council is consulted before any procedural rules are changed and it reviews various matters that are referred to it. However, the Council on Tribunals has little real power and is certainly not able to overturn the decisions of any tribunal.

Advantages of tribunals

Tribunals have five main advantages over the courts. These are outlined in Box 11.3.

Disadvantages of tribunals

Tribunals have four main disadvantages. These can be described as follows.

(i) Lack of openness
Hearings held in private are open to suspicions about fairness.

(ii) Lack of independence
The Franks Committee in 1957 said that tribunals should be open, fair and impartial. Impartiality means independent decision-making without a tendency to favour one side over the other. Leggatt felt that independence was the most important feature of a proper tribunal system, but in relation to administrative tribunals it was clearly lacking. A key recommendation of the Leggatt Report was to have all the tribunals supported by a new Tribunals Service. If tribunals were administered by an organisation that was separate from government departments and, therefore, not in any way linked to them, they would be more truly impartial.

(iii) Legal aid is not available
While the private citizen may not be able to afford legal representation, the government departments and employers that defend cases have access to high quality legal advice and representation. At the same time, legal aid is unavailable for almost all tribunal hearings. Is this fair? Leggatt put forward a number of recommendations. These included:

- voluntary advice groups, such as the Citizens Advice Bureaux, should be funded so that they can offer legal advice
- tribunal Chairs should be trained to give such assistance as they legitimately can to claimants
- in complex cases, where legal representation really

Box 11.3 *Advantages of tribunals*

(i) Quicker than the courts
The ordinary court system is worryingly slow in hearing and deciding cases. From the start of a legal action to the day of the trial may take years. Tribunals are much quicker. Having said that, the Leggatt Report commented on increasing delay in employment tribunals. This is partly because the number of claims they deal with has risen considerably in recent years.

(ii) Cheaper and more accessible
Bringing a claim to tribunals is much cheaper than a court action. Tribunals involve virtually no financial risk for those bringing claims. Costs are not normally awarded to the loser and it should be possible for many claimants to represent themselves. No court fees are awarded in relation to tribunal proceedings. Tribunals are also cheaper for the state as the tribunal members are not paid as much as County Court and High Court judges. Straightforward documentation and the absence of the kind of complicated rules of procedure that are found in the courts also enables ordinary citizens greater access to justice, at least in theory.

(iii) Expertise
As mentioned above, there are advantages to be gained from the specific expertise provided by lay tribunal members alongside the more general legal expertise of the Chair. For example, in disputes over disablement or invalidity benefits, doctors sit as tribunal members.

(iv) Privacy
Tribunals are usually conducted in private, away from the unwanted press attention that a court appearance can bring. A major exception to this is employment tribunals.

(v) Reduces overloading of the courts
As the courts have become more and more congested, it is obvious that if many cases were transferred from tribunals back to the ordinary courts the legal system would suffer, especially as the courts are more expensive to run.

was needed, legal aid should only be provided as a last resort.

(iv) Tribunals may not really be accessible
This point is related to the issue of legal aid not being available. In 1979, the Royal Commission on Legal Services recommended that tribunal procedures should be reviewed and simplified. It was felt then that the original idea that tribunals would be accessible because applicants could represent themselves was under threat. More than 20 years later, little seems to have changed in this respect. Leggatt argued that tribunals are increasingly failing to

provide a simple, accessible system of justice where users can represent themselves. The report said that employment tribunals, in particular, were gradually becoming as formal and complex as the courts and were losing their original user-friendliness.

11.3 Alternative dispute resolution

Negotiation

The cheapest and quickest way of resolving a dispute is, of course, simply to contact the person with whom there is a dispute and communicate with them directly, in an attempt to settle the disagreement. This can be done before lawyers, the courts or alternative methods of dispute resolution are involved. If it does not work, solicitors may negotiate on behalf of their clients, though the longer this

negotiation between lawyers carries on, the more it costs. Negotiation outside the court may also lead to a settlement after, as well as before, a legal action has been started.

Other than informal negotiation, the parties may try some form of 'alternative dispute resolution' (ADR). This term embraces a number of different ways of resolving a civil dispute by a neutral third party without turning to the courts:

● **arbitration** is where a person or persons are appointed to act in a similar way to a judge and provide a solution to a dispute, having heard both sides

● **mediation** involves someone helping parties to reach a compromise without actually imposing a solution

Activity 11.2

Legal aid for tribunal applicants?

In Scotland, legal aid is now available so that employees can hire a lawyer to represent them at a tribunal in cases which are seen as too complicated for the applicant to present effectively on their own. The Scottish Executive acted to pre-empt possible claims under the Human Rights Act that people who can't afford to pay for a lawyer to represent them are not able to bring an effective case to an employment tribunal. The Human Rights Act makes the European Convention on Human Rights part of UK law (Article 6 of the Convention sets out the right to a fair trial). It seems very possible that public funding for employment tribunal applications will soon extend to other parts of the United Kingdom too. At present, in England and Wales, legal aid funding is only granted when cases go to the Employment Appeal Tribunal where the case can be won or lost on complex points of law.

This artist's impression shows Mary Archer giving evidence at an industrial tribunal in Bury St Edmunds on 4 September 2002. Jane Williams, who was the personal assistant to Mary Archer for 13 years, was claiming unfair dismissal.

A study into disability discrimination claims in employment tribunals suggested that an applicant who is not legally represented is twice as likely to lose as one who goes to the tribunal with a lawyer to argue their case for them.

One change already announced by the government is that tribunals will be given powers to make orders for costs of up to £10,000. This is a response to concerns from employers that disgruntled employees have increasingly been prepared to bring unreasonable, 'opportunist' claims before a tribunal. The change fuels the argument for legal aid because applicants could be deterred from making legal claims if, in the event of the tribunal's decision going against them, they risk having to pay a substantial bill for their employer's lawyers.

Martin Phillips, Legal Director of Lawrite, a company that runs an employment law advice website, said:

'There is little doubt among experienced employment lawyers that applicants in all but straightforward cases will be less likely to succeed without representation. Few applicants have the knowledge and skill to properly prepare and present their cases.'

Adapted from information provided by Lawrite.

(a) **What is the appeal route from employment tribunals? (2)**
(b) **Put forward three arguments for providing legal aid to tribunal applicants in England and Wales. (9)**
(c) **Using this material, and other parts of the unit, give two arguments against providing legal aid to tribunal applicants in England and Wales. (6)**

- **conciliation** is similar to mediation but goes a little further. Suggestions can be made as to how a settlement could be reached.

In recent years, the number of disputes where ADR has played a part has increased significantly. The present government sees the wider use of ADR as a key part of reforming the civil justice system. The use of ADR was strongly favoured in the Woolf Report and when the new Civil Procedure Rules came into effect in 1999, judges were under a duty to encourage parties to settle out of court (see Unit 10, Section 10.5). The Court of Appeal ruled in *Dunnett v Railtrack (2002)* that cost penalties would be imposed if parties did not try mediation in certain sorts of cases.

Arbitration

Arbitration is a private process by which an independent person, called an 'arbitrator', resolves a dispute by making a legally binding decision. An arbitrator is often a recognised expert in the particular field that is the subject of the dispute. In some cases, the arbitrator may be a lawyer. By agreeing to arbitration, parties are normally agreeing to let the arbitrator, rather than a judge in a court of law, decide how the dispute should be resolved. The Chartered Institute of Arbitrators (CIA) is the market leader in the provision of consumer disputes by arbitration and other forms of ADR. The CIA administers schemes for the Association of British Travel Agents (ABTA), British Telecom and Consignia, among others. Written contracts between the company and the consumer may contain a dispute resolution clause something similar to the one recommended by the CIA. The standard CIA clause reads:

> 'Any dispute or difference arising out of or in connection with this contract shall be determined by the appointment of a single arbitrator to be agreed between the parties, or failing agreement within fourteen days, after either party has given to the other a written request to concur in the appointment of an arbitrator to be appointed by the President or Vice President of the Chartered Institute of Arbitrators.'

Sometimes arbitration is conducted on paper. In other words, the parties put the points they wish to make in writing and send it off to the arbitrator without actually appearing at a hearing. Where an arbitration hearing is held, the parties agree among themselves whether one arbitrator or several acting as a panel will hear the case, whether evidence is given on oath or not and other procedural matters.

Although London is a major centre for international arbitration between businesses, the wait for an arbitration hearing can mean that arbitration takes almost as long as a court action. In addition, the law on arbitration has become increasingly complex. Because of this, the Arbitration Act 1996 was passed, with the intention of reforming the law and making arbitration more user-friendly - see Box 11.4.

Box 11.4 *The Arbitration Act 1996*

The Arbitration Act 1996 begins with a statement that parties should be free to agree how their disputes are resolved and that, although the courts may intervene in cases that are decided by arbitration, the circumstances for such intervention are limited. Although the Act sets out rules governing arbitration, these rules only come into operation when the parties have not made their own rules within an agreement. In other words, if you do not like the rules in the Arbitration Act, make sure you write them out of your contract.

Under the Act, where one party seeks to start a court action, even though the arbitration agreement forbids this, then the other party may request the court to stop this litigation. On the other hand, if both parties agree, arbitration may be abandoned in favour of a court action.

There are grounds for requesting intervention from the courts during arbitration, but these are limited to serious irregularities. For example, a party can go to court when the arbitrator is clearly not a suitable person to conduct the arbitration or has acted improperly during the proceedings. In addition, arbitration proceedings are always open to challenge through judicial review. This is something that cannot be altered by contract.

Mediation

With arbitration, the arbitrator acts in a similar way to a judge. Mediation on the other hand, involves a mediator helping parties to reach a compromise without actually imposing a solution upon them. The role of a mediator is to talk to both sides and act as a neutral go-between. The mediator tries to establish where the two sides might agree, without offering an opinion as to who has the better case. It is not the role of a mediator to solve the dispute, but merely to help the parties involved find a way of solving it. A more formal method of mediation in commercial disputes is a 'mini trial'. Both sides put their case to a panel consisting of a decision-maker from the two sides and a neutral adviser. Once all the arguments have been heard, the panel tries to reach a decision with the neutral adviser acting as a mediator if the other two panel members are unable to reach agreement.

Mediation is very cost effective. Commercial disputes involving a million pounds may be settled within a day. As the delays in arbitration have grown, an increasing number of companies have turned to mediation. One advantage is that it is a relatively non-confrontational way to settle disputes compared to court action. Judge Butter, a major supporter of the mediation process, has pointed out that many mediations end up with the parties shaking hands and leaving together. Commercial mediation may even include agreement about how the two businesses involved will do business in the future in a way which will avoid further disputes. This is not something that happens very often in the courts of law.

The Family Law Act 1996 made changes to the law on divorce and gave the courts powers to encourage strongly the use of voluntary mediation in certain divorce cases. Trials were conducted in a number of areas before the scheme went national, however. The results of these trials were disappointing, as fewer than 10% of divorcing couples in the pilot areas were prepared to use mediation. Of those that did, 40% stated after a preliminary information meeting that they were more convinced of the need for legal representation to protect their rights. In June 1999, the government announced that it was shelving plans for mediation in divorce cases under the Act.

This change in policy suggests one of the limitations of ADR in general and mediation in particular. Someone who is involved in a serious dispute may not feel, and indeed may not actually be, strong enough to get very much from a relatively informal bargaining process. Mediation requires active participation and decision-making. An experienced lawyer acting on behalf of a party in the courts may sometimes be more likely to achieve what that party is seeking and prevent them from being manipulated by the stronger opposition.

Conciliation

Conciliation goes a step further than mediation because the mediator takes a more active role in suggesting grounds for compromise and the best option for reaching settlement. One of the functions of the Advisory Conciliation and Arbitration Service is to attempt to resolve disputes between trade unions and employers through conciliation. This is discussed below.

The Advisory Conciliation and Arbitration Service (ACAS)

ACAS offers a range of ADR services in the field of disputes between employers and employees. Although funded by the Department of Trade and Industry, ACAS is not a government department and is fully independent

Activity 11.3

Richie Woodall and mediation

Richie Woodall after successfully defeating Sugar Boy Malinga to win the WBC super middleweight championship of the world in Telford on 28 March 1998.

Richie Woodall, WBC middleweight boxing champion, was a worried man when just weeks away from a big fight to retain his belt, a contractual dispute with his promoter Frank Warren was still proceeding through the High Court. Unless this was resolved speedily, the fight could not take place. The court approved an attempt to settle the dispute outside court. Mediation with the help of the Centre for Effective Dispute Resolution (CEDR) was arranged. CEDR were called in on a Thursday morning and within 24 hours had been able to arrange a venue, a mediator and the necessary documentation.

Although the two sides had been in dispute for months, settlement was reached within a day. The terms of the settlement were confidential and not, therefore, available to the press. Woodall and Warren issued a joint press statement announcing that: 'It was important to all concerned to have brought this matter to a speedy conclusion. We have shaken hands and look forward to resuming our successful partnership.'

(a) Using this material to illustrate your answer, explain some advantages of mediation. (6)

(b) The High Court readily agreed for an attempt to settle out of court to be attempted. Why is such encouragement from the court now more common than it used to be? (2)

and impartial. It employs around 700 staff, based in offices throughout the UK.

Under statute, ACAS offers conciliation to both sides in unfair dismissal claims before the claim can be taken to an employment tribunal (ET). Where conciliation is agreed, the conciliation officer advises the parties of the strength of their position. Each side may be told what the other said but, if the application case ultimately goes to tribunal, this information cannot be used in evidence without the permission of the relevant party.

The scheme is successful in the sense that two-thirds of cases are either withdrawn or settled through conciliation. On the other hand, a study by Dickens in 1985 showed that awards after an ET hearing were generally higher than those achieved through conciliation. This may be taken as evidence that employees do not have equal bargaining power with employers.

Because ETs have become increasingly overloaded ACAS has recently introduced an arbitration scheme as an alternative to a Tribunal hearing in unfair dismissal cases.

Advantages and disadvantages of ADR
The advantages of ADR are outlined in Box 11.5.

Disadvantages of ADR
There are five main disadvantages to the use of ADR.

(i) Unequal bargaining power
This can be a particular problem in cases that are settled through mediation and conciliation. With both of these, it may be wrong to assume that a process involving informal negotiation will involve a fair exchange of views. In employment and divorce cases for example, it may be that one side is effectively able to dominate the other, by fair means or otherwise, and get exactly what they want without giving very much away. Such behaviour may represent a continuation of the patterns that have existed in a relationship for some time. Proper legal representation, and 'arm's length' dispute, may be a better option for a 'weak' party.

(ii) Lack of legal expertise
Where a dispute involves difficult legal points, an arbitrator or mediator is unlikely to have the same expertise as a judge (though some arbitrators are experienced lawyers).

(iii) No system of precedent
It may not be easy to predict the outcome of a case decided through arbitration. Arbitrators neither create, nor are bound by, precedent.

(iv) Enforceability
Much of the advantage of ADR is lost if the 'losing side' does not actually make compensation. To enforce a decision, it will then be necessary to take the matter before the courts. This involves exactly the kind of expense and delay that ADR is designed to avoid.

(v) A court action may still be required
With both mediation and conciliation, it is possible that after a great deal of effort no agreement can be reached and the parties end up in court. This is unusual however. The Centre for Effective Dispute Resolution (CEDR), for example, say that over 80% of the cases it is involved with are settled.

Box 11.5 *Advantages of ADR*

The advantages of ADR are:

(i) Speed
Settling a case through ADR is usually much quicker than proceedings in the courts.

(ii) Expertise
A specialist arbitrator is able to find a reasonable solution using expert knowledge of acceptable and normal practices within the trade or industry in question. A judge is far less likely to be able to draw on specialist knowledge in this way.

(iii) Privacy
The parties may well prefer to avoid the bad publicity and media attention that often comes with a court appearance. With ADR, hearings or negotiations are conducted without the presence of the press or the public.

(iv) Parties may remain on good terms
This particularly applies with mediation and conciliation. The aim is to find a compromise solution that is acceptable to both parties. Court proceedings are likely to be more bruising and end in the judge finding for one side or another, without regard to compromise.

(v) Cost to the parties
Partly because ADR proceedings are much less formal and time-consuming than the court system, any form of ADR is a much cheaper option. The Centre for Effective Dispute Resolution claims that average cost savings made in mediation cases it handles are £86,000. Arbitration can be expensive however. Legal representatives are often used and the fees of the arbitrator can be heavy.

(vi) Cost to the state
Every case resolved through ADR saves government money and frees up resources within the court system.

Summary ● ● ●

1. What is the difference between a court and a tribunal?

2. What are the advantages and disadvantages of tribunals?

3. What is the difference between an administrative tribunal and a domestic tribunal?

4. What are the different types of ADR and how do they differ?

5. What are the advantages and disadvantages of ADR?

Case study Tribunals and arbitration

Item A *Social security appeal tribunals (SSATs)*

What are social security appeal tribunals for?

The Benefits Agency, part of the Department for Work and Pensions, deals with payment of a wide range of state benefits, such as Income Support, Child Support and Industrial Injuries Benefit. The laws governing entitlement to benefits are complex and give the Benefits Agency a fair degree of discretion. Appeals by benefit claimants from formal decisions by employees of the Agency are dealt with by a social security appeal tribunal (SSAT).

All SSATs are organised by the Appeals Service which, in essence, is an agency of the Department for Work and Pensions. It is responsible for the administration of SSATs: organising when and where appeals will be heard and providing tribunals with administrative support.

Who sits on SSATs?

An SSAT may consist of one, two or three members, depending on which benefit is being dealt with. In many cases the Chair is legally qualified, while other members are not. The Lord Chancellor appoints all tribunal members. Members receive training on relevant laws and in tribunal practice and procedures.

What is a SSAT hearing like?

SSATs are able to conduct a hearing solely on the papers put before them, but the claimant is encouraged to attend so that questions can be put. If there is an oral hearing, the claimant may decide to come on their own, with a representative, perhaps from a Citizens Advice Bureau or another voluntary organisation, or with a friend.

Each SSAT has a clerk, employed by the Appeals Service. The clerk is not there to make decisions about appeals but to assist in the administration and smooth running of the hearing. The Benefits Agency is represented by one of their staff, called a Presenting Officer.

Procedural rules require hearings to be in public, but it is very unusual for a member of the public to attend and the claimant may request a hearing in private. The tribunal rooms contain ordinary office furniture, and all those present sit around a large table. The way in which the tribunal actually hears an appeal varies according to the benefit being considered, the number of members and the issue the tribunal has to decide. Each Chair will, to some extent, have developed their own way of conducting a hearing.

However the appeal hearing actually proceeds, the aim of the tribunal is to provide a fairly informal setting in which everyone, particularly the claimant, has the opportunity to put forward information that will enable the tribunal to obtain a full picture before making a decision. Often the claimant speaks first, to explain why they think the original decision of the Benefits Agency to refuse payment was wrong. The Presenting Officer is then asked to explain the reasoning of the person who made the original decision. The claimant then has a final chance to make points that have not already been discussed. At some point the tribunal members ask questions.

The claimant is given a brief written decision and explanatory notes. If the claimant disagrees with the decision, they may request a further written 'Statement of Reasons'.

Source: Appeals Service website.

Item B *Arbitration and the travel industry*

Nearly all travel agents are members of the Association of British Travel Agents (ABTA). One aspect of membership means that the written terms under which holidays are sold include a dispute resolution clause, setting out the requirement for arbitration.

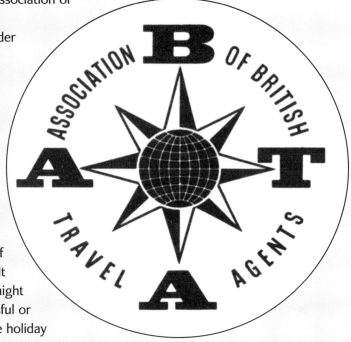

Under the ABTA arbitration scheme, well over 1,000 disputes between travel agents and consumers are taken to arbitration every year. Suppose, for example, a holidaymaker booked a room with an en suite bathroom and sea views but actually got a sink in the corner of the bedroom and a panoramic view of a multi-storey car park. If negotiation with the travel agent did not result in satisfactory compensation, the consumer might have to resort to arbitration. Whether successful or unsuccessful, the consumer (claimant) and the holiday company (respondent) are legally obliged to comply with an arbitrator's final decision, subject to any appeal made by either of the parties.

How does ABTA arbitration work?

Cases are conducted on a documents-only procedure. There is no formal oral hearing. The arbitrator makes an award based on the documents and evidence submitted by the parties in dispute. The parties should state their case clearly and produce all relevant supporting documents. The arbitration procedure takes approximately seven weeks from the date that the application for arbitration is received. A small registration fee of up to £164 is payable. A compensation award can be made up to a total amount of £15,000. If a claim fails, there is no requirement to pay the other side's legal costs.

The scheme was set up to allow the parties to present their cases without the need for legal representation. The holiday companies often have in-house legal staff or may employ solicitors to help them, but arbitrators do not expect claimants to have legal representation, though they may if they choose to.

The Schedule of Claim and supporting evidence (called 'the Bundle') is the most important part of the case. This is where the complaint against the holiday company is set out. The claimant tries to prove to the arbitrator that they should be awarded compensation. Letters, videos or photos can be used to support a claim. The arbitrator decides the case purely on the arguments and evidence presented by the parties. The parties must prove their cases on the balance of probability to the satisfaction of the arbitrator.

If the claimant is unhappy about the result of an arbitration award and wishes to appeal through the Chartered Institute of Arbitrators (CIA), a statement must be supplied to the CIA setting out the reasons why the award is 'one that no reasonable Arbitrator should have reached on the basis of the documents presented'. The CIA appoints a Review Arbitrator.

Questions

(a) Using Item A, complete the following tasks.

   i)   Explain whether a social security appeal tribunal is an administrative or a domestic tribunal. (2)

   ii) Why were tribunals like these set up? (4)

   iii) The Franks Committee in 1957 saw impartiality as an essential characteristic of a tribunal. Explain what was meant by this and comment on the extent to which SSATs appear to be impartial. (6)

   iv) How would implementation of the Leggatt Report proposals change the organisation of SSATs? (3)

   v) Edward is a former refuse collector who left school at 16 with no formal qualifications. He was made redundant five years ago and, since then, has been out of work. He relies on various state benefits and has virtually no savings. Two months ago his Income Support was drastically reduced. Edward feels that this decision was made on the basis of inaccurate information but he has been unable to convince the Benefit Agency and has been forced to apply to an Appeal Tribunal. There is no Citizens Advice Bureau in his area, so Edward will represent himself.

      Discuss what problems Edward may have in putting forward his case at the tribunal hearing. What changes in the system do you suggest that might deal with these? (10)

(b) Using Item B, complete the following tasks.

   i)   Explain how, other than appeal through the CIA, a claimant might take further action in response to an obviously unfair arbitration. (2)

   ii) Describe the similarities between arbitration (such as that in the ABTA scheme) and litigation. (6)

   iii) Give four ways in which arbitration is different from a court action. (8)

12.1 Introduction

After someone has been charged with a criminal offence by the police, they face trial in either the Magistrates' Court or the Crown Court. This unit examines the role of these courts.

About 95% of criminal charges are heard in the Magistrates' Courts. Magistrates are involved in determining whether a defendant is guilty or innocent and the appropriate sentence. They are sometimes called 'Justices of the Peace' and are mainly unpaid, part-time judges who live in the community the court serves. Although they receive training, they are not qualified lawyers. In a few courts, professional lawyers called District Judges also carry out the work of a magistrate (confusingly, this is also the name given to some judges in the County Court). Magistrates normally exercise their duties as part of a bench of three, with assistance and advice on matters of law from a legal adviser, also known as the clerk. The Chair of a bench is in charge of the conduct of the trial, and is assisted by two other magistrates, known as 'wingers'. District Judges sit alone, though a clerk assists them. It is usual for the defendant to be represented in the Magistrates' Court by solicitors. A solicitor from the Crown Prosecution Service represents the prosecution (for further discussion of the role of magistrates, see Unit 16). The role of the Crown Prosecution Service is described in Box 12.1.

Box 12.1 *The Crown Prosecution Service*

In 1986, a separate prosecuting authority, called the Crown Prosecution Service (CPS), was set up. The CPS covers the whole of England and Wales. While the responsibility to gather evidence and the decision to charge a person with a criminal offence remain a matter for the police, the decision to prosecute is made by the CPS. In most instances, a CPS lawyer is the prosecution advocate in the Magistrates' Court. The Head of the CPS is the Director of Public Prosecutions (DPP), a senior government lawyer.

More serious criminal cases are tried in the Crown Court by a judge and jury. The judge, an experienced and able professional lawyer, rules on issues of law and is responsible for seeing that the trial proceeds within the law and in the interests of justice. The judge also decides the sentence, if the jury finds the defendant guilty. The jury is made up of 12 members of the public chosen at random (see Unit 15). The advocates in Crown Court trials are usually barristers rather than solicitors. The Crown Court is a much more formal and intimidating environment than a Magistrates' Court. Procedures are more formal and complex. Cases generally take longer and the trial is more expensive.

The publication of the Auld Report in 2001 and a government White Paper in 2002 suggest that the government intends to make significant changes to the criminal justice system - see Box 12.2 on page 100.

12.2 Bail

Bail

Once they have been charged, defendants have to wait some weeks before their trial is held. Even when the due date is reached, the trial may be adjourned (postponed to a later date) for some reason. During the period before trial, the court has to decide whether the defendant should be given bail or remanded in custody. The law regarding the powers of the court to grant bail is is set out in the Bail Act 1976.

The police also make bail decisions when a suspect has been arrested and brought to a police station.

The statutory presumption for bail and exceptions to it

The Bail Act 1976 created a statutory presumption of bail. This means that the court is obliged to grant bail unless it is clear that one of the exceptions set out within the Act is applicable. In essence, the courts need to have a good reason for not allowing a defendant to be at liberty before trial.

However, there has been concern that too many defendants commit offences while on bail. A study conducted in Bristol, for example, showed that over one-third of all those charged with burglary were on bail for another offence at the time of arrest.

The reasons for remanding a defendant are outlined in Box 12.3 on page 100.

Amendments to the Bail Act

In response to public concern about dangerous offenders being given bail and committing further offences, a number of amendments to the Bail Act 1976 were made in the 1980s and 1990s to make it harder for the courts to grant bail in certain types of case.

Under Section 153 of the Criminal Justice Act 1988, a court is required to give reasons for granting bail in relation to those charged with murder, manslaughter or rape. Under Section 26 of the Criminal Justice and Public Order Act 1994, the statutory presumption in favour of

Box 12.2 *The Auld Report and the White Paper of 2002*

There is a debate about the perception that the population at large has of the courts and the relationship between that perception and the level of crime. Most people are much more aware of the work of the criminal courts than the civil courts. Serious crimes are widely reported in the press. As a result, many people have a view on whether defendants are guilty or not guilty and what sentences should be given. Because of this level of public interest, it is important that the criminal courts not only do their job well but are also seen to be doing so. In other words, the courts need to send out the right message to maintain public confidence. At the same time, courts aim to send a message to potential offenders - to deter criminal behaviour. On both counts, there have been problems. Regardless of reality, many people continue to believe that the criminal courts are unduly soft on offenders and that people found guilty of committing serious offences spend hardly any time in prison. As far as deterrence is concerned, the government published a White Paper in July 2002 which pointed out that most crimes are committed by a relatively small number of persistent offenders and that the signals being sent out by courts to these offenders were not helpful. The government highlighted several problems:

> 'Too few criminals brought to justice; too many defendants who offend on bail; too slow to bring them to trial; too many guilty go unconvicted; too many without the sentence they and society need.' (The *Justice for All* White Paper, July 2002)

The government has expressed a commitment to making major improvements in the criminal justice system. Its aims include 'reducing crime and the fear of crime and their social and economic costs' and 'dispensing justice fairly and efficiently and to promote confidence in the law'.

Significant changes to the legislative framework within which the criminal justice system operates seem likely. The White Paper follows on from the wide-ranging Criminal Courts Review by Lord Auld, known as the Auld Report, which was published in 2001. Lord Auld acknowledged the government's ambition to reform. At the same time, he cautioned:

> 'We should not expect too much of the criminal justice system, the courts in particular, as a medium for curing the ills of society.'

Further details on the Auld Report and the White Paper are given below.

Box 12.3 *Reasons for remanding a defendant - the statutory exceptions*

Under the Bail Act 1976, if the offence charged is one that is punishable with imprisonment, the court may refuse bail if it believes that one of the following conditions applies:

- the defendant would fail to appear before the court
- another offence would be committed while the defendant was on bail
- the course of justice would be obstructed
- it is necessary to detain the defendant for their own protection (or in the case of a juvenile, for their own welfare)
- more time is needed to gather information about the defendant
- the defendant has previously failed to appear in court after being bailed.

What should the court take into consideration?

In deciding whether the defendant is likely to skip bail, commit another offence, or obstruct justice, the court should consider:

- the nature and seriousness of the offence
- the character, previous record and family and community ties of the defendant
- the behaviour of the defendant when on bail in the past
- the strength of the prosecution's evidence.

to refuse bail in such cases, merely that it is not bound by the statutory presumption. Under Section 56 of the Crime and Disorder Act 1998, a defendant charged with murder, attempted murder, manslaughter, rape or attempted rape can only be granted bail if the court believes there are exceptional circumstances.

Bail conditions

Bail is usually subject to certain conditions. Failure to comply with these conditions means that the defendant will be remanded. Some examples of bail conditions are:

- reporting daily or weekly to a police station
- residence at a particular address
- surrendering any passport held
- not going to particular places.

Personal recognisances and sureties

A personal recognisance is where the court orders that the defendant must pay a specified sum if they fail to surrender to the court. The court may also ask for sureties. A surety is a person who promises to pay a particular sum in the event that the defendant fails to turn

bail in relation to any person charged with a crime that could be tried in the Crown Court and where the alleged offence took place while the defendant was already on bail was removed. This does not mean that the court has

up at court when required to do so. This system is different to that in many countries in that the surety does not have to pay the money in advance.

12.3 Mode of trial

Selecting the appropriate type of court for a case is called 'allocating mode of trial'. Criminal charges involving adults are either heard in the Magistrates' Court, or in the Crown Court. Most hearings involving offenders below the age of 18 are heard in the Youth Courts.

Activity 12.1

(a) Consider arguments for and against granting bail to each of the following defendants. (6 marks each)

Sulinder, aged 30, is an accountant. She has a husband, three children and a comfortable home. Sulinder is alleged to have defrauded one of her clients of several thousand pounds.

Sulinder

John, aged 35, has had a number of convictions for shoplifting in the last five years. He is currently charged with stealing a pair of jeans worth £30 from a store. John lives in a squat with his girlfriend. He is unemployed.

John

Tina, aged 22, has been charged with dealing in heroin. She was caught with a very considerable amount of heroin in the back of her car. She lives with her parents. Tina has worked as a secretary for the same employer since she left school at 16.

Tina

(b) Assuming that the magistrates did feel that bail should be granted, suggest suitable bail conditions for each defendant.

Summary offences

Summary offences are less serious crimes that can only be tried in the Magistrates' Courts. Trial by magistrates is sometimes called 'summary trial'. The majority of summary offences are motoring offences, but minor assaults and criminal damage of up to £5,000 are also summary offences. Magistrates have limited sentencing powers. The maximum prison sentence that magistrates may impose is six months (the *Justice for All* White Paper proposed that this limit should be raised to 12 months). The maximum fine is £5,000. Magistrates also have the power to impose other sentences, including one of a range of community sentences (see Unit 21 for types of sentence).

Indictable offences

Indictable offences are cases heard by a judge and jury in the Crown Court. An indictment is the formal document that sets out the charge or charges against the defendant. Indictable offences include murder, rape and serious assaults. Initially these cases appear in the Magistrates' Court, simply for the purpose of transferring them to the Crown Court.

Triable-either-way offences

Either-way offences are ones that may be heard in the Magistrates' Courts but where the defendant has a right to opt for a trial by jury in the Crown Court. They include theft, burglary, and assault causing actual bodily harm. There are a number of stages in processing either-way offences. The first stage is to ask whether the defendant pleads guilty or not guilty. If the defendant pleads guilty, the case will be automatically be heard by magistrates, although the court has the power to send it to the Crown Court for sentencing when it is felt that the limited sentencing powers of the magistrates are likely to be insufficient.

If the defendant pleads not guilty, a decision has to be made by the magistrates as to whether or not it is appropriate to transfer the case for trial in the Crown Court. This is done in the **mode of trial hearing**. The court must consider the following factors:

- the nature of the case
- whether the surrounding circumstances make the offence particularly serious
- whether the magistrates have adequate powers to punish the defendant
- comments made about the mode of trial by the defence and the prosecution.

If the court decides that summary trial is appropriate defendants must be asked whether they consent to this. If they do, there can be a summary trial. If, on the other hand, the defendant wishes to exercise their right to be tried by a jury, the magistrates will proceed to a stage known as 'committal proceedings' - a preliminary to trial in the Crown Court.

The pre-trial process is shown in diagram form in Box 12.4.

12.4 Proposals for reform in relation to mode of trial

1. The Mode of Trial Bill

In 1999, the government introduced into the House of Lords the **Criminal Justice (Mode of Trial) Bill**, the first of two unsuccessful legislative attempts to remove the defendant's ability to choose jury trial in either-way cases. It was estimated that this would mean 12,000 fewer Crown Court trials, producing a yearly saving of £105 million.

2. The Auld Report and the White Paper of 2002

Lord Auld felt that the considerable differences in the practices, procedures, management and funding of the Crown Court and the Magistrates' Court resulted in inefficiency. He proposed that the two systems should be replaced by a unified criminal court with three divisions:

1. The Crown Division would be as the Crown Court is now, but deal with indictable cases only.

2. The District Division would have a Crown Court Judge or a District Judge sitting with two magistrates to hear the more serious either-way cases. This would be an entirely new kind of court.

3. The Magistrates' Division would operate as the Magistrates' Courts do now but only hear summary cases.

The White Paper of 2002, *Justice for All*, adopted the Auld proposal to integrate the two criminal courts. It also proposed to allow Crown Court Judges to conduct trials in Magistrates' Courts.

Auld also recommended that the defendant's right to elect (choose) jury trial should be abolished, and that the magistrates alone would decide on mode of trial.

12.5 Committal proceedings and transfer proceedings

All cases appear before magistrates first of all. This may be a simple formality as the first step to proceeding on to a Crown Court trial, or it may be the beginning of a trial in the Magistrates' Court (see Box 12.5). In some either-way cases, magistrates have a role in reviewing the

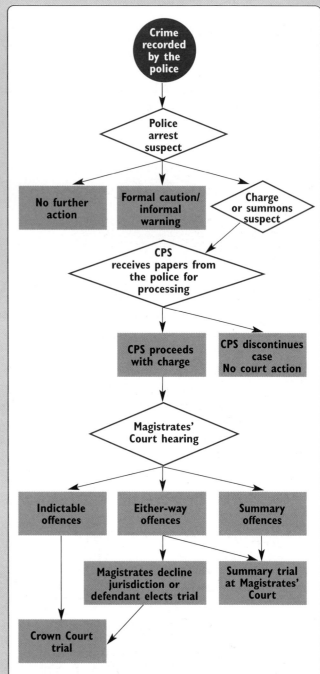

Box 12.4 *The pre-trial process*

Notes

1. *Although the majority of prosecutions are handled by the Crown Prosecution Service, certain offences are still prosecuted by the police, while some are prosecuted by private organisations or government agencies such as the Inland Revenue.*

2. *A case will be under continual review, and may be discontinued at any stage before the hearing at the Magistrates' Court or the prosecution may offer no evidence. In addition, the charge may be altered up to the final decision of the court.*

3. *Magistrates may commit to Crown Court for sentence.*

This diagram shows the various stages that take place after a crime is recorded by the police.

> **Box 12.5** *A summary of the jurisdiction of Magistrates' Courts*
>
> 1. Try summary cases.
>
> 2. Try either-way offences (unless the defendant has elected for trial in the Crown Court).
>
> 3. Decide whether there is sufficient evidence for a Crown Court trial in committal proceedings (either-way offences only).
>
> 4. Hold a first hearing for indictable offences.
>
> 5. Issue warrants for arrest.
>
> 6. Decide whether defendants should be granted bail.
>
> 7. Try cases in the Youth Court (where the defendants are not younger than ten years old and no older than 17).

strength of the case for the prosecution and, if it is insufficient, preventing the need for a Crown Court trial. This initial review is known as the 'committal proceedings'.

Committal before 1998

Committal proceedings were originally a kind of scaled-down trial of the case, held by the magistrates before all Crown Court trials (whether in relation to either-way or indictable offences) to establish whether there was sufficient evidence to justify a trial. Witnesses were called to give evidence and both the defence and prosecution were able to put arguments.

Committal today

Under Section 51 of the Crime and Disorder Act 1998, indictable offences are now transferred directly to the Crown Court after brief **transfer proceedings** in the Magistrates' Court where the magistrates do no more

Activity 12.2

No country in the world has courts of lay magistrates like those in England and Wales. Magistrates usually sit in panels of three and administer the vast majority of criminal justice. Magistrates' Courts deal with 95% of all prosecuted crime. Lay magistrates - about 30,400 of them - handle 91% of that work. The remaining 9% is dealt with by a much smaller number of District Judges (Magistrates' Courts). The Auld Report was generally positive towards magistrates but also commented that:

> 'District Judges, because of their legal knowledge and experience and because they sit full-time and alone, are significantly faster and otherwise more efficient than magistrates who need to confer with each other and often take the advice of their court clerk.'

District Judges, Lord Auld said, deal with cases more quickly without loss of judicial fairness, or general courtesy.

The interior of a Magistrates' Court (it is forbidden to take photos when the court is in session).

The Auld Report feels that the magistracy has a number of strengths. Magistrates, while not wholly representative of the communities they come from, bring: 'an important symbolic effect of lay participation in the system which should not be under-valued'. Magistrates are public spirited individuals who have a fair degree of training, procedural knowledge and experience. Jurors are not volunteers. If a person is selected for jury service they are required to do it by law. Magistrates may be vulnerable to case-hardening - in a way that juries are not - but, on the other hand, they only sit for between 30 and 70 days a year. They have a clerk to advise them on the law when they are considering their verdict and they are obliged to explain their decisions. Jurors, on the other hand, receive no training, retire to consider their verdict without the presence of a legal adviser and need give no reason for their decisions.

An artist's impression of a scene inside Bow Street Magistrates' Court in January 2003. The suspect, Samir Asli (second from right) is before Magistrate Timothy Workman. Samir was charged under the Terrorism Act.

(a) Define the following terms: (i) lay magistrates (ii) District Judges (Magistrates' Courts). (6)

(b) Why are District Judges (Magistrates' Courts) able to deal with cases more quickly than lay magistrates? (6)

(c) What advantages do magistrates offer over a jury? (10)

than consider whether to grant bail and deal with other straightforward matters. This is not a preliminary scrutiny of the evidence in the manner of committal proceedings. Proper committal proceedings are only held now in relation to either-way offences. They are usually held through an examination of written witness statements.

12.6 Trials in the Magistrates' Courts

Procedure where the defendant pleads guilty

The basic sequence of events in a Magistrates' Court with a guilty or a not guilty plea is outlined in Box 12.6.

Youth Courts

Defendants not younger than ten years old and no older than 17 are tried by magistrates sitting in a special Youth Court. This applies to summary offences and some indictable offences. In relation to homicide, other very serious charges and some cases where the defendant is jointly charged with an adult, the youth may be tried in the Crown Court. Three magistrates hear cases in the Youth Court. At least one must be a man and one must be a woman. All three receive special training. The sentencing powers of a Youth Court are different from those of a normal Magistrates' Court.

Box 12.6 *Sequence of events in a Magistrates' Court*

If the defendant pleads guilty

The Crown Prosecution Service provides the court with a summary of the facts.

↓

Details of any previous convictions are provided to the court, along with other information about the defendant's background.

↓

Various written reports, such as pre-sentence reports (prepared by a probation officer) or medical reports are considered by the court.

↓

The defence is given an opportunity to explain anything that might incline the magistrates towards being lenient.

↓

After this has all been completed, the magistrates decide what sentence is appropriate.

If the defendant pleads not guilty

The prosecution makes a short speech outlining what the case is about.

↓

Prosecution witnesses are then called to give evidence and are questioned by the prosecution. Witnesses may be asked questions by the defence as well (cross examined).

↓

The defence may then make a submission of no case to answer to the magistrates. This means that the defence feels that the prosecution is so weak that there is little or no evidence of the defendant's guilt. Only a small number of cases are discontinued at this stage.

↓

The next stage is for the defence to call any witnesses it may have, who are subject to examination (by the defence) and cross examination (by the prosecution).

↓

The defence may then make a speech setting out what are the weaknesses of the prosecution's case. Further speeches are not usually allowed.

↓

Magistrates then leave the courtroom to consider their verdict.

↓

If the verdict is guilty, information is gathered prior to passing sentence in the same way as with a guilty plea.

↓

If the defendant is found not guilty they are obviously free to go.

Youth Courts are designed to be less intimidating and formal than the adult courts. In general, members of the public are not allowed to watch cases and there are tight restrictions on the press. Parents of defendants under the age of 16 must always attend court and, sometimes, the parents of those who are 16 or over are asked to attend.

Appeals from the Magistrates' Court

There are two appeal routes from the Magistrates' Court. Which route is used depends upon whether the appeal is on a point of law (an 'appeal by way of case stated') or whether it is for other reasons. The two routes are set out in Box 12.7.

Judicial review

Both prosecution and defence may also challenge the decision of the Magistrates' Court or that of the Crown Court acting in its appellate capacity (ie when it has heard an appeal from the Magistrates' Court) by way of an application to the High Court (Queen's Bench Divisional Court) for judicial review. This is concerned with issues such as whether the court acted in excess of its jurisdiction or whether there was some irregularity in the decision-making process. A claim for judicial review can only be made with the permission of the High Court.

The House of Lords

Further appeal is possible to the House of Lords in the following limited circumstances:

1. The Divisional Court certifies that a point of law of general public importance is involved.

2. The Divisional Court or the House of Lords gives leave to appeal because the point is regarded as one that the House of Lords should consider.

12.7 Trials in the Crown Court

As explained above, the Crown Court hears all cases involving trial on indictment and some either-way offences. The Crown Court has the power to grant bail in the same way as the Magistrates' Courts. It also hears appeals from those convicted in the Magistrates' Court.

Pre-trial matters

A preliminary hearing known as a **plea and directions hearing** is held about a month before the trial itself. At this hearing, defendants are asked whether they plead guilty or not guilty. If a defendant pleads guilty, the judge will, wherever possible, sentence the defendant immediately.

Where the defendant pleads not guilty at a plea and directions hearing, the prosecution and defence summarise what they see as the crucial issues in the case.

Box 12.7 *Appeals from the Magistrates' Court*

1. Appeals to the Crown Court

Only the defence can use this route of appeal. If the plea was not guilty in the original trial, the defendant may appeal (a) against conviction and/or (b) against sentence. If, on the other hand, the defendant pleaded guilty, they may only appeal against sentence.

Appeals of this kind are heard by a Crown Court Judge sitting with between two and four magistrates. Where the appeal is about conviction, the hearing takes the form of a complete retrial. The Crown Court may leave the conviction unaltered or reverse it. Where the appeal is about sentence, the court may increase or decrease the original sentence but can only increase it up to the maximum that the Magistrates' Court would have been able to award.

Only a small number of appeals are made from the Magistrates' Court to the Crown Court. In 2000, the figure was 14,000. Further appeal is possible from the Crown Court to the Court of Appeal. This is explained in the section on appeals from the Crown Court in Section 12.7 below.

2. Appeal to the Queen's Bench Divisional Court

High Court Judges sit in the Queen's Bench Divisional Court to hear appeals by way of case stated. These appeals are quite different from those in the Crown Court since they are concerned with points of law. Both the prosecution and the defence have the right to appeal, but such appeals are fairly rare.

What is a 'point of law'?

In any criminal case two basic questions have to be answered:

1. What kinds of behaviour are defined as unlawful?

2. Has the defendant behaved in one of the ways that are defined as unlawful?

The first question requires an understanding of the common law and the legislation that defines an offence. In many trials, this is not too difficult. The law sets out categories of behaviour (theft, assault, criminal damage and so on) which must be treated as unlawful. If, as a matter of fact, the defendant's behaviour is shown to come within one of these categories, the defendant will be found guilty.

On the other hand, there may, occasionally, be room for doubt as to whether the defendant's behaviour was actually unlawful. The issue is not so much, 'did the defendant do this?' but rather, 'was this behaviour unlawful?'. On an appeal by way of case stated, the appeal is made because it is felt by one side or the other that the magistrates made a mistake about the law.

Argument is made on the basis of the facts ascertained by the magistrates. This is what is meant by 'case stated'. The Magistrates' Court provides details of the facts and what their decision was. The Divisional Court decides whether to confirm or reverse the decision of the Magistrates' Court by looking at the interpretation and application of the law rather than the facts. Sometimes, having decided on a different interpretation of the law, they simply send the case back to the magistrates for the lower court to return to the case and implement the law correctly.

The judge can then give directions aimed at organising the trial properly. For instance, the defendant and the prosecution might agree that certain evidence is not disputed and so particular witnesses need not attend trial. This sort of planning obviously helps to avoid time being wasted during the trial itself. The time saved can be used to help reduce the list of cases that are waiting to be heard

There is another way to save valuable time in court. It is not uncommon for defence and prosecution to negotiate before trial about the possibility of a charge being dropped in return for the defendant pleading guilty to a similar but lesser charge (which will obviously tend to mean a lighter sentence). This is called **plea bargaining**.

Under Section 48 of the Criminal Justice and Public Order Act 1994 the court is allowed to reduce the sentence it would otherwise give by taking into account the stage at which the defendant indicated an intention to plead guilty. This encourages a defendant to admit their guilt sooner rather than later so that there is no need to waste time preparing for a full trial.

Crown Court procedure

When a defendant pleads guilty, the process of sentencing is similar to that described in the section on Magistrates' Courts above. Sentencing decisions are solely a matter for the judge. Where the defendant pleads not guilty, the procedure described in Box 12.8 is followed.

Proposals for reforming the jury system

The Auld Report contained strong criticisms of the jury system (see also Unit 15). Apart from the proposals regarding mode of trial discussed above, recommendations were made which would have the effect of reducing the use of juries. One of these was that, as an alternative to trial by judge and jury in serious and complex fraud cases, the trial judge should be empowered to direct such trials alone. Lord Auld also recommended that, in all cases presently heard in the Crown Court, the defendant should be able to choose trial by judge alone, without a jury.

Appeals from the Crown Court - appeals by the defendant

The defendant may wish to appeal against conviction or sentence, or perhaps both. The appeal route here is to the Court of Appeal (Criminal Division). The rules are set out in the Criminal Appeal Act 1995. In fact, the appeal process has two stages. The first step is to obtain leave (permission) to appeal from either the Court of Appeal itself or from the trial judge. Only if leave is obtained can the second stage, the actual appeal hearing, take place.

Box 12.8 *Procedure in a Crown Court when a defendant pleads not guilty*

Members of the jury are sworn in (see Unit 15).

↓

The prosecution makes an opening speech summarising the facts of the case and what arguments will be put forward.

↓

Prosecution witnesses give evidence. The defence may cross examine these witnesses.

↓

When the prosecution has put all of its evidence forward, the defence may make a submission that there is no case to answer. If the judge agrees, they will direct the jury to acquit the defendant.

↓

If the trial continues beyond the prosecution case (which it usually does), the defence then makes its opening speech.

↓

Defence witnesses give evidence and are cross examined.

↓

The prosecution makes a closing speech, summarising the points in the evidence that indicate guilt.

↓

The defence makes a closing speech, highlighting weaknesses in the prosecution's evidence. It is important to remember that, to convict the defendant, the jury must be satisfied that guilt has been proven beyond all reasonable doubt.

↓

The judge sums up the case to the jury and explains relevant criminal laws.

↓

The jury then retires to consider its verdict in the privacy of the jury room, without anyone else being present.

↓

The jury's verdict is read out in open court.

↓

If the verdict of the jury is guilty, the judge then sentences the accused.

Leave to appeal

The idea of obtaining leave to appeal is to prevent unnecessary appeals from defendants who are simply clutching at straws, without any realistic hope of changing either conviction or sentence. Where the evidence against the defendant is overwhelming, an appeal against conviction might reasonably be seen as a waste of the court time. On the other hand, there will always be some cases where the decision of the jury seems unsatisfactory or where the judge seems to have been much too hard when sentencing the defendant. In these cases, the Court of Appeal is able to consider the case again. When leave to appeal is considered by the Court of Appeal, the application is considered by a single judge sitting in private. If this judge refuses to give leave, further application may be made to a full Court of Appeal.

What are the grounds for allowing an appeal?

When the Court of Appeal has heard an appeal and decided that the conviction or sentence is wrong, the appeal is 'allowed'. When it is felt that the correct decision was made, the appeal is 'dismissed'.

Section 2 of the Criminal Appeal Act 1995 states that the Court of Appeal: '(a) shall allow an appeal against conviction if they think that the conviction is unsafe; and (b) shall dismiss such an appeal in any other case.'

Appeals from the Crown Court - appeals by the prosecution

The right to appeal by the prosecution is much more limited than that of the defence. But there is some scope for appeal against either acquittal or sentence.

Appeal against an acquittal

In general, the prosecution cannot appeal against a verdict of not guilty in the Crown Court. The sole exception is in relation to cases where an acquittal was the result of interfering with the jury, known as 'jury nobbling'. This is where the defendant or their associates find some way of intimidating or otherwise influencing a member of the jury. If there has actually been a conviction for interfering with decision of the jury in this way, the prosecution may apply to the High Court for the acquittal to be quashed (set aside). If such an application is successful, the defendant can be retried for the same offence.

Appeal against sentence

The prosecution may feel that a sentence is too lenient, but they have no right to appeal on this issue as such. However, under Section 36 of the Criminal Justice Act 1988, the Attorney General can apply for leave to refer an unduly lenient sentence to the Court of Appeal (the Attorney General is the senior legal adviser to the government). This power is available in all cases tried in the Crown Court (whether indictable or either-way).

Activity 12.3

Explain which court or courts may currently hear an appeal from the magistrates in the following cases. (6 marks each)

In Janet's trial for shoplifting, her solicitor advises her that an appeal should be considered, as there appears to have been a suggestion of mistaken identity by witnesses.

Janet

Sid was acquitted of theft. The Crown Prosecution has just discovered that the Chair of the magistrates was his uncle.

Sid

The solicitor representing Geoff, who has been convicted on a charge of 'obtaining by deception' under the Theft Act, feels strongly that the court has misinterpreted the meaning of the relevant section of the Act, with the result that Geoff was wrongly convicted.

Geoff

Appeals from the Court of Appeal to the House of Lords

Either the prosecution or the defence may make a further appeal to the House of Lords. Leave to appeal must be obtained from either the Court of Appeal or the House of Lords. The Court of Appeal must, in addition, certify that a point of law of general public importance is involved. There is no right of appeal to the Lords on matters of fact. There are usually only one or two criminal appeals per year in the Lords.

Proposals for reform to the appeal system

As with appeals from the Magistrates' Court, Lord Auld regarded appeal routes from the Crown Court as unnecessarily complicated. He recommended abolition of appeal from the Crown Court to the High Court by way of case stated and its replacement by appeal to the Court of Appeal.

12.8 The Criminal Cases Review Commission

The role of the Criminal Cases Review Commission (CCRC) is to review the convictions of those who believe they have either wrongly been found guilty of a criminal offence, or wrongly sentenced. Such cases are sometimes referred to as 'miscarriages of justice'. The Commission can seek further information relating to a case and carry out its own investigations, or arrange for others to do so.

What is a miscarriage of justice?

There have been cases where defendants spent many years in prison protesting their innocence, claiming throughout, that there were serious flaws in the way in which their trial was conducted or in the credibility of evidence that was put by the prosecution. The Birmingham Six, for example, were six men wrongly convicted of involvement in IRA bombings. They had their convictions quashed after 16 years in prison. Although the number of such cases is small, there was growing concern in the 1980s and 1990s that the appeal system did not always serve the interests of justice.

The CCRC does not have the power to overturn convictions or sentences. It merely refers cases back to the courts. It may refer a Crown Court case to the Court of Appeal or a case heard in the Magistrates' Court to the Crown Court. The CCRC can only consider cases in which an appeal through the ordinary process has failed. Caseworkers and administrative staff support the 14 members of the Commission. Many members of the Commission do not have a legal background and can therefore be seen as independent of the judiciary and the legal profession.

Activity 12.4

When, in 1996, the law on defendant appeals from the Crown Court was changed, Professor Smith, a respected criminal law academic, expressed concern. He argued that a conviction might be seen as safe but also unsatisfactory. The Court of Appeal might be convinced that a defendant in a particular case was guilty, so the conviction could be regarded as 'safe'. But suppose that the police, in breach of the Police and Criminal Evidence (PACE) Act 1984, had improperly obtained some of the evidence? For example, the police might have obtained a confession from the defendant during questioning in circumstances that amounted to breach of the PACE rules. Dismissing an appeal against conviction in these circumstances would be undesirable. It would have the effect of allowing the police to disregard rules that help protect all defendants from injustice (although it might be felt that *in particular cases* no injustice had in fact occurred as the right verdict was reached).

(a) **What were the grounds for appeal by the defendant from the Crown Court to the Court of Appeal before 1995? (4)**

(b) **Did the Criminal Appeal Act 1995 make the grounds for appeal wider or narrower in the view of Professor Smith? (2)**

(c) **What Act regulates the powers of the police and, in effect, the admissibility of evidence gathered by the police? (2)**

(d) **What argument is put by Smith regarding appeals where the police have broken the rules about the way that a suspect is treated in the police station? (8)**

Summary ● ● ●

1. When is bail granted or refused?

2. What determines which court a criminal case is heard in?

3. What are committal proceedings and transfer proceedings?

4. What procedure is followed in a Magistrates' Court and in a Crown Court?

5. When are appeals allowed from Magistrates' Courts and Crown Courts?

6. What were the main recommendations of the Auld Report and the government White Paper published in 2002?

Case study   ● *The government White Paper published in 2002*

The government White Paper of 2002

The government White Paper on criminal justice published in 2002 contained some radical proposals. It featured proposals to:

● allow for trial by judge alone in certain sorts of cases
● increase the rights of the prosecution to appeal
● combine the behind-the-scenes administration of the Crown Court and the Magistrates' Court into one system.

Another controversial proposal was eliminating the double jeopardy rule in certain cases.

The double jeopardy rule is the very long established principle that a person may not be tried twice for the same crime. The rule came under public scrutiny after the collapse of the high profile case against men accused of murdering Stephen Lawrence, the young man killed in a racist attack in London in 1993 (see Unit 9, Section 9.3).

A tribute to Stephen Lawrence. It was after the trial of men accused of Stephen Lawrence's murder collapsed that the double jeopardy rule came under public scrutiny, resulting in the 2002 White Paper's recommendation that defendants be tried for a second time in 'grave cases'.

The Home Secretary asked the Law Commission to consider whether there should be a change to the rule, following the Stephen Lawrence case and other similar cases. The Law Commission recommended that the rule should remain, but new exceptions to the general rule might be made in relation to murder cases. This recommendation was adopted in the government White Paper published in 2002. This contained a proposal to allow a defendant to be tried a second time: 'in grave cases where compelling new evidence has come to light'.

There are two main arguments against such a reform. John Wadham, from the pressure group Liberty, is one of those who has argued that it would be wrong to put people through the ordeal of time in prison while on remand and the stress of a trial twice over. The other argument is that it would be almost impossible to conceal from a jury that a retrial had been ordered. The dates of events mentioned in evidence and possibly the testimony of witnesses would lead the jury to work out that an earlier trial had taken place, even if they did not recognise the case after having been exposed to earlier media reports. This would inevitably prejudice the chance of a fair trial.

Questions

(a) What was the report that influenced many of the proposals for new law contained in the 2002 White Paper? (2)

(b) Suggest why combining the Magistrates' Courts and the Crown Court into one organisation might be a good idea. (3)

(c) It is proposed that prosecution rights of appeal should be increased. If a defendant is acquitted in the criminal courts, explain the extent to which the prosecution may appeal under the existing rules. (10)

(d) What are the White Paper proposals to 'allow trial by judge alone'? (8)

(e) What justifications might be given for increasing trial by a judge alone or magistrates rather than a jury? (10)

(f) Give examples of why the White Paper might be seen as a threat to the rights of defendants. (10)

(g) Give two reasons why it is unlikely that a defendant in any second trial would be allowed bail if the double jeopardy rule was reformed. (8)

13.1 Introduction

The legal profession has two main branches. If you require the services of a lawyer for something that is not a dispute, such as buying or selling a house, or drawing up a will, you will probably go to a local solicitor. Solicitors can also offer help and advice in relation to disputes that involve the law. The role of barristers, broadly speaking, is to represent clients in court hearings, though this is not all they do. Barristers are sometimes called 'counsel'. Two separate professional bodies govern the two branches. In the case of solicitors, this is the Law Society. In the case of barristers, it is the Bar Council.

In addition to solicitors and barristers, other less highly qualified people are involved in providing legal services. The most important of these are legal executives.

13.2 Solicitors

What do solicitors do?

When solicitors act for a client in private practice, they form a contract, a legally binding agreement, with the client - to provide legal services in return for a fee. However, this is a special kind of contract where the solicitor has a strict obligation to act professionally, be completely honest and to put the interests of their client first.

Solicitors deal with a broad range of legal issues in both civil and criminal law. They may act for individuals, businesses or other organisations. The activities they are involved in are outlined in Box 13.1.

At one time, solicitors could only appear in the Magistrates' Courts and the County Courts. In recent years, however, they have been given greater rights to appear in the higher courts. Nevertheless, the traditional idea that barristers work in the courts and solicitors carry out legal work outside the courtroom is still a valid generalisation.

How solicitors practice

There are 80,000 solicitors practising in England and Wales today. Annual earnings for a qualified solicitor range from £20,000 or £30,000 per year to £400,000 and above. Most solicitors work in private practice either on their own, or as part of a partnership. Being a partner means being in business as a self-employed person and receiving a share of profits rather than a fixed salary.

Partnerships range in size tremendously. Some small firms operating in a town or a city have less than half a

Box 13.1 *The activities solicitors are involved in*

The activities solicitors are involved in include:
- preparing a case for trial (litigation)
- drawing up the documentation required for the sale or purchase of land and buildings and negotiating with the buyer or seller (this kind of legal work is called 'conveyancing')
- preparing a will and dealing with the financial affairs of a deceased person (this area of work is known as 'probate')
- offering legal advice to clients involved in commercial affairs such as starting up a company or in relation to tax law
- acting as a legal adviser to employees or employers in dismissal and other employment cases
- acting for a husband or wife in a divorce and dealing with related issues such as financial maintenance and the custody of children.

dozen partners and a small team of administrative staff. There are also some giant firms (see Box 13.2). One firm, Clifford Chance, for example, has 665 partners operating in 19 different countries. The larger the firm, the more likely it is that a solicitor will specialise in a particular type of legal work. In smaller firms, partners may have a more varied workload, perhaps visiting a police station to talk to a client who has been arrested in the morning, and drawing up documents necessary to sell a house for another client in the afternoon.

Box 13.2 *Solicitors' partnerships*

Eversheds is one of the largest law firms in the world, with over 4,000 staff, over 2,000 of whom are legal and business advisers. In addition to its offices in the UK, Eversheds has 17 offices in Europe and three in Asia.

Some solicitors, rather than working for themselves, are employed as legal advisers for organisations such as the Crown Prosecution Service, local government or a variety of commercial businesses. As competition for work has intensified, solicitors have increasingly preferred the security of working as an employee. In 1990, there were 9,147 solicitors working for companies. By 2000, this number had almost doubled.

Increasing competition

At one time, only solicitors could be paid to do conveyancing. But since much of this work, particularly in relation to residential property, is quite straightforward, the government eventually came to the view that the monopoly was no longer justifiable. It was felt that, so long as they were appropriately trained, others could be allowed to do this work. This would increase competition and have the effect of reducing the high price which solicitors charge for conveyancing. The Administration of Justice Act 1985 allowed for **licensed conveyancers** to set up in business, purely to provide legal services in the property market. Under the Courts and Legal Services Act 1990, banks and building societies were also allowed to do conveyancing for their customers.

To what extent are solicitors entitled to be advocates?

An advocate is someone who speaks for a client in the courts of law. The rights of a person to appear before a judge are known as 'rights of audience'. Solicitors have for many years been entitled to appear in the Magistrates' Courts and the County Courts. Rights of audience in the High Court and the Crown Court were, until 1990, very restricted, however. To take out an action in those courts therefore, it was necessary to pay for the services of both a solicitor and a barrister.

The first major change to this state of affairs came in the Courts and Legal Services Act 1990. Solicitors were given the right to apply to the Lord Chancellor for a certificate of advocacy to appear in the higher courts. To be given a certificate, the applicant was required to demonstrate experience of advocacy and pass a short course on the rules of evidence. Those applying for advocacy certificates were either accepted or rejected by the Lord Chancellor's department.

The Access to Justice Act 1999 provided that, in principle, all solicitors should have full rights of audience before all courts, subject to meeting certain training requirements. The Law Society and the Bar Council now deal with the provision of advocacy certificates. The Access to Justice Act 1999 also set up procedures for other bodies, such as the Institute of Legal Executives and the Crown Prosecution Service, to grant rights of audience.

The functions of the Law Society

A council of elected members and an elected President control the Law Society. The Law Society has a number of roles. These are outlined in Box 13.3.

Box 13.3 *The role of the Law Society*

The Law Society plays the following roles:

1. In order to practice, all solicitors must have a **Practising Certificate** which is issued by the Law Society.

2. The Law Society sets strict standards of professional conduct that solicitors are obliged to follow. These standards exist to protect the public. For example, if a client provides money to a solicitor to purchase a property on their behalf, or for other purposes, there are strict accounting rules about how the solicitor should record and deal with this money.

3. If a solicitor fails to meet professional standards, they are liable to be disciplined by the Law Society's Solicitors' Disciplinary Tribunal. They may have their Practising Certificate withdrawn.

4. The Law Society supervises the professional education and training of solicitors.

5. The Law Society also provides support and services to solicitors, acting as an association to further the status of the profession.

Becoming a solicitor

There are three different routes to becoming a solicitor. The three starting points are:

- obtaining a law degree
- obtaining a degree in a non-law subject
- entry through training as a legal executive, which does not require a degree.

A law degree

Law is one of the most popular subjects to study at University. In the year 2000, 82,000 people applied to do law degrees. For those who have passed their law degree, the next step is to obtain a place on a one-year **Legal Practice Course** (LPC) - either at one of the Law Society's training centres or at one of the universities permitted to run the course. This is a vocational course. In other words, it involves training and it is work related, whereas a law degree involves academic study. LPC students are trained in negotiation, drafting legal documents and accounts, for example.

The fees for the LPC are several thousand pounds. Unless students have parents who can afford to pay their fees and any living expenses, the LPC year is difficult to fund, as it is often impossible to obtain a local authority grant and, where one is available, it will only cover a small part of the total expenditure. Loans under the Student Loan system are not available for study beyond degree level. The LPC may be studied part-time over two years, when students may work to help pay for the course.

After passing the LPC, a two-year **training contract**, must be obtained. During these two years, the trainee is employed by a firm at a modest rate of pay and works under the supervision of a solicitor. Alternatively, the trainee might work for one of a number of other organisations carrying out legal work, such as the Crown Prosecution Service or a local authority. After successful completion of a training contract, including a short period of study on a **Professional Skills Course**, a person may be admitted to the Law Society as a qualified solicitor.

A degree in a subject other than law

The training route here is the same as that for a law

graduate except that, before commencing the Legal Practice Course, trainees must pass the Common Professional Examination (CPE), which involves a one-year course covering particular areas of law (the CPE may also be studied over two years on a part-time basis).

Institute of Legal Executives (ILEX) qualifications

It is possible to become a solicitor without obtaining a degree. Legal executives do routine legal work under the supervision of a solicitor. Although it may take a long time to qualify as a solicitor in this way, legal executives are paid a basic salary during the time they are training. To become a solicitor via ILEX it is necessary to be over 25, be a Fellow of the Institute and have five years experience in legal employment. Fellows of ILEX obtain exemption from some parts of the CPE. However, it is still necessary to study, usually on a part-time basis, for those parts of the CPE from which being a legal executive does not provide exemption. Legal executives are also required to pass the LPC. Most people taking the ILEX route are exempt from the two-year solicitor's training contract, but they must pass the Professional Skills Course.

Criticisms of the current training process

There are three main criticisms of the current training process. These are outlined in Box 13.4.

Complaints against a solicitor

Lawyers have never been popular with the British public and, recently, their professionalism has been called into question. In 2001, the consumer magazine *Which*

Activity 13.1

Jayesha is 16 years old. She is interested in becoming a solicitor, but is unsure which training route is right for her.

(a) **For each of the training routes explain to Jayesha how long it will take to qualify (assuming that any degree course takes three years full-time study). (8)**

(b) **Jayesha does not like the idea of building up huge debts. Briefly outline what you see as the advantages and disadvantages of the three training routes in light of this. (4)**

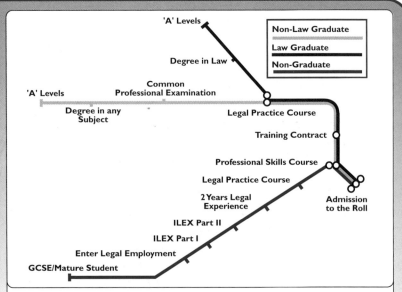

This diagram, devised by the Law Society, shows the various routes that can be taken before being admitted to the Law Society as a qualified solicitor.

Box 13.4 *Criticisms of the current training process*

1. Only the relatively wealthy can afford to train as a solicitor

An increasing number of students on all degree courses struggle to fund their degree. On top of that, virtually no government funds are available to help with the very considerable cost of the postgraduate Legal Practice Course. This is likely to deter those students from less well-off families who are considering a career as a solicitor.

2. Solicitors without a law degree are under-qualified

It is surprising perhaps that trainee solicitors who do not have a law degree only need to study six areas of law for one year on the CPE to reach the same point as a law graduate, who will normally have studied law for three years. Does this mean that some entrants to the profession are under-qualified?

3. There is a severe shortage of training contracts

Another way of looking at this is to say that too many students are enrolled on professional courses. No matter how well a trainee solicitor does in the college-based stage of their training, for a third or more of trainees it may prove impossible to find a training contract with a firm of solicitors. At least a third of those who pass the LPC every year come up against this problem. It seems a pity that students should be allowed to run up debts and spend a lot of time studying, only to find that they cannot qualify.

conducted a survey of 343 people who had used a solicitor:

- 40% said they had not been treated with courtesy and respect
- 60% said their solicitor had made a basic and potentially serious mistake.

Some complaints against solicitors involve dishonesty and misconduct. For example, solicitors may grossly overcharge or misuse money that they were supposed to be holding for clients. The majority of complaints, however, concern inadequate professional services. When a client feels they have a serious problem with their solicitor, there are three courses of action:

- the complaint can be taken to the Office for the Supervision of Solicitors

- a complaint may be made to the Legal Services Ombudsman
- an action against the solicitor may be started in the courts in contract or negligence.

The Office for the Supervision of Solicitors

The Law Society set up the Office for the Supervision of Solicitors (OSS) in 1996, to deal with complaints about solicitors and to regulate their work. It was created in response to criticisms about the efficiency of its predecessor, the Solicitors' Complaints Bureau, (which was also part of the Law Society). The Office is, to some extent, independent of the Law Society (the Law Society provides funding but cannot become involved in individual cases). Another way in which the independence of the Law Society is safeguarded is the involvement of appointed lay people in policy-making.

The OSS tries to conciliate complaints. In other words, it helps an aggrieved client and the solicitor reach agreement. If this cannot be achieved, it has the power to reduce bills, award compensation to the client or to discipline any solicitor.

The OSS has, like its predecessor, struggled to deal with the volume of complaints it receives within anything approaching a reasonable timescale. The government has warned the Law Society that it will be forced to take steps to deal with this itself unless the problem is tackled urgently. Indeed, the Access to Justice Act 1999 contained a provision that would enable the Lord Chancellor to appoint a Legal Services Complaints Commissioner.

The Legal Services Ombudsman

The Courts and Legal Services Act 1990 created the role of Legal Services Ombudsman (LSO). The LSO investigates the way in which complaints are dealt with by the professional bodies involved in legal services. The LSO is not a lawyer and is completely independent of the legal profession. After investigating a complaint, the LSO might take a number of steps:

- recommend that the professional body investigates the original complaint again
- require the professional body to pay compensation to the claimant
- require the lawyer concerned to pay compensation to the client.

A court action

The relationship between solicitor and client is based on a contract. It follows that if the solicitor fails to provide the service they have agreed to provide, or only provides it in part, the client will normally have the right to sue.

Naturally, this contractual relationship works two ways and a solicitor may sue for unpaid fees.

Solicitors also owe a duty of care to their clients, so it is possible for clients to take out an action in negligence where that duty has been broken. Solicitors are required to take out professional negligence insurance, to provide for this eventuality. The only special exception to the right to sue in negligence used to be in relation to advocacy, that is, work involved with actually appearing in court. However following the recent House of Lords ruling in *Arthur JS Hall and Co. v Simons and Other Appeals (2000)*, it appears that this immunity has been removed, so that both solicitors and barristers may now be sued for negligence while acting for a client in court (this case is discussed further in Section 13.3 below).

13.3 Barristers

What do barristers do?

In 2000 there were slightly over 10,000 practising barristers in England and Wales, which is far fewer than the number of practising solicitors. The public image of barristers is one of bewigged lawyers appearing in court, but, in fact, barristers also spend time on other sorts of work. They research and write up opinions on a particular point of law where they have been asked by a solicitor for advice. They also work on important documents known as 'pleadings', which must be produced in preparation for a

trial. Whatever work they are involved in, barristers are expected to maintain high standards of honesty and integrity. They have a strong duty to the courts and the interests of justice as well as to their client.

At present, it is not possible for a claimant to instruct a barrister to act. A solicitor must do this on behalf of their client. However, in recent years, an exception to this rule in relation to other professionals, such as accountants and surveyors, has been created. There is debate in some quarters as to whether direct access should be increased further.

Barristers are not allowed to form partnerships, except with lawyers in other countries. Barristers are self-employed. However, they are able to share the cost of employing staff and maintaining offices by forming a **chambers**, a loose association that is something less than a partnership. Every chambers employs a barrister's clerk, who has a key role within the office. When a solicitor first approaches a chambers to offer them a case, initial contact is with the clerk who then allocates work to barristers. The clerk also negotiates a fee on behalf of the barrister.

The cab rank rule - never turn a client away

If a solicitor offers work on behalf of a client and the barrister is available to take it, then work should not be refused on the grounds that the client or the nature of the case is disapproved of. This is known as 'the cab rank

Activity 13.2 Do solicitors provide good customer service?

In 1999, the Office for the Supervision of Solicitors (OSS) received 23,000 complaints that had not been successfully resolved between solicitors and their clients. That's an average of one complaint for every three solicitors. To make matters worse, the OSS had a backlog of a staggering 16,000 cases. Ann Abraham, the Legal Services Ombudsman (LSO), is critical of the OSS and solicitors in general: 'Although nearly nine out of 10 people complained to their solicitor before registering a complaint with the OSS, 80% of those people said that their own solicitor had done nothing to attempt to resolve the complaint. By its own admission, the Law Society's ability to protect the public is now in jeopardy.' But David McNeil, a spokesman for the OSS, said: 'There are roughly 11 million legal transactions a year. Given that most people use solicitors for emotionally stressful transactions, such as house purchases and wills, where the potential for misunderstanding is correspondingly high, then our record begins to look substantially better.' Tony Biles, acting Chair of the consumer group Campaign Against Solicitors, Action for Independent Adjudication says the problem stems from the fact that the Law Society is ultimately judge and jury over its own members. 'The only real answer is to have an independent body', he commented.

Adapted from the *Guardian*, 12 July 2000.

Ann Abraham.

(a) **Briefly explain the role of the OSS. (4)**

(b) **What criticisms can be raised against the OSS? (6)**

(c) **What can a client who feels they have received poor service do, apart from complain to the OSS or contact the Legal Services Ombudsman? (3)**

rule'. If you want a cab, you get into the one at the top of the queue on a 'first come, first served basis'. There is no need to discuss whether the driver wishes to take you to your destination. There are limited exceptions to this rule. For example, the barrister may obviously decline a case on the basis of prior commitments to another client.

Senior barristers - Queen's Counsel

When a barrister has been practising for ten years or more they may apply to the Lord Chancellor to become a Queen's Counsel (QC). This is sometimes known as 'taking silk' because of the silk robes that QCs wear (see Box 13.5). Solicitors who have had a High Court advocacy certificate for ten years may also apply (in fact, only a tiny proportion of QCs are solicitors). In recent years, an average of 70 new QCs per year have been appointed. There was criticism of the secrecy surrounding the Lord Chancellor's method of selection, but, since 1999, reasons have been given to unsuccessful applicants.

Barristers who are not QCs, no matter how experienced they may be, are known as 'junior counsel'. Until 1977, the rule was that when a QC appeared in court they had to be assisted by a junior counsel. This rule was dispensed with in 1977, but, in some cases, two barristers may, nevertheless, still appear.

Becoming a QC can be important in terms of professional development, as judges are usually selected from those barristers who have become QCs. And, of course, QCs are able to charge higher fees. Annual earnings for QCs at the top of their field range from £150,000 to £2 million. In 2000, 26 QCs apparently earned over £1 million a year.

The functions of the Bar Council

The Bar Council, which is made up of senior members of the profession, is the professional body for barristers in England and Wales. It has a number of different roles:

- it deals with the rules relating to qualification and conduct of barristers
- it deals with complaints against barristers
- it puts the Bar's view on matters of concern about the legal system to government and others, and acts as a source of information about the Bar.

The training of barristers

There are three starting points on the path to becoming a barrister. These are:

- taking a law degree
- taking a degree in a non-law subject
- entry as a mature student, which does not require a degree.

The last route is subject to stringent conditions and few people join the Bar in this way. A first class or upper second class degree is normally required. As with training to become a solicitor, there is both an academic and a vocational ('on the job') stage to training. Qualified barristers are also required to undergo a certain amount of further training for the first three years after they have qualified. Whichever route is taken, all barristers have to be a member of one of the historic **Inns of Court**:

- Lincoln's Inn
- Inner Temple
- Middle Temple
- Gray's Inn.

All of the Inns are situated in London.

Those who have a law degree

After obtaining a degree, the trainee barrister must join one of the Inns of Court and spend one year full-time or two years part-time on the **Bar Vocational Course** (BVC). This can be studied at the Inns or one of several other centres that have been approved by the Bar Council. Unless students have parents who can afford to pay their fees and any living expenses, this is difficult to fund, as it is often impossible to obtain a local authority grant and, where one is available, it will only cover a small part of the total expenditure. The course cannot be funded under the government's Student Loan scheme. Although the Bar Council makes some money available for student grants,

---

Box 13.5 *QCs*

This photo shows QCs in their wigs and silk robes.

this is only sufficient to fund a small proportion of those who study on the course. Course fees are up to £8,750 per year.

During the BVC, students must spend a certain amount of time at whichever Inn they have joined. Until as recently as 1997, this involved the archaic tradition of dining at least 12 times during the year at the Inn. The idea behind this was that students would benefit from contact with experienced barristers, but in reality the only people they were likely to meet were fellow students. The matter of Inn dinners merely added to the total cost of training, especially for those studying outside London. Since 1997, the requirement has been modified a little. Attendance involves participation in educational events and may take the form of four weekends, or six full days, instead of 12 evenings.

The purpose of the BVC is to ensure that students intending to become a barrister acquire the skills and knowledge to prepare them for working in the profession. Skills taught include:

- how to prepare a case
- drafting documents
- interpersonal skills such as interviewing clients and appearing in court.

Students also study the rules of evidence and professional ethics.

After passing the BVC, the next step is to secure a **pupillage**, which is essentially a form of apprenticeship with a barrister. Pupillage lasts for one year. The barrister supervising pupillage is known as a 'pupil master'. In the first six months, pupils shadow their pupil master. In the second six months, they may be permitted to appear in court. Competition for a limited number of pupillages is fierce but, from 2003, all pupils became entitled to an annual award of not less than £10,000 and to receive reasonable travel expenses. The Bar Council also requires pupils to attend further training courses.

A degree other than law

Those students who do not have a law degree need, like trainee solicitors, to take the Common Professional Examination. After this they then join one of the Inns of Court, study for the Bar Vocational Course and become pupil barristers in just the same way as law graduates.

Criticisms of the barrister training process

Critics of the current system have raised the same kind of complaints as those raised against the training of solicitors. The three main criticisms are outlined in Box 13.6.

Complaints against a barrister

Complaints against a barrister can fall into a number of

Box 13.6 *Criticisms of the barrister training process*

1. Only the relatively wealthy can afford it

An increasing number of students on all degree courses struggle to fund their degree. On top of that, government funds are not available to help with the considerable cost of the Bar exam fees. This seems likely to deter people from less well-off families who are considering a career as a barrister. On the other hand, the introduction of a £10,000 salary for pupil barristers is a step forward, as, until recently, pupils earned very little money.

2. Barristers without a law degree are under-qualified

It is seems odd that trainee barristers who do not have a law degree are only required to study six areas of law for one year on the CPE to reach the same point as a law graduate, who will normally have studied law for two more years.

3. There is a shortage of pupillages and places in chambers for the newly qualified

Competition for a limited number of places for pupil barristers is described by the Bar Council itself as 'intense'. The competition within the profession is such that a large number of training barristers find it difficult to earn an acceptable living for several years after they have qualified. It often proves hard to find a place or 'tenancy' in chambers, which is really the only way to gain work.

different categories. First, complaints involving professional misconduct involving some element of dishonesty or serious incompetence. Second, complaints in which it is alleged that a barrister has provided a poor service.

Investigation by the Bar Council

The Bar Council has a complaints procedure and will investigate complaints of professional misconduct and inadequate service. It has a number of powers to deal with justified complaints. These include permanent or temporary suspension from the Bar, a fine, repayment of fees or compensation of up to £5,000. The complaints procedure is overseen for the Bar Council by the Complaints Commissioner, who is not a lawyer.

Legal action in the courts

When a solicitor instructs a barrister, there is only a

contract between the barrister and the solicitor, not between the barrister and the client. This means that the client cannot sue the barrister for breach of contract (although recent developments in contract law may mean that such an action will be possible in the future).

Action in negligence against barristers was until recently limited to pre-trial work which was not closely connected with the conduct of a case in court and written advice on points of law. This was decided in *Saif Ali v Sydney Mitchell & Co. (1980)*. The case of *Rondel v Worsley (1967)* established that a client could not sue for professional negligence in respect of work done by a barrister when appearing in court. However, following the recent House of Lords ruling in *Arthur JS Hall and Co. v Simons and Other Appeals (2000)*, it appears that this immunity has now been removed in relation to both civil and criminal litigation. The leading judgement in this case was given by Lord Hoffman, who said that, in light of changes in the legal system and the law of negligence since 1967, public policy no longer required that advocates should be immune from claims in negligence.

The Legal Services Ombudsman (LSO)

The LSO investigates the way that complaints are dealt with by the professional bodies involved in legal services. An explanation of the LSO's role is given in Section 13.2 above.

13.4 Legal executives

Legal executives work within a firm of solicitors, carrying out relatively routine legal work under the supervision of a solicitor. The professional body for legal executives is the Institute of Legal Executives (ILEX - see Box 13.7 on page 118) which has 22,000 members. Legal executives normally work in one particular area of law, such as conveyancing or probate.

To become a fully qualified legal executive (a Fellow of ILEX) it is necessary to have at least four GCSEs at C or above. Mature students may be accepted on the basis of work experience. Training is on the job, but trainees also need to study part-time for exams. Training normally takes about four years. As discussed earlier, Fellows of ILEX can pursue further training to become solicitors.

Activity 13.3 Would you like to be paid up to £416 an hour?

Judges have expressed concern for some years about over-staffing and the high level of fees paid to QCs in long criminal trials and childcare cases. A few years ago, the House of Lords demanded to know why four QCs were claiming fees of up to £416 an hour. In 2001, Mr Justice Butterfield asked why, in the Old Bailey trial of 11 Afghans suspected of terrorism, the taxpayer had been required to fund a separate QC and junior counsel for each defendant when some had called no witnesses or put forward any evidence (the defence lawyers were funded through legal aid). At the same time, many junior barristers are finding it increasingly difficult to make a decent living.

One Bar Council member said that unless changes were introduced: 'We face a shrinking bar and upheaval in the lives of our rank and file'. Less money is available from the government for legal aid. Fewer cases are being brought in some kinds of work because legal aid has been removed altogether. At the same time, solicitors and others have gained new rights to appear as advocates, so competition for work is becoming fiercer.

If the 'rank and file' really are finding life difficult, the way forward could be to open up new markets and find other ways for juniors to use their skills. Civil practitioners could be allowed to take instruction in advisory work direct from the public. This in turn should have the effect of reducing the cost of legal services to the consumer.

Adapted from the *Guardian*, 27 April 2001 and the *Times*, 10 October 2000.

Mr Justice Butterfield

(a) **When did it cease to be compulsory for two counsel to appear when a QC is involved? What is the current position? (1)**

(b) **Why might QCs argue that they are entitled to be paid higher fees than other lawyers? (4)**

(c) **When can a barrister be instructed without having a solicitor as intermediary present? Why would increased direct access benefit the consumer? (6)**

Box 13.7 *ILEX*

This document was produced by ILEX

Summary

1. How does the job of solicitor differ from that of barrister?

2. How do people train to become solicitors and barristers?

3. What role does the Law Society and Bar Council play?

4. What would you do if you wanted to pursue a complaint against a solicitor or a barrister?

5. What is a 'legal executive'?

Case study ● *Sex, race, class and the legal profession*

Item A Ethnicity and educational background of lawyers

Are there sufficient numbers of black and Asian people in the legal profession? While the proportion of the total UK population from ethnic minority groups is 8.7%, 5% of solicitors with Practising Certificates come from ethnic minorities, 9% of barristers and 2% of QCs. In 1994, a Law Society study on entry into the legal profession found that 47% of white students successfully found articles compared to 21% of Asian students and 7% of black students. Even after factors such as A level results and type of university were taken into account, differences remained.

Stephen Migdal, from the University of the West of England, says that one-third of all places in commercial law firms go to Oxbridge graduates. Students with a public school education dominate Oxford and Cambridge Universities.

What problems does the narrow social background of lawyers create? First, there is a danger that some good legal brains will not be working within the legal system

A training session for solicitors. Just 5% of solicitors are black or Asian. The census of 2001 showed that black and Asian people made up 8.7% of the population as a whole.

because they have been handicapped by prejudice or lack of opportunity. Second, if the legal profession is overwhelmingly male, middle class and white, some sections of society might feel wary about consulting a lawyer and will be less likely to obtain their legal rights. Third, the composition of the legal profession will obviously influence the composition of the judiciary. Many would argue that it is desirable for the judiciary to reflect a wide range of backgrounds. Apart from anything else, what credibility does the legal system have if lawyers are themselves breaking sex and race discrimination laws?

Adapted from the *Times*, 2 April 2002; the Lord Chancellor's speech to the Association of Women Barristers (2002); Migdal, S., *Go forth and Multiply*, UK Centre for Legal Education, 2001; Halpern, D., *Entry into the Legal Professions, Law Society*, 1994; press release by the Bar Council, April 2002.

Item B *Gender and the legal profession*

Academics, and even some sections of the legal Establishment, have, for some time, been concerned that the legal profession as a whole comes from a narrow social background in terms of class, sex and race. Is there any evidence for this? And if it is true, what are the implications?

While it is true that women now make up more than half of entrants to the legal profession, of the 113 new QCs appointed in 2002, only 12 were women. The Chair of the Association of Women Barristers was quoted in the *Times* on 2 April 2002 as saying: 'No wonder only 6% of the High Court bench are women and two of 36 Court of Appeal judges'. It is worth noting that about 15% of those with over 15 years experience as a barrister are female. Lord Irvine, the Lord Chancellor, said in a speech to the Association of Women Barristers that he recognised that women lawyers struggle to maintain their careers while bringing up children, saying:

'They may face prejudice - perhaps a belief among their seniors, or among their clerks, that women with family responsibilities are not really committed to their work. They may not be considered for more challenging or high profile cases. They may lose ground in the competition to keep up with their male peers. But none of this is a reflection on their intellectual abilities or legal skills. Many women lawyers find themselves disadvantaged in their careers simply by circumstances.'

Questions

(a) Briefly summarise evidence in Items A and B that points to (i) sexism and (ii) racism within the legal profession. (6)

(b) Using Items A and B and other parts of the unit, explain why people from low-income families who wish to enter the legal profession, are likely to find it difficult. (4)

(c) How could the Lord Chancellor influence the composition of the legal profession? (3)

(d) Judging from Items A and B and your own knowledge, why might it be argued that it is desirable for lawyers to come from a wide range of backgrounds? (8)

(e) Identify issues other than apparent discrimination that may be giving the legal profession a bad image. (6)

14.1 Introduction – the role of the modern judge

'The part of a judge at a trial of a civil action is to listen to the evidence, only himself asking questions of witnesses when it is necessary to clear up any point that has been overlooked or left obscure, to see that the advocates behave themselves seemly [properly] and to keep to the rules laid down by law; to exclude irrelevancies and discourage repetition, to make sure by wise intervention that he follows the points that the advocates are making and can assess their worth; and at the end to make up his mind where the truth lies.' (Lord Denning in *Jones v The National Coal Board (1957)*)

Judges need to ensure the proper conduct of a trial, including the way that evidence is presented to the court. They must ensure fair treatment of all the parties involved. They should be able to analyse and evaluate the arguments put before the court and reach a decision at the end of the trial. In a civil case, the judge has to decide whether to find for the claimant or the defendant and what damages, if any, should be awarded. In a criminal case, in the Crown Court, the judge has to provide a summary of the facts and the law for the jury and, if the defendant is found guilty, determine an appropriate sentence.

The quote above, though almost 50 years old, provides a fair summary of the role of a modern judge. Having said that, judges have also been given new tasks in the last few years. For instance, judges are obliged under the Human Rights Act 1998 to assess whether legislation is compatible with the rights set out in the European Convention on Human Rights (see Unit 3). And while it remains true that English courts operate an adversarial system, in which judges decide a case based upon the evidence put before them by opposing advocates, the Woolf reforms place a new duty on judges in the civil courts to actively manage the conduct of a trial (see Unit 10).

What kind of people are judges? They are often ridiculed as being old men who are out of touch with the realities of life for ordinary people (see Box 14.1). Lord Chief Justice Parker once remarked:

'A judge is not supposed to know anything about the facts of life until they have been presented in evidence and explained to him at least three times.'

Though this is an exaggeration, it is undoubtedly true that the judiciary is dominated by elderly, white males who have progressed from a privileged life in chambers to a privileged life as a judge. According to a survey carried out by *Labour Research* on Circuit Judges and those in the High Court, Court of Appeal and House of Lords published in December 2002:

- 60% of judges went to Oxbridge
- 67% attended public school (the percentage is higher if Circuit Judges are excluded - 83% of judges in the High Court and above went to Oxbridge and 79% attended public school)
- only 8% of these judges were women (there were seven female High Court Judges out of 109, two female judges in the Court of Appeal out of 36 and no female Law Lords)
- fewer than 1% of these judges were from an ethnic minority group (no judge in the High Court or above was from an ethnic minority group)
- the average age of judges was over 60.

Box 14.1 *Who are the judges?*

Judges are seen as wise protectors of fairness and the truth. This may or may not be true, but perhaps one can have some sympathy with Sir John Dyson, the High Court Judge, when he wrote that:

> 'Judges are ordinary human beings trying to do a difficult and important job conscientiously and with sensitivity.' (quoted in the *Guardian*, 7 May 1996)

Leading judges

Each of the higher courts is led by a judge who is both the most senior judge and in charge of how the court overall is organised and administered. Box 14.2 lists the leading judges in order of seniority.

14.2 Superior judges

The method of appointment, training, and type of work undertaken varies between different judges. Judges can be put into two broad categories:

- superior judges
- inferior judges.

Superior judges work in the High Court and above. Inferior judges work in the Crown Court and County Court. Those who sit on tribunals and Magistrates' Courts are also classed as inferior judges. The different types of judges are examined below, in order of their seniority within the hierarchy. Box 14.3 on page 122 shows the hierarchy as a whole.

Lords of Appeal in Ordinary

Lords of Appeal in Ordinary sit in the House of Lords, acting as the highest court of appeal within the United Kingdom. They are often known as 'Law Lords'. There can be between seven and 12 Law Lords. Normally, they sit in a panel of five. The work of the Law Lords is to hear appeals on a point of law, whether it relates to a civil or criminal case. The Lord Chancellor is entitled to sit as a judge in the Lords, but rarely does so. The Law Lords are also entitled to vote and take part in debates of the House of Lords as a legislative chamber. It should be noted that not all members of the House of Lords are entitled to act in a judicial capacity, only the Lords of Appeal in Ordinary.

The caseload in the Lords is much smaller than that in other courts. Judges in the House of Lords are normally appointed from the ranks of Court of Appeal Judges.

Appointment to the Lords is made by the monarch. This does not mean that the monarch appoints Law Lords, but rather that the Prime Minister makes a decision based on a list of names drawn up by the Lord Chancellor. In practice, the first choice of the Lord Chancellor is rarely refused. Those chosen to become Law Lords do not apply

---

Box 14.2 *Leading judges*

The Lord Chancellor
The Lord Chancellor is the most senior judge in the United Kingdom. The person in this role is also a government minister in charge of a department with responsibility for:

- the effective management of the courts
- the appointment of judges, magistrates and other judicial office holders
- the administration of legal aid
- involvement in carrying through a wide range of government civil law reforms.

In addition, the Lord Chancellor is the Speaker of the House of Lords. Further discussion of the Lord Chancellor's role can be found in Section 14.5 below.

Lord Chief Justice
The holder of this position is the second most senior judge in the English legal system. The Lord Chief Justice is the President of the Criminal Division of the Court of Appeal and technically the most senior judge in the Queen's Bench Division of the High Court, though the Lord Chief Justice only occasionally sits there.

Master of the Rolls
This person is in charge of the Civil Division of the Court of Appeal (the official title is 'President of the Civil Division'). Perhaps the most influential, and certainly the most famous judge of the post-war period, Lord Denning, was Master of the Rolls for some years.

President of the Family Division of the High Court
The post holder is the most senior judge in the Family Division and also has responsibility for the organisation of the High Court.

Vice Chancellor of the Chancery Division of the High Court
The Vice Chancellor is in charge of the day-to-day operation of this part of the High Court (technically the Lord Chancellor is the head of the Chancery Division, but, in practice, very rarely sits there).

Senior Presiding Judge for England and Wales
This post was created by the Courts and Legal Services Act 1990. It involves responsibility for administration of the Crown Court. The Senior Presiding Judge is appointed from the Lords Justices of Appeal.

---

for an advertised vacancy. Instead, they are invited to accept the post, after a range of judges and others have been consulted. How the selection process works has never really been revealed.

Lords Justices of Appeal

Lords Justices of Appeal hear cases in the Court of Appeal. Normally, three judges sit in a Court of Appeal

Box 14.3 *Superior judges*

Name of Judge	Court(s)	Qualification	Appointment system	How dismissed?
Lords of Appeal in Ordinary	House of Lords	a) Held high judicial office (eg Court of Appeal) for two years b) Advocate in High Court or above for 15 years	Appointed by the monarch on advice from Lord Chancellor	By the monarch, following a vote in both Houses of Parliament
Lords Justices of Appeal	Court of Appeal	a) Presently High Court Judge b) High Court advocate for ten years	Appointed by the monarch on advice from Lord Chancellor	By the monarch, following a vote in both Houses of Parliament
High Court Judges	High Court Crown Court (serious cases only)	a) Circuit Judge for two years b) High Court advocate for ten years	Appointed by the monarch on advice from Lord Chancellor	By the monarch, following a vote in both Houses of Parliament

case. They are usually appointed from the ranks of High Court Judges. Those lawyers who have had a qualification as a High Court advocate for at least ten years are also eligible, but it is very rare to become a Court of Appeal Judge in this way. Lords Justices are appointed in much the same way as Law Lords (by invitation only). The first woman to become an Appeal Court Judge in England and Wales, Elizabeth Butler-Sloss, was appointed in 1998. Whereas judges in lower courts tend to specialise in civil or criminal cases, Lords Justice of Appeal sit in both the Civil and Criminal Divisions. Although a minority of cases are appealed to the Court of Appeal, the number of cases dealt with every year by the Lords Justices is far greater than in the Lords. In December 2002, there were 36 Lords Justices of Appeal.

High Court Judges

As well as hearing cases in the High Court, High Court Judges also hear serious cases in the Crown Court. To be eligible to become a High Court Judge, a person must either have been a Circuit Judge for two years or entitled to practice in the High Court for at least ten years. Current eligibility rules were introduced by the Courts and Legal Services Act 1990 (CLSA). The Act introduced changes to the rights of audience of lawyers and, therefore, the qualifications required to become a superior judge. Essentially, the Act made it possible for solicitors to become High Court Judges for the first time, as they became eligible to receive High Court advocacy certificates. Obviously the impact of the CLSA on the composition of the judiciary can only be a very gradual one. For the time being, nearly all High Court Judges are former barristers. In time, more solicitors will have ten years experience of High Court advocacy. Again, appointment is by the Crown, after advice from the Lord Chancellor and by invitation only.

In December 2002 there were a total of 109 High Court Judges. Although technically all judges may sit in any Division, in practice they usually specialise in one of the three.

For some years the High Court has had a permanent backlog of cases, causing unacceptable delays for litigants. To deal with this, the Lord Chancellor has increasingly used Deputy Judges of the High Court who are appointed on a temporary basis.

14.3 Inferior judges

Circuit Judges

Circuit Judges work in the Crown Court or (occasionally) in the County Court. One method of qualifying for appointment as a Circuit Judge is progression from judicial office as a Recorder. The second is holding an advocacy certificate for the Crown Court or the County Court for a minimum of ten years. The third method of qualifying is having been something like a District Judge, Social Security Commissioner or Chair of an Employment Tribunal for a minimum of three years. Whereas superior judges are almost without exception former barristers, about 10% of Circuit Judges practised as solicitors. Circuit Judges, and all other inferior judges, are selected following advertised vacancies with a relatively open selection process. In December 2002, there were 617 Circuit Judges.

Recorders and Assistant Recorders

These part-time judges hear cases in the Crown Court or (occasionally) in the County Court. Their jurisdiction (right to hear cases) is much the same as that of a Circuit Judge, but they hear less complex or serious cases. Applicants must have held a Crown Court or County Court advocacy certificate for at least ten years, though, in practice, it is rare to appoint someone with less than 15 years' experience. Normally an applicant is appointed as an Assistant Recorder for two to three years before being invited to become a full Recorder. There were 1,324 Recorders in May 2002. Appointment as an Assistant Recorder is by the Lord Chancellor following advertisement and an open competition.

District Judges

District Judges work in the County Court, hearing straightforward civil cases. To become a District Judge, a lawyer needs to have had a general qualification for seven years. This means they have a right of audience in all proceedings in any part of the Supreme Court (High Court or above) or all proceedings in County Courts or Magistrates' Courts. Appointment is made by the Lord Chancellor, following advertisement and an open competition. In May 2002, there were 415 District Judges.

District Judges (Magistrates' Court)

Magistrates are usually lay people (ie unpaid and without legal qualifications). They sit in court on a part-time basis. However, in some areas, notably in London, it is difficult to find enough people to be magistrates. Full-time, paid lawyers are therefore appointed to hear cases. These were formerly known as 'stipendiary magistrates'. The qualification is a seven-year general qualification. Appointment is made by the Lord Chancellor, after advertisement. In May 2002, there were 103 judges of this kind.

14.4 Selection and removal of judges

If judges are to be independent of government when they decide cases, rather than acting merely as servants of government, it is important that they have a high degree of job security and cannot easily be removed from post when their decisions are unpopular with government. This explains why judges in the High Court and above can only be removed from office by the Crown after presentation of an address to both Houses of Parliament. This has never happened.

Inferior judges have less security of tenure. They can be removed by the Lord Chancellor on the grounds of misconduct or incapacity. However, such action is very rare. The last time it happened was in 1983 when a Circuit Judge was found guilty of smuggling alcohol and tobacco. In 1994, the Lord Chancellor wrote to judges, setting out the kind of behaviour that might lead to removal. The list included drink driving and causing offence through sexist or racist conduct.

Some judges, such as Recorders and Deputy High Court Judges are appointed on fixed-term contracts. The Lord Chancellor does not have to give reasons for not renewing such contracts. This has sometimes led to the suspicion that a contract has not been renewed because the views of the judge are seen as non-conformist rather than because of lack of ability.

Box 14.4 *Inferior judges*

Name of Judge	Court(s)	Qualification	Appointment system	How dismissed?
Circuit Judges	a) Crown Court b) County Court	a) Presently Recorder b) Crown Court or County Court advocate for ten years c) District Judge or certain other minor judicial office for three years	Advertisement/open competition and appointed by the monarch after advice from Lord Chancellor	By Lord Chancellor on grounds of incapacity or misbehaviour
Recorders / Assistant Recorders	a) Crown Court b) County Court (occasionally)	Crown Court or County Court advocate for ten years	Advertisement/open competition and appointed by Lord Chancellor	By Lord Chancellor on grounds of incapacity or misbehaviour, or contract not renewed
District Judges	County Court	Seven years general advocacy qualification	Advertisement/open competition and appointed by Lord Chancellor	By Lord Chancellor on grounds of incapacity or misbehaviour
District Judges (Magistrates' Court) - paid magistrates	Magistrates' Court	Seven years general advocacy qualification	Advertisement/open competition and appointed by Lord Chancellor	By Lord Chancellor on grounds of incapacity or misbehaviour

The selection of judges

Before putting forward names to the Prime Minister for appointment and before appointing judges to the lower courts, the Lord Chancellor consults a range of other people to obtain views on the individuals under consideration. For some years, there have been suggestions, denied by successive Lord Chancellors, that the consultation process is too secretive and can operate unfairly. In 1999, the Law Society showed its disapproval by withdrawing from the present appointments system. Slapper and Kelly neatly sum up widespread criticisms. Lord Irvine was appointed Lord Chancellor when the Labour government came to power in 1997:

> 'Even Lord Irvine's repeated insistence on the objectivity of the judicial appointments process has done little to remove the suspicion that, because it still relies on the sounding of the senior members of the judiciary and professions, it remains in the final analysis restrictive, conservative and unfair, especially to minority groups.' (Slapper G. & Kelly D., *The English Legal System*, 2001 p.208)

The Commission for Judicial Appointments

In 1999, Sir Leonard Peach was asked to conduct an independent examination of the current appointments process. Peach recommended that a Commission for Judicial Appointments should be set up to monitor how the appointments process worked in practice and to handle complaints from unsuccessful applicants. It was recommended that the Commission would simply have an independent overview, not actually have any role in the appointments process. Decision-making would remain in the hands of the Prime Minister and the Lord Chancellor. The recommendations of the Peach Report were implemented and the first Commissioners were appointed in 2001.

Claims by the Law Society, the Bar Council and others that the appointments process is biased and unfair must be taken seriously, as many of those making such criticisms have witnessed the system at first hand. On the other hand, the selection of new judges by a process of consultation among a range of existing judges can be seen not only as reasonable but even as the best way to gauge the professional skills of the people under consideration. If the appointments process was left to people outside the judiciary and the legal profession, their decision might be more unbiased but how would they take an informed view on, for example, the depth of a candidate's legal knowledge and their ability to work under pressure? Practising judges and lawyers may be much better placed to do this.

The judicial appointments procedure for open competitions

Where there is an open advertised competition for judicial appointments, prospective applicants are sent an

Activity 14.1

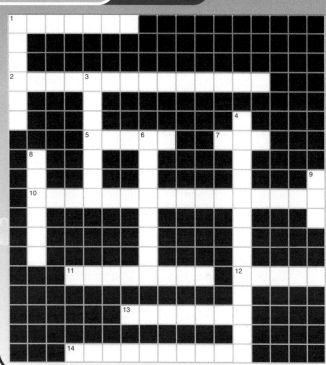

Across

1 This MR was never landlord of the Queen Vic (7)
2 Responsible for appointment of judges (4, 10)
5 Helps a judge during the trial (5)
7 Must be hot under this in the summer! (3)
10 A bit more than governor of the Bentley (6, 2, 3, 5)
11 Somebody who works in the County Court (see also 12 across) (8, 5)
12 See 11 across
13 A Lord of Appeal in Ordinary (3,4)
14 Sounds like Margaret never deviates! (10)

Down

1 A devil of a judge (6)
3 This judge does laps, while hearing cases in the Crown Court and the County Court (7)
4 A judge who hears smaller civil claims (8, 5)
6 Small children make a racket with this judge in the Crown Court (8)
8 The first woman in charge of this part of the High Court has a name like a drunken servant (6)
9 Judges teaching judges (3)

Answers can be found on page 162

application pack containing an application form, a job description, the criteria for appointment and information about who will be invited to provide feedback on the applicants.

The three stages of the appointments procedure for judges up to and including Circuit Judges are application, consultation and interview. The successful candidates are those who best demonstrate that they meet clearly stated selection criteria. The main points from the criteria are listed in Box 14.5.

The consultation process has been criticised by some as too secretive. For example, Marcel Berlins wrote in the *Guardian* on 11 December 2000 that:

'Those consulted by the Lord Chancellor submit their comments in confidence, and candidates often have no idea why they have been rejected; nor do they have any realistic opportunity of challenging what has been said or thought about them.'

In fact, the Lord Chancellor has specified that any allegation of professional misconduct made about a candidate in the course of consultation should be disclosed to the candidate and that they should be allowed to respond. Unsuccessful candidates are also given feedback interviews and told about the content of the assessments.

Box 14.5 *Main criteria used for appointing judges*

The main criteria used when appointing judges are as follows:

- legal knowledge and experience
- intellectual and analytical ability
- decisiveness
- communication and listening skills
- integrity and independence
- fairness and impartiality
- understanding of people and society
- maturity and sound temperament
- courtesy
- commitment, conscientiousness and diligence.

Advocacy is not included in these criteria as Lord Irvine, the Lord Chancellor, made it clear that he does not regard advocacy experience as an essential requirement for judicial office. While judges are required to have been barristers for the required number of years, the kind of work they did is less important. For example, a barrister who has practised primarily in the civil courts may become a Circuit Judge hearing criminal cases in the Crown Court.

Activity 14.2 Who are the judges? (1)

Table 1: Selected judges in the Queen's Bench Division of the High Court

Name	Date of Birth	Date of Appointment
Lord Woolf (Lord Chief Justice)	2.5.33	6.6.00
Sir Patrick Neville Garland	22.7.29	14.10.85
Sir Michael John Turner	31.5.31	7.11.85
Sir Thomas Scott Gillespie Baker	10.12.37	1.1.93 (HC FD 10.10.88)
Sir Douglas Dunlop Brown	22.12.31	4.6.96 (HC FD 19.1.89 CJ 11.7.80)
Sir Michael Morland	16.7.29	17.5.89

HCFD stands for High Court Family Division   CJ stands for Circuit Judge

Table 2: Judicial salaries in England and Wales

Judge	Annual salary (2001-02)
Lord Chief Justice	£171,375
Master of the Rolls	£162,213
Lords of Appeal in Ordinary	£157,699
Lords Justice of Appeal	£149,897
High Court Judge	£132,603
Circuit Judges	£ 99,420
District Judges (outside London)	£79,767

(a) Using Table 1, complete the following tasks.
   (i) Calculate the age of each of the judges shown in Table 1 at the date they were appointed to the Queen's Bench.
   (ii) Calculate their present age.
   (iii) What does this tell us about the judiciary? (2)
(b) Using information on the income of solicitors and barristers in Unit 13 (Sections 13.2 and 13.3) and Table 2, comment on how issues of pay might influence an experienced and successful lawyer who is considering becoming a judge. (6)

Activity 14.3 Who are the judges? (2)

Judges at the opening of Parliament. Most judges are white males who have been educated at public school and Oxbridge.

Table 1: The percentage of judges who are female (as at 1 June 2002)

Type of judge	Female (%)
Lords of Appeal in Ordinary	0
Lords Justice of Appeal	6
High Court Judges	6
Circuit Judges	10
Recorders	12
Assistant Recorders	19
District Judges	18
District Judges (Magistrates' Court)	18

Table 2: The percentage of judges who are black or Asian (as at 1 June 2002)

Type of judge	Black or Asian (%)
Lords of Appeal in Ordinary	0
Lords Justice of Appeal	0
High Court Judges	0
Circuit Judges	1.1
Recorders	2.9
Assistant Recorders	5.8
District Judges	2.8
District Judges (Magistrates' Court)	2.9

Source: Lord Chancellor's Department website.

Table 3: Percentage of those with long service in the legal profession who are women or black or Asian

Lawyer	% women	% black or Asian
Solicitors - over 15 years experience	15.4	*
Solicitors - over 20 years experience	10.9	*
Barristers with over 15 years experience	14.4	5.4
Barristers with over 20 years experience	10.8	4.4

* Relevant figures are not available.

Note: The average length of legal experience of all those appointed through open competition in 2000-01 was just under 21 years.

About 50% of the UK population is female and 8.7% of the population is from ethnic minority groups. In light of this, what comments would you make on the information provided in Tables 1-3? Does the data suggest that the Lord Chancellor is failing to appoint enough women or black and Asian people to the judiciary? (12)

Judicial training

The Judicial Studies Board (JSB) was set up in 1979, following the Bridge Report which set out the most important objective of judicial training as:

> 'To convey in a condensed form the lessons which experienced judges have acquired from their experience.'

The JSB provides training for all full-time and part-time judges in England and Wales in the skills necessary to be a judge. The training is provided by judges for judges. Most of the training provided is for inferior judges and, in particular, Recorders. Assistant Recorders have compulsory training. They must attend seminars on procedure and sentencing before they can sit on their own in the Crown Court. They also have to attend some further training on sentencing. The JSB also has an advisory role in the training of lay magistrates and tribunal members.

The Equal Treatment Advisory Committee, set up in 1991, provides advice and support for all the other committees. In 1996, it started a programme of race training for judges that was the first of its kind in the world. Sir John Dyson, who chaired the committee, said:

> 'A few judges have come to the seminars with great reluctance, protesting that they are colour blind and do not need any lessons in how to conduct a fair trial. The majority, however, realise that they can unwittingly behave in a prejudiced manner and cause offence to members of ethnic minorities, and that they can be helped to reduce the risk of such behaviour by training.' (*Guardian*, 7 May 1996)

Training is also provided on gender and disability awareness issues.

14.5 The position of judges within the UK constitution

A constitution is a system of rules which describes:

- the relationship between the different parts of the state (the government, Parliament and judges)
- the powers of government
- the relationship between government and the citizen.

There are three principles underlying the UK constitution. These are:

- the separation of powers
- the rule of law
- the supremacy of Parliament (see Unit 3).

Judges and the separation of powers

Under the theory of the separation of powers, it is crucial that those involved in one part of the state should not have too much control and influence through links to another part, as this could lead to corruption or other abuse of power. In a constitution with a clear separation of powers, the executive, legislature and judiciary are separate and independent of one another and, therefore, more able to act as a restraint on each other to the benefit of ordinary citizens. It is not desirable for a judge also to be a member of Parliament or of the executive, for example.

As was pointed out above, it is very difficult for the government to remove superior judges. This helps them to maintain a distance from government. They can only be removed on the grounds of misconduct or incapability after a petition has been put to both Houses of Parliament. Clearly, for example, a High Court judgement that has the effect of creating a law that is inconsistent with government policy does not amount to misconduct. So, judges have little to fear as long as they do their jobs properly. On the other hand, it is often argued that the role of the Lord Chancellor is wholly inconsistent with the concept of separation of powers.

The role of the Lord Chancellor and the separation of powers

Not only is the Lord Chancellor in charge of the administration of the justice system, including the appointment of judges, but as Speaker of the House of Lords, the Lord Chancellor also has a significant role to play within the legislature. Still greater potential for abuse of power arises by virtue of the fact that as a Cabinet minister, the Lord Chancellor is very much part of the executive. If the government loses a general election, the sitting Lord Chancellor is replaced by someone from the political party forming a new government. A number of previous Lord Chancellors were very active in politics well before they were appointed. For instance, Lord Hailsham, Lord Chancellor while Margaret Thatcher was Prime Minister, had previously been an MP for many years.

Critics argue that there is a danger that decisions about courts made at the highest level are taken in light of purely political priorities. They also argue that the fact that the Lord Chancellor has a role in all three camps creates a danger of abuse of power. Lord Steyn, the Law Lord, has stated:

> 'The proposition that a Cabinet minister must be the head of our judiciary in England is no longer sustainable on either constitutional or pragmatic grounds.'

Joshua Rozenberg, the legal journalist, put it more bluntly:

> 'Riding three horses is difficult enough at the best of times.' (the *Daily Telegraph*, 20 February 2001)

An example of the difficulties the Lord Chancellor faces is given in Box 14.6.

> ### Box 14.6 *Lord Irvine and the 'cash for wigs' affair*
>
> The actions of Lord Irvine, the Lord Chancellor who was appointed when Labour came to power in 1997, have, at times, been criticised. In February 2001, he wrote to lawyers known to be Labour supporters, inviting them to attend a fund-raising dinner at which they would be asked to pledge a minimum of £200 to the Labour Party. Leading lawyers claimed that they had been put under unfair pressure. Predictably, there were calls for Lord Irvine's resignation from Opposition MPs in the Commons.
>
>
>
> *Derry Irvine who became Lord Chancellor after New Labour won the general election in May 1997.*
>
> Michael Ancram, then Conservative Party Chairman, said:
>
> > 'When the Lord Chancellor is dealing with lawyers over whom he has enormous powers of patronage in the future, when he is eventually going to decide who becomes judges, when he is in a sense the custodian of the independence of the judiciary, then he has to be clearly non-political. He has stepped over that line.' (quoted in the *Daily Telegraph*, 20 February 2001)
>
> Against this, the Lord Chancellor has always taken care not to become involved in cases of a political nature or those where the government has a direct interest. This is, in any event, necessary under Article 6 of the European Constitution on Human Rights which requires that cases be heard by an independent and impartial tribunal established by law. Case law has established that 'independent' includes independence from the executive and the legislature. It would seem that, if the Lord Chancellor sat as a judge, this might be in breach of the Human Rights Act 1998 (see Unit 3).

14.6 Judicial independence

An essential part of the separation of powers is judicial independence. What is meant by independence in this context? Judges need to be independent in several ways. They should be separate from the legislature. They should be able to make rulings without fear of being sacked or disciplined by the government. They should be immune from challenge in the courts by aggrieved parties when acting in a judicial capacity and they should be free from the suspicion of any form of bias. So, are UK judges independent?

Independence from the legislature

Full-time judges are not permitted to be Members of the House of Commons. On the other hand, the Law Lords are able to take a full part in parliamentary debates. In fact, any judge who is a peer may vote in the Lords. It is customary for the Law Lords not to take part in debates on very political issues. However, in the past, they have been prepared to be active in the Lords on a number of issues, notably radical Conservative proposals on sentencing in the mid-1990s. In addition, as already mentioned, the Lord Chancellor is the Speaker of the House of Lords.

Independence from the executive

Judges should not show political bias. In private, a judge may be sympathetic or hostile to the government of the day, but this should not influence how cases are decided. This is particularly relevant in judicial review cases when it may well be a decision of a government minister that the court is being asked to review.

Although the majority of judicial review cases are decided in favour of the government, the courts have not shown themselves to be afraid of deciding against the government in some fairly high profile cases and, in this sense, could be said to have a healthy degree of independence. Examples of cases where the courts have decided against the government are given in Box 14.7 on page 129.

Freedom from bias

Judges should not only act impartially but also avoid giving the **impression** of bias. This is to prevent public confidence in the courts being undermined by suspicions of bias. Having said that, judges are only human. They carry with them opinions and values that, even if subconsciously, must influence them in the courtroom. A judge might be biased on the basis of views formed through their education and background, for example. In the 1920s Lord Scrutton said:

> 'I am not speaking of conscious partiality, but the habits you are trained in, the people with whom you mix, lead to your having a certain class of ideas of such a nature that when you deal with other ideas you do not give as sound and accurate judgements as you would wish.'

Box 14.7 *Judicial review cases where the courts have decided against the government*

In *M v Home Office (1993)*, the House of Lords ruled that a finding of contempt of court could be made against a government minister in either their personal or official capacity.

In *R v Secretary of State for Foreign Affairs, ex parte World Development Ltd (1995)*, the Queen's Bench Divisional Court severely embarrassed the government when it ruled that the Secretary of State had exceeded his powers by granting aid to the Malaysian government for the construction of the Pergau Dam, in order to make it easier to secure an agreement to purchase arms from Britain.

In *R v Secretary of State for the Home Department, ex parte Venables and Thompson (1997)*, the House of Lords decided that the Home Secretary had misused his powers in relation to the defendants in the Bulger case by sentencing them to detention during her Majesty's pleasure.

In *R v Secretary of State for Education and Employment, ex parte National Union of Teachers (2000)*, the Divisional Court held that the Education Minister had exceeded his powers in attempting to alter the contracts of teachers when introducing performance related pay. This was because the teaching unions had not been properly consulted.

Immunity from prosecution

Judges have the power to make court orders that can have an immense impact on the life of the party concerned. If an order for damages is made, this may lead to the financial ruin of a defendant. In family law cases, parents can be separated from their children by court order. Being sent to prison is of course something that has a tremendous impact. Without immunity from prosecution, a judge, in evaluating the facts and the law involved in a case and then making one of these court orders, might be worried about the possibility that a party would take legal action for huge amounts of damages against the judge in person, for example due to some negligence in the way the judicial task was exercised, or for libel. Clearly this could lead to injustices, as judges would sometimes be afraid to make certain decisions. Not only that, there would be many more cases in the courts if litigants challenged the way judges worked as well as or instead of a normal appeal. For this reason, things said or done by judges in court cannot be the subject of a court action. For example, in *Sirros v Moore (1975)*, a judge ordered someone's detention. The Court of Appeal recognised that the detention had been unlawful but ruled that no action could be taken against the judge, as he had acted in good faith in his judicial capacity.

The issue of judicial independence was raised by the Pinochet case - see Box 14.8.

Box 14.8 *The Pinochet case*

In 1973 the elected government of Chile was overthrown in an armed coup led by General Augusto Pinochet. President Allende and others were killed in the fighting. After Pinochet came to power many more people were killed and tortured by his associates over a period of some years, with the General's knowledge. By 1998, however, the country was returning to democracy and the General had received an amnesty in Chile. In poor health, he came to Britain for medical treatment.

Pinochet was arrested, under the terms of an extradition warrant issued in Spain, in relation to his alleged involvement in various crimes during the 1970s. He challenged this on the basis that he had diplomatic immunity (a right to avoid court action in the UK as a member of a foreign government). The case was eventually appealed to the House of Lords. Amnesty International, which campaigns worldwide against torture and imprisonment for political reasons, was given permission to give written evidence. Lord Hoffman, one of the Law Lords hearing the case was, in fact, an unpaid director of Amnesty and his wife was an employee. The House of Lords rejected the claim for diplomatic immunity by a 3:2 majority. Lord Hoffman was part of the majority.

Lord Hoffman, the Lord of Appeal in Ordinary whose links with Amnesty International allowed General Pinochet to escape extradition to Spain.

Because of this link between one of the judges and Amnesty, lawyers acting for Pinochet asked the Lords to set the appeal aside. This was the first time the House of Lords had been asked to conduct a form of judicial review on itself. The House was forced to admit that the failure of Lord Hoffman to reveal a relevant interest invalidated the decision reached in the original Lords hearing. A new hearing in the Lords was set up, with a specially extended committee of seven members. In this re-hearing the same decision was reached, that Pinochet did not enjoy diplomatic immunity, though the basis of the decision was significantly different.

Not surprisingly, the whole affair has not reflected well on the Lords. While nobody questions that Lord Hoffman was entitled to be involved with such a worthwhile cause as Amnesty International, he was wrong not to declare his involvement or withdraw from the case in the first place. It is a basic and well established rule that nobody should be a judge in a cause that they are involved in. This is sometimes known by the phrase ***nemo judex in causa sua***.

Activity 14.4 Avoiding bias

The Lord Chancellor's office published *Guidance on Outside Activities and Interests* in June 2000. The guidance document begins:

'Judges must ensure that while holding full-time judicial office they conduct themselves in a manner consistent with the authority and standing of a judge. They must not, in any capacity, engage in any activity which might undermine, or be reasonably thought to undermine, their judicial independence or impartiality.'

It goes on to say that where any question of bias arises, judges should follow the guidance in cases such as the Court of Appeal judgement in *Locabail (UK) Ltd v Bayfield Properties Ltd and Another (1999)*. Judges must not undertake any other paid work, other than being paid royalties as an author. Nor should they be involved in any activity that limits their ability to perform their judicial duties. They should conduct their personal affairs in a way that minimises the possibility of 'conflict or embarrassment'. If any doubt arises on the application of these principles, a judge should seek guidance from a senior colleague, Head of Division or the Lord Chancellor.

Activities and interests that will usually be permissible
There is normally no objection to a judge having shares in a company.

There is, in principle, no objection to members of the judiciary speaking on technical legal matters, which are unlikely to be controversial, at lectures and conferences. It is well established that the writing of books and articles is not incompatible with holding judicial office.

Activities and interests that may not be permissible
No judge should hold a directorship in a profit-related organisation. Any person holding such a directorship is, therefore, expected to resign from it on appointment to judicial office. Judges involved in charitable activities should be on their guard against circumstances that might be seen to cast doubt on their judicial impartiality or conflict with their judicial office. Judges should not be involved in any kind of political activity. Judges are expected to end all professional contacts with former partners and clients and to terminate connections with their former chambers.

(a) Explain why being involved in 'charitable activities' led to the suggestion of bias in the Pinochet case. **(3)**

(b) The guidance says that judges who are uncertain as to what the rules are should ask their Head of Division for advice. If a judge hears cases in the Family Division of the High Court, who will this be? **(2)**

(c) A male judge has been regularly photographed by the newspapers in various London clubs while dressed as a woman. Comment. **(4)**

(d) Justice Poppycock has a large number of shares in Pills R Us plc, a major drug company which until recently has made substantial profits as the only manufacturer of a particular product. Gluck plc, a fierce rival of Pills R Us, have now brought out a rival drug that will badly affect Pills R Us's sales and profits. At the same time, Gluck are in the High Court as defendants in a negligence case. Judge Poppycock will be the judge in this case. Is this acceptable? **(6)**

What is defined as judicial bias?

For a brief period the Pinochet case raised the possibility that the courts would face an increase in actions challenging judicial decisions. However, the Court of Appeal in *Locabail (UK) Ltd v Bayfield Properties Ltd and Another (1999)* delivered clear guidance on what might or might not be treated as judicial bias. In their judgement the Court of Appeal ruled that there is a well established common law rule that judges should be disqualified from hearing cases in which they have any kind of financial interest. An example would be ownership of shares in a company that was a party to the action (see *R v Gough (1993)*).

A list of other specific circumstances that might be thought to give rise to the danger of bias, (including factors such as religion, age, employment background, education, class, or sexual orientation) was provided in the judgement. These could not be grounds for a claim of judicial bias. Various other circumstances, such as membership by the judge of a society or other body or

previous articles written by the judge would only give grounds for an objection in exceptional circumstances.

A personal friendship, close acquaintance or animosity between the judge and any member of the public involved in the case could create a real danger of bias.

Summary

1. What is the judicial hierarchy?

2. How are different judges appointed and trained?

3. What sort of people tend to become judges?

4. What is the position of judges within the British constitution?

5. What is meant by judicial independence?

6. What criticisms have been made of the post of Lord Chancellor?

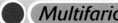

Case study ● *Multifarious Lord Irvine*

The three roles played by the Lord Chancellor

The 'cash for wigs' affair highlighted the many roles played by the Lord Chancellor at the same time. Lord Irvine is the judge who appoints his fellow judges. When he sits as a judge, he does so as the most senior Law Lord. He has been described as a government 'heavyweight' who chairs Cabinet committees on important constitutional reforms. In the House of Lords he 'umpires' political debates as the Speaker.

Although Lord Irvine rarely sits as a judge and avoids hearing appeals in which any government department is involved, many now say that he should hang up his judicial wig for good. In

The Lord Chancellor plays a role in each of the three branches of government - as the most senior judge (the judiciary), as a member of Cabinet (the executive) and as Speaker of the House of Lords (the legislature).

McGonnell v United Kingdom (2000), the European Court of Human Rights considered the impartiality and independence of the Bailiff of Guernsey. The Bailiff, who is appointed by the monarch, is head of the island's judiciary, presides over sittings of its Parliament and has considerable powers in the matter of creating legislation. The Court of Human Rights concluded that in light of Article 6 of the European Convention on Human Rights, which requires that trials should be conducted by an independent and impartial court, any person who is directly involved in creating legislation should not judge any case concerning its application. Why should the position of the Lord Chancellor on the mainland be any different?

In the controversial matter of the fund-raising dinner, Paul Boateng, then Home Office Minister, said on behalf of the government:

'To suggest that what we have here is an abuse of power is absolute nonsense'.

Few would doubt that Lord Irvine appoints QCs and judges on merit. It is worth noting that he (a Labour Party supporter) happily appointed Edward Garnier, a Conservative MP, as a part-time judge. However, the Lord Chancellor has created the unfortunate impression that there is no difference between the interests of the government and the interests of the Labour Party.

Adapted from the *Daily Telegraph*, 20 February 2001 and the *Times*, 27 February 2001.

Questions

(a) What are the 'multifarious', or multiple, roles of the Lord Chancellor? (8)

(b) What is meant by the separation of powers? (6)

(c) How does the position of the Lord Chancellor undermine the concept of judicial independence? (6)

(d) Briefly summarise the system for the selection of judges. Who has influence over this other than the Lord Chancellor? (8)

(e) How easy is it for a Lord Chancellor to remove a judge who might be seen as 'troublesome' by the government? (6)

(f) Why might problems faced by the Bailiff of Guernsey be of interest and concern to the Lord Chancellor? (8)

(g) Evaluate the arguments for and against reform of the position of Lord Chancellor within the legal system. (12)

15.1 Introduction

A jury is a group of people chosen at random from the general public to decide issues of fact in some criminal and civil trials. Juries try serious criminal cases in the Crown Court. The task of the jury is to consider the evidence and then reach a verdict of 'guilty' or 'not guilty'. If a jury finds the defendant guilty, the judge then decides the appropriate sentence, within the law. However, it is the jury which has the final say as to whether a person is sentenced or whether they are able to walk free from the court.

Juries also try some civil cases, such as libel, in the High Court or in a County Court. Juries also sometimes serve in a Coroner's Court.

Many people regard the jury as an invaluable element of the justice system because ordinary people, not the state, determine whether a person is convicted. This helps to prevent possible abuse of power by state officials. The historian E.P. Thompson summed up the view of some commentators when he wrote:

'A jury attends in judgement not only upon the accused but also upon the humanity and justice of the law.'

Others, however, argue that the system of trial by jury is, for a variety of reasons, in need of reform.

15.2 The jury panel and jury selection

There are three stages to setting up a jury:

1. Juries are selected at random from those people aged between 18 and 70 whose names are entered on the electoral register. The electoral register (or electoral roll) lists those eligible to vote in parliamentary or local authority elections.
2. From the list selected, **panels** of jurors - groups larger than 12 - are drawn up.
3. Juries of 12 are then selected at random for individual cases.

People are selected for jury service at random so that there can be no suggestion of the court selecting people who they think are more likely to convict a defendant. Completely random selection does not of course eliminate the possibility of bias. There is no guarantee that a randomly selected group of people will be in any way representative of the population as a whole. A randomly selected jury might be all male, or all female, and, since only around 8% of the population is black or Asian, it is very likely to be all-white.

Jury vetting

Jury vetting is the process of checking the background of potential jurors. The term is used in relation to two types of check - see Box 15.1.

Box 15.1 *Jury vetting*

1. Police checks

The first kind of jury vetting is routine police checks to identify those with criminal convictions. As explained below, convictions may mean that a person is disqualified from acting as a juror. Since the Court of Appeal decision in *R v Mason (1980)*, police checks on potential jurors have been regarded as entirely legitimate.

---

2. Political vetting

The second kind of jury vetting - political vetting - is controversial as it undermines the principle of random selection. It first came to light in 1978 in a case known as the ABC trial, (after the initials of the defendants) which concerned breaches of the Official Secrets Act. It emerged that the police had examined the political views of the jurors to help the prosecution to exercise their right to have certain individuals removed. Because of this, a re-trial was ordered. The Attorney General published guidelines in 1980 that set out when political vetting of jurors is permissible. The current version of the guidelines states that political vetting may be justified only:

- where issues of national security are involved
- where part of the trial is held *in camera* (ie behind closed doors and not open to the press or public)
- in terrorist cases.

Political vetting can only be carried out with the permission of the Attorney General.

Disqualification

Although almost everyone over the age of 18 qualifies for jury service, there are certain people who cannot be part of a jury. The eligibility rules for jury service, which are found in the Juries Act 1974 (as amended by later legislation), are set out below.

1. Criminal convictions

Those who have been sentenced at any time to a term of imprisonment or youth custody for five years or more are disqualified from jury service for life.

Those who, within the last ten years, have received criminal sentences such as a prison sentence, a community rehabilitation order or other community-based orders are disqualified (being fined does not, therefore, disqualify a person). Those currently on bail do not qualify for jury service.

2. Mental disorder or mental health problems

People who are resident in a mental hospital or receiving regular treatment for a mental disorder or mental health problem are ineligible for jury service. In addition, judges have the power to disqualify a person on the grounds of mental health problems.

3. Legal profession or related occupation

People are not qualified for jury service if they are, or ever have been, a judge, a lay magistrate or someone involved in certain senior capacities in a tribunal. People who, within the last ten years, have been a solicitor, barrister or employed in one of a wide range of other jobs within the courts and the criminal justice system (for example as a probation officer, police officer, or employee of the CPS) are also ineligible.

4. The clergy

Priests and ministers of any religious denomination are not eligible for jury service. Nor are people who live in a convent or monastery.

5. Not resident in the UK

People are not eligible for jury service unless they have lived in the United Kingdom, the Channel Islands or the Isle of Man for a total of at least five years since the age of 13 and are eligible to vote in parliamentary or local authority elections.

6. Physical disabilities

Under the Criminal Justice and Public Order Act (CJPOA) 1994, there is a presumption that a person with a disability should serve unless the judge has clearly established that the person will not be able to perform the role. The courts have ruled that profoundly deaf people can only act as jurors with the aid of a sign language interpreter, but, as only jury members are allowed in the jury room when the verdict is being considered, this prevents profoundly deaf people from serving.

15.3 Can people avoid doing jury service?

Jury service may be **deferred** (postponed to a different date sometime within the next 12 months) or a person may be **excused** from jury service altogether. Where a person is excused from jury service, they will only do jury service if their name happens to be selected at random from the electoral register again some time in the future. Being excused is only permitted if the Jury Summoning Officer is satisfied that it is not reasonable to expect the juror to do jury service during the next year.

Although jurors can claim for loss of earnings and travel expenses, many people see jury service as inconvenient. The self employed, who may be concerned about losing business if they are not available for work, and people with senior management jobs, are examples of people who may well be reluctant to commit themselves to unpaid public service. Unless a person has been excused or allowed to defer jury service to another date, failure to attend on the specified date can lead to a hefty fine. The occasions where it may be possible to avoid jury service are set out in Box 15.2.

Box 15.2 *Being excused from jury service*

1. Being excused by right

There are certain grounds where a person may be excused without requiring the agreement of the court. Grounds for excusal as of right include:

- being over 65
- having already done jury service within the past two years
- being a Member of Parliament
- being a member of a religious group whose beliefs are not compatible with jury service
- being employed within certain 'essential' occupations such as the medical profession (including dentistry) or the Armed Forces.

2. Deferral at the discretion of the judge

Anyone with problems that makes jury service extremely problematic can ask to the court to allow them to defer their jury service. The sorts of reasons that may be accepted by the court are illness or important hospital appointments and family events such as holidays that have already been booked. Work commitments are not usually a valid reason for deferring service.

15.4 Can the parties influence who is on the jury?

Suppose that, for one reason or another, either the defence or the prosecution comes to believe that one (or more) jurors is likely to be biased either for or against the defendant. Suppose, for example, that a skinhead is on trial and the prosecution see a person who looks like a skinhead among the potential jurors or suppose that the defendant is accused of assaulting and robbing an elderly lady and there are four stern-looking female pensioners in the jury. Can the defence or prosecution do anything? The answer is that, before the trial starts, counsel for the defendant and the prosecution are given a chance to see the proposed jurors and they do have certain powers to require a person to withdraw from a jury under the Juries Act 1974, even though this runs against the idea of random selection of a jury.

Challenge for cause by the defence

The defence may challenge any number of potential jurors 'for cause'. In other words, the defence can show the judge that there is a good reason why a specific juror should not serve on the jury hearing the case of a specific defendant. A Practice Direction issued by the Lord Chief Justice, however, stated that jurors were not to be excluded on the grounds of race, politics, occupation or religion. This means that challenge for cause will generally be confined to a fairly narrow range of reasons. One sort of acceptable reason would be where a potential juror is personally known to the defendant or is involved in the facts of the case in some way.

Activity 15.1

State with reasons whether the following people are necessarily obliged to serve on a jury:

1. **A solicitor**

2. **A 71-year-old bus driver**

3. **A man who has a hospital appointment to have his tonsils removed**

4. **A woman who was fined a year ago for shoplifting**

5. **A Conservative MP**

6. **A 40-year-old pub landlord**

7. **A man who served 12 years for manslaughter but since his release in 1980 has never been in trouble with the police**

8. **A magistrate's clerk**

(3 marks each)

Challenge by the prosecution

The prosecution has two separate rights of challenge. First, the prosecution has the right to challenge for cause (in the same way as the defence). And second, the prosecution also has the right to ask jurors to **stand by**, without having to give a reason. In this instance, a person is asked to go to the bottom of the list of potential jurors. Technically, that person may still end up serving on the case they were initially allocated, as other jurors may have to drop out altogether, but it is unlikely that they will do so. For example, in a case where the prosecution asks a juror to stand by but two other people from the jury panel then fall ill and some others are excused as of right, the juror asked to stand by then has to return to the 12-member jury. In reality, however, this does not happen very often.

The Attorney General has issued a Practice Note stating that the Crown should only ask jurors to stand by in two exceptional circumstances:

- where a potential juror was 'manifestly unsuitable' - for example, an illiterate person in a complex case requiring the jury to read a large number of documents

- in national security cases where jury vetting has been approved by the Attorney General and the potential juror is shown to represent a security risk.

Defence and prosecution challenge the whole jury

Under Section 5 of the Juries Act 1974, either side may require a whole new jury if they are able to show that the jury has been chosen in an unrepresentative or biased way. This is known as challenge 'to the array'. In *R v Ford (1989)* it was held that this sort of challenge could not be used in an attempt to obtain a multi-racial jury.

15.5 The role of the jury in criminal trials

Jury trial is used in relation to indictable offences and can be used in triable-either-way cases. Indictable offences such as murder, rape and some drugs offences are always tried in the Crown Court. Either-way offences are those where the accused may choose to be tried either in the Magistrates' Court or in the Crown Court (see Unit 12). Either-way offences include a number of offences of violence, including threats to kill and inflicting grievous bodily harm, indecent assault, theft, and most burglaries. In fact, the number of jury trials taking place every year represents a very small proportion of the total number of criminal trials. Magistrates deal with over 95% of criminal trials.

Activity 15.2

Before the trial of *R v Aperson* began, the jury caused a bit of a stir. One juror blew a kiss to the black defendant, who waved back and shouted out 'Hello Gladys!'. Mr Smith, another juror, who was wearing wearing a T-shirt with a racist slogan across it, greeted this with a scowl.

Explain whether Gladys or Mr Smith may be removed from the jury. (6)

During a Crown Court trial, the jury is passive, simply listening to the case as it develops. The judge is in charge and is responsible for making sure the case is presented to the jury in an accessible, understandable and balanced way. The judge also settles any legal argument and advises the jury on the law. The judge acts as a kind of filter through which information is passed. The judge often knows considerably more about the case than the jury as some defence or prosecution evidence may have been regarded as inadmissible by the judge and the jury is not allowed access to the criminal record of a defendant.

The role of a jury is to determine issues of fact, not law. Part of the judge's role is to make sure that the behaviour at issue is unlawful. In many cases this is relatively straightforward. The judge also examines legal questions as to what kinds of evidence can be put before the jury. The judge has to be alert to the jury being influenced by evidence that is, by its very nature, unreliable. This is particularly important in a criminal trial where the prosecution must prove their case beyond all reasonable doubt.

Some types of evidence, such as hearsay evidence, cannot be put before a jury in court. Hearsay evidence is, in simple terms, information obtained second hand - for example, a witness saying: 'I know he said that because Fred told me he had'.

The essence of a trial is that the prosecution presents evidence that could show certain criminal activity was carried out by the defendant. The defendant denies that the charges brought have a factual basis. Which version of

the facts is regarded as the true one is a matter for the jury alone. Box 15.3 gives an example of how this works.

> **Box 15.3** *Questions of law - R v Ireland and Burstow (1997)*
>
> In some cases, issues of law are more difficult to work with. For example, well-established common law rules define an assault as any act which makes the victim fear that unlawful force is about to be used against them. This means that the victim must have feared the immediate infliction of force. In the 1990s, several defendants were tried for assault on the basis of behaviour that did not easily fit this category of behaviour. In *R v Ireland and Burstow (1997)*, for instance, the victim was harassed by someone making numerous silent telephone calls. While this was obviously
>
>
>
> *R v Ireland and Burstow (1997) was concerned with harassment over the phone.*
>
> antisocial in the extreme, the question was whether it amounted to assault in terms of legal principles. This was an issue of law, which the judge was required to consider. When the judge decided that such behaviour could amount to assault, the jury considered whether the right man had been charged and factual issues of that kind.

In the courtroom, members of the jury are merely observers, watching and listening. Paper and pens are provided for the jury to use. These can only be used in the courtroom and the jury room and cannot be taken home. At the end of the trial, notes made by the jury are destroyed. When the prosecution and the defence have called all of their witnesses and made closing speeches, the judge sums up the facts of the case and explains relevant laws to the jury. The jury then retires to the jury room to decide whether the defendant is guilty or innocent.

Reaching a verdict

When the jury considers its verdict in private, it elects a **foreman** (who may be a man or a woman). The foreman speaks for the jury when it delivers its verdict to the court. Plenty of time is allowed to discuss the evidence and to reach a verdict. No other people are allowed into the room while the jury considers and no contact with the outside is permitted, except by giving a note to the usher. What takes place in the jury room must be kept secret. Under the Contempt of Court Act 1981 (s.8), it is an offence to obtain or disclose any details of what happened while the jury was deliberating.

If the jury wants the judge to clarify or explain anything about the case, it may send a note. The jury then returns to the courtroom and the judge gives as much help as possible, but no new evidence can be given at this stage.

Unanimous and majority decisions

The verdict of the jury is given by the foreman in open court. Before the Criminal Justice Act 1967, the jury had to be unanimous to reach a verdict, whether the verdict was innocent or guilty. Since the Criminal Justice Act 1967, a judge may permit a majority decision. In 1967, the government was of the view that jury trials resulted in too many acquittals and that permitting majority decisions would help convict more criminals. Although unanimity fits in with the concept of being satisfied beyond all reasonable doubt, it also makes 'jury nobbling' more likely. Jury nobbling occurs when the defendant or their associates finds some means of intimidating or otherwise influencing a member of the jury.

The judge initially requires the jury to reach a unanimous decision. If, after at least two hours (the judge waits much longer in complex cases), the jury has not been able to reach unanimity, the judge can call it back and tell jury members that a majority decision is permissible. The rules for majority decisions are given in Box15.4.

When the jury cannot reach a verdict, which is known as a 'hung jury', the prosecution is entitled to request a retrial. Retrials are comparatively rare.

15.6 The role of the jury in civil trials

Until the mid-19th century all cases in the common law courts were decided by judge and jury. Since then, there has been a steady decline in the use of the jury in civil trials. Today, under the Supreme Court Act 1981, jury trials are only found in cases of defamation, false imprisonment, malicious prosecution and fraud. Even then, a judge may deny the claimant the right to jury trial for certain reasons, such as lengthy examination of documents or complex scientific evidence. Under the County Courts Act 1984, jury trials may be held in the County Court as well as the High Court. Juries are also used in certain Coroners' Courts (courts which investigate the circumstances of a death).

Box 15.4 *Majority decisions*

No. in jury	Majority decision
12	10 to 2 11 to 1
11	10 to 1
10	9 to 1

Whether the verdict is guilty or not guilty, a majority decision is only permissible with a full jury of 12 people when the votes are at least ten to two. In other words, up to two people may disagree with the majority, but the verdict will still be accepted.

If there are less than 12 people on the jury - for example, if one or more of the jurors falls ill during the course of a trial - then the following rules apply:

● where there are 11 jurors, the majority verdict must be ten to one
● where there are ten jurors, the majority verdict must be nine to one
● if there are only nine jurors the verdict must be unanimous - the jury is not allowed to fall below nine people.

Under the Juries Act 1974, where the jury convicts a defendant on the basis of a majority decision, the foreman of the jury must give details of the number of jurors agreeing and disagreeing in open court. There is no requirement to reveal the size of a majority where the defendant is acquitted.

Where they are involved in civil cases, juries have two roles. First, the jury decides whether the claimant or the defendant has the strongest case. So, as with a criminal trial, the jury makes decisions on issues of fact. Second, in civil cases the jury also goes on to determine the amount of damages that should be paid.

Criticisms of the use of juries in civil cases are outlined in Box 15.5 on page 137.

Can jury decisions in civil trials be overturned?

In *Grobbelar v News Group Newspapers Ltd (2001)*, the claimant, a former goalkeeper for Liverpool FC, was accused by the *Sun* newspaper of accepting money to fix matches. Despite a very strong prosecution case, he had been acquitted in a criminal trial and then went on to bring a libel action against the *Sun*. The jury in this separate civil trial found that Grobbelar had, in fact, been libelled and awarded him £85,000 damages. It is important to remember when considering this decision that the standard of proof required in a civil trial is lower then that in a criminal trial. The Court of Appeal found

Box 15.5 *Criticisms of the use of juries in civil cases*

The main criticism of the use of juries in civil cases is that they are unpredictable when awarding damages. Whereas judges have to determine how much damages should be awarded by looking back to similar cases, juries do not. The amount that a party may be awarded in a jury trial can vary widely and it is difficult for lawyers to predict what damages their clients might win. In 1975, the Faulks Committee expressed doubts as to whether juries should be used to assess damages. It certainly seems that juries have, on occasion, awarded unreasonably high amounts, especially in defamation cases. In *Aldington v Watts and Tolstoy (1989)* damages of £1.5 million were awarded by a jury. This case was taken to the European Court of Human Rights which ruled that the amount awarded was so disproportionate that it amounted to an infringement of Tolstoy's right to freedom of expression under Article 10 of the European Convention on Human Rights (see Unit 3, Section 3.4 for details on this convention). Another example of excessive awards for damages is *John v Mirror Group Newspapers Ltd (1996)*, where the jury awarded £350,000 for libel.

Because of cases like these, under Section 8 of the Courts and Legal Services Act 1990, the appeal courts were given the power to alter the size of awards made by juries. Then, in 1996, the Defamation Act extended the role of judges in defamation cases. This included giving judges the power to set levels of compensation where the defendant has offered to make amends.

the jury decision very hard to accept and said that on a balance of probabilities, no reasonable jury could fail to believe that, in essence, the story printed by the *Sun* was true (if an allegedly defamatory statement is shown to be true, there has been no defamation). This is a very rare example of appeal judges setting aside the decision of a jury, though the House of Lords later reversed their decision.

15.7 Should the jury system be reformed?

The system of jury trial has traditionally been much revered as a way of bringing the good sense and judgement of ordinary people into the legal system. Some judges and academics have made much of its importance within English law, and it is sometimes said to be an essential feature of any democratic society. Lord Devlin

said juries are 'the lamp that shows that freedom lives'. At the same time, criticisms of the justice provided by jury trial have been made. The strengths and weaknesses of juries are examined in Box 15.6.

Box 15.6 *Strengths and weaknesses of the jury - a summary*

Strengths

1. Jury trial is highly regarded by the public.
2. Using ordinary members of the public to decide whether an accused is guilty or not guilty may prevent biased decisions, if judges are seen as too likely to be supportive of the prosecution viewpoint.
3. In cases such as the Ponting trial (discussed below), jury verdicts may be seen as having a corrective effect on unfair or unjust laws.

Weaknesses

1. Research for the Runciman Commission in 1992 suggests that juries too often have difficulty in understanding or remembering evidence.
2. A study by Baldwin and McConville showed that in 25% of the jury decisions examined, legal professionals involved felt that the verdict was probably the wrong one.
3. Some critics argue that too many people manage to avoid doing jury service.
4. In cases which receive a lot of media attention, a jury may be unduly influenced by press coverage before the trial.
5. Random selection does not guarantee a jury that is representative of the population as a whole. This might disadvantage black and Asian defendants.

Research and reports on juries

Proposals for reform of the jury system must come from knowledge of its strengths and weaknesses. But research and analysis of the jury system in England and Wales is severely restricted by the existence of the Contempt of Court Act 1981 (Section 8) which makes it an offence to investigate what happens in the jury room. It would be wrong, however, to say that there is no research on the performance of juries, as there is a significant amount of worthwhile research on real juries in other countries such as the USA. In addition, some UK researchers have found ways of conducting worthwhile investigation into juries without breaking the law. This research is outlined in Box 15.7.

There have been two major government inquiries into the jury system in recent years. First, the Royal Commission on Criminal Justice, known as the '**Runciman Commission**',

Box 15.7 *Research into juries*

1. McCabe & Purves (1974)

In 1974, Sarah McCabe and Robert Purves conducted a study based on 30 cases heard by shadow or mock juries. They were observed trying to reach a decision after hearing real trials. The researchers reported:

> 'The shadow juries showed considerable determination in looking for evidence upon which convictions could be based.'

They also saw the danger in relying on a hunch about guilt. The summary of results went on to say that:

> 'There was little evidence of perversity in the final decisions of these thirty groups.'
> (Sarah McCabe and Robert Purves, *The Shadow Jury at Work*, 1974, p.60)

2. Baldwin & McConville (1979)

A far less favourable view of juries emerged from research conducted by John Baldwin and Michael McConville in 1979. They investigated 370 jury trials. The researchers asked the trial judge, the defence solicitor, the prosecuting solicitor, the police and the defendant whether they had any doubts about the decision of the jury. The study suggested a considerable disagreement between juries and the other key people in a trial. Acquittals were seen as doubtful or highly questionable by three or more respondents in 25% of cases. Baldwin and McConville felt that their study showed that the jury's verdict in some cases was affected by sympathy for the defendant or hostility towards the victim.

conducted a major survey of 800 contested cases in the Crown Court in 1992. It made several recommendations for reform of juries. Second, the wide-ranging Criminal Courts Review by Lord Justice Auld, known as the **Auld Report** was published in 2001. Darbyshire, Maughan and Stewart compiled a review of all the major research up to 2001 for the Auld Report. The findings and recommendations of Auld and Runciman will be referred to in the discussion of specific issues below. Some of the key proposals made in the Auld Report were adopted by the government in the proposals for legislation contained in the White Paper *Justice for All*, published in July 2002.

Public approval and public representation

There is considerable evidence that jury trial is highly regarded among the population as a whole and that the public believe juries do a good job. Helena Kennedy has argued that the opportunity to see the courts in action and participate in that process maintains public trust and confidence in the law. A survey of 900 members of the

Activity 15.3

Juries in libel and slander cases

Elton John.

When Elton John was awarded £350,000 in damages from the *Sunday Mirror* for libel by a jury in *John v Mirror Group Newspapers (1995)*, the Court of Appeal had no doubt that the amount was excessive in comparison to the amount that a judge would have given in a personal injury case. Damages were reduced to £75,000. Giving the judgement of the court Sir Thomas Bingham said:

> 'It is, in our view, offensive to public opinion, and rightly so, that a defamation plaintiff should recover damages for injury to reputation greater, perhaps by a significant factor, than if that same plaintiff had been rendered a helpless cripple or an insensate vegetable.'

Lord Bingham also said that, if the judge gave guidance by suggesting an upper and lower figure, this did not mean that the jury could not choose a figure outside of this bracket but 'the process of mentioning figures would, in our view, induce a mood of realism'. The Court of Appeal took a similar approach in *Thompson v Metropolitan Police Commissioner (1997)* which was a case involving unlawful acts by the police, another type of case where juries have at times awarded astronomical amounts to claimants.

When the Faulks Committee examined the use of juries in defamation cases in the early 1970s, it recommended that a judge sitting alone would be preferable to the use of a judge and jury in some libel and slander cases, such as complex cases and ones where technical legal points were involved. It stopped short, however, of recommending that juries should no longer be used at all. In relation to setting the level of damages, the Faulks Committee felt that this should be taken away from jurors. They simply lacked the required knowledge and experience. It was suggested that the jury should determine whether the damages were to be 'substantial/moderate/nominal or contemptuous' and the judge should fix the specific amount.

(a) In what kinds of action does a jury determine the amount of damages? (4)

(b) Why did the Court of Appeal in *John v Mirror Group Newspapers* feel that the amount of damages awarded by a jury was too high? (4)

(c) When does a judge have the power to set the level of compensation, under the Defamation Act 1996? (4)

(d) How do suggestions for fixing the level of damages differ between the Court of Appeal and the Faulks Committee? (6)

public commissioned by the Bar Council, the Law Society and the Criminal Bar Association showed that 85% felt that jury trial was fairer than trial by a judge and 81% believed that a system with juries produced better justice. It is also worth noting that 66% of those interviewed were opposed to proposals in the Auld Report, which would have the effect of reducing the number of jury trials by two-thirds.

However the Auld Report has put forward some strong reasons for not accepting the view that jury trial should not be reformed. These are summarised in Box 15.8.

Box 15.8 *The Auld Report's arguments against jury trials*

1. The jury is not truly democratic and does not represent all sections of the community because jurors are selected at random. Only those who are selected participate in the trial process.
2. Over the last two centuries: 'judges have been more instrumental than juries in declaring and protecting the rights of citizens'.

Lord Auld (Robin Auld QC), a Lord Justice of Appeal.

3. The use of juries did not prevent the miscarriages of justice uncovered in the late 1980s and early 1990s arising, in the main, from falsification or concealment of evidence.
4. If the jury system is so valuable, why does a jury hear only 1% of all prosecuted crime?

Do juries provide fairness where the law is unjust?

As juries, unlike judges, are not bound by precedent or statute and do not even have to give reasons for their verdict, they are free to acquit or convict someone on the basis of what they as individuals think is fair. There are some cases where the jury verdict is inexplicable unless it is seen as a decision to ignore the facts of the case or the law. These are known as **'perverse verdicts'**.

An example of a perverse verdict is provided by the case of *Ponting (1984)*. Ponting was a civil servant who was charged under the Official Secrets Act 1911 for leaking information about the sinking of an Argentinian ship, the *General Belgrano*, during the Falklands war. This did not pose a threat to the success of the Armed Forces in the war, though it did seem to cause political embarrassment

to the government. At his trial, Ponting did not deny that he had leaked information but claimed that he was not guilty, as he had acted in the public interest. He felt that the public should know what really happened, rather than the official version. The judge said that there was no such defence under the Act. This effectively meant that the jury had to convict Ponting, as he had admitted committing an offence. Nevertheless, they acquitted him. This was regarded by some people as the right thing to do, even though it was in defiance of the law.

The Auld Report is critical of the 'attractive notion of a blow for freedom' that many attach to perverse verdicts of this kind. Auld points out that juries are not democratic and should not be allowed to override the will of Parliament.

It was recommended in the Auld Report that the law should be changed so that juries have no right to acquit defendants in defiance of the law.

Media influence

Jurors should listen to evidence and deliberate on their verdict with an open mind and without being influenced by preconceptions about the case and the defendant. In practice, this may prove very difficult where there has been widespread media coverage of a case before it even reaches trial. The question is whether this prevents defendants from receiving a fair trial. Box 15.9 explores this issue.

Box 15.9 *Media coverage and jury trials*

A good example of a case where there was a huge amount of media exposure is *R v West (1996)*. Rosemary West was involved in the murder of ten girls and women. After the bodies were discovered, there was a huge amount of attention paid to the case in the newspapers and on television. It would no doubt have been virtually impossible to find 12 people who had no prior knowledge of West and who, therefore, were likely to have an entirely unbiased viewpoint. After her conviction in the Crown Court, West appealed on the basis that the media coverage had prevented her from receiving a fair trial. The Court of Appeal rejected the appeal. They said that, if it were allowed, defendants in gruesome murder cases would never be convicted. In such cases, the judge can warn the jury against bringing opinions formed from media coverage into consideration when deliberating on their verdict.

Fred and Rosemary West.

Activity 15.4

The murder of Jill Dando and conviction of Barry George

Jill Dando.

Can you remember where you were when the news that TV presenter Jill Dando had been shot dead was first broadcast on the television and radio? In Michael Mansfield's closing speech for the defence at the trial of Barry George, who was accused of the murder of Dando, he said that her killing was, in that sense, comparable to the death of Princess Diana.

Dando was shot dead on the doorstep of her London home. There were no witnesses to the killing, and very few clues to work on. During a year-long police investigation, the media ran stories on the 'hunt for Jill's killer' on a daily basis. The public was invited to puzzle over detailed speculation about the identity of a suspicious man in a blue suit seen running from the area. As time wore on, a detailed theory about a politically motivated Serbian assassin killing someone seen as 'the voice of the BBC' emerged. The police thought that the killer might have had two lookouts. At one point a policeman was suspended for leaking information to the media. Then Barry George, an eccentric loner, was arrested. Speculation intensified before his trial when details of his past, including obsessions with celebrities, emerged.

The jury in the Jill Dando murder trial was given a warning not to be led by the desire to make someone pay for Dando's death when deciding their verdict. Mr Justice Gage told the jury to ignore the publicity surrounding Dando's murder and to put aside any feelings of anger, sympathy or prejudice. He asked the jury to concentrate on the evidence they had heard in court with a 'cool head and a dispassionate view'.

In July 2001, Barry George was convicted of the murder of Jill Dando, after an eight-week trial. Many of the lawyers and reporters who attended the trial had anticipated an acquittal, but the jurors convicted on a 10:1 majority, after many hours spent considering their verdict. A year later, the Court of Appeal agreed to review the conviction on the basis that key prosecution evidence had been shown to be unreliable.

(a) What problems would the jury in this case have faced when trying to fulfil their proper role? (6)

(b) Do you think that, if the case had been tried by a judge alone, without a jury, the decision-making process would have been more objective? (6)

Do jurors understand or remember evidence?

Lawyers are not notorious for oversimplification. A Crown Court trial may feature lengthy scientific or other expert evidence and complex legal points. Some jurors might find this difficult to follow and, as a consequence, might not reach a verdict after proper consideration of the evidence. Research has suggested that such problems frequently occur.

In the Crown Court study carried out for the Runciman Commission, jurors were asked:

> **Do you think the jury as a whole was able to understand the evidence?**

Only 56% said that all the members of the jury were able to understand the evidence, while 41% said that most understood.

Fraud trials pose a particular problem. They can involve complicated evidence about accounting procedures, which might confuse a jury. Fraud trials also tend to be quite long. The Auld Report said that complex fraud cases were 'fertile ground for error and injustice that are, in the main, undetectable by way of appeal'.

The Auld Report recommended that the judge should be empowered to give the jury a series of written factual questions, tailored to the law and to the issues and evidence in the case.

The composition of juries

In the Auld Report, concern was expressed about the very large numbers of people who are summoned but are excused or defer jury service. A 1999 Home Office research project showed that, in a sample of 50,000 people summoned for jury service in June and July 1999, only one-third was available for service, about half of whom were allowed to defer their service to a later date.

The Auld Report was concerned that, too often, juries were deprived of the experience and skills of a wide range of professional and otherwise successful and busy people. Auld felt that the large number of jurors being excused created the impression that: 'jury service is only for those not important or clever enough to get out of it'.

Black and Asian people and juries

In cases where an all-white jury takes part in the trial of a black or Asian person the question arises as to whether the black or Asian person can be sure of a fair trial since there is the danger that some jurors might have views that prejudice the outcome of the trial. Dr. Penny Darbyshire's analysis of research on juries for the Auld Report says that there is evidence that the race of jurors can adversely affect the verdict in cases where either the defendant or the victim or witnesses are of a different race from those on the jury. One solution to this problem might be for the defendant to exercise the right to challenge jurors. Another would be for the judge to require some jurors to be of the same ethnic group as the defendant or victim or witness.

Under present law, however, deliberately creating a multi-racial jury is not possible. The Court of Appeal ruled in *Thomas (1989)* that a judge could not influence the composition of the jury by directing that a multi-racial jury be empanelled. Lord Lane said that there was no principle that juries should be racially balanced as that assumes that jurors of a particular race would be incapable of giving an unbiased verdict. In 1993, however, the Runciman Commission recommended a change in the law. This proposal is outlined in Box 15.10.

> **Box 15.10** *The Runciman Commission proposal*
>
> The Runciman Commission recommended in 1993 that, in exceptional cases with 'a racial dimension' involving a black or Asian defendant or victim, judges should have the power to order the selection of a jury consisting of up to three people from ethnic minority groups, where they were persuaded that it was needed. The Auld Report made similar recommendations and also suggested methods of widening the pool of potential jurors so as to include better black and Asian representation countrywide. An argument against such reforms is that they would interfere with the principle of random selection.

15.8 Alternatives to jury trial

If it is accepted that jury trial is not always desirable, other options include trial by:

- a judge alone
- a panel of judges
- judges and lay assessors together.

Trial by a judge alone

One possibility is for the single Crown Court Judge to act as both judge of law and fact. One argument against this is that judges may become 'case hardened'. In other words, they might become cynical about the need to assume that a defendant is innocent until proven guilty because they hear a great many similar cases. It is also said that a single judge would be unable to draw on the same pool of understanding and experience as 12 people from different backgrounds.

On the other hand, judges are trained to evaluate cases as lawyers and, therefore, do not have the same difficulties with complex fraud trials as juries. In fact, defendants in such trials are able to opt for trial by a judge alone in many other countries. The popularity of this approach comes partly from its provision of a simpler and speedier procedure than trial by jury. Judges can get to grips with complex facts much more quickly than juries. If trials are quicker, they are also cheaper. Allowing judges to decide questions of fact has the advantage that they would be required to give reasons for their verdicts, and the decisions of judges can be challenged in the appeal courts, whereas the decisions of juries cannot.

Trial by a judge alone has been tried before. Box 15.11 examines what happened.

> **Box 15.11** *Diplock Courts*
>
>
>
> In 1973, the Northern Ireland (Emergency Provisions) Act was passed, abolishing jury trial in favour of trial by a single judge in Northern Ireland cases involving terrorism, due to a lack of confidence in the ability of jurors to bring in a fair verdict. Lord Diplock headed an inquiry into the problem. His report revealed various problems including intimidation of witnesses by terrorists and the danger of perverse acquittals of Loyalist terrorists by mainly Protestant juries. The Diplock Committee recommended that judges should replace juries in certain criminal trials. These non-jury courts were known as 'Diplock Courts'.
>
> *Lord Diplock.*
>
> The Auld report argued that Diplock Courts had earned 'a fair degree of public acceptance'. He recommended that defendants, with the consent of the court after hearing representations from both sides, should be able to opt for trial by judge alone in all cases now tried on indictment. The 2002 White Paper *Justice for All* adopted this proposal. It also proposed trial by judge alone 'in serious and complex fraud trials, and in some other complex and lengthy trials or where the jury is at risk of intimidation'.

A panel of judges

Many of the possible attractions offered by replacing the jury with a single judge are also present if a panel of judges were used. The verdict could be explained, the judges would be more skilled in analysis and more able to understand the law, and the trial would be quicker and cheaper than jury trial. The disadvantages are also similar. The possibility of case-hardened judges still arises and nearly all judges come from the same social background (and so a panel of judges would not reflect the broad range of experience that a jury reflects). There might also be practical problems with finding enough suitable judges, and such a system would be more expensive than trial by a single judge.

The use of magistrates or other lay assessors with judges

The most dramatic change to the criminal justice system proposed within the Auld Report was the creation of an intermediate court to deal with either-way offences, consisting of a judge and two lay magistrates (see also Unit 12). Under these proposals, only the judge would be able to determine questions of law. The judge would not sum up the case but would retire with the magistrates to reach a verdict. In fact the concept of an intermediate court was not adopted within the White Paper *Justice for All.*

The Auld Report said that this intermediate court would draw on the strengths of trial by judge and the use of lay magistrates. Although they are not legally trained, magistrates are effectively part-time volunteer judges. So, one advantage of such a system would be considerably shorter trials than with a judge and jury, since the magistrate members would be familiar with the procedures of the court, together with much of the law required. However, if it is seen as important to draw members of a decision-making court from a wide selection of people and bring in differing opinions, a disadvantage would be that magistrates come mostly from middle-class and upper-class backgrounds (though not necessarily from the same restricted social circles as judges). When jurors are selected randomly from the electoral register, they obviously contain a much wider range of people.

Summary

1. How are juries selected?

2. Can people avoid serving on juries?

3. Can the parties influence who is on a jury?

4. What role is played by the jury in (a) criminal trials and (b) civil trials?

5. Should the jury system be reformed?

6. What are the alternatives to the use of juries?

Case study | Trial by jury

The problem of secrecy

What goes on behind the jury room door and how do 12 ordinary people reach the verdict that could put someone in prison for years? Try asking them and you could face a large fine and a spell in prison yourself. In 1992, the *Mail on Sunday* was found guilty of contempt of court and fined £75,000 for publishing interviews with jurors in the Blue Arrow fraud trial about how they reached their verdicts.

"The jury will ignore that last remark…"

No-one questions the general principle that justice must not only be done but be seen to be done. Yet, a veil of secrecy hangs over the jury room. Researchers are banned from questioning jurors to find out how the system works in practice and how it could be improved. The Court of Appeal has even refused to inquire into what happened in the jury room when faced with a claim that some irregularity made a conviction unsafe. In the words of Lord Devlin, the jury is 'the lamp that shows that freedom lives'. But, says Clare Dyer, legal editor for the *Guardian*, 'the lamp must not be lit too brightly - it could show up the warts and dent public confidence'.

In New Zealand, the law is less strict and research into real juries is possible. A major study was conducted there for the New Zealand Law Commission in 2000. The research team interviewed 312 jurors as well as many judges. A key finding was the considerable difficulty that many jurors had with understanding the requirements of the law. 'Fairly fundamental' misunderstandings of the law emerged during deliberations in 35 of the 48 cases. Is it surprising that ordinary people find it hard to grasp difficult concepts - such as the burden and standard of proof, the elements necessary to prove an offence and rules of evidence - when they have heard them only once from the judge and were given no written record? Suggestions from the authors of the report include more guidance for jury foremen, providing the jury with a written summary of the judge's summing up on the law, more help with flow charts and other aids in cases with several defendants, and more encouragement to ask the judge questions.

Adapted from *Juries in Criminal Trials*, New Zealand Law Commission, 2000.

Questions

(a) Under which UK Act is questioning jurors on what happened in the jury room unlawful? (2)

(b) In which sorts of cases are jurors most likely to experience difficulties? (6)

(c) How can a jury seek assistance after it has retired to consider its verdict? (3)

(d) What arguments can be made for relaxing the law in respect of research into juries? (6)

(e) What are the arguments against such a reform? (6)

(f) Discuss the value of jury trial as a way of providing justice. (10)

16 Magistrates

16.1 Introduction

Lay people - people who are not professional lawyers - play an important part in the delivery of justice within the legal system. They may be part of a jury (see Unit 15). They may sit on administrative tribunals (see Unit 11). Or they may hear cases in one of the many local Magistrates' Courts. This unit examines the role played by magistrates, sometimes known as 'Justices of the Peace' (JPs), in England and Wales.

The Lord Chancellor's Department website contains basic guidance about the work of a magistrate. It states:

'Laws in this country are made and enforced on behalf of the people. It is a tradition that ordinary people, untrained in the law, should take part in the legal process - either as members of juries or as magistrates.'

The use of the word 'tradition' often implies that something is widely regarded as of value simply because it has been around for a long time. This is certainly true of the use of magistrates for hearing cases, which goes back at least 800 years in England. But more than that, the quotation above implies that the magistracy is given a role in the law because it is somehow felt to be more democratic, more representative, than the use of paid, full-time judges.

What do magistrates do?

Magistrates are involved in judging issues of fact and law in a trial. Unlike a jury in the Crown Court, magistrates also determine the appropriate sentence. Magistrates normally exercise their duties as part of a bench of three, with assistance and advice on matters of law from a legal adviser, also known as the 'clerk'. The Chair of a bench is in charge of the conduct of the trial, and is assisted by two other magistrates, known as 'wingers'. Each magistrate has a say in reaching a verdict and deciding what sentence should be passed. Magistrates' Courts try about 95% of criminal cases. All summary offences are heard in the Magistrates' Courts. The majority of offences triable-either-way are also heard by magistrates (see Unit 12). Only a jury hears the most serious offences, known as 'indictable offences'. The Magistrates' Court also sits as a Youth Court, to hear criminal cases involving those under the age of 18. Magistrates are drawn from a special panel for this purpose.

The other work done by magistrates is outlined in Box 16.1.

Box 16.1 *Work done by magistrates (other than hearing criminal cases)*

1. The awarding of antisocial behaviour orders

Since the introduction of the Crime and Disorder Act 1998, Magistrates' Courts have been able to award antisocial behaviour orders (see Unit 21). These are civil orders, but criminal sentences may be used if they are breached.

2. Hearing civil cases

Magistrates also handle certain sorts of civil cases. They hear civil cases involving:
- the enforcement of debts owed to the utility companies (gas, electric and water)
- debts owed to local authorities for council tax
- non-payment of television licences.

3. Hearing cases involving family law

Some magistrates, who are part of the special family panel, specialise in cases involving family law. These include:
- some cases under the Children Act 1989 (adoption proceedings and applications for orders for residence or contact with children)
- the setting of maintenance payments (for spouses and children)
- awarding personal protection and exclusion orders sought by victims of domestic violence, under the Domestic Proceedings and Magistrates' Courts Act 1978.

4. The granting, renewing and removal of licences

Magistrates grant, renew and remove licences for selling alcohol in public houses, off licences and other licensed premises.

Magistrates are expected to undertake a fair share of the work of the Bench (group of magistrates) to which they belong. A magistrate must sit for at least 26 half days each year and try to be available to sit for up to 35 half days each year. Magistrates are also required to undergo a certain amount of training.

Who can be a magistrate?

The Lord Chancellor appoints magistrates after consultation with local Advisory Committees, who conduct a selection process. Eligible candidates may apply or their names may be suggested for consideration. The

Lord Chancellor will not generally appoint a person under 27 or over 65. Magistrates must retire at the age of 70.

Applicants must live within the area in which they wish to be a magistrate. They should have a reasonable degree of knowledge of the area to which they wish to be appointed and are expected to have lived in that area for at least a year. Applicants should be in good health so that they are able to listen to cases for a long time without losing concentration. Those with a disability are not discouraged from applying.

Under s.50 of the Employment Rights Act 1996, employers are required to give employees reasonable time off work to be a magistrate, though there is no requirement to give paid time off.

The following people are not eligible to be a magistrate:

- Members of Parliament
- people in the Armed Forces
- people working in the criminal justice system such as police officers, prison officers or employees of the Crown Prosecution Service (applicants with a spouse or partner in such employment are also ineligible)
- those convicted of a serious offence or a number of lesser offences
- undischarged bankrupts (those made bankrupt whose financial affairs are still being regulated by court order).

This is not a complete list. Other grounds for excluding an application from consideration may emerge during the selection process.

What kind of personal qualities are needed to be a magistrate?

Factors such as occupation are far less important than general personality and character. There are six key qualities sought in the selection process. These are outlined in Box 16.2.

16.2 The social background of magistrates

In the introduction to this unit it was suggested that magistrates are given a role in the law because it is somehow felt to be more democratic, more representative, than the use of paid, full-time judges. If this is true, then the composition of the bench in each area should reflect as far as possible characteristics of the population in general, and characteristics of the local population in particular. The degree to which the magistracy is representative may be assessed in a number of ways,

Box 16.2 *The six key qualities needed to be a magistrate*

An artist's impression showing magistrate Timothy Workman sitting at Bow Street Magistrates' Court in London in January 2003.

1. **Personal character**
   For example, applicants must have the respect and trust of others, and must be able to maintain confidentiality.
2. **Understanding and communication**
   The sort of things that are looked for include the ability to absorb documents, identify what is relevant and what is not, and the ability to communicate effectively.
3. **Social awareness**
   This includes respect for different cultures, and understanding of the local community.
4. **Maturity and sound temperament**
   Maturity does not mean of advanced years, it indicates qualities such as regard for others, the ability to learn from advice and the ability to work with others. 'A sound temperament' refers to qualities such as courtesy and determination.
5. **Sound judgement**
   This involves the ability to think logically and approach decisions in an objective way, without prejudice.
6. **Commitment and reliability**
   It is important that the applicant is happy about committing considerable amounts of their own time and will attend court when agreed. The applicant will also need to show that they have the support of their employer.

including by gender, social class, income, age and ethnic origin. Lord Chancellors since the 1960s have also sought to move towards the right balance regarding political sympathies.

Is the magistracy representative?

The Auld Report concluded that:

'The fact that the magistracy is not a true reflection of the population nationally or of communities locally is confirmed by a number of studies.'

The main study referred to was that carried out by Morgan and Russell for the Home Office in 2000.

The Morgan and Russell study showed that the magistracy is, at least, gender balanced. Almost 50% of magistrates are women. Harry Mawdsley, Chair of the Magistrates Association has pointed out that, since men overwhelmingly dominate the professional judiciary, the lay magistracy is, at present, the only place that women can make a contribution to the criminal justice system.

On a national basis, black and Asian people are under-represented. The 2001 census revealed that black and Asian people make up c.8.7% of the population as a whole. The proportion of magistrates from black and Asian groups on a national basis in 2002 was as follows:

- 2% African-Caribbean magistrates
- 2% from the Indian sub-continent or of Asian origin
- 1% other non-white magistrates.

In terms of socio-economic status or class, Morgan and Russell conclude that magistrates are overwhelmingly drawn from professional and managerial groups. They are, as a result 'disproportionately middle class, and almost certainly financially well-off, compared to the population at large'.

The magistracy is also not representative of the general population in terms of age. Two-fifths is comprised of retired people. This imbalance is made worse by their ability to sit more often than those in work.

It would seem that the majority of magistrates are likely to vote Conservative in elections, even in many areas where Labour traditionally does well. It might be that this is a reflection of the fact that most magistrates are middle class.

Why is the magistracy not representative?

The Lord Chancellor, Derry Irvine, has made it clear that he wants the magistracy to be more representative, and has taken steps to try and encourage a broader range of people to become involved. But why has the problem arisen? The factors which play a part are outlined in Box 16.3.

16.3 The training of lay magistrates

Although there is no requirement for lay magistrates to be legally qualified, they are required to attend training courses. The content of the training is supervised, though not delivered by, the Judicial Studies Board (See Unit 14, Section 14.4). The main elements of this training are outlined in Box 16.4 on page 147.

Box 16.3 *Factors which ensure the magistracy is not representative*

1. Loss of earnings

People on lower incomes are not likely to be able to afford to become magistrates. Although an allowance is paid for transport and meals, the loss of earnings allowance is modest. Employers are not required to pay staff while sitting as magistrates.

2. Time spent working as a magistrate

Not everyone is willing or able to commit themselves to an absolute minimum of two half days per month, especially if this means a loss of earnings. There has been a trend for British workers to work longer hours in recent years, which obviously does not help.

3. Lack of public awareness

The Auld Report was critical of the amount spent on trying to attract members of the public to become magistrates. It pointed out that, while the government spent £4.7 million on publicity for the Territorial Army, only £35,000 was spent on raising awareness of the magistracy.

4. Inconsistent approach

Advisory Committees are left to devise their own methods to recruit magistrates. The Auld Report noted that there were considerable variations in the way that committees go about this from area to area. Some, it claimed, are too reliant on drawing from a network of 'the great and the good', such as local councillors, school governors and so on.

In 2001, the Judicial Studies Board had a trivial budget for training magistrates: £175,000 out of a total of over £5 million. Considering that magistrates hear 95% of criminal cases, critics argue that this is unacceptable. The Magistrates' New Training Initiative (MNTI - see Box 16.4 on page 147) has also been criticised as too complex in the Auld Report and elsewhere. There are no less than 104 'competences' that must be met. It is also said that the MNTI has not been implemented consistently across the country - some areas provide better training than others. The Magistrates' Association, a group that represents and supports magistrates, does a great deal to make up for the patchy nature and lack of consistency in training, with its own training unit.

Box 16.4 *The main elements in magistrates' training*

1. The Magistrates' New Training Initiative (MNTI)

The MNTI is a 'competence-based' training and appraisal scheme. This emphasises practical skills required, such as the ability to summarise evidence and approaches to handling witnesses. Specially trained magistrates observe and assess new recruits in action.

2. National guidance

Magistrates receive occasional national guidance on specific matters. For example, before the Human Rights Act 1998 was implemented, magistrates received considerable training.

3. National training courses

Advice and residential national training courses for Chairs of benches are provided when they are selected.

4. Database

A database of approved training materials has been set up.

Activity 16.1

The recruitment problem

Smaller companies may not be ready to let their staff have time off to be magistrates. 'I was secretary to my husband's firm, and he always said that if I had just been another employee, he'd never have allowed me time off', said Anne Knight, a Justice of the Peace. Local councils, and organisations such as banks and building societies look more favourably on the idea. But schools are increasingly reluctant to give staff time off to sit on the local bench. Many head teachers have tight budgets and are not keen at the idea of getting supply teachers in. As a result, teachers now have to limit their sittings to school holidays. The time commitment is considerable. The minimum number of half day sittings a magistrate must attend in one year is 25, though 35 is preferred. There is a danger that only retired colonels and non-working people will want to become magistrates, although people who are not working normal business hours, such as those in call centres or the leisure industry, and the self employed, may have less of a problem.

Adapted from the Guardian, *3 October 2001.*

(a) Can an employer be required to give an employee time off to be a magistrate? (3)

(b) Does the magistracy have a good gender balance? (2)

(c) Dave is a self-employed painter and decorator with a wife and three children. How easy might he find it to commit himself to being a magistrate? (6)

16.4 District Judges (Magistrates' Courts)

Most magistrates are lay people. But a small number of magistrates are professional lawyers who are employed to work as magistrates where it has proven difficult to recruit sufficient numbers of lay magistrates. This type of magistrate is called a 'District Judge' (there are two sorts of District Judges - the other sort hears cases in the County Courts - see Unit 14, Section 14.3). District Judges were formerly called 'stipendiary magistrates'. In May 2002, there were 103 District Judges, compared to over 30,000 lay magistrates.

The Lord Chancellor appoints District Judges. Only barristers or solicitors who have practised for seven years are eligible. The majority are solicitors. District Judges tend to be mostly male (about 84%), white (about 98%) and middle-aged (more than 50% are aged 45-54, though, in the main, they are younger than magistrates). Both the Auld Report and the Runciman Royal Commission recommended that there should be a more systematic approach to the role of these professional judges in the summary trial system to make the best use of their special skills and qualifications. However, some people criticise the use of professional magistrates on the grounds that, if there were better systems for finding lay magistrates, it would not be necessary or desirable to have them.

16.5 Justices' clerks and other legal advisers

Every court is assisted by a legal adviser, or clerk, who is responsible for the administration and smooth running of the court and providing legal advice, where required, to magistrates. Although many of these advisers are legally qualified, some are not. The government decided that, starting from 1 January 1999, all legal advisers must qualify as a barrister or solicitor within ten years.

In addition, legal advisers are supervised by a justices' clerk (also known as a 'senior clerk') who is always qualified as a barrister or a solicitor. A recent re-organisation has led to a significant reduction in the number of justices' clerks, with the result that many of them now serve several benches and hundreds of magistrates spread over a large geographical area.

16.6 An evaluation of the work done by magistrates

Representative?

As noted above, key sections of the population are not represented in proportion to the size of each group. This may have a detrimental effect on the quality of the decision-making process. For example, a white, middle-aged and middle-class magistrate may well have a poor insight into the behaviour and attitudes of a black, young, and working-class male witness or defendant.

On the other hand, it could be argued that magistrates should be representative in the sense that what is most important is that they try to act in a way that reflects the concerns and interests of their local community as a whole. In other words, magistrates should take decisions that reflect the interests of everyone, not just those of the particular race, generation, and class to which they themselves belong. According to this argument, what decent, law-abiding people need from the criminal justice system does not vary all that widely between one social group and another. Looked at from this point of view, magistrates may or may not be representative. There is no real evidence either way.

Public confidence?

Another reason that is traditionally advanced for retaining the lay magistracy is that the public is said to have more confidence in lay justice than it does in professional judges. In fact, there is significant evidence that members of the public are deeply ignorant about criminal trials. In 2001, a large-scale survey carried out by Professor Andrew Sanders for the Institute of Public Policy Research (IPPR) showed that:

'The public knows little about how the magistracy works. One third...did not know that the majority of magistrates are lay people. They also hugely underestimated the proportion of cases heard in the lower courts. The role of the magistracy is not visible to the public.'

Cost effective?

A trial using lay magistrates is significantly cheaper than a Crown Court trial by judge and jury. If District Judges

The Auld Report on criminal justice, published in 2001, said that a whole range of broad, overlapping and vague notions had to be taken into account when considering the debate over whether lay or professional justice is better. These notions, it said, include: 'public confidence, lay justice, people's or citizens' justice, "participative

Lord Auld (Robin Auld QC), a Lord Justice of Appeal.

democracy", "locality" or community justice, magistrates as "surrogate jurors", judicial independence and, the right to a "fair" trial.' In support of District Judges, the Auld Report said, are the more concrete qualities of 'legality, consistency, speed and other efficiency and effectiveness'. The Auld Report recommended that, in summary trials, work should be divided between District Judges and magistrates as follows:

- District Judges and magistrates should not routinely hear cases together, but there might be occasions when this would be an advantage
- there should be no significant increase in the number of District Judges
- District Judges should deal with cases of legal or factual complexity, urgent cases, and long cases.

Harry Mawdsley, Chair of the Magistrates Association, recognises that cases which involve difficult legal concepts and cases which seem likely go on for a long time would be more efficiently and expertly handled by a District Judge. But, he says that there is a feeling among his members that stipendiaries should take their fair share of the more mundane work. 'They should do some road traffic and we should not see them taking a chunk of work that is reserved just for them', he says. If Justices of the Peace are only allowed to tackle routine offences, their numbers will decline, argues Mawdsley.

Adapted from the Auld Report, Review of the Criminal Courts of England and Wales, 2001 and the Times, 9 January 2001.

(a) What are the differences between a District Judge and a lay magistrate? (3)

(b) What advantages might District Judges have over lay magistrates? (5)

(c) What are the possible drawbacks of using District Judges? (8)

entirely replaced lay magistrates, thousands of new judges would have to be recruited. Each judge would have to be paid a considerable salary. At present a District Judge earns about £90,000 a year. In addition, there might be difficulties in recruiting sufficient numbers of lawyers with the right ability and experience. On the other hand, District Judges can deal with cases considerably faster than lay magistrates so the cost might be less than it at first appears.

Local knowledge?

It is sometimes said that magistrates have the advantage of local knowledge. This may be useful where, for example, knowledge of local road conditions helps understand evidence presented in court. On the other hand, local magistrates are more likely to recognise repeat offenders. They may have strong views about local issues - for example, problems on particular housing estates. This sort of knowledge could make it harder for the magistrate to consider objectively whether or not a defendant is innocent and to determine a fair sentence.

High conviction rates?

Some critics argue that lay magistrates, unlike juries, are in danger of becoming too close to the police and the Crown Prosecution Service, with the result that they become biased towards the prosecution. Obviously, magistrates encounter people from both organisations on a regular basis. But supporters of the current system argue that such a charge is unfair to most magistrates, not least because their training seeks to make them aware of such a danger.

If magistrates really do tend to believe the prosecution more than the defence, a high conviction rate compared to jury trial would be expected. A 1985 study of 305 Magistrates' Court trials and 320 Crown Court trials by Julie Vennard for the Home Office revealed that the acquittal rate in the Crown Court was 57% compared with 30% in the Magistrates' Courts. However, Vennard was not able to explain this marked difference in outcome. It could be that juries are too ready to acquit rather than that magistrates are too ready to convict.

Inconsistent sentencing?

Concern has been expressed at the very considerable variation in sentencing practices between different benches. This inconsistency is unsurprising in one sense

given the enormous numbers of cases dealt with by magistrates every year. Magistrates in one area may have tougher attitudes than those in another area when it comes to sentencing for a particular type of offence because the offence is more common. Home Office research published in 1995 showed, for example, that while 70% of those driving while disqualified were sent to prison in West Derbyshire, nobody was jailed in Cirencester, Gloucester or Beverley.

Do legal advisers have too much influence?

There has been some suspicion that court clerks may have too much influence over the decision-making process of magistrates. Clerks are often legally qualified and always more experienced in the work of the courts than lay magistrates. Some clerks often go with their magistrates when they withdraw to consider their verdict, though they may only do so when invited by the bench and they should only advise the magistrates in the exercise of their power.

With these issues in mind a Practice Direction issued in 2000 set out rules aimed at preventing clerks from unfairly influencing magistrates 'behind closed doors'. The rules are:

● magistrates may seek the advice of their legal adviser, including reference to notes

● such advice should normally be given in open court

● any legal advice given to the justices other than in open court should be repeated in open court and parties to the case may put forward comments on the advice.

Summary

1. What do magistrates do?

2. Who are magistrates and what skills do they have?

3. How representative are magistrates?

4. What role is played by District Judges, clerks and other advisers?

5. What are the arguments for and against using magistrates to judge the vast majority of cases brought before the courts?

Case study — People's justice?

A Magistrates' Court in action

In Court 3 of Bexley Magistrates' Court, one defendant is a barber from south London, about 20, African-Caribbean, smartly dressed, with no previous convictions. He drove a car without insurance and does not have a licence. Along with his guilty plea, the young man wrote a letter of explanation to the court. A relative urgently needed his help, so he got in the car, but he now regrets it very much. While this letter is read out, he stands in the dock, head bowed in remorse, hands behind his back as though handcuffed, and when addressed by the Chair of the bench he answers politely. A case-hardened professional

The interior of Court One at Bow Street Magistrates' Court. Photographing the court when it is in session is prohibited.

judge would see him off in a minute. But the three magistrates are entertained by a wonderful performance and let him go with a modest fine. This is what people's justice is all about.

Magistrates are amateurs and whereas the clerks, ushers, solicitors and security guards who are so respectful to them are paid a salary, those on the bench are allowed only expenses (and some choose not to claim them). Preparation involves a series of induction evenings, training days and visits to prisons and Young Offenders' Institutions. Once a JP has been vetted, approved, trained and sworn in, which may take up to two years, there are regular appraisals, under the MNTI. Even then, they will only be a 'winger'. To become the Chair, the person in the middle who does the talking, you need a minimum of five years' experience.

Why would anyone want to be a magistrate? One person said: 'I'm the sort of idiot who puts his hand up when volunteers are needed', and another spoke of reaching the age where 'you feel it's time to put something back in'. A third admitted 'an itch to sort out people's lives for them'.

Magistrates around the country are struggling to cope with the workload and in recent years there has been a drive from the government to modernise the administration of the courts. One trend has been the merger and closure of courts. Back in the 1960s, there were about 800 Magistrates' Courts in England and Wales. A decade ago there were 600. Now, there are slightly over 400 and they continue to disappear at the rate of 20 a year. Greater efficiency is the idea: a centralised modern court complex in place of scattered, Victorian piles. But when people have to travel 20 miles to the next town because their local court is no longer there, it's difficult to see the benefits. Any economic gains are minor in comparison to what's being lost, namely the concept of local and visible justice - 'justice of the people, by the people, for the people'. What does this mean if the judges come from leafy, up-market, middle-class areas and those being judged live on benefits in rough estates? Letting professionals take over from laypeople would only widen the social divide. For all its confusion and slowness, the current system works pretty well.

Adapted from an article in the *Guardian*, 4 April 2002.

Questions

(a) Explain what is meant by the following abbreviations and terms used in the material:
(i) MNTI, (ii) JP, (iii) winger (iv) clerk (3 marks each)

(b) In what way is 'local justice' seen as being under threat? (4)

(c) What does the material imply about the way that lay magistrates regard defendants compared to the way in which 'professional judges' regard them? Is this difference a good thing or not? (8)

(d) What is meant by 'people's justice'? (5)

(e) Using this material and other parts of the unit, summarise the arguments for and against the use of lay magistrates to provide 'people's justice'. (12)

17.1 Introduction

If the law of our country applies to everyone (see Box 17.1), it seems only fair that everyone should have access to advice and assistance from lawyers. This is important in civil cases and even more important in relation to criminal cases when the reputation and liberty of the accused is often at stake. However, there is always a danger that some people, particularly poorer and less well-educated members of society, will find it difficult or impossible to receive this advice and assistance. There are a number of reasons why, in practice, access may be limited.

First, to be represented by a solicitor can cost a great deal of money. If a claimant ends up with what they want from instructing a solicitor, this may seem like money well spent. Costs can normally be recovered from the losing side. But many people involved in legal claims are understandably nervous that they will end up spending huge sums on fighting a legal battle, only to lose the case. In this case, legal costs are money wasted. Those on modest incomes may feel they cannot, therefore, afford legal action, even though they actually have a strong case, due to a fear of losing their savings or running up debts.

Second, ordinary people often find the legal world intimidating, incomprehensible and hard to access. They are unsure about what services a solicitor can provide. And some people, such as those living in rural areas, may find it difficult physically to access a lawyer who can help them, especially in relation to more specialised cases.

Box 17.1 *Access to the legal system*

A judge once said that the law courts of England are open to all people like the doors of the Ritz Hotel.

Despite these fears, there are a number of ways in which people with limited amounts of money can receive the support of a legal expert. A number of charitable and voluntary groups, such as Citizens Advice Bureaux, offer some degree of legal advice and help. Lawyers sometimes do a proportion of their work without charging. Most importantly, however, government funding, or legal aid, offers free or subsidised access to a lawyer for people on smaller incomes. The nature of legal aid in England and Wales has recently undergone dramatic change, so it is worth beginning with an overview of the old system.

A brief history of legal aid

Since 1945, the state has provided some degree of help with legal costs to ordinary people. This has taken the form of subsidising the fees required by legal professionals in private practice, rather than funding lawyers to work solely for the government. The availability of this support has varied over the years, but, initially, it was available not just to the poor. It was also available to those on modest incomes. When the scheme first started in 1949, about 80% of the population were eligible for some degree of legal aid, though this was available only for civil cases to begin with. Legal aid for criminal cases was first made available in 1964.

Eligibility for legal aid depended on a **means test**, as it does today. A person's income and savings are assessed. If these fall below certain levels, legal aid can be awarded. In addition to a means test, some cases were subject to a **merits test**. A merits test involves looking at how strong a case the client has, and whether the case should be funded by the state. The idea of a merits test is also used in the current system.

Until very recently, the philosophy behind legal aid was that it was 'demand-led'. This meant that the government funded all legal aid claimants who applied, so long as they came within the eligibility rules. In effect, the Legal Aid Board was given a blank cheque. This might be fair in principle, but for various reasons the amount of taxpayers' money spent on legal aid grew to what many regarded as unacceptable levels. From the 1970s onwards, the government regularly altered the means test so that a smaller and smaller proportion of the population could claim legal aid. By 1993, only 40% of the population was eligible for legal aid.

Under the old system, lawyers were paid on a case-by-case basis, usually at rates or fees set in regulations, but in some cases on the same basis as a privately-funded lawyer. Once legal aid had been granted there were few methods or incentives for promoting value for money or monitoring the quality of the service provided by lawyers. A solicitor was paid by the hour. They might work efficiently and effectively or they might not. As Lord Irvine, the Lord Chancellor, said in a BBC interview:

> 'The vice of the old legal aid system was that you could walk into any solicitors' practice anywhere in the country and if you qualified for legal aid the solicitor could take it forward from beginning to end, even if he lacked the skills and experience for it.'

So, however incompetent the solicitor, the Legal Aid Board had to foot the bill.

In the late 1990s, the government proposed radical changes to the legal aid system because legal aid expenditure was seen as being out of control. Over a six-year period, total expenditure on legal aid increased by £529 million, from £1,093 million in 1992/93 to £1,622 million in 1998/99, a rise of 48%. This compares with general price inflation of 16% over the same period. It was also felt that some cases which deserved legal aid were not receiving it, while more dubious cases were being funded.

17.2 The Access to Justice Act 1999 - general principles

The Access to Justice Act 1999, which came into force in 2000, introduced a completely new system of legal aid. In relation to those sections of the Access to Justice Act that deal with legal aid, the unspoken aim of the legislation was to replace demand-led provision with the concept of controlled and planned government spending. The government has sought to move away from merely subsidising private practice for doing as much legal aid work as they choose. The total amount of money available is now limited and the funding body seeks to regulate the way that solicitors carry out legal aid work. The Act introduced changes which are outlined in Box 17.2.

17.3 The Criminal Defence Service (CDS)

The purpose of the CDS is to ensure that, in the interests of justice, people suspected or accused of a crime have access to advice, assistance and representation. There are four different ways in which a person may be able to obtain legal aid from the Criminal Defence Service. Each of these is explained below.

1. The Duty Solicitor scheme
People who are arrested and brought to a police station are entitled to contact their own solicitor for help or

Box 17.2 *Changes introduced by the Access to Justice Act 1999*

1. The Legal Aid Board was abolished. In its place, a new body with wider powers called the **Legal Services Commission (LSC)** was created. The LSC is accountable to the Lord Chancellor.

2. The LSC has been given responsibility for the **Community Legal Service**. The Community Legal Service fund provides legal aid in civil and family cases under substantially different arrangements from those in operation before 2000.

3. The LSC is also in charge of the **Criminal Defence Service**, that provides a reformed system of criminal legal aid.

4. Spending priorities must be set. A limit is set on total spending and it is up to the LSC, in partnership with others, to ensure that this money is targeted where it is needed most.

5. The LSC has to provide the best possible value for money when buying legal services. This includes working with organisations outside the legal profession, such as local councils and voluntary groups, who are also involved in the provision of legal services.

6. Only legal service providers who have shown that they meet the quality standards set by the LSC are allowed to recover costs from work that they have been contracted to do for the Community Legal Service and the Criminal Defence Service.

7. The Act created new rules to increase the use of **conditional fee agreements** between lawyers and clients in personal injury cases. Under these agreements, also known as 'no win, no fee' contracts, lawyers either charge no fees or a much reduced fee, unless they win the case.

alternatively to obtain free legal advice and assistance from a solicitor with a firm taking part in the Duty Solicitor scheme. This is a rota of some of the solicitors in the area who have agreed to be on call at particular times in order to be available to people at a police station when

Activity 17.1

Michael Mansfield QC.

Legal aid spending runs out of control

A 1999 report by the National Audit Office said that, of £597 million granted in legal aid by the overstretched Magistrates' Courts in England and Wales during the previous year, nearly £78 million was given with either no evidence that the applicant was entitled to it or insufficient evidence. This was the seventh year in a row that the Audit Office had been critical of the way that money was allocated on criminal legal aid.

During the late 1990s the Lords investigated the amounts charged to legal aid by top barristers in four separate cases. In one Lords appeal, Michael Mansfield QC charged £416 per hour in a case that was being funded by legal aid. Court officials reduced this by half. Mr Mansfield ran up a £20,000 bill for his work on an appeal in a murder conviction. This covered 48 hours preparation and the first day in court. In another case, the fees claimed by counsel had risen by 400% as the case went up through the appeal system. One proposal has been made that criminal QCs should not be able to earn more than £200,000 a year from legal aid work. This is equivalent to the earnings of a senior hospital consultant. But would this be fair to those defendants on legal aid?

Adapted from articles on BBC News website, 5 February 1999 and 18 June 1998.

(a) What percentage of the total amount allowed by magistrates for criminal legal aid in 1998 was improperly paid out? (2)

(b) Using this material, give two explanations for excessive public expenditure on legal aid. (6)

they have been arrested. A Duty Solicitor can give advice on police powers of detention, the nature of any charges that have been brought, what rights the suspect has during detention and questioning and so on. In addition, the Duty Solicitor scheme is available to unrepresented defendants who need basic advice and assistance when they appear as defendants in the Magistrates' Courts. The Duty Solicitor scheme is entirely free to the user.

2. The Advice and Assistance scheme

If a person requires further help from a lawyer, after leaving the police station, they may apply for this under the Advice and Assistance scheme. For example, the accused can obtain general legal advice, help with writing letters, help with negotiating with the police, obtaining the opinion of a barrister and preparing a written case. Payment cannot be made for representation at court under this scheme. The scheme is means tested. The solicitor fills in a form showing details of how much money the client has and this is used to calculate eligibility (the means test is explained in detail in Box 17.3).

Box 17.3 *The means test*

'Means' refers to the amount of money that the applicant has access to. The resources of the applicant can be considered under two headings: income and capital. Details of both income and capital must be provided in the application forms that solicitors send to the LSC on behalf of their clients. Capital refers to things like savings, shares, valuables such as jewellery, and in some cases the value of a house. Whichever type of assistance is sought, eligibility is calculated in much the same way:

- if the applicant's income and capital are above the maximum allowed they are not eligible

- if income and capital are between the maximum and the minimum limits, then, with some forms of legal aid, the applicant is required to make a contribution to solicitor's costs, the amount to be contributed depending on the exact amount of the applicant's income and capital (this is called a 'sliding scale' of contributions)

- if the applicant's financial resources are below a minimum level they are not required to contribute to costs at all.

3. Advocacy Assistance

Advocacy Assistance covers preparation of the case by a solicitor and initial representation in the Magistrates'

Court or the Crown Court, but not work connected to any appeal. Advocacy Assistance can also be used for prison disciplinary hearings. It is means tested.

4. Representation

Representation covers the cost of a solicitor for preparing a case for court and appearing in court, including an appeal. If needed, the cost of a barrister is also covered. To apply, the claimant's solicitor must fill in a form showing details of income and capital and send it to the court where the case is to be heard. The court will grant this form of legal aid where it is in the interests of justice to do so. This includes providing assistance to those who may go to prison or lose their job, do not speak English, or have cases involving substantial arguments on points of law. A person might be asked to pay a contribution by the judge if the case involves a hearing in any court other than a Magistrates' Court.

17.4 The Community Legal Service

The Community Legal Service (CLS) provides funding for legal advice and representation in civil cases by solicitors operating under a Legal Services Commission contract (sometimes they are called 'franchised' solicitors). There are several different sorts of help available under the Community Legal Service. All are subject to a means test and most of them are subject to a merits test. Details on the means test are given in Box 17.3.

The figures used for the maximum and minimum limits vary from one type of legal aid to another but, as a generalisation, anybody who earns over £25,000 per year is unlikely to receive funding. The disposable rather than 'gross' income of the applicant is used to calculate entitlement. This means that things like mortgage repayments and other essential living expenses are deducted from income to find what the applicant has left to spend on 'non essentials'.

The merits test

The merits test involves assessing the likelihood of applicants winning their case. Most cases can only be funded if the chances are seen as 50% or greater. In borderline cases, funding may still be granted if a case is of significant public interest or is of overwhelming importance to the client, for example because the physical safety of the client is at stake. The Legal Services Commission will also look at whether the amount of money that could be gained from winning a case justifies the likely costs.

Statutory charge

In some forms of civil legal aid, the statutory charge is

used. This means that, if a legal aid applicant wins a CLS funded case, they will have to use some or all of the money they win to repay the CLS. It is indicated below where the statutory charge applies.

Legal Help and Help at Court

These two services enable people to get help from a solicitor until their costs reach a total of £500. Legal Help can be used for general advice, writing letters, negotiation, obtaining a barrister's opinion and preparation of a written case if the client has to go before a court or tribunal. Help at Court can be used for appearance in court at a particular hearing, without formally acting for the client in the whole proceedings. Both services are means tested. Although no contribution is required from the client, the statutory charge applies in relation to family or clinical negligence cases.

Legal Representation

Where a person needs to go to court, they may be advised by their lawyer to apply for the higher level of funding available through Legal Representation. Legal Representation is subject to both a means and a merits test. The two types of provision are outlined in Box 17.4 on page 156.

Family Mediation

Mediation is where a third party helps the two sides (in the case of family mediation, a husband and wife in the process of divorce) to reach an agreed compromise (see Unit 11). The government favours the use of mediation, as it is always cheaper than a court action. Family Mediation can be used for family disputes relating to children, money and property. Mediation can be used in addition to Legal Help or Approved Family Help. It is means tested, but no contribution is required.

Approved Family Help

Approved Family Help is short of Full Representation but provides legal help in family cases where there is a contested court action.

Support Funding

Support Funding provides partial funding for personal injury cases (excluding medical negligence) and some multi-party actions (a case in which a large number of people bring claims of the same type) in certain circumstances. These are where the client is bringing a case under a 'conditional fee agreement', but it is unusually expensive so justifies some assistance from the LSC. The case continues on a private basis but the solicitor is paid limited amounts by the LSC during the case towards the total legal costs. This is intended to

Box 17.4 *The two types of Legal Representation*

1. Investigative Help

Where the prospects of a successful claim are unclear, Investigative Help can be used to investigate the strength of a proposed claim. It is only granted where the prospects of success are not clear and investigation by a lawyer seems likely to be expensive. Investigative Help is not available in family cases.

2. Full Representation

In principle Full Representation can cover all work needed to take legal proceedings to trial and appeal, although the LSC may impose conditions on the extent of funding. This is awarded more often than Investigative Help. The statutory charge applies where money is recovered.

Although Legal Representation may be used in nearly all courts, it is NOT available for the majority of cases in the following categories:
- personal injury cases arising from negligence (other than clinical negligence) - these cases should instead normally be pursued under conditional fee agreements
- business cases
- cases involving disputes about a company, trust or partnership.

It is never available for the following matters:
- boundary disputes
- libel and slander.

make the risk of losing the case more acceptable to a solicitor since, under a conditional fee agreement, clients do not usually have to pay their solicitor if the case is lost. There are two types of Support Funding:

1. Investigative Support.
2. Litigation Support.

The statutory charge applies.

Box 17.5 on page 157 summarises the various types of aid which are available.

Quality standards and contracting

Under the new arrangements, legal aid funds can only be made available to firms that satisfy the quality control requirements of the Community Legal Service (CLS) or the Criminal Defence Service (CDS). A detailed contract between the LSC and the firm regulates aspects of how the partnership is run and exactly what service is provided to the client.

17.5 Advantages and disadvantages of the new legal aid system

The advantages of the new legal aid system are as follows.

1. The new system should provide better value for money
Whereas under the previous system, lawyers were paid regardless of whether they were doing a good job, the insistence that quality standards are followed by legal aid providers should lead to a more cost effective use of taxpayers' money.

2. A ceiling has been placed on legal aid spending
The enormous year on year increases in total legal aid spending will no longer occur.

3. Many cases taken outside the scope of legal aid
Legal aid is no longer available for personal injury cases. It is expected by the government that conditional fee agreements will be used instead. This reduces the financial risks that often deter people from taking expensive court action. The increased use of conditional fees has been seen as a means of increasing access to justice while reducing the need for legal aid and the size of the legal aid budget. However, sections of the legal profession have been critical of conditional fee arrangements.

The disadvantages of the new legal aid system are as follows.

1. New merits test in civil cases criticised
The new test has been criticised on the grounds that the extent to which a case is likely to be won is not the only way of deciding whether it deserves to be funded.

2. The increase in red tape and lower pay
Since the implementation of the new Act, solicitors have complained at the freeze on legal aid rates paid by the LSC. Contracting had a poor start when solicitors threatened court action over the criminal payments offered. There have also been complaints about bureaucracy and the very tough standards demanded by the LSC.

3. Reduction in firms offering legal aided work
In 2000, it was estimated that 5,000 out of the 11,000 solicitors' firms offering legal aid services would no longer do so in future. The Lord Chancellor, Derry Irvine, has argued that there may be fewer providers but they will provide a better service. The Law Society on the other hand has expressed concern that soon there may not be enough legal aid solicitors to meet the public's needs.

Box 17.5 *Types of government-funded aid*

Table 1: Summary of the Criminal Defence Service

Type of help	Covers	Contribution required?
Duty Solicitor scheme	Free basic advice and assistance at the police station or Magistrates' Court.	No
Advice and Assistance	Help from a solicitor other than court appearance. Means tested.	No
Advocacy Assistance	Preparing case and initial representation in Magistrates' or Crown Court. Means tested.	No
Representation	Cost of preparing case for court and appearing in court, including appeal. No means test but court may only approve where it is in the interests of justice.	Yes

Table 2: Summary of the Community Legal Service

Type of help	Covers	Contribution?	Statutory charge
Legal Help and Help at Court (up to £500 worth)	Mainly general advice.	No	Yes (except some family cases)
Legal Representation	Work needed to take legal proceedings to trial (and appeal).	Yes	Yes (except some family cases)
Family Mediation	Family disputes relating to children, money and property.	No	No
Approved Family Help	'Help with mediation' (just advice). 'General family help' (negotiations where no mediation in progress).	No Yes	No Yes
Support Funding	Partial funding in unusually expensive cases.	Yes	Yes

4. The end of demand-led funding will reduce access to justice

Setting strict limits on legal aid spending creates the potential for some applicants being denied legal aid when the budget has run out. This 'first come, first served' approach seems unfair.

17.6 Conditional fee arrangements

Conditional fees are also known as 'no win, no fee' agreements. A lawyer provides professional legal services for the client on the understanding that no fees will be charged unless the case is won. This has been permitted under the law in England and Wales since the Courts and Legal Services Act 1990, but changes made under the

Access to Justice Act 1999 were designed to encourage far greater use of such a system. Lawyers may offer conditional fee arrangements to their clients in all civil cases except those involving family law. Legal aid is no longer available for personal injury cases, except those involving medical negligence. It is expected by the government that, in future, conditional fees will be used instead. The thinking behind this is as follows.

The legal costs involved in bringing a court action, or defending one, are very substantial and this deters some people from enforcing their rights. If a court case is lost, the expense has been for nothing. It should be remembered that, as a general rule, the losing side in court has to pay the costs of the winning party. Under a

Activity 17.2

(a) Identify which form of legal aid the following people might make use of. (5 marks each)

Derek has been arrested and taken to the police station.

Derek

Serena purchased a nearly new car from a local garage recently. After 50 miles the engine fell out. The garage refused to repair the vehicle and Serena wants to know whether she could take the company to court.

Serena

Dave is going through divorce proceedings. His wife, Jasmine, is making demands for a level of financial maintenance that Dave sees as unreasonable. Dave's lawyer has suggested that this could be settled without the need for an expensive court hearing.

Dave

Jasmine

Jane wishes to plead not guilty to a charge of shoplifting which will be heard in the local Magistrates' Court.

(b) What tests must be satisfied before legal aid will be granted in any of these cases? (5 marks each)

Jane

conditional fee arrangement, however, the financial risks to the client are largely removed. It can be argued that allowing such arrangements increases access to justice. Many of those with relatively limited incomes, who would not otherwise be prepared to take a risk even though they may have a strong case in law, are now able to justify engaging the services of a lawyer.

What are the fees if the case is won?

Lawyers who take on cases on the basis of a conditional fee arrangement charge a higher fee than normal. The difference between a normal fee and the conditional fee is known as the 'success fee' or 'uplift'. As a rule, the more uncertain the case, the higher the success fee is likely to be. Since the Conditional Fees Arrangements Order 1998, the maximum uplift is 100%. Most solicitors have adopted the Law Society recommendation that the success fee should be equivalent to not more than 25% of the damages awarded to the successful claimant. This is known as 'the cap'. Box 17.6 shows an example.

Box 17.6 *Conditional fee arrangements (1)*

Lynton has been injured at work and feels that he may be able to claim compensation for the negligence of his employer. He consults a solicitor. She gathers details of the case and after careful consideration says: 'Normally, if we have to go to court I would charge £5,000 to act in a case like this. However, on a no win, no fee basis I would charge £10,000, bearing in mind that if you lose in court, I will not charge anything for my services. The uplift, if we do win, will be £5,000.'

What about the other side's costs?

As mentioned earlier, the losing side in court has to pay the costs of the winning party. This presents an obvious problem to someone who has a conditional fee arrangement with their own lawyer but who loses the case. Although they do not have to pay legal fees to their own lawyer, they still have to pay the other side's costs and the disbursements (other costs associated with the case such as fees paid to expert witnesses) of both sides. Insurance policies are available to cover this, although the premiums (payments made to the insurance company) can sometimes be very high. For this reason, conditional fee arrangements are not entirely without risk. A party to a case could spend a significant amount of money on insurance costs.

Can the winning party recover the insurance premium from the loser?

At one time, the cost of insurance could not be recovered from the other side. So, if a successful claimant recovered damages and costs from the defendant, the value of compensation received was effectively reduced by the amount of any insurance premium. Since the Access to Justice Act came into force, however, the winning party may recover both their own costs, including any uplift and the cost of conditional fee insurance from the other side. An example is given in Box 17.7.

Box 17.7 *Conditional fee arrangements (2)*

After meeting with his solicitor, Lynton is told he should expect to obtain £25,000 damages from his employer. Using the figures from the example in Box 24.1, if the case is won the defendant (the employer) will be liable to pay Lynton the following amounts: damages (£25,000); the legal costs of Lynton (£10,000); and the insurance premium paid by Lynton (which, purely for the purpose of this example, is treated as £1,500). This comes to a total of £50,000.

If on the other hand the case is lost, Lynton will incur the following expenditure: the employer's legal costs (£10,000, which is recovered from the insurance company); and the insurance premium (£1,500). Although Lynton will not have to pay his own solicitor any fees, the case has still cost him £1,500.

The advantages of conditional fees

For claimants, the advantages of conditional fees include:

- there are no worries about having to pay enormous legal fees
- with no win, no fee, the lawyer has an obvious incentive to try hard to win the case
- there is no time delay while a legal aid application is processed.

In one sense defendants also benefit, as the conditional fee system should reduce the number of claimants making unjustified claims.

Finally the taxpayer benefits, as the amount of cases funded by legal aid is reduced.

The disadvantages of conditional fees

Critics of the conditional fee approach have highlighted the disadvantages outlined in Box 17.8.

17.7 Help offered by the legal profession

1. Cheap interviews

Many solicitors offer regular advice 'surgeries' at their premises, where individuals can have a half-hour initial discussion about any legal problem either for free or at a greatly reduced cost. This is probably more to do with generating business for the practice than offering a public service but, nevertheless, it can provide increased access to justice for those who might not otherwise consult a solicitor. The Law Society has also endorsed a commercially-run telephone service called Accident Line. If someone thinks they have a potential personal injury claim, they can ring up and arrange to meet a personal

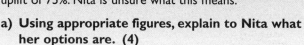

Activity 17.3

Nita has been advised that she may be able to sue her local council for injuries caused by falling down some steps in poorly maintained council premises. Her solicitor says that he would charge £8,000 to represent her. She is afraid to start a court case, as she is a single parent on a fairly low income with savings of just £2,000. However her solicitor has offered a conditional fee arrangement, with an uplift of 75%. Nita is unsure what this means.

Nita

a) **Using appropriate figures, explain to Nita what her options are. (4)**

b) **How likely is it that Nita's solicitor will fight for every last penny of compensation? (3)**

Box 17.8 *The disadvantages of conditional fees*

1. In the USA, where personal injury lawyers have been able to offer something like conditional fees for some years, an undesirable 'ambulance chasing' culture has emerged, to some degree. This has damaged the public image of the legal profession.

2. There is a danger that lawyers will be prepared to settle a case for smaller amounts of damages than should be obtained so that they can recover their fee.

3. Some personal injury cases, which, in the past, might have been funded by legal aid will not reach court because the claimant cannot find a lawyer prepared to accept a conditional fee arrangement and cannot afford to pay legal costs.

4. As discussed above, a large insurance premium for the policy covering the other side's legal costs will sometimes deter otherwise deserving claimants from starting a court action. Conditional fee arrangements are not always risk-free for claimants.

injury solicitor for a free consultation. This is an easy way for potential claimants to be put in contact with a lawyer who can act on their behalf, often on a conditional fee basis.

2. Pro bono advice and representation

'Pro bono' is the term used when a barrister acts for someone without charging. Many members of the Bar have done some unpaid work in the past on an informal basis, but, in 1996, the Bar *Pro Bono* Unit was established. The unit offers the services of barristers prepared to provide legal advice and representation in deserving cases where public funding is not available or where the applicant is unable to afford legal assistance. Since it was set up, more than 1,500 people have been helped.

17.8 Advice Agencies

Citizens Advice Bureaux (CAB)

Five million people seek advice from one of 2,000 local offices every year. Many of these people go to the CAB for advice on a wide range of legal issues. The majority of those working in CAB offices are volunteers. The National Association of Citizens Advice Bureaux is an association of charities who are reliant on donations, though the recently established Legal Services Commission has plans to provide funding for some CAB work in the future.

Advice and guidance can be offered on a range of matters, typically debt problems and advice on benefits. CAB can also put people in contact with other organisations and agencies, such as local solicitors who do legal aid work.

Law Centres

Law Centres aim to provide free legal advice, and possibly representation, in areas where people are unlikely to be able to afford to pay a solicitor. Law Centres provide the kind of services required by local residents. Most commonly, they deal with housing, welfare, employment, discrimination and immigration cases. Although many of those who work at Law Centres are volunteers, qualified solicitors also help at some sessions.

Trade Unions and other organisations

Members of many trade unions are able to obtain free or low-cost legal advice and assistance on employment matters from a solicitor as one of the benefits of membership. Organisations such as the AA offer help with the law relating to motoring, and some charities offer specialist help on the issues that they are concerned with.

Summary ● ● ●

1. How did the legal aid system work before 2000?

2. How has the legal aid system worked since 2000?

3. What sort of aid is provided by the CDS and CLS and in what circumstances?

4. What impact has the introduction of a new system of providing legal aid made?

5. What are conditional fee arrangements?

6. What are the advantages and disadvantages of conditional fee arrangements?

7. What sort of legal aid is provided by the legal profession?

8. What sort of legal aid is offered by advice agencies?

Case study | Legal aid

Item A *The new rules*

The implementation of new eligibility rules in 2001 increased the number of people entitled to publicly-funded legal advice and representation from 16 to 21 million people. Some people will receive free legal services. Others will receive it at a reduced cost. Bodies such as the Law Society and the National Association of Citizens Advice Bureaux (Nacab) congratulated the Lord Chancellor's department on the change, which followed two decades of declining state aid. Criminal solicitor Rodney Warren, who chairs the Law Society's Access to Justice Committee, said:

> 'Twenty years ago, almost all the people who came to my firm - a high street, provincial practice - would have qualified for legal assistance. But it got to the point where nobody qualified unless they were out of work.'

Many lawyers, however, are concerned that the changes could turn out to be cosmetic. A major problem is that thousands of law firms stopped doing publicly-funded work because they found the system that replaced legal aid last year did not pay them sufficient and involved too much paperwork. The number of firms offering legal services through legal aid halved over a two-year period. Alison Green of Nacab said: 'It is a bit of a geographical lottery. It can mean that some people face a 50-mile round trip to get legal help.'

Another issue is that, while the eligibility rules were relaxed, there has been no increase in the overall budget from the Legal Services Commission (LSC). Although most firms hope to be able to help all those who come along for advice, they will probably have to introduce new criteria to decide who to help with more complicated casework, especially if representation at a court or tribunal is required. Some people may not get help. Those providing LSC funded services will need to prioritise.

A leaflet produced by the Criminal Defence Service.

Adapted from the *Observer*, 2 December 2001.

Item B *Ambulance chasing or the road to justice?*

David Lock was elected Labour MP for Wyre Forest in 1997 and served as Parliamentary Secretary in the Lord Chancellor's Department. He was defeated by Dr Richard Taylor in the 2001 general election.

Mr David Lock, a junior minister in the Lord Chancellor's Department, strongly defended conditional fee arrangements when giving evidence to a committee of MPs. He said that conditional fee agreements tackle the fundamental problem of the British legal system, which is that it is open to very few people unless they are legally aided:

> 'The majority of people - those above income support level - have been unable to litigate because they cannot afford to pay lawyers' fees if they lose. In practice, they have been excluded from access to justice...Conditional fee agreements are giving hundreds of thousands of people access to justice who could not previously have contemplated going to law.'

Lord Irvine, the Lord Chancellor, has also stoutly defended the use of conditional fees in personal injury cases instead of legal aid.

Lord Irvine.

Sources: Evidence given by David Lock to the Fifth Commons Standing Committee on Delegated Legislation, 16 March 2000.

Questions

(a) Using Item A, complete the following tasks.

   (i)   What is the 'Legal Services Commission'? (2)

   (ii)   Explain why some people will receive free legal services and others will have to pay something towards legal costs. (6)

   (iii) What particular Community Legal Service scheme (or schemes) will a person seeking representation by a lawyer in court apply for? (4)

   (iv)   Discuss the extent to which recent changes to the nature of legal aid in England and Wales have increased access to justice. (12)

(b) Using Item B, complete the following tasks.

   (i)   What argument does David Lock make in Item B in favour of conditional fee deals? (3)

   (ii)   The government wishes to increase access to justice. If it is the case that 'the majority of people - those above income support level - have been unable to litigate', what alternative does the government have, other than encouraging the use of conditional fees? Use Items A and B in your answer. (2)

   (iii) If a potential personal injury claimant is not eligible for legal aid, outline three ways in which they might obtain legal advice and help. (9)

Answers to crossword on page 124	Across		Down
	1 Denning	11 District	1 Devlin
	2 Lord Chancellor	12 Judge	3 Circuit
	5 Clerk	13 Law Lord	4 District Judge
	7 Wig	14 Magistrate	6 Recorder
	10 Master of the Rolls		8 Family
			9 JSB

18 *Actus reus*

18.1 Introduction

To prove someone guilty of committing a crime, the prosecution usually needs to show two things:

1. It is necessary to show that the accused committed the relevant criminal act. This is known as the *'actus reus'* of the offence.

2. It is necessary to show that the accused intended that criminal act (or, sometimes, merely that the accused was reckless). Another way of putting this is to say that the accused had the required state of mind at the time the act was committed. This is known as the *'mens rea'* for the offence.

'Actus reus' and *'mens rea'* are Latin terms. The first means 'guilty act', the second means 'guilty mind'.

To help understand the concept of *actus reus* and *mens rea*, imagine that Alex is very angry with Bryn. Alex goes to Bryn's house, with the intention of attacking him with a baseball bat. However, Bryn is not in, so Alex never acts on his intention to assault Bryn. In this situation, Alex has not committed a crime. He had thoughts that amounted to the *mens rea* of assault. But these thoughts were not combined with action. They could not amount to a crime, as there was no *actus reus*.

18.2 Voluntary acts

One way of defining *actus reus* is to say that it involves an act, in other words *doing* something. For instance, the *actus reus* for theft is taking property that belongs to another. This nearly always requires the accused to take active steps to do something, whether it is breaking into a car, opening a bag or removing something from a shop.

To result in criminal liability, conduct must normally be voluntary. In other words, it should be conduct caused by the free will of the defendant in some way. In very rare cases, such as those involving sleepwalking, there is not a sufficient link between the will of the defendant and the act committed to identify it as voluntary. So, a voluntary action is one involving some degree of physical control on the part of the defendant. In *Hill v Baxter (1958)*, the court gave hypothetical examples of how the driver of a vehicle might lose control in a way that could be seen as involuntary. These included being attacked by a swarm of bees, being hit on the head by a flying stone, or having a heart attack at the wheel.

Note that it is very unusual for conduct under the influence of drugs or drink to be regarded as involuntary.

18.3 Omissions

Can an omission amount to *actus reus*? An omission involves failing to do something whereas an act involves doing something. If Carl hits Dave, this is obviously an act and amounts to an assault. On the other hand, suppose that Ali and Jasmine are on a busy street. Ali steps off the pavement and is hit by a car which he (foolishly) fails to see. Jasmine sees the car approaching but does nothing to warn Ali. This omission on the part of Jasmine would not make her criminally liable for any injury caused to Ali. As a general rule, only acts, not omissions, can make a person guilty of an offence. However, there are a number of exceptions to this rule.

Exceptions to the rule on omissions

An Act of Parliament may create a situation where an omission may be the *actus reus*. For example, it is an offence under Section 6 of the Road Traffic Act 1988 to refuse to blow into a police breathalyser. In addition to these **statutory exceptions**, there are five common law exceptions to the rule on omissions. In each of these categories of case there is a duty to act, and a failure to act may amount to *actus reus*. The common law exceptions are set out below.

1. Where a family relationship exists
Parents of young children and husbands and wives are under a duty to protect each other from serious harm. In *Downes (1875)*, the defendant failed to call a doctor to treat his very sick child. The parent was a member of a religious sect which believed in the power of prayer over medicine. When the child died, Downes was convicted of manslaughter.

2. Where the defendant has assumed responsibility for a person
If the defendant has voluntarily taken on the task of looking after someone vulnerable, they have a duty to prevent harm occurring to that person, even if the person does not have a close family relationship to the defendant (see Box 18.1 on page 164).

3. A duty arising from an official position
Police officers and some others are under a duty to protect the public.

In *Dytham (1979)*, a police officer witnessed an attack on the victim. He did not intervene to help the victim or call for help. In fact, he drove away from the scene of the crime. The officer was guilty of wilfully and without reasonable excuse neglecting to perform his duty.

Box 18.1 R v Stone and Dobinson (1977)

The defendants were cohabiting. Stone's mentally ill sister, Fanny, lived with the couple, and they looked after her. Fanny developed a serious eating disorder and was confined to bed. The defendants made halfhearted attempts to get medical help over a period of time, but somehow or other Fanny never saw a doctor. Because of this neglect she became severely ill and malnourished, and eventually died. When her body was found it was clear from the squalor of the room and Fanny's thinness that she had been virtually abandoned. The Court of Appeal found Stone and Dobinson guilty of manslaughter. Judge Lane said that this situation was not the same as that of the drowning stranger. The defendants had undertaken to care for Fanny and having done so should have taken proper care of her after she became bed-bound. Their omission could be treated as the cause of death. If prompt medical help had been obtained, Fanny would have had a good chance of recovery.

4. Under a contract

The defendant may have a duty to act under a contract. This is especially likely under some contracts of employment - see Box 18.2.

Box 18.2 Pittwood (1902)

A railway employee was employed to keep a level crossing gate shut whenever a train was about to pass. He forgot to shut the gate, with the result that a man was killed when he tried to cross the line with his hay cart and was hit by a train. The gatekeeper was held liable for manslaughter.

5. Where the defendant has started a chain of events

If a chain of events has led to harm being caused, it may be the case that a person can be held as accountable for having originally created a dangerous situation. That person had a duty to take steps to prevent harm occurring - see Box 18.3.

Box 18.3 R v Miller (1983)

Miller dropped a burning cigarette onto his mattress.

Miller was squatting in a house. One night he fell asleep while lying on a mattress smoking a cigarette. When he woke up he saw that he had dropped the cigarette in his sleep and that the mattress was smouldering. He did nothing about it; he simply moved to another room and went back to sleep. The house eventually caught fire. The defendant's conviction for arson was confirmed by the House of Lords. Lord Diplock said that the crime of arson may be committed by not only doing something that could cause a fire but also, where the defendant had created the danger, by failing to take steps to put the fire out or call the fire brigade.

Activity 18.1

In each case, consider whether the defendant (D) will be liable for the death that occurred. For this activity, you only need to consider whether D had *actus reus*.

(a) **D is walking in the country on a cold winter afternoon. She comes across a large, deep lake. A man is in the middle of this lake, apparently drowning. D does nothing to try to rescue him. (4)**

(b) **D, a hospital surgeon, is on call. This means she may be rung up at home and called into the hospital when necessary. D is telephoned but she chooses to finish a game of chess before setting off for the hospital. This takes thirty minutes. As a result of the delay, a patient who has been admitted as an emergency case suffers serious injuries. (4)**

18.4 Causation

The issue of causation is about dealing with cases where harm might be said to have been caused by a number of different things, one of which was the act or omission of the defendant. These cases throw up difficult questions about whether or not the defendant has *actus reus*. For example, a number of causation cases involve a criminal attack followed by inadequate medical treatment (see below). If the victim dies, should the original attacker be seen as the cause of death, or the doctors who were at fault? One way of describing situations where injuries, deaths or other potentially criminal consequences have a number of causes is to say that there is a **'chain of causation'**. If, after the act of the defendant, something else occurred which is regarded as being the true cause of the harm, it is said that the chain of causation has been broken.

To show *actus reus* it is necessary to show that:

- the defendant's conduct was the factual cause of the harm
- the defendant's conduct was in law the cause of the harm
- there was no intervening act which broke the chain of causation.

Factual causation

To establish that the defendant's behaviour act was, in the particular facts of the case, sufficient to justify conviction, the question that has to be answered is known as the 'but for' test - would the victim have escaped harm **but for** the defendant's act? This is explored in Box 18.4.

On the other hand, in different circumstances, the chain of causation may be broken, so that even though a defendant appears blameworthy they cannot be held responsible for what has happened - see Box 18.5.

Legal causation

Where there is factual causation, the courts are reluctant to accept arguments that the chain of causation has been broken. For example, the mere fact that the behaviour of a defendant was not the only cause of death, or that events took an unexpected turn, will rarely excuse liability. But, in exceptional circumstances, even if there is factual causation linking the defendant to a crime, the defendant may not be accountable in law.

The 'thin skull' or 'eggshell skull' rule

In some cases, the victim is peculiarly susceptible to harm in a way that the great majority of people are not. These are sometime known as 'thin skull' or 'eggshell skull' cases. The idea is that a person with a very thin skull will suffer

Box 18.4 *R v Pagett (1983)*

A police officer firing a gun.

The defendant shot at the police while holding his girlfriend in front of him as a human shield. The police fired back in self defence and a police bullet killed the girlfriend. Did the defendant have the *actus reus* for murder? What should be seen as the cause of her death? The defendant was found to have caused the death of the woman. The victim would not have died but for the actions of the defendant.

Box 18.5 *White (1910)*

A son gave his mother poison, but before it had a chance to take effect, she collapsed, suffering from what turned out to be a fatal heart attack. The son was not guilty of murder, as he had not caused her death (he was, however, guilty of attempted murder).

far more from a blow to the head than someone with a normal skull. The question is whether a person is liable for the death of a person with a thin skull if they strike that person with what would not be a fatal blow to the vast majority of people. The answer to the question is that the person who caused death in this way would be liable. In this kind of case, the courts have, for a long time, been clear that the defendant must take victims as they find them. Of course, thin skulls are not the only kind of vulnerability covered by this principle - see Box 18.6.

Box 18.6 *R v Blaue (1975)*

The victim of a stabbing was a Jehovah's witness. Because of her religious beliefs, the victim refused to have a blood transfusion in hospital and, as a consequence, died of her wounds. In a subsequent murder trial, the Court of Appeal rejected the defendant's argument that this refusal of treatment broke the chain of causation and said the defendant must take the victim as he found her. This was an application of the thin skull rule.

Intervening acts

When there is a combination of reasons for death or injury occurring, and the conduct of the defendant is only one of these reasons, the question to be asked is whether the defendant's act was the significant one in a chain of events. If there is an event that is treated as more significant, it is said that there has been an **intervening act**. This raises the question how significant a cause of harm the defendant's behaviour needs to be before they are liable. The answer to this question can be seen in *R v Cheshire (1991)* - see Box 18.7.

Box 18.7 *R v Cheshire (1991)*

The defendant shot his victim in the leg and stomach after an argument in a fish and chip shop. The victim was in hospital for some weeks. As part of his treatment a tube was inserted into his windpipe. Due to fairly rare complications, caused by the tube, he died. This was at a time when the original injuries were no longer life threatening. Evidence was given that the doctors had been negligent in the way that they treated the victim. On appeal, the Court of Appeal reviewed when, in general terms, medical negligence would break the chain of causation. Judge Beldam said, dismissing the appeal:

'It is not the function of the jury to evaluate competing causes or to choose which is dominant provided they are satisfied that the accused's acts can fairly be said to have made a significant cause to the victim's death.'

So, the lesson of *R v Cheshire (1991)* is that, to establish *actus reus*, it is sufficient to show that the defendant made a **significant contribution** to the cause of

Box 18.8 *R v Jordan (1956)*

The victim was stabbed by an attacker and admitted to hospital. Two serious mistakes were made by the doctors involved. At the time of these mistakes the original wound had virtually healed. The immediate cause of death was pneumonia resulting from bad medical care. Judge Hallet said:

'It is sufficient to point out here that this was not normal treatment.'

The murder conviction of the man causing the stab wounds was quashed. The Court of Appeal felt that the mistakes were in some way out of the ordinary. Doctors might make mistakes when treating the victim, but this does not alter the fact of the attacker's liability for harm caused. Only when the mistakes of doctors, and the consequences of those mistakes, are exceptionally serious can they be said to overshadow the original attack as the cause of death.

death. Only in very exceptional cases will the courts permit the negligence of doctors to break the chain of causation. An example of such an exception is *R v Jordan (1956)* - see Box 18.8.

Intervening acts and foreseeability

If the intervening act was predictable or foreseeable it does not normally make any difference to the liability of the defendant. For example, in *R v Pagett (1983)*, discussed above, it was reasonably foreseeable that the police would return the fire of the accused, thus endangering the life of the woman the defendant used as a human shield. Another example is that of *Roberts (1971)* in which a woman jumped from a car travelling at something between 20 and 40 mph to avoid the sexual advances of the defendant. The defendant argued that her decision to jump was the true cause of her injuries. Nevertheless, the defendant was held liable for assault, as it was reasonably foreseeable that a woman might react in this way.

On the other hand, if the victim acts in an unreasonable or unforeseeable way, this may break the chain of causation - see Box 18.9.

Box 18.9 *R v Williams and Davis (1992)*

The appellants gave a lift to a hitchhiker and allegedly tried to rob him. He jumped from the car, which was travelling at about 30 mph, and died from head injuries caused by falling into the road. The Court of Appeal quashed a conviction for manslaughter on the basis that the judge had misdirected the jury on the issue of causation. The Court of Appeal said that, in cases like this, the jury should consider firstly whether the action of the defendant was reasonably foreseeable and secondly whether it was in proportion to the threat of harm.

Summary ●●●

1. What is the difference between actus reus and mens rea?
2. When is conduct regarded as being involuntary?
3. Can an omission amount to actus reus?
4. What is a 'chain of causation' and when is it broken?
5. What are the 'but for test' and the 'thin skull rule'?
6. What is an 'intervening act' and how might it affect liability?

Case study • Actus reus

Item A *Actus reus*

Under English law, people have no general duty to help or protect strangers, those people with whom they have no relationship. Even if there is some kind of relationship, there is not necessarily a duty to act. For example if you have a business relationship with a person you would not be legally required to try and rescue them from a dangerous situation. We might hope that

The water in this lake is shallow enough for the man to wade into. Is he guilty of a crime if he fails to take steps to rescue the child?

someone in such a situation would feel some kind of moral obligation, but this is one situation where the criminal law does not enforce morality. However, the closer a relationship is, the more likely it is that the criminal law will punish certain omissions, notably where someone loses their life.

What kind of relationships will give rise to a duty to act? One example is that of the bond between parents and their children. Another is that of husband and wife. But the crucial factor is not whether there is a blood relationship or marriage, but whether one party relies on the other. In *R v Gibbins and Proctor (1918)* a man and a woman lived together with the man's young daughter. Both were found guilty of murder when they failed to give the child food and she died. On the other hand, in *Shepherd (1862),* it was held that there was no duty to act owed by a parent to an independent 18-year-old daughter.

It will depend on the facts of each case whether the court is prepared to conclude that a relationship is close enough to create a duty to act. The rule as it stands is open to criticism, however. Suppose that a man can easily rescue a child from danger, for example in water that is too deep for the child but shallow enough for the man to wade into. If the child is a stranger, the man is not criminally liable if he ignores the fact that the child is drowning. Is this morally justifiable? In certain countries an offence has been committed if anyone fails to take steps to protect or rescue another from serious harm, when they might have done so without risk of harm to themselves.

Item B *Bill and Rod*

Bill and Rod have been drinking together all night. They walk home from the pub. Half way to the street in which they both live, they have a violent argument. Bill punches Rod hard. He falls over the kerb and badly sprains his ankle. Bill leaves Rod hopping about and carries on alone. Rod limps towards home at a much slower pace. However,

he has only gone a hundred metres when a puma attacks him. The puma has escaped from a local zoo a few hours earlier. Rod is unable to move quickly enough to escape into a late night shop that is just feet away (but for the sprained ankle, he would have been able to). The puma leaps at Rod and badly mauls him.

Questions

(a) Using Item A and other parts of the unit, complete the following tasks.

   (i) Will the parents of a 21-year-old son, living away from home, have a duty to get medical help for their son if he falls seriously ill? (4)

   (ii) If a lifeguard, employed at a local swimming pool, does nothing to help someone she does not know from drowning, can she be criminally liable for the death? (4)

   (iii) Put forward arguments for and against the current state of the criminal law regarding a duty to act. (8)

(b) Using Item B, discuss whether, under the criminal law, Bill would be regarded as having caused the injuries Rod sustains. (8)

19.1 Introduction

To convict a person of a criminal offence, the prosecution must prove beyond all reasonable doubt that the defendant committed the crime. Crimes generally have two component parts: the *actus reus* or physical act (which was examined in Unit 18) and the *mens rea* or mental element. To prove *mens rea*, the prosecution needs to prove that the defendant had a particular state of mind when the crime in question was committed.

It is important to remember, however, that motive and *mens rea* are quite separate things. Motive is the reason for doing something. *Mens rea* is forming the necessary intention. Motive is irrelevant in relation to criminal guilt. This can be illustrated by looking at an example.

Suppose that Joe has become an alcoholic. He has been told by his doctor that he must stop drinking, or he is seriously in danger of dying from liver failure. Jan, his wife, is very worried. She attempts to persuade Joe not to go to the pub. Joe ignores his wife's expressions of concern and starts to leave the house. Jan knocks him unconscious with a frying pan to prevent this. We may feel that Jan's motive is very different from, for example, a street mugger, but nevertheless she has the *mens rea* for a criminal offence. This difference can be dealt with when sentencing the defendant. One person convicted of assault may receive a more severe sentence than another. But the degree of wrongdoing is not relevant to the decision about guilt.

19.2 Different types of mens rea

There are two kinds of *mens rea* - intention and recklessness. These are outlined in Box 19.1.

19.3 Intention

With some offences, such as murder and theft, the law requires that the prosecution must prove intention. Recklessness is not sufficient to obtain a conviction. Another example can be seen in Section 18 of the Offences Against the Person Act 1861. Wounding or causing grievous bodily harm is the *actus reus*. The *mens rea* is that the defendant must intend to wound or cause grievous bodily harm or resist arrest. If the defendant did not intend one of these then an offence has not been committed under s.18.

For example, suppose that a speedboat is driven at excessive speed on the River Thames by a person who has consumed large amounts of alcohol and suppose that an accidental collision occurs - the speedboat hits another craft and someone is seriously injured. No offence has been committed under Section 18 (although a less serious offence has been committed in these circumstances). The person in charge of the speedboat did not intend to injure the victim.

Foresight of consequences

For the prosecution to prove an intentional assault they must produce evidence that shows that the defendant desired the consequence of his action. In some cases this is difficult, as defendants who plead not guilty rarely reveal what was really going on in their minds when they committed a criminal act.

In some cases, though, it is very hard to accept a defence that the defendant's *mens rea* was anything other than intention. An example can be seen in the case of *Moloney (1985)*. The defendant was a soldier on leave who had been drinking heavily with his stepfather, with whom he was on good terms. The evidence was that the two men had held a contest to see who could load a gun and be ready to fire first. Moloney won, and stood pointing his gun at his stepfather, who teased him by saying that he would not dare fire. By his own admission, Moloney pulled the trigger. In evidence he said, 'I never conceived that what was I doing might cause injury to anybody. It was just a lark.'

The question is whether we can accept the notion that the defendant is not guilty of murder. Instinctively, one feels that Moloney must have known at the time that he pulled the trigger what would happen to his stepfather. In cases like this it might be assumed that defendants were

---

Box 19.1 *The two kinds of mens rea*

Intention

If something is done intentionally, it is done on purpose. If a person feels angry towards another person, they may physically strike out. This is a deliberate action and if some kind of harm occurs, then this harm was probably intended.

Recklessness

The Oxford Dictionary defines reckless as meaning: 'lacking caution, regardless of consequences, rash'. In criminal law, it might be helpful to think of recklessness as being similar to extreme carelessness. Recklessness means that the defendant realises that there was a serious risk of something unlawful occurring but, without actually desiring it to happen, carries on regardless.

able to predict the consequences of their action. This is usually referred to as '**foresight of consequences**'.

Under Section 8 of the Criminal Justice Act 1967 a jury can conclude that a defendant intended a result of their action. They can do this when that result was a **natural and probable cause** of the defendant's actions. For example, any jury would tend to think that if someone pulls the trigger of a gun when it is pointed at another person then the natural and probable consequence of that result would be serious injury or death. However a jury can also take into account other evidence, some of which may point towards the defendant's innocence.

In *Woollin (1998)*, a man threw his very young baby towards his pram. The pram was against a wall only three feet away. The baby suffered fatal head injuries. On appeal, the House of Lords set out how a judge should explain the need to prove intention to a jury. This can be summarised in Box 19.2.

Box 19.2 *How a judge should explain the need to prove intention.*

1. In most cases, it is sufficient to tell the jury simply that they must be satisfied that the defendant intended the consequences (such as serious harm) of their actions.

2. In some cases, however, the jury may find the necessary intention if they feel that the consequence was a virtual certainty as a result of the defendant's actions **and** the defendant appreciated that this was the case at the time.

3. The jury should make their decision after consideration of all of the evidence.

19.4 Recklessness

In ordinary English, being reckless means taking an unjustified risk. In the criminal law the word has a similar but slightly different meaning.

Subjective recklessness

The nature of '**subjective recklessness**' was defined in *R v Cunningham (1957)*. The defendant in this case broke into a gas meter to steal money from it. As a result, damage was caused to a gas pipe. This meant that gas seeped into the house next door, where Cunningham's mother-in-law was sleeping. She became very ill because

of the gas leak. Cunningham was charged with the offence of 'maliciously administering a noxious thing so as to endanger life'. On appeal, his initial conviction was quashed because of a misdirection to the jury.

In examining whether or not the defendant had *mens rea*, the Court of Appeal provided a definition of recklessness. Looking at the words used in the relevant Act, the Court of Appeal said that 'maliciously' meant that either intention or recklessness could provide *mens rea*. A definition of recklessness was:

> '**foreseeing a serious risk of the type of harm that actually occurred, but choosing to go ahead anyway**'.

Recklessness is about identifying a serious risk but carrying on regardless. The two-stage test for identifying this kind of recklessness is outlined in Box 19.3.

Box 19.3 *The two-stage test for identifying subjective recklessness*

1. Did the defendant foresee a possibility of an unlawful consequence occurring? In the case of *R v Cunningham (1957)*, did the defendant foresee injury to others, caused by the escaping gas?

2. Was the risk unjustifiable or unreasonable?

If the answer to both of these questions is yes, the defendant has been reckless.

What is central to subjective recklessness is the 'risk analysis' of the defendant. Sometimes a person may not actually perceive a risk that any reasonable person would, in which case they have not been reckless. For example in *R v Stephenson (1979)*, the defendant crept into a hollow in the side of a large straw stack to sleep. Feeling cold, he lit a fire of twigs and straw inside the hollow. Predictably, the stack caught fire. At his trial for arson, evidence was put that he suffered from schizophrenia, which could prevent him from having the same ability as a normal person to identify risks. As recklessness was subjective, the Court of Appeal felt that this actual lack of foresight could mean that someone was not reckless in a criminal sense.

Subjective recklessness is the test used in almost all criminal offences where recklessness is a possible *mens rea*. It is used for all non-fatal offences against the person.

Objective recklessness

Since the case of *R v Caldwell (1981)*, the courts have

also used a second type of recklessness in relation to some offences. 'Objective recklessness', often referred to as 'Caldwell recklessness', involves asking whether a reasonable person, rather than the defendant, would have identified a risk. If the answer to that question is yes, and the risk was unjustifiable, recklessness is shown. So, if the defendant in *R v Stephenson (1979)* was judged by the objective standard (in other words what a normal person would have thought in his shoes), he would almost certainly have been found guilty since a reasonable person would have identified the obvious risks of starting a fire beside a stack of straw. Objective recklessness is not applied to non-fatal offences against the person.

19.5 Transferred malice

Under the principle of 'transferred malice', when an injury intended for one person falls by accident on another, a person should still be convicted of an offence. A number of possible situations are considered in Box 19.4.

19.6 Coincidence of actus reus and mens rea

Consider the following example.

> John loathes his little five-year-old brother, David. He finds his attention-seeking tantrums hugely irritating. One day, David is loudly demanding chocolate from his mother in the garden. John picks up a small plastic toy in a rage and hurls it from close range at David's head. The toy sails over David's head, missing him by a tiny fraction. It lands harmlessly on the lawn. Later that day, while John and David are eating a meal, John

---

Box 19.4 *Examples of transferred malice*

1. Suppose that the defendant causes the *actus reus* by a different method than he intended. For instance, imagine that Syd and Ali are both on a small boat. Syd shoots Ali intending to kill him. In fact, Ali is only hit in the leg, but as he collapses he falls from the boat into the sea and drowns. It is a long-established rule that in this situation the defendant is nevertheless liable.

Syd and Ali.

2. The defendant is mistaken as to the identity of his victim. For example, Sue shoots a man who she believes to be Fred, but in fact is Harry. Again, it is well established that the defendant is liable for the death. The defendant has the *mens rea* for murder and the fact that someone dies means that there is also *actus reus*.

3. Lynton poisons a glass of wine with the intention of killing Sophia. In fact, Jennifer picks up the glass by mistake and dies after drinking from it. Lynton will nevertheless be liable for the death, even if he could not have known that Jennifer would drink from the glass. The authority for this principle is *Latimer (1886)* where the defendant swung a belt at a man with whom he had argued. The belt hit the face of a woman standing nearby.

4. Roger and Simon quarrel in Simon's garden one night after a party. Roger throws a rock at Simon, but his aim is poor and he only succeeds in smashing a small garden statue. Roger was unaware that the statue was there when he threw the rock. There may be no *actus reus* for assault on Simon but the question is whether Roger is liable for criminal damage. In fact, Roger is not liable for criminal damage because the doctrine of transferred malice does not apply where the *actus reus* is different from the *mens rea*. Only if the *actus reus* intended and the *actus reus* caused are the same can malice be transferred from one to the other. This rule was established in *Pembilton (1874)*.

accidentally knocks over a pot of boiling hot tea which spills onto David's hand, burning him.

For offences that require *actus reus* and *mens rea*, both should be present at the same time. In the example above, when John threw the toy he had *mens rea* for assault but he did not have *actus reus*. Later, when the teapot was spilt, John had *actus reus* but no *mens rea* (the spill was purely accidental). There was no coincidence between the *mens rea* and the *actus reus*.

Continuing act

There is one situation where it might seem at first sight that the *mens rea* and *actus reus* do not coincide, but the courts still consider that an offence has been committed. This is where there is a '**continuing act**'. In other words, there is a sense in which *actus reus* stretches over a significant period of time and, at some point during that period, the defendant has *mens rea*. The leading authority for this is *Fagan v Metropolitan Police Commissioner (1968)*. Fagan was asked by a police officer to park at the side of the road. He followed this instruction and in the course of doing so, accidentally drove onto the officer's foot. To begin with, Fagan did not realise this had happened, but when the police officer asked him to move he refused to do so. After repeated requests, he eventually moved the car.

The question was whether Fagan was guilty of assault. The Court of Appeal said that the *actus reus* was still continuing when Fagan formed the *mens rea*. In other words, Fagan had criminal intention after having accidentally injured the officer but during a time when the car was still parked on the officer's foot. The two elements of a crime could be treated as occurring at the same time.

19.7 Strict liability

As a general rule, to be guilty of a criminal offence requires proof of both *actus reus* and *mens rea*. With some offences, however, only *actus reus* is required. It is not necessary to show that the defendant had *mens rea*. These are known as strict liability offences.

An example of a strict liability offence is illegal parking. It is conceivable that a person who parks on double yellow lines does not realise that they have done so. But an offence has been committed whether the driver has acted intentionally or not. Not even recklessness needs to be shown to convict someone of a strict liability offence. Other examples of strict liability offences include:

- trading standards
- food safety laws

- polluting waterways and other environmental offences
- the sale of alcohol, tobacco or lottery tickets to under-age children.

Which offences are strict liability?

Unfortunately, statutes do not always specify whether *mens rea* is required for a particular offence. This has sometimes caused problems for the courts. There are two general questions, either of which can help decide whether an offence is one of strict liability. These are:

1. Do the words used in the Act imply strict liability?
2. Is the offence really criminal or merely 'regulatory'?

Do the words used in the Act imply strict liability?

In the Privy Council case of *Gammon Ltd v Attorney General of Hong Kong (1985)*, it was stated that even if a statute did not specify whether an offence was one of strict liability, the words used might nevertheless indicate this. Key words are outlined in Box 19.5.

Box 19.5 *Key words in statutes and strict liability.*

1. **'Cause'**
   In *Alphacell v Woodward (1972)*, the defendant company was accused of polluting a river when equipment designed to prevent discharge into a river from the company's premises failed. There was no evidence that the defendants had been negligent or were aware of the mechanical failure that led to material being discharged. The wording of the relevant statute made it an offence to 'cause' polluted matter to enter into a river. The House of Lords held that, in the normal meaning of the word, the defendants had 'caused' the pollution to enter the water, as their activities had led to it. Their conviction was upheld.

2. **'Possession'**
   The word 'possession' is found in a number of statutes, for example those relating to illegal drugs. Use of this word generally indicates strict liability.

3. **'Knowingly'**
   On the other hand, use of the word 'knowingly' in a statute is taken to indicate that *mens rea* is required.

Criminal or 'regulatory'?

If there are not any words that provide clues about the need for *mens rea*, it is well established that the courts should start from the presumption that all criminal offences require *mens rea* - see Box 19.6.

> ### Box 19.6 *Sweet v Parsley (1970)*
>
>
>
> *A cannabis plant.*
>
> The defendant let rooms to students in a property in which she did not normally live. She exercised no control over the students other than collecting the rent and occasionally shouting at them to be quiet on one of her occasional overnight stays (she kept one room in the house for her exclusive use).
>
> During a police search, cannabis was found on the property. Although the defendant did not know that her tenants were using drugs, she was convicted of being concerned in the management of premises being used for the smoking of cannabis contrary to Section 5 (b) of the Dangerous Drugs Act 1965. On appeal to the House of Lords, Lord Reid said that, where the wording of an Act gave no clear indication as to whether *mens rea* was required, there was a long-standing common law presumption that Parliament did not intend to make criminals of persons who were in no way blameworthy in what they did. He went on to say, '…we must read in words appropriate to require *mens rea*'.
>
> The defendant's conviction was quashed.

However, in *Gammon Ltd v Attorney General of Hong Kong (1985)*, Lord Scarman stated that a distinction should be made between offences that are 'truly criminal' in character and those that are concerned with an issue of 'social concern'. This second category is likely to be regarded as strict liability offences. Social concern cases are sometimes described as regulatory offences. These are offences which:

- deal with matters of public welfare such as health and safety or road traffic
- do not damage the reputation of the defendant
- are unlikely to involve a prison sentence.

The arguments for and against strict liability are summarised in Box 19.7.

> ### Box 19.7 *Arguments for and against strict liability*
>
> **1. Arguments for strict liability**
>
>   (i) Strict liability removes the need to prove *mens rea* in appropriate offences, reducing the cost of running the courts.
>
>   (ii) In relation to 'social concern' offences, strict liability encourages companies to ensure that the law is not broken.
>
>   (iii) While convicting business operators without the need to prove *mens rea* may be tough on some defendants, it is preferable to the widespread public harm that would result from unregulated business practices. For example, if a restaurant broke food safety laws, a large number of people eating there might become ill.
>
> **2. Arguments against strict liability**
>
>   (i) Punishing defendants regardless of their guilt or innocence in the normal sense might be seen as unfair.
>
>   (ii) Some opponents of strict liability argue that there is no evidence that people take more care to avoid harm to others because of the existence of strict liability. It might even be the case that those who are aware that they can be prosecuted regardless of lack of *mens rea* do not place a high priority on taking proper steps to prevent harm.

Summary ● ● ●

1. In what way is mens rea different from motive?

2. What is meant by 'foresight of consequence' and how does it relate to intention?

3. How has 'recklessness' been defined?

4. When must actus reus and mens rea coincide?

5. What is 'strict liability'?

Case study ● *Mens rea*

Item A *Intention or recklessness?*

(i) Simon, the spoilt son of a millionaire, flies a light aircraft. Simon swoops down to ten feet above the swimming pool at his father's house as a practical joke. A guest at the house is about to dive from the top board but is so startled by the low flying plane that he falls against the side of the pool, causing a serious head injury.

Simon flies over the swimming pool at his father's house.

(ii) *DPP v K (a minor) (1990)* A pupil at a school took some acid from a laboratory. When he thought that he was about to be detected, he panicked and put the acid into a hot air dryer in the toilets. Another boy suffered injury when he used the dryer and the acid was blown out onto his face.

(iii) Alan pours petrol through the letterbox of a man who owes him money and is very late paying the debt. He sets light to the petrol. He merely intends to frighten the man and give him a warning, not to hurt anyone. A child that was in the house is severely burnt in the fire caused by Alan's action.

Item B

(i) Carol, a disc jockey, is charged with using a radio station for broadcasting without a licence contrary to the Wireless Telegraphy Act 1949. She is able to show in court that she believed she was making a demonstration tape and genuinely did not realise that the station was broadcasting. The purpose of the Act is to prevent unlicensed broadcasts on the grounds of public safety. Such broadcasts may interfere with the communication systems of the emergency services and air traffic control for instance.

Carol

(ii) John runs a newsagent in which he is allowed to sell lottery tickets. He sells a ticket to Tina, who is a very mature looking girl of 15 (she wears make up and is almost six foot tall). John is charged with selling a lottery ticket to a person under the age of 16.

John

(iii) Helen runs a pub. She allows a local band to practice in the function room one morning every week, while the pub is closed. She has noticed a strong smell of cannabis coming from the room from time to time but did not see a need to make a fuss, as the room is not open to the public at this time. After a police raid, Helen is charged with being concerned in the management of premises being used for the smoking of cannabis contrary to s.5(b) of the Dangerous Drugs Act 1965.

Helen

Questions

(a) In each of the cases in Item A consider whether the *mens rea* should be regarded as intention or recklessness. Explain how you reached your conclusions. (6 marks each)

(b) In each of the cases in Item B explain whether the offence is likely to be seen as one of strict liability. Also explain which of the following defendants should be regarded as having committed an offence. (6 marks each)

20 Non-fatal offences against the person

20.1 Introduction

There are a number of offences against the person within the criminal law, ranging from murder to common assault. The term 'assault' has two meanings. The wider, more general, meaning involves some kind of attack by one person on another. In the law, the term also has a more narrow meaning. Assault is the least serious offence of a range of different offences, all of which involve threatening or actually causing harm. The most important non-fatal offences against the person are explained in this unit. The least serious of these are common law offences (created by judges through precedents). These are:

- common assault
- battery.

The others are all contained within the Offences Against the Person Act 1861. In order of seriousness, these are:

- Section 47 assault occasioning actual bodily harm
- Section 20 wounding and grievous bodily harm
- Section 18 wounding and grievous bodily harm with intent

20.2 Common law assault

Common law assault is an offence that is tried in the Magistrates' Court and carries a maximum sentence of six months imprisonment. Common Assault comprises two elements:

- assault
- battery.

Broadly speaking, if someone threatens violence but does not actually make physical contact with the victim there has been a common assault. The application of force means that there has been a battery. Box 20.1 examines the *actus reus* of assault.

Fear of immediate violence

Threatening violence in circumstances where it is clear that the threat cannot be carried out immediately, though it may be very unpleasant behaviour, will not usually amount to common assault. For example, imagine that a man is standing at an underground train station and another man is shouting threats and making aggressive gestures from a train as it pulls out of the station. It is clear that violence cannot occur in the immediate future, so there is no *actus reus* of the offence.

Box 20.1 *Actus reus of assault*

In *R v Ireland and Burstow (1997)* the House of Lords ruled that the *actus reus* of assault is present when the accused puts the victim in fear of immediate and unlawful force being used against them. Examples of assault include:

- threatening someone by pointing a gun
- shouting out to a stranger 'I am going to kill you'
- waving a fist in an aggressive way
- throwing something that could cause injury.

On the other hand, the threat of violence has sometimes been regarded as immediate for this purpose where there is a real possibility of an attack in the immediate future. In *Smith v Chief Superintendent, Woking Police Station (1983)*, a woman looking through her bedroom window at night saw a man standing in the garden. She was badly scared and feared that he would smash the window to enter the room and attack her. It was held that the *actus reus* of assault was present.

Harassment and stalkers

During the mid-1990s there was considerable media attention given to the problem of stalkers:

'Stalking can be broadly described as a series of acts which are intended to, or in fact, cause harassment to another person. Stalkers can have a devastating effect on the lives of their victims, who can be subjected to constant harassment at home, in public places, and at work, to the extent that they feel that they are no longer in control of their lives.' (Home Office, *Stalking - The Solutions: A Consultation Paper, 1996*)

Stalkers may make obscene or menacing phone calls or persistently follow their victim. There have been problems in prosecuting the worst stalkers with an offence that carries a sentence that is adequate for the seriousness of the crime. Although an offence may have been committed under the Telecommunications Act 1984 or the Malicious Communications Act 1988 for instance, these and other crimes are only summary offences (in other words they carry a maximum sentence of six months imprisonment).

In response to media coverage of the problem, the government created the Protection from Harassment Act 1997 that creates two criminal offences of harassment. The more serious of these is under Section 4(1) which involves pursuing a course of conduct that causes the victim to fear that violence will be used against them. The maximum penalty is five years imprisonment.

An important case was *R v Ireland and Burstow (1997)*, outlined in Box 20.2.

In *Constanza (1997)*, a stalker made repeated silent

telephone calls and sent 800 letters to his victim. The last two letters were interpreted by the victim as clear threats. The Court of Appeal held that the assault was committed when the victim read these letters as there was a 'fear of violence at some time *not excluding the immediate future*'. This seems a surprising decision, if assault involves a threat of immediate violence. As Clarkson and Keating have commented:

> 'While the recipient of a telephone call might conceivably fear that the call is from a nearby call-box or mobile phone and that the caller will be at her door in a minute or two, it seems inconceivable that she would apprehend such immediate violence upon receipt of a letter.' (*Criminal Law Text and Materials*, Clarkson, C.M.V. and Keating, H.M., 1998)

Words can negate an assault

In the old case of *Tuberville v Savage (1669)*, the defendant placed his hand on his sword hilt and said to another man, during a quarrel: 'If it were not assize time, I would not take such language from you'. The defendant was saying that he felt restrained from attacking the other man because he knew that there were law officers in the area at that time. For this reason there could be no possibility of fear of immediate force.

On the other hand, in cases where the threat of violence is conditional on an action by the intended victim, an assault may have been committed. In *Read v Coker (1853)*, for instance, the victim was told that he would get his neck broken unless he left the premises straight away. In such a case, there clearly is a threat to use immediate force. The victim can only avoid this threat by actively doing something.

Mens rea of assault

The *mens rea* of assault is either intention to put the victim in fear of immediate unlawful violence or recklessness as to whether this happens. Recklessness is measured here by the 'Cunningham' (subjective) test explained in Unit 19, Section 19.4. In other words, the defendant must actually realise that there is a risk that their actions or words could cause someone to fear immediate unlawful violence.

20.3 Battery

Actus reus of battery

Battery differs from assault in that unlawful force has not only been threatened but also actually applied. A defendant may be charged with assault and battery at the same time. For example:

Box 20.2 *R v Ireland and Burstow (1997)*

In *R v Ireland and Burstow (1997)*, the House of Lords court ruled that not only threatening actions but also words could be sufficient for an assault. In fact, in this case, silence was enough. The defendant made many unwanted telephone calls to three separate women. He remained silent when they answered the phone. All of the victims suffered significant psychological symptoms. In fact, the defendant was convicted of assault occasioning actual bodily harm under Section 47 of the Offences Against the Person Act 1861. To convict under this offence,

R v Ireland and Burstow (1997) was concerned with harassment over the phone.

there must have been an assault. The established common law rule is that assault involves a fear of immediate personal violence. Lord Steyn pointed out that the Protection from Harassment Act did not cover cases where the victim feared that violence **might** be used against them. It only covered cases where the victim feared that violence **will** be used. Lord Steyn, therefore, extended common law assault to cover a situation where the victim feared the possibility of immediate personal violence. He said that the victim need only fear that 'the caller's arrival at her door may be imminent'. By extending assault in this way, the courts are able to convict some stalkers of the Section 47 offence, which carries a maximum sentence of five years.

● waving a fist in an aggressive way and then punching the victim

● throwing something that could cause injury and making contact with the victim.

It is possible that a battery occurs without there being an assault. For example if an object is thrown from behind the victim.

A battery need not involve any kind of pain of injury. The merest touch is sufficient. In *Wilson v Pringle (1986)*, the Court of Appeal said that there was a battery when a hostile touching or contact of some form occurred. For example in *Lynsey (1995)*, there was a battery when the defendant spat in the face of a policeman. In *R v Ireland and Burstow (1997)*, it was held that psychiatric injury could also amount to battery. If the defendant causes any injury, even if it is slight, it is likely that they will be charged with one of the statutory offences explained below.

Mens rea for battery

The *mens rea* for battery is either intention to apply unlawful physical force or subjective recklessness.

Activity 20.1

In each case, explain whether there has been an assault and/or a battery. (5 marks each)

a) **Linda, aged 16, is told to be home at 11 pm by her mother. She sneaks home at midnight. Her mother shouts that she will kill her.**

b) **A teacher loses his temper with a badly behaved pupil who is running past him. He grabs one of the boy's ears and pulls it.**

c) **A man stops a woman in an alley late at night and says: 'Come with me or I will hurt you'.**

c) **Stewart has an obsession with Margaret. He writes to her and says that he is angry because she wants nothing to do with him.**

20.4 Assault occasioning actual bodily harm

Under Section 47 of the Offences Against the Person Act 1861, 'any assault occasioning actual bodily harm' is an offence for which the defendant may be sentenced for up to five years. The offence is triable-either-way, so the case may be heard in the Magistrates' Court or the Crown Court (see Unit 12).

Actus reus

There are two elements to the *actus reus*. Firstly, there must have been the *actus reus* for assault or assault and

battery. In addition this assault must have caused 'actual bodily harm'. In *Miller (1954)*, it was held that this means 'any hurt in or injury calculated to interfere with health or comfort'. As explained above, a battery may involve physical contact but not injury.

Further explanation was provided in *R v Chan-Fook (1994)* where the court commented:

> 'The word "actual" indicates that the injury (although there is no need for it to be permanent) should not be so trivial as to be wholly insignificant.'

For example, if a person is struck in the face, there ought to be some kind of bruising for there to be anything more than common law assault and battery.

Actual bodily harm (ABH) may include psychological injury, though in *R v Chan-Fook (1994)*, it was said that a medical condition of some kind is necessary, rather than emotions such as fear or panic on their own (these emotions may well occur as part of a medical condition). In both *R v Ireland and Burstow (1997)* and *Constanza (1997)*, discussed in relation to assault above, the defendants were charged under Section 47. Both cases involved psychological injury.

Mens rea

The *mens rea* for assault occasioning ABH is either intention to put the victim in fear of immediate unlawful violence or recklessness as to whether this happens (so, it is identical to that of assault or battery). But supposing the defendant, while intending to do something that would only amount to the *actus reus* of an assault or battery, ends up causing actual bodily harm? Is there *mens rea* for the more serious offence in this situation? The answer to these questions is found in *R v Savage (1992)* - see Box 20.3.

Box 20.3 *R v Savage (1992)*

The defendant, Savage, intended to throw a pint of beer over the victim, who was the new girlfriend of her husband. As she threw the beer, she accidentally let go of the glass. The glass broke and cut the other woman's wrist. Her defence was that she lacked *mens rea* for a s.47 offence. She had not seen the risk that the glass might break. This might be seen as a valid argument - on the grounds that it is not fair that someone can be guilty of an offence for which the maximum sentence is five years when they only intended to commit a battery, which is an offence carrying a maximum sentence of six months. The interpretation given to Section 47 by the House of Lords, however, is that there is no requirement that the defendant foresee actual bodily harm. Lord Ackner said that: 'the prosecution are not obliged to prove that the defendant intended to cause some actual bodily harm or was reckless as to whether some harm was caused'. Savage was therefore guilty of an offence under s.47.

20.5 Section 20 - wounding and grievous bodily harm

Section 20 of the Offences Against the Person Act 1861 states that:

> 'whosoever shall unlawfully and maliciously wound or inflict any grievous bodily harm upon any other person...shall be guilty of an offence'.

Conviction for an offence under Section 20 carries a maximum sentence of five years imprisonment.

Actus reus

There are two alternative types of injury under Section 20. One of these is 'wounding'. *JJC v Eisenhower (1984)* was important in determining what, exactly, this means - see Box 20.4 below.

The second type of injury under Section 20 is grievous bodily harm (GBH). The difference between actual bodily harm and grievous bodily harm was suggested in *DPP v Smith (1961)* when the House of Lords ruled that grievous meant 'really serious'. This harm might be life threatening but it need not necessarily be so. GBH can include really serious psychological harm.

Whether the harm caused is sufficient to amount to GBH is a question of fact to be determined by the jury in each case. As a generalisation, attacks with weapons, such as guns, knives or clubs will nearly always result in wounds or GBH. On the other hand, attacks with fists may only result in actual bodily harm. Any injury that requires hospital treatment is likely to be regarded as wounding or GBH rather than a Section 47 offence.

Notice that the word 'inflict' is used in relation to GBH. In *R v Ireland and Burstow (1997)* - see Box 20.2 above - it was decided that Section 20 does not require an assault or battery, though there are very few cases where the harm caused is not the result of an assault.

Mens rea

The *mens rea* of Section 20 is present when harm was intended or when the defendant was reckless as to whether some harm was caused. Recklessness is judged by the subjective test.

Suppose that the defendant did not foresee the full extent of the injury that actually occurred. In other words, suppose that the defendant only foresaw a lesser injury than that required under Section 20. The question then arises as to whether the defendant has *mens rea* for Section 20. This question was answered in *Parmenter (1991)* - see Box 20.5.

Box 20.5 *Parmenter (1991)*

A father throwing his child into the air.

In *Parmenter (1991)*, the defendant injured his three-month-old baby while throwing him in the air and catching him, in play. Parmenter said that he had often played with older children in this way and did not realise that there was any risk of injury. He was acquitted of a Section 20 offence on appeal to the House of Lords. The Law Lords who heard the case, however, held that it was unnecessary for a defendant to have foreseen the degree of harm required by Section 20. Foreseeing only minor harm is enough.

Box 20.4 *JJC v Eisenhower (1984)*

It was held in *JJC v Eisenhower (1984)* that a wound for this purpose means causing a cut or a break in 'the whole skin'. What does this mean? The skin has two layers. The outer layer is called the epidermis and the inner layer, which, among other things, contains nerve endings, is called the 'dermis'. For a wound under s.20 (also for s.18) both layers must have been penetrated. Internal bleeding does not count as wounding for the purposes of Section 20.

The picture (right) shows a cross-section of the skin. A wound under s.20 would require penetration of the whole of the epidermis and dermis.

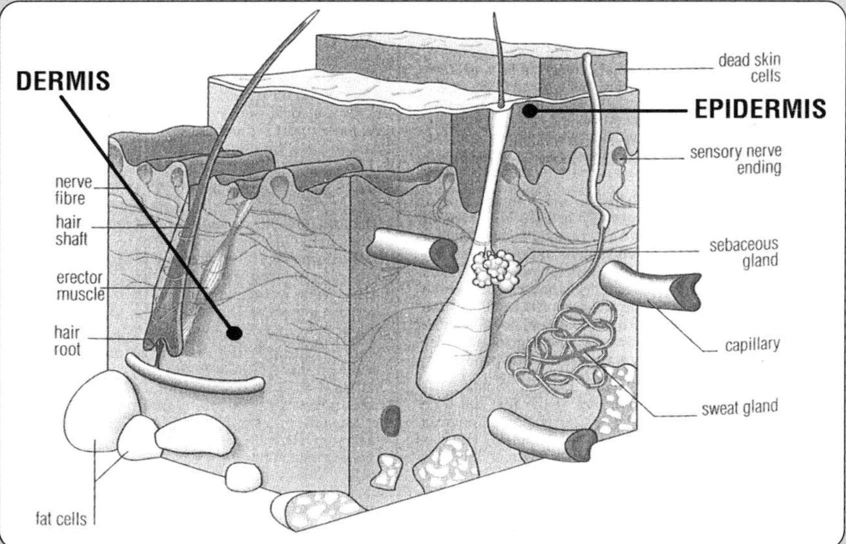

20.6 Section 18 – wounding and grievous bodily harm (with intent)

Section 18 of the Offences against the Person Act 1861 states:

'Whosoever shall unlawfully and maliciously by any means whatsoever wound or cause any grievous bodily harm to any person, with intent to do some grievous bodily harm to any person, or with intent to prevent the lawful apprehension...of any person, shall be guilty of an offence.'

The maximum sentence for this offence is life imprisonment.

Actus reus

The *actus reus* for Section 18 is almost the same as the *actus reus* for Section 20. Both offences involve 'wounding' and 'grievous bodily harm'. The only difference is that in Section 20 the word 'inflict' is used, whereas in Section 18 the word 'cause' is used. In *R v Ireland and Burstow (1997)*, however, it was said that there is little or no difference between the meaning of these words within the Act.

Mens rea

The *mens rea* for Section 18 differs from that of Section 20. Section 18 is an offence of specific intent. In other words, it is necessary for the prosecution to prove that the defendant had intention. Mere recklessness will not be sufficient. Remember that a jury can conclude that where the action of a defendant is virtually certain to cause GBH and the defendant realises that this is so, the jury may assume that the GBH was intentional (see Unit 19, Section 19.3).

If you read both Section 20 and Section 18 carefully you will see that the words 'with intent' are not only present in the latter, and it is this that makes it an offence of specific intent. However the *mens rea* can be satisfied in one of two ways:

1. Intent to do some grievous bodily harm to a person.

2. Intent to avoid arrest. This is the meaning of the part of Section 20 that deals with resisting or preventing 'lawful apprehension of any person'. So, an attack on a police officer who is seeking to make an arrest can amount to a Section 18 offence, even though the defendant might argue that the intention was to escape arrest rather than injure a police officer.

Box 20.6 on page 181 gives a summary of non-fatal offences against the person.

Activity 20.2

Mustafa has sustained a leg injury in the course of a rugby match. He is using a walking stick while recovering from this injury. One evening Mustafa goes to a party. He gets into an argument with Sam, another guest, which threatens to become violent. As Mustafa is a big, strong man, Sam thinks it is best to make a swift exit. He shouts one final insult at Mustafa as he walks from the sitting room into the kitchen. Mustafa goes to tap Sam with his walking stick, though not very hard. He merely intends to give the fleeing Sam a light smack on the leg to humiliate him. However as Mustafa swings the stick, Sam slips and falls in the kitchen doorway, on a highly polished wooden floor. The stick catches Sam in the eye, causing him some pain, though not an injury which requires medical treatment.

Discuss, using any appropriate cases, whether Mustafa should be charged with common law assault and battery or an offence under Section 47 of the Offences Against the Person Act 1861.

Box 20.6 *A summary of non-fatal offences*

Type of offence	Actus reus	Level of harm	Mens rea	Maximum sentence
Assault	Causing victim to fear immediate unlawful force	None	Intention or recklessness	6 months
Battery	Application of unlawful force - hostile contact	None	Intention or recklessness	6 months
S.47 Offences Against the Person Act 1861	Assault or battery causing ABH	ABH (usually slight)	Intention or recklessness	5 years
S.20 Offences Against the Person Act 1861	Act or omission causing wound or GBH (no need to prove assault)	Cut (wound) or grevious (really serious) bodily harm	Intention or recklessness	5 years
S.18 Offences Against the Person Act 1861	Act or omission causing wound or GBH	Cut (wound) or grevious (really serious) bodily harm	Intention	Life

ABH = actual bodily harm   GBH = grievous (really serious) bodily harm

20.7 Non-fatal offences against the person – which offence should be charged?

The law on assault has come in for a great deal of criticism. These criticisms include:

1. It is may be difficult for the jury to understand the law in this area.
2. It seems hard on defendants that for a conviction under Section 47 (actual bodily harm) only the *mens rea* for assault and battery need be shown.
3. Similarly, it seems surprising that having the *mens rea* for Section 47 is sufficient for a conviction under Section 20 (grievous bodily harm).
4. It seems illogical that Section 47 and Section 20 both carry the same maximum sentence of five years, although s.20 involves more serious harm.
5. It is also illogical that even a minor cut is equal to GBH in the sense that it creates the possibility of a s.20 charge.

In 1993, the Law Commission produced a report recommending substantial changes to the Offences Against the Person Act 1861. Five years later the government produced a consultation paper and a draft Bill, but by May 2003 no Act had yet been passed.

In practice, the Crown Prosecution Service uses guidelines identifying what offence should be charged in relation to particular levels of harm. This helps to reduce the effect of some of the inconsistencies in the law on assault.

An assault involving a battery that results in harm that technically constitutes ABH contrary to s.47 should be charged as a common assault, where the injury consists only of:

- a graze, scratch, or abrasion
- a bruise (including a 'black eye')
- swelling
- a reddening of the skin
- a superficial cut.

The following injuries should normally be charged under s.47:

- damage to a tooth or teeth
- temporary blindness or deafness, or temporary loss of other senses.
- extensive bruising
- a displaced broken nose
- minor fractures
- cuts requiring stitches
- psychiatric injury that goes beyond fear and panic, when confirmed by expert evidence.

Section 20 of the 1861 Act should only be used for those wounds considered to be serious, ie on a par with grievous bodily harm. Injuries that should be charged with GBH include those involving:

- permanent disability or loss of a sensory function
- permanent visible disfigurement (unless it is minor)
- broken or displaced limbs or bones
- harm involving sufficient loss of blood to require a transfusion
- lengthy treatment or incapacitation.

Summary ● ● ●

1. What are the different non-fatal offences against the person?

2. Why is the case of *R v Ireland and Burstow* (1998) important?

3. How does assault differ from battery?

4. What is the actus reus for an assault occasioning actual bodily harm?

5. What is the difference between offences under Section 18 of the Offences Against the Person Act 1861 and those under Section 20?

Case study ● Non-fatal offences against the person

Item A *Three different scenarios*

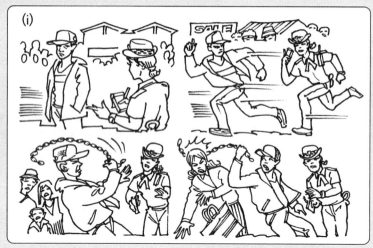

(i) Josh, a member of a criminal gang, is approached by a police officer, who wishes to arrest him. Josh runs off into a crowded shopping street, with the police officer hard on his heels. Josh pulls a length of chain from his coat and swings it in the air, to scare the police officer rather than hit her. However he hits a passer-by with the chain, causing a cut on the head that requires stitches.

(ii) John pushes Dave from a car moving at 20 mph. Dave manages to roll himself into a ball as he is pushed out of the car door, so escapes with bruising and some nasty grazes on his arms and legs.

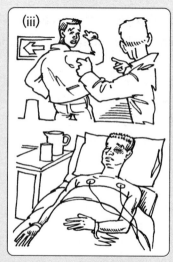

(iii) Phil is attacked in the street by Robert, the ex-husband of Phil's girlfriend. He has a black eye and suffers from internal bleeding.

Item B *The Rough House*

The Rough House Night Club is a venue that has more than its fair share of trouble. Ron walks into the club holding a gun in his hand, as the music stops playing. He sees Yvonne, whom he knows, and points the gun at her as a joke and to show off. Yvonne sees the gun and screams out: 'Look out, there's a man waving a gun over here!' Everybody in the crowded room panics and rushes for the stairs. Because the building is in a poor state of repair, the stairs will not take the strain of so many people at once. Tim finds himself being thrown to the floor as the stairs collapse. He has a broken ankle and damaged ligaments in one leg.

Item C *A pub brawl*

In a busy pub, Jim accidentally stands on John's foot. John winces and angrily shoves Jim against a table. Eddie the bouncer intervenes to prevent a fight, and throws both men out of the club into a badly lit yard. Tina, Jim's hot tempered girlfriend, has followed them out. She mistakes Roger for John and stabs him with a knife, though not fatally.

Item D *A violent quarrel*

Phil has a violent quarrel with Ned in the street. He swings a punch at him, intending to hit him on the nose. Ned stumbles and falls. As he falls he hits his head on the edge of a road works sign, causing him to sustain an injury that needs six stitches.

Questions

(a) In each of the cases outlined in Item A, explain what type of non-fatal offence you feel the defendant might be charged with. (6 marks each)

(b) Look at Item B. For criminal liability to be shown, the prosecution must prove *actus reus* including causation (see Unit 18, Section 18.4 for information on causation), and *mens rea*.

   (i)   Briefly explain what is meant by each of these three terms and indicate how the law of causation could apply to this situation. (15)

   (ii) Discuss Ron's criminal liability for Tim's injuries. (10)

(c) Read Item C and discuss the criminal liability of John and Tina. (15)

(d) Read Item D and discuss Phil's criminal liability for the attack on Ned. (10)

21.1 Introduction

Criminal cases are heard in either the Magistrates' Court or, where the offence is more serious, in a Crown Court before a judge and jury. Until the court reaches a verdict, the person alleged to have committed a crime is known as the 'accused' or the 'defendant'. If a defendant is found guilty, they become the 'offender'. The focus then switches from deciding whether someone has committed a crime to deciding upon an appropriate sentence.

The purpose of this unit is to examine what the aims or principles of sentencing are and to explain the types of sentences that the courts may award for a criminal offence.

21.2 Aims of sentencing

When a person is given a sentence for breaking the law, what exactly is the aim? It is obvious that there is any number of possible answers to this question. Perhaps different people should be treated in different ways. Most people would agree that sentences should vary to reflect not only the nature of the crime but the individual who is being sentenced. However, there is room for all kinds of debate on this.

Who decides what is an appropriate sentence?

The framework is set out by Acts of Parliament which lay down what types of sentence are possible for an offence and the minimum and maximum sentence available for particular crimes. A few offences carry only one possible sentence. For example, a person found guilty of murder must receive a sentence of life imprisonment. In the case of most offences, however, the courts, within the framework laid down by Parliament, are able to exercise their discretion as to exactly what sentence an offender receives

There are four main theories behind, or philosophies of, sentencing. These can be summarised as follows:

1. **Retribution** means seeking recompense or vengeance of some kind for the wrong done.

2. **Deterrence** means discouraging both the offender and the population as a whole from committing crimes. Offenders are 'made an example of'.

3. **Rehabilitation** means the sentence is aimed at reforming the offender or, in a sense, making them learn better ways.

4. **Incapacitation** means protecting society by locking up offenders to prevent them from doing harm.

No one of these theories is used on its own within the

courts at any given time. All of them are applied in day-to-day practice. The sentence received by an individual depends on factors such as the individual views of the judge involved, the background of the offender, the nature of the offence committed and the particular facts of the case. On any given day, one criminal may receive imprisonment as retribution while another does community service with the aim of rehabilitation. However, the history of the past 50 years of the criminal justice system is a history of regular swings from one sentencing principle to another. Sometimes retribution or deterrence is seen as the most appropriate overall aim, sometimes rehabilitation. Each idea has moved in and out of fashion among government policy-makers. From 1991 to 1997 for example, retribution was seen as the key principle of sentencing. This was a result of the Criminal Justice Act 1991. Since the Crime (Sentences) Act 1997, there has been something of a shift towards deterrence.

21.3 Retribution

The word 'retribution' in modern times is associated with ideas of punishing the offender on the basis of what justice demands, or to some extent, as a public expression of disapproval (see Box 21.1). Until the late 19th century, criminal punishment, which was much harsher than it is today, was seen as satisfaction of the victim's desire for revenge. The state was acting on behalf of victims and their families to prevent people taking the law into their own hands. In addition, punishment by the state satisfied a public need for vengeance. Such ideas seem barbaric to

Box 21.1 *A public execution*

A public hanging at Newgate prison. The last public hanging took place in 1868. The death penalty was abolished in 1965.

many people today, although the strength of the public reaction to some paedophile cases raises the question as to whether sentencing as a safety valve for public outrage still has a place in our legal system.

Just deserts

The phrase 'just deserts' suggests that criminals should be punished on the basis of what justice demands. The Conservative government of the early 1990s championed this sentencing policy. The 1990 White Paper *Crime, Justice and Protecting the Public* attacked deterrence and rehabilitation as justifications for punishment and explored the just deserts model. In line with the White Paper, the Criminal Justice Act 1991 introduced new sentencing rules to be used by the courts. These rules restricted judicial discretion and were aimed at ensuring that particular sentences were given for particular crimes. The key aim was uniformity of sentencing between different cases.

Although it might be thought that just deserts would lead to longer prison sentences, one attraction of the approach is that excessively severe sentences given for the purpose of deterrence or protection of the public become unacceptable. It may be seen as unfair that those who receive a sentence of imprisonment as a deterrent, for example, are given a longer term than many others who have committed the same offence previously. In other words, there is less disparity between sentences when the discretion of the courts is restricted.

Some have argued that the Criminal Justice Act 1991 has led to a failure to give longer sentences for those who persistently offend. One recommendation of the Halliday Report in 2001 was that the just deserts philosophy should be retained, but modified so that the severity of sentences increases when an offender has sufficient relevant and recent previous convictions.

Reparation

A simple form of retribution is reparation. This involves the offender making amends in some way directly to the victim. This may be through the payment of compensation or some form of service provided to the victim. An offender may also be required to make reparation to society as a whole, which is sometimes called 'restitution'. Doing work in the community under a community punishment order is one example of restitution.

21.4 Deterrence

Deterrence, unlike retribution, is concerned with looking at the future behaviour of an offender. This philosophy of sentencing says the prospect of punishment or making an example of offenders can reduce crime. Deterrence takes two forms. These are outlined in Box 21.2.

Box 21.2 *The two forms of deterence*

In the 1970s and 1980s, football hooliganism was seen as a growing problem and severe sentences were passed to deter football fans from engaging in violence. This photo was taken at Upton Park in October 1975. The game between West Ham United and Manchester United was held up for 19 minutes due to fighting on the terraces.

Individual deterrence

Individual offenders may be deterred from committing further offences by virtue of the sentence they receive. This is an argument for 'tough' sentences, particularly for younger offenders. The Conservative government of the 1980s introduced the notion of the 'short, sharp shock' for young offenders, with deterrence in mind.

General deterrence

As well as deterring an individual offender from committing crimes in the future, public awareness of the sentence the offender receives might have a deterrent effect on others. This is the idea of general deterrence. It operates on two levels. First, the level of sentence set by Parliament for a particular offence creates a type of on-going deterrence. Everybody is aware that committing crimes involves the risk of punishment, sometimes severe punishment. Second, when from time to time a particular type of crime is seen as a special menace, tough sentences may be passed by judges to make an example of those who are caught. This is known as giving an exemplary sentence. For example, during the 1970s and 1980s football hooliganism was seen as a growing problem and severe sentences were passed to send a message to violent football fans (in *R v Whitton (1985)* a Crown Court judge passed a life sentence on a football hooligan, although the Court of Appeal later reduced this to three years).

Does punishment deter criminals?

The idea of deterrence often receives popular support. There is a common sense appeal to the notion that those who behave in antisocial ways will think twice before committing a crime if they know they will really be made to suffer for it. It seems logical that this will cause the incidence of crime to fall. Moreover, where there is widespread public concern about increases in the levels of a certain type of behaviour, such as football-related violence or mugging, deterrent sentences may also satisfy a public appetite for retribution. However, there are at least four criticisms that can be levelled against deterrence as an aim of sentencing.

1. Crime statistics

Crime statistics do not altogether support the idea of individual deterrence. Reconviction rates in the UK after a first offence are about 50%. When 'short, sharp shock' detention centres were created by the Criminal Justice Act 1982, they were considered to have virtually no effect on reconviction rates and just six years later were abolished.

2. The effectiveness of deterrence is linked to the perceived likelihood of being caught

The experience of Denmark is often given as illustration of this point. The entire Danish police force was arrested during the Second World War by the occupying German army. Normal police work was carried out by a hastily-formed 'watch corps'. The crime rate rose rapidly. For example, the number of robberies in Copenhagen rose from ten per month in 1943 to over 100 per month after the disbanding of the police force in 1944. The courts issued very severe sentences to act as a deterrent but this had no apparent effect on levels of crime.

3. Offenders may not stop and think before they commit crimes

Crime may be committed on the spur of the moment. This point was considered in the government White Paper published in 1990:

'But much crime is committed on impulse, given the opportunity presented by an open window or an open door, and it is committed by offenders who live from moment to moment...It is unrealistic to construct sentencing arrangements on the assumption that most offenders will weigh up the possibilities in advance and base their conduct on rational conduct. Often they do not.'

4. General deterrence depends on publicity being given for exemplary sentences

Public knowledge regarding either the possible sentencing range for offences or the sentences handed out for individual crimes is limited. Research considered by the Halliday Report showed that:

'The public is badly under-informed about sentencing severity, and believes it to be more lenient than it is.'

In part this is due to reporting in the press. Newspapers tend to highlight cases where, they suggest, the sentence is too low rather than focusing on stiff sentences.

Activity 21.1

Consider whether fear of punishment is likely to deter individuals from committing offences in each of the situations below. In each case explain your answer.

(1) **A convicted burglar walking past a luxury home in a quiet residential street that has keys left in the front door. (4)**

(2) **A Real IRA terrorist who is plotting to plant a car bomb in a major city. (4)**

(3) **The father of two children who is invited to take part in a plan to smuggle a large consignment of heroin into the country. (4)**

(4) **An extremely intoxicated man. (4)**

(5) **A woman who has suffered years of physical abuse at the hands of her husband is standing in the kitchen. She knows that her husband is about to attack and sees a row of knives in a knife rack within range. (4)**

(6) **A person with a very low mental age. (4)**

21.5 Rehabilitation

The aim of rehabilitation is to reform offenders, to encourage them to see how they can behave differently in the future. The Oxford Dictionary gives one meaning of rehabilitation as: 'to restore to effectiveness after training'. Rehabilitation usually involves education and other help to enable the offender to develop into a more useful member of society. In the 18th century, reformers argued for a system of punishment that combined deterrence with rehabilitation. Lengthy solitary confinement, often seen as a harsh form of retribution today, was seen as an opportunity to feel remorse and find the resolve to reform. Rehabilitation does not necessarily lead to soft option sentences. Cross points out that, during the 1960s, judges sometimes passed long prison sentences purely to allow time for retraining (Cross, *Punishment, Prison and the Public*, 1971).

Critics of the modern British prison system point out that very little is done to reform offenders in prison. However, community rehabilitation orders and community punishment orders (see Section 21.14 below) are examples of sentences aimed largely at rehabilitating. Both involve supervision in the community with the aim of guiding offenders into becoming law-abiding people and helping them keep away from trouble. Rehabilitation within the community is often seen as particularly appropriate to younger offenders.

Criticisms of rehabilitation

There are a number of criticisms that have been made of the rehabilitative model. These are outlined in Box 21.3.

Box 21.3 *Criticisms of the rehabilitation model*

1. Loss of human dignity

Rehabilitation may lead to unacceptably harsh treatment of the offender, who becomes the subject of experiments. In some countries, rehabilitative treatment has meant having electrodes planted in the brain. During the 1970s, experiments with hormone drug treatment were inflicted on sex offenders. While most people would accept that offenders must expect to lose some of their civil rights, can the use of human guinea pigs in this way be justified?

2. Discrimination against the disadvantaged

Bottoms argues that judgements are made by members of the middle-class Establishment who believe that the educated and privileged are less likely to need reforming than the uneducated and poor.

3. Unjust sentences

It is possible that those found guilty in less serious cases end up serving longer sentences than those who have committed serious offences when the rehabilitative model is applied. An offender who is perceived, rightly or wrongly, not to have reformed may be kept in prison until their sentence is finished, while a person who is perceived as having made 'improvements' (but is nonetheless guilty of a more serious offence) has a shorter sentence because they are released early.

21.6 Incapacitation (protection of the public)

It is undoubtedly true that while offenders in prison are removed from general society they are not able to re-offend (or, at any rate, they can only re-offend within prison). In this limited sense, incapacitation has value. However, keeping people in prison is hugely expensive and nobody could seriously argue that locking up all criminals for life is a viable option. As prisons have long been regarded as training grounds for criminals, it might be reasonably argued that they are counter-productive. Only a very small number of highly dangerous offenders are permanently imprisoned.

In the case of a certain type of serious offender who it appears is very likely to re-offend, there may be a case for permanently removing them from society. This might particularly apply to violent offenders. However, can we be certain that predictions of dangerousness are accurate? Is it acceptable to imprison someone for life solely on the basis of incapacitation? Clarkson and Keating argue that it is not, partly because it is hard to tell if someone will always be dangerous and partly because:

'It is wrong in principle to punish someone for what

they might do in the future.' (Clarkson & Keating, *Criminal Law*, 1998)

However, Clarkson and Keating do say that incapacitation may be acceptable where people have persistently shown themselves unable to learn from previous convictions and sentences received.

Incapacitation may take forms other than imprisonment. The death penalty is obviously an effective form of incapacitation, but so are driving bans and curfews. One attraction of sentences such as these is that they make it much harder for the dangerous driver or the drunken hooligan to re-offend but are much cheaper on the public purse than prison.

21.7 Do reconviction rates indicate the value of a sentencing philosophy?

Evidence to establish the success of policies designed to deter people from committing crime can be gathered by measuring the number of offenders who re-offend. A person who re-offends is known as a 'recidivist'. The number of people in the population re-offending is called the 'level of recidivism'. If recidivism is lower than it was before the introduction of deterrent policies, those policies could be regarded as a success. It could be argued that potential criminals have been deterred by the sentences they know they may receive. Much the same approach to measuring the success of rehabilitative policies can be used. If policies are put in place to rehabilitate prisoners, any fall in the reconviction rate might be regarded as a consequence of this approach.

However there are several difficulties in adopting this simple cause and effect model. Crime figures are notoriously unreliable as statistical evidence. Recorded crime figures do not indicate the amount of undetected crime, which may alter with changes in policing methods and the sophistication of criminals. Also, the sentence an offender receives is only one of many factors that will have an impact on levels of crime at any given time. Many changes in society, for example levels of poverty, may also have an effect.

Those who argue primarily for retribution or protection of the public are less concerned with reconviction rates. The focus here is on dealing with the offence that has been committed, rather than having an impact on the offender's future behaviour.

Reconviction rates

Home Office statistics from 1994 provide a summary of

national reconviction rates (see Box 21.4). They suggest that too many offenders get into trouble with the law again, whatever sentence they receive. For those starting community penalties or discharged from prison in 1994, about half were reconvicted within two years. There were no real differences between reconviction rates for custody and for all community-based sentences. Nor did an analysis of reconviction rates by type of community sentence reveal significant variations. Those who have offended repeatedly very often continue to offend. Over two-thirds of those with seven or more convictions were reconvicted within two years.

The two factors most clearly linked with reconviction are age and gender. Approximately 56% of men were reconvicted, compared to 45% of women. There is a particular problem with younger offenders - 70% of offenders under 21 were reconvicted within two years. Chart (ii) in Box 21.4 shows reconviction by age.

Box 21.4 *Reconviction rates*

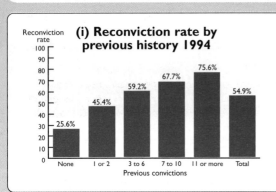

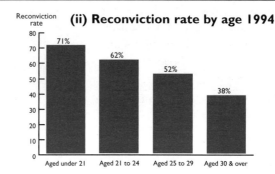

Chart (i) shows reconviction rate by previous history.

Chart (ii) shows reconviction by age.

Activity 21.2 Crime pays in Greenland?

Greenland is perhaps the best place in the world to serve a prison sentence. The island's only prison, Anstalten for Domfaltde (Institution for Convicts) allows its hundred or so inmates to travel to paid outside jobs in Nuuk, the capital of Greenland, every day. Their wages are paid into special accounts which are managed by the prison's head guard who also acts as a kind of financial adviser. Prisoners are given a £40 per week spending allowance and can request further withdrawals to buy consumer goods. After serving a few months of their sentences, the Anstalten convicts have often acquired video players and a wardrobe of new clothes. From Monday to Friday they drive themselves from the prison to their jobs every morning, and return at the end of the day, to a night behind prison bars (possibly calling in at the video shop on the way).

The Community Centre in Greenland's capital, Nuuk, at the time of elections in November 2001.

Some people in Greenland think that the inmates of Anstalten live a life that is virtually indistinguishable from anyone else. Jorgen Meyer, Director General of the island's police force, defends the prison regime in Greenland, however. He claims that the brutality of traditional prisons only serves to make prisoners tougher and often they will re-offend. Only some, more serious, offenders are sent by sentencing magistrates to a conventional prison in Denmark (Greenland is a semi-independent region of Denmark).

Repeat offenders are as common in Greenland as in Denmark. As a proportion of the population, the number of people being sent to prison is higher in Greenland than in Denmark. Meyer admits that:

'Greenland's inhabitants are becoming more and more convinced that the punishment for crime on the island is inadequate.'

Adapted from 'Greenland calls time on the good life in prison', *Daily Telegraph,* 21 October 2001.

(a) What term can be given to a person who persistently re-offends? (2)

(b) Explain what seems to be the dominant philosophy of sentencing in Greenland. (6)

(c) Does the approach to sentencing seem to have an effect on the amount of crime in Greenland? (5)

(d) To what extent does the sentencing system in Greenland meet the aims of retribution and deterrence? (10)

(e) Suggest reasons why some more serious offenders are sent to a conventional prison in Denmark. (6)

21.8 Types of sentence

The types of sentences and the maximum sentence that can be passed in relation to an offence are laid down by Acts of Parliament. Within this framework, the courts have to decide how lenient or severe a sentence should be for a particular offender. Until the Criminal Justice Act 1991, judges relied solely on what is known as the tariff system.

The tariff system

The term 'tariff system' is used to describe the approach used by judges in setting a sentence. This involves referring to broad guidelines laid down by the Court of Appeal. It is based on **proportionality**. In other words, people with similar backgrounds who commit similar offences in similar circumstances should receive similar sentences. However, the tariff system allows for proportionality to be given less weight in relation to offenders in certain categories. This is called 'passing an individualised sentence'.

Individualised sentences

Individualised sentences are passed when the court is seeking to deal with the individual needs of the offender rather than just provide a proportionate sentence. An example of an individualised sentence is where the focus is on reforming rather than punishing the offender. This may be appropriate for a younger offender or cases where offenders have a record of committing fairly minor crimes over a long period of time and appear not to have responded to prison sentences. Mentally ill offenders may be detained in a hospital or be given probation with a requirement that psychiatric treatment is undertaken.

Tariff sentences

If it is felt that there are no grounds for giving an individualised sentence, the tariff system itself is applied. The tariff system has two stages. The first is calculating the initial tariff sentence. This involves finding the appropriate place to put the offender within the range regarded as standard to each type of factual situation. The second stage is to apply secondary tariff principles. In other words, the initial tariff may be reduced by mitigating factors or increased by aggravating factors.

Mitigating factors

Mitigating factors are those that suggest a less severe punishment than the facts of the case otherwise indicate. Examples are shown in Box 21.5.

Aggravating factors

The presence of aggravating factors may lead the court to pass a more severe sentence. The Court of Appeal has

---

Box 21.5 *Mitigating factors*

Provocation
If for example, a person convicted of assault in a pub brawl was the subject of great ridicule or had been the victim of racist abuse, this could reduce the sentence that would otherwise be given.

Youth or old age
A young offender may be regarded as having been led astray by an older accomplice for example. An old and frail person might not be sent to prison as they would find it harder to bear than a younger person in good health.

Intoxication
An impulsive punch in the face when under the influence of drink by a person that is normally placid, can be seen as different from a premeditated attack.

Previous good character

Attitude and behaviour after the offence was committed
Did the offender show remorse? Did the offender voluntarily compensate the victim? Has the offender cooperated with the police?

Pleading guilty
The defendant who admits guilt is perhaps part way to realising that what they have done is inexcusable. An early guilty plea can mean that a sentence is reduced by up to one third.

---

stated that the correct way to deal with aggravating factors is to ignore any mitigating factors rather than going straight to giving a more severe sentence than the initial tariff.

Aggravating factors are outlined in Box 21.6.

21.9 The offender's background

Before passing sentence, the court needs to gather information on a number of factors.

1. Whether the offender has previous convictions

2. Background information about the defendant's circumstances
This will include information on family circumstances, employment, behaviour since the offence was committed and so on. To gather this information, the court requests the preparation of a **pre-sentencing report (PSR)** by the

Box 21.6 *Aggravating factors*

Examples of aggravating factors are as follows:
- the fact that an offence was racially motivated (Criminal Justice and Public Order Act 1994)
- the fact that a victim was very young or very old, or can otherwise be seen as particularly vulnerable
- in rape cases, the effect of the crime on the victim - all rape victims will suffer distress and shock, but if the victim suffers particular psychological harm, a heavier sentence will be given
- in some cases, particularly motoring offences, the use of drink or drugs - the Court of Appeal once warned those who took part in 'a motorised pub crawl' could expect more severe sentences for the offence of causing death by reckless driving
- a carefully planned offence will be treated more severely than one that was committed on the spur of the moment
- the fact that an offence was committed while the offender was on bail
- the presence of relevant previous convictions (relevance is judged by whether the convictions were for the same kind of offence).

probation service. A PSR influences decisions such as whether to give a custodial or a community sentence.

3. Medical reports
Medical reports are particularly important if the court is considering the use of special powers to commit the offender to a mental hospital under the Mental Health Act 1983 (see page 194).

4. The financial situation of the offender
The financial position of the offender is particularly relevant when the court wishes to impose a fine.

Activity 21.3 Guidelines in relation to appropriate sentences for rape

The initial tariff

Except in very exceptional cases, rape is a serious crime that justifies an immediate custodial sentence.

Rape committed by an adult without aggravating or mitigating circumstances.. 5 years

Rape committed by two men together or following a kidnapping (or various other circumstances)............................... 8 years

The defendant has raped several women .... 15 years

The defendant's behaviour indicates serious psychological problems and he is likely to remain a danger indefinitely .... Life

The secondary tariff

Some aggravating factors	Some mitigating factors
Violence, over and above that necessary to commit the rape, is used.	A guilty plea - especially important because of the distress a victim suffers in court.
A weapon is used to frighten or wound.	The behaviour of the victim where it 'was calculated to lead the defendant to believe she would consent to sexual intercourse'.
The defendant has previous convictions for rape or other serious offences involving violence or sexual crimes.	Previous good character, though this is only 'of minor relevance'.
The effect upon the victim is of special seriousness.	

Fred is accused of raping Sue. He has pleaded guilty. He has no previous convictions for rape. Evidence suggests that the likelihood of him offending again is slight, and that he has shown considerable remorse. For many months after the attack, Sue suffered from bad nightmares and depression. Her doctor has signed her off for several months from work.

Suggest an appropriate sentence for Fred, based on the 1986 Court of Appeal guidelines set out above. (6)

The tariff system - an illustration

In *R v Billam (1986)*, the Court of Appeal, Criminal Division, laid down guidelines in relation to appropriate sentences for rape. Some of these have been summarised in the form of the table in Activity 21.3.

21.10 The Powers of the Criminal Courts Act 2000

The Powers of the Criminal Courts Act 2000 consolidates two important pieces of legislation from the 1990s, namely the Criminal Justice Act 1991 and the Crime Sentences Act 1997.

The Criminal Justice Act 1991

Until 1991, judges relied solely on the tariff system. This allowed for a considerable degree of judicial discretion. The Criminal Justice Act 1991 (CJA) was passed, in part, because of the Conservative government's concern that the severity of sentence received by an offender seemed to depend largely on which judge and which court the offender was sentenced in. In some places, much more lenient sentences were passed than in others. The aim of the legislation was to create more consistency of sentencing between courts than the tariff system alone seemed to produce and to focus the courts on simply ensuring that offenders received no more nor less than they deserved. The Act sought to set up the form of retribution known as 'just deserts' as the primary aim of sentencing. This was achieved by reducing the amount of discretion given to judges. Severe sentences could not be passed as a deterrent. They must be justified by the offence committed.

The effect of Section 1(2) is that imprisonment is only to be used if the offence is so serious that it is the only sentence which can be justified. In the case of violent or sexual offenders, only imprisonment will protect the public from serious offences.

Section 2(2) of the Act specifically prohibits sentences passed to make an example of the offender.

The intention of the CJA and what has actually happened are two different matters however. The Court of Appeal stated in *R v Cunningham (1993)* that the 'seriousness' of an offence within the meaning of the Act should not be interpreted in isolation. This, therefore, enables the courts to take other matters into consideration. This raises the question of whether the tariff system has really been reformed. The Halliday Report *Making Punishments Work: a Review of the Sentencing Framework for England and Wales,* published in 2001, noted that:

'The statute law leaves a great deal to discretion, to a degree that is bound to result in inconsistency of approach.'

The Crime Sentences Act 1997

The Crime Sentences Act 1997 left the framework set up by the Criminal Justice Act 1991 largely untouched, but reintroduced deterrence - discouraging the offender and the population as a whole from committing crimes through sentencing - as a government policy. The main change created was the introduction of minimum sentences for repeat offenders in relation to certain offences. This is known as the 'two strikes' rule - see Box 21.7.

21.11 Prison

For offenders aged over 21, a custodial sentence means being sent to prison (see Box 21.8). Although sections of the British public may view our legal system as too lenient, the fact remains that Britain has more people serving life than any other country in Western Europe. At the end of 2001, there were more than 68,000 people in prison, which is 51% more than in 1990. For every 100,000 people in the UK, 125 are in prison. According to 1999 Home Office research findings, these figures place the UK at about the mid-point in the world list. Within the European Union, only Portugal has a higher rate of imprisonment. Russia has the highest prison population rate in the world, with 685 per 100,000 people.

Joe Levenson, a member of the Prison Reform Trust, which campaigns for change within prisons, wrote in 2000 that:

Box 21.7 *The two and three strikes rules*

The two strikes rule
Under Section 109 of the Powers of the Criminal Courts Act 2000, if an offender over the age of 21 commits a second offence where that offence is defined as a serious one, they should be given a life sentence. Serious offences for this purpose are offences such as manslaughter, attempted murder, rape and armed robbery.

The three strikes rule
Under Section 110 of the Powers of the Criminal Courts Act 2000, if an offender over the age of 18 is found guilty of a Class A drug trafficking offence for a third time, a minimum sentence of seven years must be imposed. Similarly, Section 111 imposes a minimum sentence of three years for a third domestic burglary.

Under Sections 109 to 111, the court may disregard the minimum sentence rules where there are exceptional circumstances.

Box 21.8 *Prison in Britain*

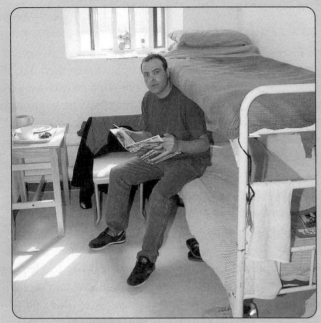

This photo shows a prisoner in Wormwood Scrubs prison.

'Although some prisons are providing safe and constructive environments for prisoners, a disturbing number of prisons are overcrowded, have little purposeful activity for prisoners and are unsafe for prisoners and staff. Unless these failing prisons are drastically improved, they will not be effective in helping prisoners to stay away from crime after release.'

Every year about a hundred people commit suicide in prison.

The early release rules

Many offenders do not serve the whole of their prison sentence. Before the Criminal Justice Act 1991, an offender could leave prison early due to good behaviour (known as 'remission') or under a system called 'parole', supervised by an agency called the Parole Board. Under this system, if an offender re-offended after release on the recommendation of the Parole Board but during the period of the original sentence, they could be taken back to prison to finish their term.

The 1991 Act abolished remission and parole, replacing them with the single concept of early release. Early release distinguishes between two groups:

- those sentenced for up to four years
- those sentenced for more than four years.

Box 21.9 describes the conditions under which prisoners may be released from prison before the end of their sentence.

Box 21.9 *Early release*

Those sentenced for four years or less

Offenders are automatically released after half their sentence. If the sentence given by the court is for more than one year, the early release is 'on licence', which means that the offender is monitored and supervised by the Probation Service. If the offender breaks the terms of their licence, the Parole Board has the power to return them to prison to finish the original sentence.

When offenders are released early, they may be released subject to a curfew. This means that the offender is expected to stay at home during night time hours. Although the early release on curfew scheme has been attacked in some quarters, only 5% of inmates subjected to curfew orders were recalled to prison between 1999 and the end of 2001, mostly for breach of curfew rather than committing further offences.

Those sentenced to more than four years

Prisoners sentenced to more than four years can be released on licence after serving somewhere between one half and two-thirds of the sentence. At what exact point an individual is released is decided on the basis of a recommendation by the Parole Board. If early release is allowed, the offender is on licence until they have served three-quarters of their sentence.

Activity 21.4

Sam is sentenced to life imprisonment for his part in the armed robbery of a post office. A shotgun that Sam fired seriously injured one of the post office staff.

Discuss when Sam might be released from prison. What is the consequence of breach of any licence under which he is released? (4)

Sam

21.12 Suspended sentences and discharge

Suspended sentences

In relation to sentences of up to two years' imprisonment, the court may order that the sentence be suspended. This means that the sentence will not take effect unless the offender commits another imprisonable offence during a period laid down by the court. This period must be between one and two years.

It might be thought that the use of suspended sentences would reduce the prison population, but it seems that, in the past, it tended to increase it. Suspended sentences were sometimes used instead of a community-based sentence and so, if an offender re-offended, they were sent to prison. The Criminal Justice Act 1991 (CJA) s.5 dealt with this by requiring the court to ensure that a suspended sentence is only given where exceptional circumstances are present and the offender would otherwise have been imprisoned. Since the CJA was passed, suspended sentences have rarely been given.

Discharge

A discharge can be given by the court to a person who has been found guilty of an imprisonable offence. The discharge may be absolute or conditional. An **absolute discharge** means that no action is taken at all. This sentence is appropriate when the offender is wrong in law but no reasonable person would wish to punish them. A **conditional discharge** on the other hand means that no punishment will be given unless the offender commits another offence within a specified time frame. In the event of this happening, the offender is brought before the court again and a sentence is determined (unlike with a suspended sentence, the offender does not know what punishment they will receive). A conditional discharge may be given to offenders where there are very strong mitigating circumstances.

21.13 Monetary sentences

Fines

A fine may be imposed for almost any offence. Offences heard in the Magistrates' Court carry a maximum fine. There is no maximum in the Crown Court. One advantage of a fine over prison is that it does not affect the employment prospects of an offender in the same way. Some research evidence suggests that the reconviction rate for those receiving a fine is lower than that for other sentences. To some extent, a sentence may vary according to the amount an offender earns, as the court can take this into account. A fine can be deducted from pay using an 'attachments of earning order'.

Other monetary sentences are outlined in Box 21.10.

21.14 Community sentences

Since the Criminal Justice and Court Services Act 2000, community sentences have been given new names.

1. Community rehabilitation orders (formerly known as 'probation')

With community rehabilitation orders, an offender is not kept in custody but is required to meet regularly with a probation officer who is there to supervise the offender and ensure that they keep out of trouble. When the court gives a community rehabilitation order, conditions will normally be attached. For example, the offender may be required to live in a probation hostel or to undertake certain activities for up to 60 days or undergo psychiatric treatment. Community rehabilitation orders may last from six months to three years. Where conditions are broken, the probation officer has the power to return the offender to court for resentencing.

Research conducted by Mair and May in *Offenders on Probation*, 1997, suggests that 90% of those receiving probation felt it had been useful, often because they felt having an independent person to talk to about problems was helpful.

2. Community punishment orders (formerly known as 'community service')

Community punishment orders require the offender to spend a specified number of hours performing unpaid work for the benefit of the community. The sort of work undertaken includes outdoor conservation projects and other physical tasks. The Probation Service supervises community punishment orders. The maximum number of hours is 240. If offenders do not turn up to carry out

---

Box 21.10 *Other monetary sentences*

Compensation orders

The aim of these court orders is to require the offender to compensate the victim of their crime, rather than make payment to the state. Examples of compensation orders include payment of money for injury or loss and the return of stolen property.

Confiscation orders

The Proceeds of Crime Act 2002 enables profits made from criminal recovery to be taken from the defendant after conviction. The purpose of confiscation proceedings is to recover the financial benefit that the offender has obtained from criminal conduct. The court calculates the value of that benefit and can order the offender to pay an equivalent sum. Proceedings are conducted according to the civil standard of proof - ie on the balance of probabilities. The Act includes provisions to set up an Assets Recovery Agency.

Forfeiture orders

Forfeiture orders are used to seize and destroy illegal material, such as drugs.

work, or otherwise breach their order, they may be taken back to court. The courts have a range of powers in these circumstances, including passing a new sentence for the original offence.

3. Community punishment and rehabilitation orders (formerly known as 'combination orders')

In certain circumstances the courts may combine community rehabilitation orders with an element of community punishment. This more flexible order provides the opportunity to give a more individualised sentence.

4. Curfew orders

Curfew orders were introduced in the late 1990s. The offender is required to remain at home or at some other place between certain hours, usually after dark. A curfew is enforced by an electronic tagging device that identifies the movements of the offender (see Box 21.11). A private sector firm undertakes the monitoring of curfews. As a separate sentence, it is quite unusual for the court to pass a curfew order. They are more commonly used in relation to prisoners on the early release scheme (see Section 21.11 above).

> **Box 21.11** *Electronic tagging*
>
>
>
> *This photo shows a police officer exhibiting the sort of electronic tag that would be worn by disgraced former Cabinet Minister Jonathan Aitken. The tag ensures that the offender's movements can be tracked.*

5. Drug treatment and testing orders

Since the Crime and Disorder Act 1998 became law, drug offenders can be sentenced to up to three years at a residential or non-residential drug centre. This is a community sentence, not a custodial one. The offender must be willing to take part in the treatment for the courts to give this sentence. Pilot schemes in 1998 suggested that the order was often successful in reducing drug-taking behaviour.

Activity 21.5

Doreen Marshall, aged 69, admitted putting 45 crushed sleeping pills into the food served to her 90-year-old mother, Cecilia. Cecilia lived in a residential home in Luton. She had been incontinent and suffering from severe depression for some years. Although she became unconscious, she later recovered. Doreen was charged with attempted murder. She told the police that she wanted her mother to sleep and to be out of her misery. She also said, 'I'm not sorry. The only thing I am sorry about is that it didn't work.'

The trial judge, Judge Rodwell, said that he was satisfied that the mother's condition was 'absolutely wretched beyond belief', and that Doreen was attempting a mercy killing. The seriousness of the offence meant that a prison sentence was necessary but because of exceptional circumstances the judge felt that the sentence could be suspended. A 12-month prison sentence was given, suspended for two years.

Adapted from the Independent, 29 September 2001.

(a) **What are mitigating factors? (2)**

(b) **What mitigating factors are present in this case? (3)**

(c) **Under what circumstances will Doreen Marshall spend time in prison? (2)**

(d) **What arguments might be put against the decision to give a suspended sentence in this case? (6)**

(e) **If Doreen Marshall had been given an immediate prison sentence what is the earliest she might have been released? (2)**

21.15 Other sentences

Brief mention should be made of some other sentences that may be used in relation to particular circumstances or types of offence.

Mental health orders

Under the Mental Health Act 1983, where an imprisonable offence has been committed, the courts have the power to order the detention of the offender in hospital for treatment for a mental or psychiatric disorder. This type of sentence is sometimes called 'sectioning', a term used because there are several different orders that may be made under different sections of the Act.

Antisocial behaviour orders

Under Section 1 of the Crime and Disorder Act 1998, the police or a local authority may apply to the Magistrates' Court for an antisocial behaviour order. The court has the power to prevent someone from doing something, for example going to a particular place or area. Antisocial behaviour orders can be issued to people of any age, but are most likely to be used against young people who are seen as harassing or distressing people in a neighbourhood, for example through persistent vandalism or intimidation of elderly people. Antisocial behaviour orders are civil orders, but criminal penalties may be applied if they are breached.

Disqualification from driving

The courts have power to impose disqualification from driving for a period of time. For a first offence of drink driving, this is normally 12 months.

21.16 Sentences for younger offenders

Except in very unusual circumstances, the courts only deal with offenders who are over the age of ten. Young offenders are dealt with by special Magistrates' Courts called 'Youth Courts' which were, until recently, known as 'Juvenile Courts' (see Unit 12, Section 12.6). Most sentences that the courts give to adults cannot be given to those under 18. The law relating to custodial sentences for younger offenders is controversial and there have been many different attempts to find the best approach by governments over the past 30 years. It is generally recognised that young offenders tend to need reform more than punishment, and it is often argued that young people are influenced to a greater extent by efforts to rehabilitate than older criminals. Sadly, the criminal justice system has a poor record in relation to the rehabilitation of young offenders, as is shown in the reconviction statistics discussed on page 188 above.

Young Offenders' Institutions

Although prison is only available for those aged 21 and over, secure custodial units called Young Offenders' Institutions exist for those aged between 18 and 21 (see Box 21.12). The maximum sentence for offenders in this age group is no different from other adults, so if necessary an offender may be transferred to an ordinary prison on reaching 21.

Box 21.12 *A Young Offenders' Institution*

This photograph shows young offenders in Feltham Young Offenders' Institution.

Detention and training orders

If the court wishes to impose a custodial sentence on an offender aged between 12 and 21, they may be sent to a special centre, rather than an adult prison. As might be expected with this age group, there is a greater emphasis on education and training than is found in prisons. Those below the age of 15 are generally only detained in custody when they are persistent offenders.

When a detention and training order is passed, the sentence must be for a period of not less than four months and not more than two years. However, the courts have additional powers in relation to very serious offences such as those involving a death or an indecent assault on a woman.

Youth Offender Panels

Since 2002, some young people going before the Youth Courts have received a **referral order**, under the Crime and Disorder Act 1998. A local Youth Offender Panel, comprising volunteers from all sections of the community, devises and enters into an agreement with the young person to make amends for their offending behaviour. This can include meeting with a victim and agreeing reparation. Panels are assisted by Youth Offending Teams, which include professionals from a range of agencies, including the police, social services, and the local health authority.

Parenting orders

The Criminal Justice Act 1991 introduced an element of parental blame. The courts have the power to fine parents if they have agreed to keep their child under control after committing an offence and a further offence is, in fact, committed. Parenting orders can also be issued where, for example, parents are required to attend guidance or counselling sessions to help them change the behaviour of their child.

Attendance centre orders

Attendance centres are run by the probation service and provide training for those sent there. This sentence is available to those under 21. The offender may be required to attend for one or two hours per week for a limited period. If the offender has received a custodial sentence in the past, an attendance centre order cannot be issued.

Action plan orders

Under the Crime and Disorder Act 1998, the new community order of action plans was created for those under 18. This followed a White Paper that argued for a sentencing option that offered 'a short intensive programme of community intervention combining punishment, rehabilitation and reparation to change offending behaviour and prevent further crime' (reparation means making amends to the victim). The offender is monitored and, over a period of three months, has to comply with conditions relating to participation in specific activities, such as training or voluntary work, keeping clear of particular places, appearing at attendance centres and reparation.

Supervision orders

Under supervision orders, those aged between ten and 17 are supervised by trained staff for the purpose of rehabilitation. This is a similar sentence to community rehabilitation orders.

Police warnings

The police can deal with young offenders without bringing the case before the courts. Where there is evidence that a child has committed an offence and the child admits committing it, the police may give a formal warning and refer the offender to a Youth Offending Team which will arrange for the child to participate in a rehabilitation scheme. However, under the Crime and Disorder Act 1998 there are limits on how many times such a warning

may be given without the offender being taken to court. Warnings should only be used where a prosecution would not be in the public interest.

Summary ● ● ●

1. What are the four main aims of sentencing and what are the advantages and disadvantages of each?

2. Do reconviction rates indicate the value of a sentencing philosophy?

3. What is the 'tariff system' and how does it work?

4. What are aggravating and mitigating factors and how do they affect the type of sentence passed?

5. Other than a prison term, what sentences can judges hand out?

6. How does sentencing differ for juveniles?

Case study ● Sentencing

Item A *The aims of sentencing*

A young man, Peter, is very badly injured in what seems to be an unprovoked attack. His attacker, John, is a known heroin addict who has been homeless for three years. Now 29, John once had a promising career as an architect, but he lost his job and his home when he turned to hard drugs after a tragic car crash in which his parents, brother and sister were all killed. John, who was also injured in the accident, was the only survivor. He spent the year following the accident in a psychiatric hospital, suffering from severe depression.

Item B *Supply of Class C drugs*

The Misuse of Drugs Act 1971 states that the maximum sentence for supply of class C (soft) drugs is five years imprisonment and/or a fine.

Tom, aged 30, is found guilty of supplying class C drugs. He has had numerous previous convictions in the past 15 years, some of them leading to short prison sentences. A pre-sentencing report shows that he is at present homeless and out of work. He pleaded not guilty at his trial. A police search showed that he had very large quantities of class C drugs on his person when arrested.

Item C *Dangerous driving*

Under the Road Traffic Act 1988, the offence of causing death by dangerous driving is punishable by up to ten years imprisonment (though it is very unusual to see the maximum penalty imposed).

Janet has been found guilty of causing death by dangerous driving. She committed this offence while driving at 54 mph in a busy town centre street, where the speed limit was 30 mph. It was after dark when the offence occurred. Last year, Janet was fined for careless driving.

Item D *Growing cannabis*

The maximum sentence for growing cannabis is six months imprisonment and/or a fine.

Jim, aged 41, is a consultant psychiatrist who has smoked cannabis since he went to university. He has no previous convictions and pleaded guilty to the offence of growing cannabis (he grew it on a sunny window ledge in his home).

A cannabis plant.

Questions

(a) Using Item A to illustrate your answer, explain the aims of sentencing. (15)

(b) Look at Item B.

   i) Explain what is meant by a 'pre-sentencing report'. (3)

   ii) Suggest what order (or orders) the court might make, taking full account of the tariff system. (6)

(c) Look at Item C.

   i) What information would the court require before passing sentence? (6)

   ii) Suggest how Janet's sentence will be calculated. (4)

(d) Look at Item D. Do you feel that a fine, a community based order or a custodial sentence is most appropriate in this case? Explain your answer. (8)

22.1 Introduction

This unit deals with some basic principles of the law of negligence. Negligence is the most significant branch of the law of torts, which deals with a variety of civil wrongdoings. Other branches of tort are briefly outlined in Unit 1. It is important to realise that liability in tort is separate from any liability under a contract. It should also be remembered that while criminal liability results in a sentence being passed in the criminal courts on the defendant, civil liability leads to the payment of damages or some other remedy being provided for the claimant - assuming, of course, that the court finds in favour of the claimant.

What is the meaning of the term 'negligence'?

In everyday language, the term 'negligence' means failure to take proper care. In legal terms, where this failure results in some kind of damage, the person who has caused it (the defendant) is liable to compensate the claimant for the damage suffered. The laws of negligence are the rules that have been developed to decide when compensation should and should not be allowed. Today, the rules of negligence are applied in a wide range of situations. Negligence claims may result for example from a road accident, from injuries at work, from careless medical treatment, or even from work badly done by an accountant or a lawyer.

Duty of care

The basis of the law of negligence stems from the idea of what is known as a 'duty of care'. This concept originated in the case of *Donoghue v Stevenson (1932)* which is illustrated in Box 22.1.

When is there liability for negligence?

For a claimant to prove liability they must prove three things. To understand the law of negligence, it is necessary to know the rules relating to each of these. The three factors that must be proven by the claimant are:

- **that a duty of care was owed by the defendant to the claimant**
- **that this duty had in fact been breached** - in other words, the defendant did something that was careless
- **that the breach caused damage** - in other words, that the loss suffered was caused by the defendant's carelessness, rather than some other cause.

Box 22.1 *The origins of negligence - Donoghue v Stevenson (1932)*

Ms Donoghue went to a café with a friend who bought her some ginger beer and ice cream. The proprietor of the café opened the ginger beer and poured out some of the contents. The bottle was opaque, so it was not possible to see inside it. When the glass was topped up, a partially decomposed snail came out of the bottle. As a consequence Donoghue became quite ill.

When somebody buys something, the law of contract applies. If a term of a contract for sale is not met, the courts will allow the person who has lost out to obtain compensation. However, the right to sue for damages relating to breach of contract is only provided to parties to the contract, namely the buyer and the seller. Donoghue was not a party to the contract, as she did not buy the drink. The question was whether there was any other way that she could recover damages for her illness, given the apparent carelessness of the manufacturer.

Lord Atkin gave the leading judgement in the House of Lords. He recognised that the law of negligence was very piecemeal. The courts had only ruled on each specific case as it came before them. If claimants could not fit their case into one of a limited number of categories, they were unable to claim in negligence. Donoghue's case, like many others, did not fit into the existing types of negligence.

Lord Atkin regretted that no broad, general, duty of care existed. He set about defining such a duty. He ruled that a manufacturer of products that could not be inspected before use owes a duty of care to all those who might be expected to consume their product. Lord Atkin set out his general test, now known as the 'neighbour test' to establish when a duty of care might arise in all manner of cases. He said:

'You must take reasonable care to avoid acts or omissions which you can reasonably foresee would be likely to injure your neighbour. Who then is my neighbour? The answer seems to be - persons who are so directly affected by my act that I ought reasonably to have them in contemplation as being so affected when I am directing my mind to the acts or omissions which are called in question.'

In other words, everyone has a duty to avoid injuring those who it might reasonably be thought would be injured by a lack of care.

22.2 Duty of care

The duty of care is a device used by the courts to identify where a defendant should be seen as having an obligation to avoid causing damage to the claimant. This is a matter of law rather than fact. Judges need to decide whether, as between two people, a duty of care should be recognised. If they decide not to recognise such a duty, the claimant will not be able to recover damages. Of course, once the higher courts have stated that there is duty of care in a particular case, this is likely to become a binding precedent so that, in similar cases in the future, the door has been opened to negligence. The courts have used the approaches outlined in Box 22.2 when deciding whether in principle a duty of care arises.

There are a number of categories of case where the detail of the rules used to decide the existence of a duty of care in some cases is somewhat different:

- a claim based on psychiatric injury (sometimes called nervous shock by lawyers) rather than physical injury
- a claim based on economic loss (which basically means loss of profit) rather than damage to property
- where the damage was caused by an omission rather than an act
- where the damage was caused by a third party rather than the defendant
- where the defendant falls into a special group, for example, the police.

Box 22.2 *When does a duty of care arise?*

1. 'Policy reasons'

Sometimes, the courts have taken the view that a duty of care should only be recognised where there are policy reasons for doing so. 'Policy', in the language of judges, means reasons that are for the good of society. This is a very vague idea, which means different things to different judges at different times. It is sometimes argued that the courts use the term to justify moulding the law in the way that they feel is appropriate, and that the good of society really has little or nothing to do with this. As a consequence of this use of 'policy', the law of negligence has, at times, developed quite slowly. The courts have been cautious, for a variety of reasons, about allowing excessive numbers of people to claim for negligence.

2. The two-stage test

In *Anns v Merton London Borough (1978)*, Lord Wilberforce put forward a new version of the test establishing whether a duty of care should be recognised. This is often called the two-stage test. The two stages are:

1. Ask whether the defendant could be reasonably be expected to foresee a risk of harm to the claimant.
2. If the answer to this question is yes, then to ask whether policy reasons existed which would prevent a duty of care arising.

Under the two-stage test, the claimant would be able to rely on the existence of a duty of care in untested negligence cases, unless it was possible to identify a good policy reason for there being no duty. Before *Anns v Merton London Borough (1978)*, no duty of care was recognised unless there was a good reason for doing so. This means that it became easier to establish the existence of a duty of care. Some judges were concerned that there would be too many negligence cases being brought in the future and that there would be an excessive widening of the scope of negligence.

3. The three-stage test (the Caparro rules)

In *Murphy v Brentwood District Council (1990)*, the House of Lords overruled *Anns v Merton London Borough (1978)*, by using the 1966 Practice Statement (see Unit 7, Section 7.6). This led to the creation of a three-stage test in *Caparro Industries plc v Dickman (1990)*. This is a more cautious test for the existence of a duty of care. The test is the one used today. It involves asking:

1. Was the damage to the claimant reasonably foreseeable?
2. Was the relationship between the claimant and the defendant sufficiently proximate?
3. Is it just and reasonable to impose a duty of care?

'**Reasonably foreseeable**' means asking whether a reasonable person would have predicted that the claimant might suffer injury or damage. '**Proximate**' in the second part of the test is a way of summarising Lord Atkin's 'neighbour test': 'persons who are so directly affected by my act that I ought reasonably to have them in contemplation'. Proximity is about closeness. It means that there must be a relationship between the two parties that is sufficient to create a duty of care. The '**just and reasonable**' element enables judges to refuse to recognise a duty of care where they feel there are good reasons for this, even though the other two stages have pointed towards the existence of a duty.

This unit just deals with the duty of care in relation to physical injury and damage to property, where the Caparro rules apply. Two cases help to illustrate the three-stage test. In the first a duty of care was recognised by the court, in the second it was not. These cases are outlined in Box 22.3.

22.3 Breach of duty

If there is a duty of care that will give rise to a liability in negligence, it is also necessary to show that the duty has been breached. Even if it is foreseeable that the claimant might suffer loss as a result of the defendant's negligence, it has to be established that the defendant's behaviour was actually careless. For example, all drivers owe a duty of care to other road users but they have not breached that

Activity 22.1

Jane witnesses an armed robbery in a bank. She is the only person to get a good look at one of the gang. When a person is arrested under suspicion, she positively identifies him as the robber. Jane will only give evidence in court if she is given police protection while at home, as she is scared that other members of the gang may harm her. The police agree to provide protection but, due to an administrative error, no officer is assigned to protect her. Another gang member seriously assaults Jane.

Jane is considering taking legal action against the police.

(a) **Briefly explain the legal test for establishing whether a duty of care exists. (6)**

(b) **Do you think that the police owe Jane a duty of care in negligence? (8)**

Box 22.3 *The three-stage test in Caparro*

Chris Eubank and Michael Watson in action during their WBO title fight at Tottenham Hotspur's White Hart Lane ground in London on 22 September 1991.

Peter Sutcliffe, the Yorkshire Ripper.

Watson v British Boxing Board of Control (2001)

The defendant, the British Boxing Board of Control, is a non-profit-making regulatory body. All those involved in a boxing match are obliged to accept and comply with the Board's requirements. In 1991, the claimant, Michael Watson, suffered a brain haemorrhage during a title fight with Chris Eubank. He received medical treatment after a delay, by which time he had sustained serious brain damage. He claimed damages in negligence from the Board. The Board argued that it owed no duty of care to the claimant. Lord Phillips of Worth Matravers, ruling in favour of Watson, said that the injuries sustained by professional boxers were not just foreseeable but inevitable. These injuries were a consequence of an activity that the Board funded, encouraged and controlled. The facts, therefore, established a relationship of close proximity between the Board and its members who were professional boxers. The claimant relied on the Board to look after his safety. It was fair, just and reasonable to impose a duty of care on the Board.

Hill v Chief Constable of South Yorkshire (1990)

Peter Sutcliffe, the notorious serial killer known as the 'Yorkshire Ripper', had already murdered a number of women when he killed the daughter of the claimant. It was argued that the South Yorkshire police were negligent in failing to catch the killer at an earlier stage. The court ruled that even if the police had been at fault in the way that they handled the investigation, they owed no duty of care to the claimant's daughter. It was held that she was not sufficiently proximate to the police. There was no special relationship as there was no reason for the police to believe that the victim was in more danger than any other woman in the area where the murders were committed. There were also policy reasons for not recognising a duty of care. There was a danger that investigations would be hindered as the police would use resources to protect the public rather than locate the killer. The police would act to avoid claims in negligence from those whom they did not protect.

duty of care until their driving falls below a certain standard.

The objective standard of care

In the law of negligence, the standard of care required is determined by considering what would be expected from a reasonable person. It is an objective standard. This means that the characteristics of the defendant are not (usually) taken into account. In *Nettleship v Weston (1971)*, Weston was learning to drive using her husband's car. Nettleship, a friend, was teaching her. She steered and controlled the pedals while he kept control of the gear lever and handbrake. He also helped with the steering at times. Weston lost control, mounted the kerb and crashed into a lamp post, despite guidance from Nettleship. Nettleship's knee was injured in the collision. The question that had to be settled in court was whether the standard of driving expected of Weston should be regarded as that appropriate to a learner or that expected from any driver. Lord Denning said:

> 'The learner driver may be doing his best, but his incompetent best is not good enough. He must drive in as good a manner as a driver of skill, experience and care, who is sound in mind and limb, who makes no errors of judgement, has good eyesight and hearing, and is free from any infirmity.'

This is a general principle, not just one that is used in relation to road accidents. The individual shortcomings of a particular defendant are not usually taken into account when deciding whether there has been a breach of duty.

It is interesting to note that, later in his judgement, Lord Denning discussed the relationship between the objective standard and insurance. All drivers are required to be insured for injury caused by negligence to others. It is the insurance company that pays damages, not the defendant. But the injured third party may be in the position of only being able to recover damages if the other party involved is liable in law. For example, a person may have comprehensive insurance as a driver, but might be injured as a pedestrian hit by a car. Lord Denning commented that, as insurance companies are in a better position to pay out than the injured party, the courts seek to ensure that a high standard is expected of drivers. This relationship between the law of negligence and insurance is a factor that has regularly influenced the way that negligence law has developed.

22.4 The objective standard - key issues

The courts have evolved various principles regarding the

detail of the objective standard, as difficult cases have come before them.

Are precautions needed when the risk is small?

1. **A reasonable person is not usually expected to go to great lengths to prevent harm where there is a very small risk of it occurring.** Two cases involving cricket grounds provide an illustration of this principle. They are outlined in Box 22.4.

Box 22.4 *Bolton v Stone (1951) and Miller v Jackson (1977)*

Surrey's Mark Ramprakash hits a six off John Woods to beat Lancashire by three wickets in the Frizzell County Championship Division One at the Oval, London on 11 May 2002.

In *Bolton v Stone (1951)*, over a 28-year period, a cricket ball had travelled out of a ground into the adjoining (little used) lane only six times. On the seventh occasion it hit a passer-by, despite the presence of a fence on the boundary. The management of the cricket club was sued for negligence. The question was whether there was a breach of duty. Would a reasonable person have taken steps to prevent this happening, for example by having a higher fence? The court held that the chances of this kind of accident occurring were so slight that the club could not be expected to take steps to guard against it.

On the other hand, in *Miller v Jackson (1977)*, the ball travelled out of the cricket ground about eight or nine times every season. When a person was injured, it was held that actions should have been taken to prevent an injury of this nature. The defendant had breached their duty of care by not doing so. The extent of the risk was much greater than in *Bolton v Stone (1951)*.

2. **Where the risk seems small but the potential harm that might occur is great, a reasonable person would be expected to take steps to deal with the risk.** In *Paris v Stepney Borough Council (1951)*, the plaintiff had only one eye. He was employed in a garage by the defendant. He was not provided with goggles for doing tasks such as welding. While he was using a hammer to remove a bolt, a piece of metal flew off into his good eye. The House of Lords, while accepting that the risk of injury was very small, ruled that the defendant was liable. The consequences of the injury for this particular defendant were very grave, as he became completely blind. The defendant ought to have taken into account the seriousness of the harm. To supply goggles to the defendant was both easy and inexpensive.

Are there any acceptable reasons for taking a risk?

Sometimes it can be acceptable to run a risk if the purpose of the activity under consideration justifies it. It is sometimes said that it is necessary to balance usefulness to society with the level of risk. In *Watt v Hertfordshire County Council (1954)*, the claimant was a fireman. He was part of a team that was rushing to the scene of a serious accident where a woman lay crushed under a car. A heavy piece of lifting equipment was held down by the claimant and two other men on the back of a lorry for a short journey. It was known that there was some risk that the equipment would move about on the lorry, but to secure it properly would have taken more time. It was important to reach the accident as quickly as possible if the life of the trapped woman was to be saved. The claimant was injured when the equipment slid on the lorry. In the Court of Appeal, Lord Denning said:

'One must balance the risk against the end to be achieved. If this incident had occurred in a commercial enterprise without any emergency, there could be no doubt that the...employee would succeed.'

In this case, however, the duty of care had not been breached.

To what lengths does the defendant have to go to prevent harm?

The defendant is only expected to do what is reasonable to prevent harm. The case of *Latimer v AEC Ltd (1953)* provides an illustration of this principle. The defendants' company owned a factory. Through no fault of the defendants, the factory floor was flooded during an unusually heavy storm. This meant that oil that was normally in a small channel spread all over the floor. Obviously this meant that the floor was slippery. Sawdust was spread as much as possible but there was not enough sawdust to cover every part of the affected area. Although there was some risk of injury, it was decided by the company that there was no need to shut the factory down. The plaintiff slipped on an untreated patch and badly sprained his ankle.

Lord Denning in the Court of Appeal said:

'So, here the employers knew that the floor was slippery and that there was some risk in letting the men work on it, but, still, they could not reasonably be expected to shut down the whole works and send all the men home. In every case, it is a matter of balancing the risk against the measures necessary to eliminate it...In the circumstances of this case, it is clear that the defendants did everything they could reasonably be expected to do. It would be quite unreasonable to expect them to send all the men home.'

Of course, a number of factors are taken into account when deciding what, in each individual case, someone might reasonably be expected to do. These include cost and the level of harm that might occur. But, overall, the courts usually accept that there is a need to be realistic.

Activity 22.2

The owners of Goldenrock Motor Racing Circuit are reviewing whether they need to improve their safety barriers for the annual Grand Prix (no changes have been made since 1992). They are aware that they need to take into account the possibility of being sued.

Here is a table of figures showing the numbers of accidents by year. The table shows which bends were involved and the number of serious injuries and deaths caused to drivers and spectators.

Year	Name of bend		
	Blackthorn	Old Glory	Hell's Gate
1993	1	2	0
1994	0	3	0
1995	0	1	0
1996	0	0	5
1997	0	0	0
1998	0	0	0
1999	0	1	0
2000	0	1	0
2001	0	1	0
2002	0	0	0

Using reference to relevant case law, advise Goldenrock Circuit. (8)

What is regarded as standard practice?

In considering what amounts to a breach of duty, the courts may be influenced by what is regarded as standard practice in a particular context. If standard practice has been followed this will be strong evidence that a defendant was not negligent. However in *Re Herald of Free Enterprise (1987)* the court ruled that standard practice was obviously dangerous and should not have been followed - see Box 22.5.

Box 22.5 *Re Herald of Free Enterprise (1987)*

The salvage operation following the sinking of the 'Herald of Free Enterprise' in 1987.

The *Herald of Free Enterprise* was a Zeebrugge car ferry, which left port one day with its bow doors not fully shut. It was unexpectedly swamped by a wave and took on a great deal of water. The ferry sank, with considerable loss of life. The defendants claimed that it was standard practice for the master of the ship not to check that the bow doors were closed before setting out to sea. The court ruled that this was negligent and, if it was standard practice, it should not have been.

The standard expected of a defendant with special characteristics

There are some situations where, because of the nature of the defendant, a higher or lower standard of care might be expected in determining whether there has been a breach of duty.

Doctors and other experts

It might seem fair to expect a higher standard of care from someone who is skilled and expert in their field than someone who is not. This has certainly tended to be the view of the courts. For example, suppose that someone is injured in the street. If a passer-by, someone without

medical training, gives first aid, they would not be expected to be able to do very much. If they fail to do something a doctor would have done, this is unlikely to amount to negligence. If, on the other hand, a doctor is treating a person with the same injuries, fewer errors and a greater level of care would be expected. The reasonable person test is inappropriate with this kind of defendant and is replaced by a higher standard of care. This is a similar idea to the concept of 'standard practice'. Professionals should be expected to conform to professional standards.

An important authority on this matter is *Bolam v Friern Barnet Hospital Management Committee (1957)*. The plaintiff agreed to undergo electroconvulsive therapy for his mental illness. As a result of the treatment he suffered severe fractures and sued the defendants in negligence claiming that:

- he should have been warned of the risk of injury
- relaxant drugs should have been administered to eliminate the risk.

At the time, many doctors believed that there were problems in administering relaxants while many others believed that this was, in fact, sound practice. The court held that the fact that medical opinion was divided did not necessarily matter, so long as there was a respectable body of expert opinion to support the action of the defendants. As a result, the defendants were not negligent.

The House of Lords slightly modified the *Bolam* approach in *Bolitho v City and Hackney Health Authority (1997)*. Lord Browne Wilkinson said that the fact that a respectable body of professional opinion supported a particular course of action did not mean that it was always acceptable. There should be a careful consideration of the relative risks and benefits of each approach by the experts. It was ultimately for the court, not for medical opinion, to determine the standard of care required of professionals in each particular case.

Children as defendants

Where a child is alleged to have been negligent, the standard of care expected is lower than that which applies to an adult. In *Mullin v Richards (1998)*, two 15-year-old girls, the defendant and the claimant, were 'sword fighting' with plastic rulers. The ruler used by the defendant snapped with the result that a piece of plastic went into the eye of the claimant, causing her serious injury. This kind of play fighting was common in the school and there was no school ban in place. The Court of Appeal held that the defendant was not negligent. Judge Hutchinson ruled that the defendant should be judged as having the same foresight as any normal 15-year-old. He stressed, however, that the test for negligence was still an

Activity 22.3

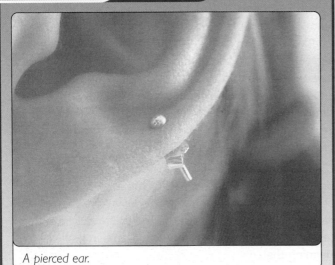

A pierced ear.

What do you feel would be the standard of care expected from a jeweller carrying out an ear piercing? Do you feel it should be that required of a reasonable person? That required of a trained nurse? Or some other standard? Explain your answer, including reference to relevant precedents. (6)

objective one, so that a 15-year-old who was more absent-minded, inexperienced or slow-witted than other children of that age might in principle still be negligent.

Ill defendants

There have been a number of appeals concerning defendants who have suddenly had an attack of some kind while driving. For example, in *Roberts v Ramsbottom (1980)*, the defendant suffered a stroke while driving and, as a result, lost control of his car and hit the claimant. Surprisingly, the court held that he should be judged by the standards of a reasonably competent driver and, on that basis, he had acted negligently. This may seem hard on the defendant, but it should be realised that underlying this decision was a desire to ensure that the claimant received compensation. The driver was insured, after all, so that it was really his insurance company that would be required to pay out.

22.5 Special characteristics of the claimant

To some extent, a reasonable person is expected to take into account the individual characteristics or vulnerability of the claimant. One example of this can be seen in *Paris v Stepney Borough Council (1951)*, discussed above. The defendant was expected to treat an employee with one eye differently from one with two eyes.

In several recent cases the courts have considered whether the intoxication of the claimant can influence what is expected of the defendant - see Box 22.6.

Box 22.6 *Barrett v Ministry of Defence (1995)* and *Griffiths v Brown (1998)*

Barrett v Ministry of Defence (1995) concerned a Navy Pilot on a remote Norwegian base controlled by the Ministry of Defence (MOD). Heavy drinking was commonplace on the base (probably because the men had little else to do in their free time). The defendant was found in a state of extreme drunkenness and taken to his room, where he was then left alone. He subsequently choked on his own vomit and died. His widow sued the MOD. In the High Court it was ruled that the officer in charge could be liable in negligence for failing to prevent drunkenness. The Court of Appeal disagreed with this decision. There was no duty of care to prevent off-duty drunkenness. However, the Court of Appeal took the view that a duty of care had arisen at the point in time when the officer assumed responsibility by moving the pilot to his room. The officer in charge had acted negligently by not fetching medical help or making sure that someone kept watch over him.

Note that in the *Barrett* case, damages were reduced on the basis of what is called 'contributory negligence'. The pilot was partly to blame by becoming so drunk in the first place.

In *Griffiths v Brown (1998)*, the claimant had also drunk too much. He called a taxi and asked to be taken to a cashpoint machine. The driver took him there, parking very near to the cashpoint but on the opposite side of the road. As the claimant crossed the road he was injured. The claimant argued that the driver, knowing that he was drunk, should not have exposed him to the risk of being run down. The court rejected this argument, saying that the driver's duty was simply to stop at a place where the passenger could get out safely. That duty was not altered by virtue of the fact that the passenger was drunk.

22.6 Res ipsa loquitur

It is generally for the claimant to prove that the defendant breached the duty of care. There is no requirement for defendants to show that they acted reasonably. However, in some cases it will seem obvious, on the basis of common sense, that the defendant must have been negligent. For example, in *Scott v London and St Katherine Docks (1865)* two sacks of sugar fell from an open hatch in the defendant's warehouse and injured someone on the ground below. The Court of Appeal held that it was possible for negligence to be assumed from what had happened, as the bags could not have fallen by themselves. In cases such as these, it is up to the defendant to establish that there has been no breach of duty, rather than the plaintiff to prove that there has. This is known as the doctrine of *res ipsa loquitur* (Latin for 'the thing speaks for itself').

The doctrine will take effect only if three conditions are met. Each of these conditions is examined in turn.

1. The accident could not have occurred without negligence

An example of this can be seen in *Ward v Tesco Stores Ltd (1976)*. The plaintiff was injured when she slipped on some yoghurt, which had been spilt on the floor of the defendant's supermarket. The Court of Appeal held that such an accident could only have occurred through a failure on the part of the defendants to keep the floor clean, and that, unless the defendants could prove otherwise, they must therefore be negligent.

2. The defendant had control

If the defendant did not have control of an activity, in the sense that another party may have caused something to happen, then it cannot be said be said that the thing speaks for itself. Two contrasting cases illustrate this.

In *Easson v LNE Railway (1944)* a train was seven miles from the station when one of its doors flew open and a passenger fell out. The plaintiff argued that this was an example of *res ipsa loquitur*, as the door must have opened due to the failure of railway staff to check that it was shut. The court held that it was perfectly possible for another passenger to have interfered with the door in the time since the train left the station and so *res ipsa loquitur* had not been shown. There was the possibility that the railway company was not the cause of the accident.

In *Gee v Metropolitan Railway (1873)*, the facts were very similar to those in the *Easson* case. However, in this case, the door of the carriage flew open just after it left the station, so the only possible cause was the failure of railway staff to shut it properly. In this case it was obvious that only the defendant could be held responsible.

3. The defendant has no alternative explanation

If the accident could not have occurred without negligence and the defendant had control, this does not mean that the defendant has been shown to be negligent. It may be that the defendant is able to put forward an alternative explanation of what happened. That is the significance of the doctrine that it is for the defendant to show that they were not negligent.

22.7 Damage

Even if the claimant has established the existence of a duty of care, and a breach of that duty has been shown, the claimant also needs to prove that the defendant was

---

Activity 22.4

The reasonable person

Whether there has been a breach of duty depends upon what the reasonable person would do. The imaginary reasonable person has been described by Lord Denning as 'the man on the Clapham omnibus' or 'the man who takes the magazines at home and in the evening pushes the lawnmower in his shirt sleeves' *(Hall v Brooklands Auto Racing Club 1933)*. Such a person is presumed to be sensible but is not required to possess superhuman foresight or caution. It has to be recognised that the standard required will vary according to the perceptions of individual judges. Lord Macmillan said in *Corporation of Glasgow v Muir (1943)*:

> 'What to one judge may seem far-fetched may seem to another both natural and probable.'

In this case, the defendants owned tea rooms in a Glasgow Park. The manageress had allowed members of a church picnic party to bring their own food and drink into the rooms because of bad weather (a small fee was paid). Two of the picnic party carried their tea urn down a passage in which some children were queuing. The urn tipped up in the crowded passage and some customers (the claimants) were scalded with hot tea. The result was a

A tea urn.

claim in negligence. It was argued that the manageress ought to have foreseen the risk from spillage and was, therefore, negligent in failing to remove the children from the passage while the urn was being moved. The case was appealed to the House of Lords.

Adapted from *Case and Commentary on Tort* by Harvey, B. and Marston, J., 1998.

(a) Briefly explain what is meant by the 'objective standard of care'. **(3)**

(b) Give arguments for and against the owners of the tea room in *Corporation of Glasgow v Muir* being liable for negligence. Do you consider that there has been a breach of duty? **(6)**

(c) Imagine that one of the customers of the tea room is injured by choking on a small stone which was found to have come from a rock cake. Explain why this illustrates the concept of *res ipsa loquitur*, and the effect of that concept on the burden of proof. **(8)**

---

the cause of the damage suffered. This applies whether the claim is based on personal injury or damage to property. In simple road traffic accidents, for instance, it is often not too hard to find witnesses to identify that it was the defendant's vehicle, rather than any other, which collided with the vehicle in which the claimant was travelling.

In other cases, the task of linking damage to breach of duty can be less clear-cut. In deciding if a defendant should be liable, the courts may be faced with one of two questions:

1. If there are a number of possible causes of damage, which should be treated as the significant one? This is the issue of **causation**.

2. How far should the defendant's liability for damage extend? This is the issue of **remoteness of damage**.

This second question is not about disputing the existence of a duty of care but about placing a limit to the extent of compensation a defendant is required to provide.

Causation - the 'but for' test

Causation is about establishing what the true cause of damage was. There needs to be a link between the action or omission of the defendant and the damage. The starting point for the courts is to consider whether, as a matter of fact, the defendant's breach of duty was the cause of damage. This is known as the 'but for' test. The test involves asking whether the claimant would not have suffered the damage 'but for' the event brought about by the defendant.

An example of a case where, despite a breach of duty, the defendant was not held liable for the plaintiff's loss is *Barnett v Chelsea & Kensington Hospital Management Committee (1968)*. The plaintiff's husband went to the defendant's casualty ward. He was found to be suffering from what was later diagnosed as arsenic poisoning. The doctor on duty did not examine him. He was simply told to go away and see his own GP. Several hours later he died. His wife brought a claim in negligence against the hospital. In the Queen's Bench Division, the judge ruled that the defendant was not liable. Even if the man had been examined and treated at the hospital, it was very unlikely that anything could have been done to save him. The effect of the poison was too far advanced. It was too late for an antidote to take effect. The negligence of the doctor was not the cause of death. It was clearly not the case that the plaintiff would have lived but for the negligence of the doctor.

A further example of the kind of approach taken by the courts is given by *Baker v Willoughby (1969)* - see Box 22.7.

Novus actus interveniens

If something happens which has the effect of breaking the link between the defendant's conduct and the damage, it is said that there has been a *novus actus interveniens* - in other words, an intervening act. In *Baker v Willoughby*

(1970) - the case described in Box 22.7 - the defendant argued that there was an intervening act (the gunshot wounds) in the hope of being found no longer to be liable. The court did not accept this argument.

An example of where a *novus actus interveniens* **was** seen as preventing the liability of the defendant is *Thompson v Blake James (1998)*. The defendant, a doctor, had advised the parents of a child not to give the child measles immunisation. This was because of her particular medical history. She might have been made ill by the jab. The child then contracted measles and, as a result, developed a rare condition that caused brain damage. The parents had, in fact, taken the advice of other doctors as well. They too recommended not immunising against measles. The Court of Appeal held that the later advice was, in effect, an intervening event. After the second opinion, the parents had ceased to rely on the advice of the first doctor.

Multiple causes

Supposing that there are a number of possible causes of damage, and although the defendant may have been negligent, it is uncertain as to whether it was this negligence or some other cause that led to the damage? In *Wilsher v Essex Area Health Authority (1988)*, the plaintiff was a baby who was born prematurely with a number of medical problems. The defendants (the hospital) administered oxygen. The baby was later found to have an incurable eye condition that caused blindness. It was argued on behalf of the plaintiff that far too much oxygen was administered and that this was the cause of blindness. The House of Lords, reversing the Court of Appeal decision, held that there were in fact five possible causes of the blindness and that the excess oxygen was only one of these. As the plaintiffs had failed to prove, on

---

Box 22.7 *Baker v Willoughby (1969)*

Due to the negligence of the defendant's employer, the plaintiff suffered an injury to his left leg. Before the court action arising from this injury, the plaintiff was shot in his injured leg by armed robbers while working in his new job. His injuries were so serious that he had to have the leg amputated. The defendant argued that he was only liable for damage from the date of the first injury to the date of the robbery. The House of Lords rejected this argument. The Law Lords held that the plaintiff was being compensated by the first employer for the limiting effect of having a bad left leg. The plaintiff was prevented from doing things he could do before. The fact that the condition of this leg was made worse at a later date did not alter the fact that he had already been deprived of the use of a good leg.

a balance of probabilities, that it was the effective cause, the defendants were not liable.

In a sense, this case illustrates a problem with the traditional 'but for' test. If the claimant cannot show the existence of a causal link between the actions of the defendant and the damage, then, however much it might be thought that the claimant deserves compensation, they will not be entitled to it.

There has been increasing recognition in the courts that strict application of the 'but for' test can potentially lead to injustices. A good example of how the courts have confronted this problem can be seen in the House of Lords appeal of *Fairchild v Glenhaven Funeral Services Ltd and others (2002)* - see Box 22.8.

Remoteness of damage

The rules on remoteness of damage are concerned with establishing when a defendant should or should not be liable to pay damages. It often seems straightforward enough to make the negligent liable for the consequences of their actions. However when those consequences are very unexpected, this might seem unfair. For example in *Re Polemis (1921)* a ship was chartered to carry tins of petrol to Casablanca. These tins leaked, releasing large amounts of petrol vapour. When the ship arrived at port to be unloaded, workers positioned heavy planks over the open hold of the ship. As a result of their negligence, one of the planks slipped and fell into the hold. As it hit the ship, a spark flew off. This in turn caused the petrol

---

Box 22.8 *Fairchild v Glenhaven Funeral Services Ltd and others (2002)*

The judgement in *Fairchild v Glenhaven Funeral Services Ltd and others (2002)* actually dealt with three appeals, all concerning workers who, through no fault of their own, had contracted the fatal disease of mesothelioma at work. This disease is caused by exposure to asbestos dust. Sufferers do not show any symptoms for 20 years or more, then suffer a painful and lingering death. In each case, there was alleged breach of duty by employers, who had failed to take reasonable care to prevent inhalation of the dust. All of the workers had been exposed to asbestos in two different jobs, each of which was with different employers. In each case, both employers were at fault. To establish liability, the claimant needed to show when the particular asbestos dust that went on to cause the mesothelioma was inhaled.

1. Was it when the claimant worked for employer A?
2. Was it when the claimant worked for employer B?
3. Or was it inhaled during employment A and B taken together?

A worker wearing a protective suit and mask removes asbestos in November 1995.

The problem was that scientific knowledge did not enable the claimant to show which of these three possibilities applied. The question was whether the claimant was entitled to recover damages against either A or B or against both A and B. The Court of Appeal said not. It did so because, applying the conventional 'but for' test of liability, it could not be said that the claimant had proved any of the following:

- against A that his mesothelioma would probably not have occurred but for the breach of duty by A
- against B that his mesothelioma would probably not have occurred but for the breach of duty by B
- against A and B that his mesothelioma would probably not have occurred but for the breach of duty by both A and B together.

So the claimant failed against both A and B. There had been breach of duty by both employers and the claimant had suffered damage as a consequence. But, because he was not able to identify precisely who was to blame, he could not show causation.

Lord Bingham, in the House of Lords, giving the leading judgement, said that these appeals showed that there were problems with the 'but for' test:

'I would suggest that...too often the traditional "but for", all-or-nothing, test denies recovery where our instinctive sense of justice - of what is the right result for the situation - tells us the victim should obtain some compensation.'

The House of Lords reversed the decision of the Court of Appeal. The workers were allowed to recover damages from both employer A and employer B, even though it had not been shown which of them was at fault (this did not mean that the amount of damages would be any more than if only one of them was liable). However the Law Lords did not disapprove of earlier cases such as *Wilsher*. They were careful to explain that they were merely allowing a new exception to the existing causation rules. It remains to be seen how this decision is interpreted in later cases.

vapour to ignite and the resulting fire caused severe damage to the ship. The owners of the ship sued the company that had chartered their vessel for damages.

Imagine for a moment that you were the person to blame for the plank slipping. Would you have expected a fire, let alone such a serious one? Does it seem reasonable to make someone liable for such a surprising outcome? In fact, the charterers were held to be liable for the damage to the ship on the basis that it was a direct consequence of their breach of duty. However, this case no longer reflects current law. The courts gradually came to the view that it was rather hard on defendants. The current test is based on reasonable foresight.

The reasonable foreseeability test

The current test for remoteness is about making the defendant liable for damage that is reasonably foreseeable. In other words, only if a reasonable person present at the time would have been able to predict the consequences of a breach of duty would the defendant be liable for the damage caused.

This principle stems from a Privy Council in a case known as the *Wagon Mound (No 1)* and *Wagon Mound (No 2)* - see Box 22.9.

How much needs to be foreseen?

The test of reasonable foreseeability leaves one question unanswered. If the type of damage is foreseeable, will the defendant still be liable if it is hard to predict the exact way in which it occurs? The established principle is that so long as the **type** of injury is foreseeable, it does not matter if the **manner** in which it occurs is not foreseeable.

In *Hughes v Lord Advocate (1963)*, workers had opened a manhole that they left unattended but covered by a small tent, surrounded by paraffin lamps. An eight-year-old boy, with a ten-year-old friend, took a ladder and one of the lamps to explore the hole. The eight-year-old tripped over the lamp, which fell into the hole, causing the paraffin vapour to ignite. There was a large explosion. The boy was thrown into the hole and suffered severe burns. The defendants argued that the particular type of burn injury was not foreseeable. The obvious risks were fire and a fall caused by the combination of the tent, the paraffin and the hole. Unexpectedly, there was an explosion rather than a fire. The defendants argued that an explosion was not reasonably foreseeable. The House of Lords ruled that the defendants were, nevertheless, liable. The type of injury was foreseeable. The damage was serious but not different in kind from that which might have been produced had the lamp spilled and produced a normal fire, rather than an explosion, in the hole.

Box 22.9 *Wagon Mound (No 1)* and *Wagon Mound (No 2)*

Greg Norman's yacht 'Aussie Rules' enters Sydney harbour in February 2003.

A ship's engineer negligently permitted a considerable amount of oil to spill into Sydney Harbour from a ship (the *Wagon Mound*). The oil drifted as a thin film on the surface of the water to a wharf some six hundred feet away. Sparks from welding operations on the plaintiff's wharf fell on to some cotton waste in the sea, which, while still smouldering, floated into the film of oil. A fire started, which caused damage to the plaintiff's wharf. The Privy Council held that, as a reasonable person would not have foreseen such damage, the defendants were not liable in negligence for it, even though the carelessness of the ship's engineer was the cause of it.

The facts of the *Wagon Mound (No 2)* are based on the same negligence by the ship's engineer, but, in this case, the damage under discussion was the fire damage of two ships. The evidence was different from that in *Wagon Mound (No 1)*. The Privy Council ruled that a reasonable person in the position of the engineer would have identified that there was a risk. Although the risk of this kind of incident occurring was slight, a reasonable person would have nevertheless taken steps to eliminate the risk. As the damage to the two ships was reasonably foreseeable, the damage was not too remote and the defendants were liable.

The 'thin skull' or 'eggshell skull' rule

Some claimants suffer more serious harm from a breach of duty by the defendant than a reasonable person might foresee. If a person with an extraordinary sensitivity (a hin or 'eggshell' skull) suffers harm, they might sustain serious injury where the vast majority of people would merely be slightly hurt. As long as the **type** of injury is foreseeable, the defendants are liable, even if the **extent** of injury is not foreseeable.

In *Smith v Leech Brain and Co (1962)*, the plaintiff was employed to dip objects into a tank of molten metal. A splash from the tank burned his lip. Unknown to the defendant employer, the plaintiff had a pre-cancerous condition and this burn led to the development of a serious cancer. The court rejected an argument that the *Wagon Mound* rule of reasonable foreseeability prevented the defendants from being liable and applied the eggshell skull rule.

Summary

1. Why is the case of Donoghue v Stevenson (1932) important?

2. When does a duty of care arise?

3. How do courts establish that a duty of care has been breached?

4. What principles regarding the detail of the objective standard have the courts evolved?

5. What are res ipsa loquitur and novus actus interveniens?

6. How do courts establish that the defendant was the cause of the damage suffered?

Case study 〉● Negligence

Item A *A fictitious case*

Dave worked for Jones Ltd, a company that refits ships. Dave was employed for some years refurbishing cruise liners. This often involved stripping out old asbestos insulation. This created a danger of contracting asbestosis, a fatal lung disease, from inhaling asbestos dust.

When Dave had problems breathing, he went to his local hospital. Sarah, an experienced doctor, failed to carry out a full check, due to a high volume of work. She suggested that Dave should go to his local GP. Dave was unable to see the GP for several days. The GP had little experience and was unable to diagnose the disease. He referred Dave back to the hospital. After three weeks, Dave attended a hospital appointment with Inderjit, a third doctor, who immediately diagnosed asbestosis. There is no known cure. Dave died of the disease in a few months.

The cruise liner 'Legend of the Seas' off the island of Dragonara, South West Mallorca in 1999. Old cruise liners often contain asbestos.

Item B *Two fictitious prisoners*

Due to a door being accidentally left unlocked, two prisoners escape from a prison in a remote area of Wales. They spend the night in an empty holiday cottage two miles away then steal a tractor. They are captured the next night 20 miles further on. Both the cottage and the tractor have been vandalised by the men.

Questions

(a) Look at Item A.

   i)   Dave's widow is considering suing Jones Ltd for negligence. Discuss whether Jones Ltd would be liable in negligence. (10)

   ii) Dave's widow is also considering suing the Health Authority who employs Sarah, for negligence. Assuming that Sarah was in breach of duty, discuss whether the Health Authority would be liable in negligence. (15)

(b) Look at Item B.

   i)   Discuss whether the prison authorities will be liable in negligence for the damage caused to the cottage and the tractor. (15)

   ii) Would your answer differ if the tractor had been struck by lightning while under the control of the two men and damaged as a result of that? (10)

23.1 Introduction

This unit explains how damages are calculated in negligence cases involving personal injury and damage to property. **The overall aim of negligence damages is for defendants to pay an amount that will restore claimants to the position that they would have been in had the tort not been committed.** For instance, one of the victims in Activity 23.1 is a keen amateur tennis player. The victim suffers injuries that will prevent her from continuing to play sports. She can claim compensation for this loss. The legal term used for a court order regarding damages is an 'award of damages'. In cases involving personal injury, damages may be awarded for physical or psychiatric harm, illness and disease.

Activity 23.1

Motorbikers.

Steve, aged 44, is a self-employed carpenter. Rebecca, Steve's girlfriend, aged 32, is a teacher. Steve and Rebecca were touring Snowdonia on Steve's motorbike. As they climbed a twisty mountain road, Steve was forced to swerve to avoid a collision with a car coming out of a side turning. He lost control of the bike and crashed. His motorbike has been completely written off.

Steve has sustained a broken arm and severe bruising. He will not be able to work for three months, but when the arm has healed he should have virtually normal use of it. Rebecca, on the other hand, has sustained a much more serious injury. Her leg is cut and badly broken in three places so that, although she will eventually be able to walk on it, she will always have a bad limp and substantial loss of mobility. Rebecca was a keen member of her local tennis club. The doctor has advised her that she should not expect to be able to play tennis again. The motorbike leathers she was wearing are ruined.

In an action for negligence, the car driver has been found liable.

Draw up a brief list that indicates what Steve and Rebecca have lost as a result of the crash, both in terms of personal injury and damage to property. (8)

The calculation of damages in personal injury involves a great deal of guesswork, as it is often very hard to know, for instance, how long it might take the claimant to recover from injuries and to what extent the claimant may be disabled. Bear in mind that a medical condition may turn out to be much better or much worse than expected. As the courts only assess damages once and for all, the award may turn out to be either too high or too low. Quite apart from this, there is the question of how much money should be provided for the loss of something that is not usually measured in financial terms. There is no simple answer to that question, but the courts are guided by the amount of damages awarded in similar cases in the past.

As well as a court action for negligence, claimants may also be able to claim on an insurance policy and claim state benefits. To some extent, the courts take this into account when calculating damages. As far as insurance is concerned, it is often an insurance company that pays damages, not the defendant. After all, this is a function of insurance companies - to cover the cost of claims made against the insured. It follows that, if the defendant is not liable in negligence for injury to the claimant, the defendant's insurance company will not be liable either. The claimant has to bear the loss.

If claimants are found to be partly at fault for damage they have suffered, the damage they would have received to compensate them for their loss is reduced accordingly. This is known as 'contributory negligence'. A simple example is failure to wear a seat belt. Or it may be that the accident itself was caused by the carelessness of both the claimant and the defendant. The court expresses any contributory negligence as a percentage. For example, if a claimant suffers damage that is assessed at £10,000 but the court rules that contributory negligence on the part of the claimant is 30% to blame, the claimant will only receive £7,000.

The other main remedy that is used in tort is an injunction. A **prohibitory injunction** is a court order ordering the defendant not to do something. A **mandatory injunction** is used to require the defendant actively to do something. However, injunctions are very rarely used in negligence cases. They are more often found in torts which can be said to involve continuing wrongs, such as defamation or nuisance.

23.2 General and special damages

Claimants usually ask the court for damages under two headings:

- general damages
- special damages.

General damages are those that cannot be calculated exactly in terms of monetary value. Special damages, on the other hand, can be calculated exactly. Most special damages are those expenses that have been incurred up to the date of the trial and can, therefore, be calculated more precisely. Some examples of each kind of damages are given in Box 23.1.

Box 23.1 *General and special damages*

General damages

Examples of general damages are:

- pain and suffering
- future loss of earnings (from the date of the trial onwards)
- the cost of care, where the claimant is disabled.

Special damages

Examples of special damages are:

- the cost of repairing or replacing a damaged car
- the cost of hiring a car while the claimant's own vehicle is out of action
- earnings lost up to the date of the trial.

Activity 23.2

Look at Activity 23.1 again. Check that you thought of everything that Steve and Rebecca might receive damages for. Next to each item on your list indicate whether it is counted as general damages or special damages. (8)

23.3 Pecuniary damages

Whether damages are general or special damages, they can also be classified as 'pecuniary' or 'non-pecuniary'. Pecuniary damages are those that involve financial loss. Examples include loss of earnings or the cost of repairs to a vehicle. Non-pecuniary damages are those that involve a loss which is not financial but where the court will nevertheless provide financial compensation, as this is all that can be done. Pain and suffering and the loss of a limb are examples of non-pecuniary loss. The categories for which damages may be recovered are known as 'heads of damage'. The most common heads of damage are examined below.

Medical expenses

The claimant may require expensive medical or nursing care for some time. Under Section 2(4) of the Law Reform (Personal Injuries) Act 1948, the claimant is allowed to claim for private medical care, despite the existence of the NHS. The Road Traffic (NHS Charges) Act 1999 enables NHS hospitals to recover the cost of treating accident victims from the defendant's insurers. Suppose that a parent or spouse has to give up work to care for a child or partner who needs constant nursing. It was decided in *Housecroft v Burnett (1986)* that, where a relative or friend has given up work to provide nursing care, lost earnings can be recovered as damages. The House of Lords ruled in *Hunt v Severs (1994)* that any damages received under this head must be passed on to the carer.

Other expenses incurred

Examples of other expenses are the cost of installing a stair lift or modifying a property in some other way. If the claimant is able to drive, they may also claim for the cost of adapting an existing car. The cost of buying a new house or a new car, on the other hand, is not recoverable as these are capital assets that can later be re-sold. This would lead to the claimant being over-compensated. Even the value of clothes that have been ruined in the accident may be recovered.

Loss of earnings

Loss of earnings can be divided into loss to date and future loss - see Box 23.2.

Box 23.2 *Loss to date and future loss*

Loss to date, or actual loss, runs from the date of the accident to the date at which damages are settled. Income tax and other deductions are made so that the claimant does not profit from damages received under this head. Loss of employment benefits such as a company car can also be taken into account.

Future loss relates to earnings after the date on which damages are assessed. These can only be based on speculation. It may be that the claimant will be unable to work for months or years, but the exact period can only be the subject of an educated guess. Even where it is known that the claimant will never be able to work again, nobody can know whether the claimant would have been made redundant or whether they would have been promoted to a job with higher pay. Those who are able to work but have a reduced earning power can be compensated for the difference between current and previous earning power.

Actuarial tables can be used in evidence to calculate future loss of earnings. These are drawn from probability statistics and are used in the insurance industry to help calculate levels of risk and premiums. Future loss is based on an assessment of the chance that various things might have happened (such as promotion) to the claimant had they not been injured.

The stages are as follows.

Stage 1 Calculate annual earnings
Net annual loss of earnings is calculated (after tax and national insurance contributions have been deducted). This is known as the 'multiplicand'. The multiplicand is adjusted to allow for promotion prospects.

Stage 2 Calculate the number of years that the disability is likely to continue
Rather than simply assuming that the claimant will work continuously until retirement, the court will reduce this figure to take into account what are called the 'contingencies of life', that is to say the fact that, even if the accident had not happened, the claimant may not have lived or worked until retirement age. A smoker, for instance, is far more likely to die early than a non-smoker.

Stage 3 Reduce the number arrived at in Stage 2 to allow for return on investment
If the claimant had not been injured they would have received a certain amount every month over a number of years. The damages they receive, on the other hand, will be paid as a lump sum in advance. This lump sum is invested and will produce an investment income that the claimant would not normally have received. To allow for this, the court assumes that the investment will earn a certain percentage rate of return every year. This is deducted from the figure in Stage 2. This deduction is known as the **discount rate**. When the discount rate has been taken off, the figure arrived at is called the **multiplier**.

Stage 4 Multiply the multiplicand by the multiplier
This gives the final amount that is paid as damages for future loss of earnings.

An example of how this works in practice is given in Box 23.3.

Lost Years
If the life expectancy of a victim has been reduced so that they will have fewer years in work, the question arises as to whether the income from the lost years between the expected date of death and retirement can be claimed. It

---

Box 23.3 *Calculating loss of earnings*

Susan, aged 55, worked in a distribution warehouse. Her take home pay (after tax and other deductions) was £9,000 per year. She was very seriously injured by the negligence of another worker who was driving a forklift truck. She will not be able to work again. Prior to the accident, Susan was in very good health for her age.

Susan

Assuming a retirement age of 65, what damages for future loss of earnings will Susan receive?

Stage 1 Calculate annual earnings
This is taken as £9,000 per year. This is the multiplicand.

Stage 2 Calculate the number of years that the disability is likely to continue
From Susan's present age to retirement age is ten years. As Susan was in very good health, there is no need to suppose that she might cease working before retirement and, therefore, no need to reduce this figure.

Stage 3 Reduce the number arrived at in Stage 2 to allow for return on investment
Susan needs to end up with £90,000 (£9,000 x 10). To allow for the income produced by investing a lump sum at (say) 5% annual return however, only 6.139 years are required. The multiplier is therefore 6.139.

Stage 4 Multiply the multiplicand by the multiplier
£9,000 x 6.139 produces a lump sum payment of £55,251. When invested as a lump sum, assuming 5% income per year, this produces a final total of £90,000.

---

was held in *Oliver v Ashman (1962)* that claims for the lost years were not recoverable. But the House of Lords overruled this case in *Picket v British Rail Engineering (1980)*. Damages for future loss of earnings are now awarded for the whole of the period that the defendant would be expected to have lived before the accident occurred.

Social security payments
It is possible that between the date of the accident and the assessment of damages the defendant was receiving social security payments. Under the Social Security Administration Act 1992 the state recovers the value of these payments from the damages payable by the defendant before damages are paid to the claimant.

23.4 Non-pecuniary damages

Pain and suffering

The award for pain and suffering is generally based on guidelines produced by the Judicial Studies Boards (see pages 127 and 146). Awards in previous cases are used as benchmarks. The amount paid depends upon the severity of the injury and the impact upon the individual defendant. In 2000, a child who had severe cerebral palsy and a reduced life expectancy was awarded £190,000 general damages for pain and suffering. A permanently unconscious claimant cannot receive damages for pain and suffering *(Wise v Kaye 1962)*.

In the Law Commission's Report, *Damages for Personal Injury (Non-Pecuniary Loss)* in 1999, it was recommended that the size of awards for non-pecuniary damages should be increased, as they were not keeping pace with inflation. This was accepted by the House of Lords in *Heil v Rankin and Another (2000)*. Where previously £150,000 had been regarded as the top level, this was increased to £200,000. Between £150,000 and £10,000 there was a gradually reducing scale of increases. Below £10,000, awards stayed the same.

Loss of faculty and amenity

Loss of faculty means loss of a limb. Again, the courts use standard guidelines to calculate the amount of an award. Loss of amenity means loss of the chance to enjoy activities that are no longer possible due to loss of faculty. For example, the keen amateur tennis player might receive damages for loss of amenity. Not being able to walk at all is an obvious loss of amenity. The amount paid depends upon the particular interests and background of the claimant. A young woman deprived of the chance to enjoy sport would deserve a higher award for that loss of amenity than a man aged 60.

23.5 Lump sum or structured settlement?

A claimant can only bring one action in respect of an incident. It is not possible to start a second action if the injury or disablement turns out to be more serious than was originally expected when damages were assessed. Damages can only be recovered once. As Lord Scarman commented in *Lim Poo Choo v Camden and Islington AHA (1980)*: 'There is only one certainty: the future will prove the award to be either too high or too low'.

Until 1989, damages could only be awarded as a lump sum, which the claimant is expected to invest to produce an investment income. Since 1989, payment may be made

Activity 23.3

A worker removes asbestos safely in 1992. The company Tiao worked for did not introduce safe working practices before Tiao had breathed in asbestos fibres.

Tiao was employed as a manager at a ship building business, with a pre-tax annual salary of £40,000. Now aged 45, he worked for the same company for 23 years, working his way steadily up the job ladder, since starting as a trainee welder. Until a year ago he was regarded as someone 'tipped for the top'. He was likely to be given promotion to director level sooner rather than later. But he is now unable to work. He has been told that he has six months to live but will suffer a slow and very painful decline. Tiao's wife has given up her work as a hairdresser to care full time for Tiao.

Tiao contracted the fatal disease of mesothelioma at work. This disease is caused by inhalation of or exposure to asbestos dust, which can cause a malignant tumour. Sufferers often do not show any symptoms for 20 years or more. There was an admitted breach of duty by Tiao's employers, who had failed to take reasonable care to prevent inhalation of the dust.

(a) **How likely is it that** *the employer* **will actually make payment for damages in a case such as this? (2)**

(b) **List the various heads of damage in this case under the headings pecuniary and non-pecuniary. (8)**

(c) **What compensation will be made for the cost of caring for Tiao? Who will receive this money? (6)**

(d) **Explain how the multiplicand will be calculated in this case (you are not expected to produce a specific figure). (6)**

(e) **What factors will reduce the multiplier? (5)**

(f) **Is Tiao entitled to the income that he would have earned from his job if he had not become ill? (4)**

as a lump sum plus periodic payments. This is known as a 'structured settlement'.

The disadvantages of lump sums are outlined in Box 23.4.

Box 23.4 *Disadvantages of lump sums*

Lump sums have the following disadvantages:

1. The payment of damages is based on guesses about what will happen in the future.

2. The lump sum may not be wisely invested by the defendant or it may not be invested at all. There is nothing to stop the claimant frittering the money away before the end of the period it was designed to cover. If this happens, the claimant may end up claiming benefits, in which case compensation has effectively been paid twice.

3. There is little incentive for the defendant to settle early. Because lump sums are paid on a once and for all basis, the defendant will tend to delay paying damages for as long as possible. The claimant's medical condition may have improved significantly by the time damages come to be assessed by the court. If the claimant has become short of money in the meantime, they may feel pressured into settling for a lower amount.

Structured settlements

Since *Kelly v Dawes (1989)* payments can be made in the form of periodic payments, if both parties agree. This system is known as a 'structured settlement'. The total amount of damages is calculated in the same way, but only part of the total is paid over as a lump sum. The rest is used to purchase an annuity. An annuity is a long-term investment in return for which the investment company provides a fixed but guaranteed annual income. The purchase of stocks and shares may produce a greater income than an annuity, but it involves greater risks. The value of stocks and shares can fall as well as rise.

Structured settlements have a number of possible advantages. First, they are useful in cases where the claimant might not cope very well with managing the investment of a lump sum, whether through ill-advised investment or being a spendthrift. This, in turn, reduces the likelihood that the claimant will end up claiming benefits and become a burden on the state. Second, the periodic payments are not subject to income tax. The income from an invested lump sum on the other hand is normally subject to income tax. The defendant can reduce the overall amount of damages paid because the claimant is receiving this tax-free income. Third, structured settlements tend to encourage early settlement.

The fundamental problem remains that the assessment of damages will almost inevitably prove to be an inaccurate calculation, whether a structured settlement is used or not. The rule that damages are only assessed once still applies.

23.6 Provisional damages and interim damages

One solution to the problem of the 'once and for all' assessment of personal injury damages is provisional damages under Section 6 of the Administration of Justice Act 1982.

How do provisional damages work?

Suppose that the claimant has been advised by doctors that it is possible (though not certain) that a deterioration in health will occur in the future as a result of the original injury. Where there is a chance of a serious deterioration, the court might order that provisional damages are paid on the basis that this disease or deterioration will not occur, then review the assessment at a later date. At the review, a further sum might be awarded. Note that this review can only take place once.

In fact, the use of provisional damages is fairly rare. This is partly because the provisional award may only be made by court order. So, there is less opportunity for the parties to reduce legal costs by settling out of court. The parties must go to court to obtain a court order. In addition, the courts do not often take the view that there is a chance of serious deterioration.

Interim damages

Another option for the claimant may be to consider seeking **interim damages**. Under the Rules of the Supreme Court there can be two separate trials. In the first trial, a decision is taken solely as to whether the defendant is liable for damages. The issue of '**quantum**' (how much damages to award) is decided at a later date in a second hearing. In the time interval between the two trials, the medical condition of the claimant may become clearer. A disadvantage of this system is that it adds to delay in receiving damages.

23.7 The Fatal Accidents Act 1976

If somebody has a family which is dependent on them and they are killed though the negligence of another, the family of the deceased has a right to claim damages. Under the Fatal Accidents Act 1976, a wide range of dependants has a right of action for loss of support. The class of people covered by the Act are shown in Box 23.5.

> **Box 23.5** *The class of people covered by the Fatal Accidents Act 1976*
>
> 1. A spouse or cohabitee of the deceased who had been living with the deceased for at least two years.
>
> 2. A parent, grandparent or great grandparent of the deceased or person who was regarded as a parent by the deceased.
>
> 3. Any child or other descendant of the deceased or any person who the deceased treated as a child within their married family (this would include adopted or fostered children).
>
> 4. Any brother, sister, aunt or uncle of the deceased, or the offspring of such a person.
>
> Adopted children, half-blood relations, step-children and illegitimate children are all treated as full relations within each of the categories above. For example, an adopted child of a brother would be treated as the child of a brother.

The amount of damages awarded to a dependant for loss of support under the Fatal Accidents Act reflects the extent to which the dependant has suffered pecuniary loss. So, if an old lady with no income lived with her son at the time she was killed in an accident, the son would not be able to receive damages, as he would not have suffered any pecuniary loss. On the other hand, if a working wife who supported her unemployed husband were killed, he would be able to claim damages under the Act.

The Act also provides that the spouse of the deceased or the parents of a minor who has never married may claim a fixed sum of £7,500 in respect of a death after 1982. This is to provide for bereavement, not loss of support.

23.8 Damage to property

It is easier to calculate compensation for damage to property than personal injury. Where property is destroyed, the measure of damages is the market value of the property at the time of the accident. Where it requires repair, damages are awarded to cover the cost of repair.

The duty to mitigate

Sometimes damage to property is increased by the failure of the claimant to take reasonable steps to prevent deterioration in the condition of damaged property. The court expects the claimant to take these steps. This is called 'the duty to mitigate a loss'. The defendant is not liable for that part of the damage that is caused by a claimant's failure to mitigate.

Suppose, for instance, that Tony is involved in a minor collision, which is due to the negligence of Bert. Bodywork on the car requires minor repair. The impact also causes the car to develop an engine oil leak, which is initially undetected. Tony notices that the engine becomes very noisy and sluggish but, over a number of weeks, fails to investigate and carries on driving the car. The car engine eventually ceases to function at all and needs very expensive repair. If Tony had taken steps to investigate and deal with the problem when it first became obvious, the cost of repair would have been much lower. Bert is liable for the damage to the bodywork. He is also liable for the damage caused to the engine by the oil leak, but only to the value of repairs that would have been needed when it became obvious that the engine was seriously malfunctioning.

Any reduction in damages caused by a failure to mitigate loss should not be confused with contributory negligence. Contributory negligence is about what happened **before** the damage occurred. The duty to mitigate deals with what happened **after** the negligent damage.

23.9 Other types of damage

Aggravated damages

Aggravated damages are awarded for mental distress. They may be awarded where the claimant has suffered particularly from the bad behaviour of the defendant. In *Khodaparast v Shad (1999)* the claimant sued her ex-boyfriend for libel. He faked photographs of her that put her in a very bad light and distributed these widely. At the trial, the defendant further claimed (among other things) that his ex-girlfriend associated with prostitutes and was having an improper relationship with her solicitor. None of this was true. The judge awarded aggravated damages to compensate the claimant for the defendant's offensive conduct in the trial.

Exemplary damages

Exemplary damages also involve paying the claimant more than would normally be appropriate. However, they go beyond being compensatory to acting as a punishment. As this is really the function of the criminal courts rather than the civil courts, exemplary damages are only used sparingly. Strict rules were laid down by the House of Lords in *Rookes v Barnard (1964)* as to when exemplary damages may be given. The three possible categories are as follows:

1. Where the defendant committed a tort in order to profit. In *Appleton v Garrett (1996)* exemplary

Box 23.6 *Types of damages*

Type of damages	General	Special	Pecuniary	Non-pecuniary
Definition	Cannot be calculated exactly	Can be calculated exactly	Involve financial loss	Involve a loss which is not financial
Examples	Future loss of earnings; Pain and suffering	Loss of earnings to date of trial	Past and future loss of earnings	Pain and suffering

Type of damages	Provisional	Interim	Aggravated	Exemplary
Definition	Damages paid subject to later review	Second hearing held to establish amount of damages	Damages awarded for mental distress caused by defendant	Damages are used as punishment
Examples	Extent of disability hard to predict	Extent of disability hard to predict	Defendant makes malicious accusations at trial	Defendant committed a tort to make a profit

damages were awarded to the patients of a dentist who deliberately carried out unnecessary treatment and charged the patients for it.

2. Where public servants have acted oppressively. For instance, if police officers commit torts while acting in the course of their duty, they may be punished for not using their powers in the interests of the community.

3. Where exemplary damages are authorised by Act of Parliament.

The various types of damages covered by this unit are given in Box 23.6.

Summary

1. What is the difference between general damages and special damages?
2. What are the most common heads of pecuniary damages?
3. How are loss of earnings calculated?
4. What are 'loss of faculty' and 'loss of amenity'?
5. How is the problem of the 'once and for all' assessment of personal injury damages addressed?
6. What is the significance of the Fatal Accidents Act 1976?
7. What is the duty to mitigate?

Case study • Tort damages

A hypothetical case

Brett hurt his finger with an axe while chopping logs. He went to the local hospital for a minor operation to reset the tendons in the injured finger, to be done under a local anaesthetic. A general anaesthetic was given, and negligently administered. Brett's heart stopped beating. He was unconscious for weeks and suffered very serious brain damage. He now requires constant nursing. He was aged 37 at the time. Brett's life expectancy has been affected by his injuries. He is now likely to live to between the ages of 57 and 70 years. The defendant agreed, in an out-of-court settlement, to pay £2.6 million, of which £850,000 was returned to the defendant to fund a structured settlement. The structured settlement provided an initial annual income of around £47,000 per year, payable for the rest of Brett's life.

Questions

(a) Briefly explain the heads of damages for which the claimant in this case will recover. Identify them according to whether they are: (i) general or special damages and (ii) pecuniary or non-pecuniary damages. (10)

(b) Explain how any social security benefits that might have been paid to the claimant will be treated in relation to damages. (3)

(c) What is meant by the term 'structured settlement'? (4)

(d) What is the alternative to a structured settlement? (2)

(e) If the claimant in this case had died as a result of the medical negligence, explain what entitlement to compensation his widow and three children would have had. (6)

(f) Suppose that, in a medical negligence case, a hospital seeks to evade liability by (falsely) claiming that the claimant's collapse was mostly due to the side effects of taking an illegal drug. Explain how the court might respond when awarding damages (6)

(g) Using the hypothetical case described above, discuss the arguments for and against structured settlements. (10)

Table of statutes

Table of cases

Index

Acknowledgements

The author would like to thank everyone at Causeway Press, especially Steve Lancaster. Thanks to Denise Kilgallon, Melanie Lanser and Nick Price for their helpful comments. Most of all thank you to Nikki, for her love and support.

Editor at Causeway Press	Steve Lancaster
Cover design	Tim Button (Waring Collins Ltd)
Page design	Caroline Waring-Collins (Waring Collins Ltd)
Graphic origination	Derek Baker (Waring Collins Ltd)
Graphics	Derek Baker / Tim Button (Waring Collins Ltd)
Reader	Wendy Janes
Cartoons	Brick, Andrew Wright

The editor and author are grateful for any comments. Please contact us:

by post: Causeway Press, PO Box 13, Ormskirk, Lancs, L39 5HP
by telephone: 01695 576048
by e-mail: steve.causewaypress@btconnect.com

Picture credits

Berridge, Clive 103t, 110; BFI 70(r); Brick 2, 5, 12, 15r, 76, 83l, 86, 135, 152; *Economist* 30; Getty Images 15l, 23, 61, 67b; Ilex 118; Labour Research 120; PA Photos 6, 7tl, 25, 36, 42tr, 50br, 55, 59l, 62, 63, 70l, 87, 94, 109, 128, 131, 138, 139br, 140, 154, 161br, 164(both), 185, 188, 192tl, 194, 195, 201; Photodisc 90(all), 101(all), 107(all), 158(all), 159, 174b, 192br, 213; *Punch* 143; Rex Features 20, 46, 47, 49, 50bl, 56, 58, 60, 67t, 74, 115, 118, 126, 165, 173, 197, 198, 200(both), 203, 204, 205, 207, 208, 209, 211, 214; Topham Picturepoint 7br, 26, 33, 38, 83br, 89, 92, 97, 103bl, 114, 117, 129, 135, 139l, 141, 145, 148, 150, 161l, 177, 179t, 184; Wright, Andrew 167(both), 171, 174t, 176, 180, 182, 196, 210, 218

British Library Cataloguing in Publication Data
A catalogue record for this book is available from the British Library.

ISBN 1 902796 65 9

Causeway Press Limited
PO Box 13, Ormskirk, Lancs, L39 5HP

Printed and bound by Legoprint SpA, Italy